CAN RELIGION SURVIVE WORSHIP

Warren L. Hickman

TO

Justin, Devin, Kevin, Kelsey, Sophia, Claire and Charlie,

and their generation

CONTENTS

CHAPTER 27   CAN RELIGION SURVIVE WORSHIP

A MAN-MADE RELIGION - SMOTHERING THE MESSAGE - CAN RELIGION POSSIBLY SURVIVE WORSHIP ?

PREFACE

History is often defined as an interpretation of the relationship of people to people, events to events, and people to events. It is never a mere listing of events and people and the times and places where they were found; which only results in a chronicle rather than a history. A good historian must always try to empathize with the people about whom he or she is writing. Among other things that means trying to place one's self in the time and place where events and people interacted.

I have approached *Can Religion Survive Worship* as an historian, not as a theologian. The gospels are examined as they were meant to be read in the political/religious environment in which they were written. For laity it presents the challenge of reading literally or figuratively.

I have tried to place myself in the sandals of the writers of the gospels in order to ask:

Who was the writer?

What was his background?

Where was the writer of a gospel or letter at the time of writing?

What was the political/religious situation then and there?

Considering the time, place and political/religious situation; why did the writer write?

What did he try to convey to his audience?

How successful does it appear that he was in achieving his goal?

Having answered these questions for myself as best I could, I then sought to see these writings as each writer would have wanted his readers to see them. Obviously, this raised further questions. Did the writers wish their readers to accept their writings as literal history, or did they write in parables in order to weave a deeper message throughout? Paul and the gospel writers, being from several different generations and locations and having quite different personal backgrounds, how did these influence the manner in which they chose to meet problems of their times? Were these the reasons for offering different and sometimes conflicting versions of events and of the teachings of Jesus?

Paul's letters have been included as a gospel. I chose to do this because Mark, who wrote the first gospel, was creating the first written version of what was being taught in the Gentile churches organized by Paul, Barnabas, and other early missionaries, and Mark's gospel provided the base and outline for the gospels of Matthew and Luke. Paul even refers to his writings as "my gospel" (Paul's Letter to the Romans 2. 16).

When writers who came after Mark wrote, they knew their writings were going to differ from, even contradict, those of the other writers. Did that mean they did not intend their writings to be taken literally? Or, did it mean that they believed what earlier writers had written was wrong? Should the twenty-first century reader see these writings as literal history, or should we seek a deeper meaning through a figurative reading? I do not attempt to judge readers or beliefs by whether one reads the gospels literally or figuratively. My concern is that whichever interpretation the reader chooses that it be made with an awareness of the motive of each writer at the time of his writing.

Those reading the gospels literally place their emphasis on the messenger which results in a religion that concentrates on worshiping the messenger. Those reading figuratively concentrate on the message and the need to teach the message. From these conflicting approaches the question arises: Can religion survive worship?

As an historian I am trying to open my eyes and ears to see and hear what each writer wanted his readers to see and hear.

Although I hope readers of all ages will find *Can Religion Survive Worship* to be thought-stimulating, I have been particularly concerned with those who are finding it difficult, if not impossible, for their religion to survive worship. This particularly affects the younger generations in a world where life expectancy is ever growing. The explosive expansion of knowledge in the natural and physical sciences, and the rapid expansion of historical and archaeological research since the Second World War, have created new challenges to confront the beliefs of younger generations. They cannot be expected to read or study the Bible with the same eyes and ears as the generations that preceded them. Their horizons are broader. *Can Religion Survive Worship* is an historian's attempt to keep those eyes and ears open in these challenging times.

* * * * * * * * * * * *

     Throughout this book the quotations from the New Testament have been taken from two major sources: *The New Oxford Annotated Bible* and *The New English Bible*. Many of the annotations herein have been taken from those sources because they relate directly to specific translations of gospel passages or letters in one or the other source.

     The original gospels and letters were written in Greek. Later, after several generations of tedious and error-prone hand copying in Greek, these were repeatedly, tediously, and with further errors translated into Latin. From Latin the bible was translated into various languages, including the King James Version (a translation we now refer to as old English, translated in 1611 AD).

     Recent translations are considerably more accurate as teams of scholars have avoided the Latin translations and have gone directly to the earliest available Greek copies; copies made well before the first available Latin translations. The computer has made possible greater accuracy in translation. Furthermore, new archaeological discoveries have brought to light copies of religious tablets and parchments unavailable to translators until recently. This led me to select the translations of *The New Oxford Bible* and *The New English Bible,* over which scores of scholars researched and worked for years to bring to the point of publication; while at the same time I recognize that other good translations are available.

     References to political, economic, military, and other social aspects of the time periods covered in *Can Religion Survive Worship* will be familiar to anyone who has taught or studied Ancient History, and can be considered common knowledge in that field.

Warren L. Hickman
April 2010

CHAPTER 1

ORIGINS OF JESUS' BIBLE

Often preached – Seldom practiced.

Few ever do step into another's shoes.

From the time humans first walked this earth they have tended to assume all other extended families, tribes, clans, nations, and states have exactly the same values and goals that they do. Little is there to indicate that we of the twenty-first century are different. With all too few exceptions humans still assume, regardless of differences in cultures, that all those of other cultures have the same desires, needs, and goals, and follow the same patterns of behavior in achieving their goals as they do.

If in the twenty-first century with our knowledge of world geography, with our knowledge of languages other than our own, and with modern tools of mass communication, we still fail to empathize with those living in other cultures, how much more difficult is it for today's Christians to walk in the sandals of those who lived two thousand years ago in Palestine?

Jesus was a teacher (his disciples called him rabbi). He brought his message to people living in a culture far different than those of the twenty-first century. He taught in a style and with methods and examples aimed at people who lived in that time and that culture;

people who were symbol-minded, not literal-minded. Those who cannot step into the sandals of one of his listeners, or into the sandals of those for whom the gospels were written, will never be able to appreciate fully the deeper message of the teacher.

What kind of land was Palestine when Jesus taught? Who were his listeners? What were their customs? Where did they come from? What did they believe? What was the basis for those beliefs? Step back four thousand years and walk in the world into which Abraham was born. From there you will be able to move on another two thousand years into the world of Jesus. There is no other way to appreciate fully and to understand fully the message of the gospels.

ABRAHAMIC ROOTS

Judaism, Christianity, and Islam share a common beginning with the life of Abraham. Yet, the roots of that Abrahamic saga reach well back into the Stone Age, and it is there that one must go to understand the beginnings from which the three Abrahamic religions have sprung.

About 5600 BC, at least 2,000 years before the end of the Stone Age, small communities of Neolithic families had domesticated sheep and settled around a large lake in Anatolia; what is today northern Turkey. Their world was small. There was no reason for them to walk more than a few miles in any direction during their lifetime. Eventually they learned to build crude stone walls that could be roofed with brush and dried grasses. They could not know that to the west lay the huge Mediterranean Sea.

Whether from an earthquake, in this region of frequent earthquakes; or from erosion during a tremendous storm; or from rising waters as the earth warmed; we do not know, but suddenly the small strip of land at the Eastern end of the Mediterranean gave way. Through a two mile wide breach burst 200 times more water per minute than pours each minute over the Niagara Falls.

Rolling on at sixty miles an hour the flood gave no warning. Waters of the lake rose so rapidly, expanding the shores approximately a kilometer a day, that families could grab only a few possessions before fleeing their homes. Only the most able would have been able to keep ahead of the growing sea. Until they reached the hills many miles from what had been the lake's shore they would not be safe, for the waters would continue to rise until they reached the level of the Mediterranean Sea. The shores of what had been a lake were now miles away and some 350 feet beneath the surface of what we now call the Black Sea.[1]

Unlike the earlier lake this was an inhospitable salt water sea. Those who had lived on the northern shores of the lake are believed to have fled to the north. Those on the southern shores appear to have migrated slowly to the south where centuries later they became part of the movement of Semitic peoples into Sumer.

Sumer was far different than the Anatolia from which those wanderers came. Sometime before 4000 BC, Sumer had become the home of an industrious people, the Ubidians, who had drained vast marshes lying between the Tigris and Euphrates rivers. For thousands of years annual floods had deposited layers of silt that made this newly arable land truly the Fertile Crescent of history. The leatherwork, metalwork, and pottery of later Ubidian craftsmen were in great demand among the less skilled neighboring peoples. Early development of the trade to which this led carried with it not only the products of their craftsmen and their farmers, but also the beliefs and customs of these early settlers of the land that would become known as Sumer.

Among those beliefs were stories of the Creation and of a Great Flood. Whenever the Tigris and Euphrates flooded the area, which to them was the only world they knew, they saw dry land being "created" as flood waters receded. There too, particularly severe floods had given birth to the stories of a great flood covering the world which was saved by a mythical ancestor of Gilgamesh of whom we shall speak further. Then later those newcomers from Anatolia brought further stories of the Great Flood that had covered the world of their ancestors when the Mediterranean broke through to create the Black Sea.

These Sumerians and Semitics had wandered into this land of the Ubidians around 3300 BC, about seven hundred years after the area had been first settled. As their numbers increased Sumerians eventually replaced the Ubidians as the leaders of what historians now refer to as the Sumerian civilization. In turn the Sumerians would be replaced by Semitic peoples who would inherit this great civilization around 1900 BC as it emerged from repeated invasions by semi-barbaric hordes.

---

[1]   Near the end of the twentieth century underwater cameras of a team searching for ancient sunken vessels in the Black Sea revealed the stone walls of those early shelters some 350 feet below the surface of the sea, and far into the sea from its present shore.

Although copper had been discovered much earlier it was of little use other than for ornaments as it had not the strength to be used as a tool. It was not until a century or two before 2000 BC that the means of making bronze was discovered and the true Bronze Age began in Egypt and Mesopotamia. That giant step from Stone Age to Bronze Age revolutionized all facets of Sumerian culture. It would be followed a couple of centuries later by another giant step, the invention of the spoked wheel, making possible horse drawn chariots. It would be still another five hundred years before Scythians and others learned to ride saddled horses. Unlike Europe the climate of Mesopotamia and North Africa lent itself to the growth of the urban civilizations which would not develop in Europe for another thousand years.

Tales and beliefs of the people of Sumer would grow to become an important part of the culture that small break-away Semitic tribes would later take with them. One dealt with Hammurabi, king from 1792 to 1750 BC, who is famous for his code of laws. According to Sumerian legend, the sun god Shamash summoned Hammurabi to whom he gave stone tablets upon which were engraved the laws for his people. A stone carving from about 1700BC, more than four hundred years before Moses is supposed to have been born, shows the god giving the tablets to Hammurabi.

A second set of legends, important for their effect upon the development of other cultures, were the tales of Gilgamesh. The Gilgamesh epics, often described as an odyssey, were carved on tablets. One of its poems tells of the gods' decision to destroy all humans. However, one of Gilgamesh's ancestors was warned by a friendly god, and was told to build a boat large enough to save his family, craftsmen of all kinds, and pairs of all animals and birds. The legend describes how this ancestor sent birds out from his boat when the torrential rains had ceased, and when those birds did not return he knew they had found land and that he was saved, whereupon he offered sacrifices to the gods.

Another Sumerian myth dealt with the death of their god Tammuz, known as the Good Shepherd, who died but was resurrected from the dead. Such resurrection stories were to become an important part of the beliefs of religious cults throughout the Middle East and Egypt. Goddesses played important roles in the myths of these cults, in some cases bringing about the resurrection of a slain god.

According to Sumerian priests, God made man from clay and upon death man returned to a house of dust. According to this religion, the purpose for which humans were created by God was to worship him through their acts and sacrifices.

Egyptians at that time were also brought up to believe in several gods, one who was killed and then resurrected. Pharaohs were supposed to have been born of virgins who had been approached by a god; a useful belief in preventing rivals from claiming the throne merely by assassinating a reigning pharaoh. Later, in ancient Greece and Rome, followers of heroic leaders such as Alexander the Great and Caesar Augustus would be taught that their leaders had been born of virgins. This always lent authority to the words and actions of such heroes who were thus supposed to be half God.

As would be true in all regions of the Middle East and Egypt for the next two thousand years after the Sumerians first came to power, heroes were capable of using magic. When a person fell ill, it was supposed that evil spirits had entered that person's body. In ancient mythology these priests and heroes were, through magic, able to cast out these evil spirits and demons.

Sumerian religion developed to the point where priests had become a powerful, if not the most powerful, element of that early urban civilization. A person's dreams were thought to be important messages which only the priests could interpret in their temples. Because man was supposedly created to worship the gods, the priests collected, as tribute to the gods, almost the entire production of farmers and shepherds. Some of this was used in temple sacrifices, but much was retained by the priests, making them some of the wealthiest citizens of Sumer.

Whether it was because of these continual collections of all they had worked and slaved to produce, or because of unrest resulting from invasions and infiltrating newcomers, or because of the sharp contrast between the life of the cities such as Ur and the more puritanical peasants, or for some other cause, historians are not sure. But, whatever the reason, according to records archaeologists discovered during the twentieth century, a clan, led by its patriarch, Terah, left the region around Ur.

THE ABRAHAMIC LEGACY

The clan of Terah, like other clans of the time, was largely an extended family. Though joined by other tribes and clans Terah appears to have remained the overall leader of this exodus.[2] Whether when this migration began around 2000 BC it had an intended destination is not known, but ultimately the wanderers arrived at Harran.

As a bird flies, Harran was no more than three hundred miles to the northwest of Ur. However, to assure water and grazing for their flocks, the nomads would have tended to follow the Euphrates to the region around Harran. Here again these nomads, who had become known as the Habiru (Hapiru),[3] were to live amid a culture that was heavily religious. Harran was already known for the religious pilgrims who traveled to this home of the worshipers of the god Sin, a cult not unlike that of the moon god of Ur. As Terah's band, including its slaves, had to adjust its travel to the need for flocks to graze, and would make other stops perhaps for months at a time, no one knows whether the trip from Ur to Harran may have taken as much as years to complete.

When reading legends of the various ancient civilizations, or the *Old Testament*, it is important to remember that chronology was usually skewed to fit the myths of the time and the mathematical patterns the writers believed should be followed. Sumerians, during the centuries when the Habiru had lived in that region, believed that before the great flood life on earth had been a paradise in which people lived to fantastic ages. Eight kings were supposed to have ruled in that unblemished world and the lives of those eight kings stretched over more than 241,000 years according to legend. It is little wonder that this culture could give birth to the story of Methuselah living 969 years.

These myths and later attempts by Hebrew writers to write history in which major events fell at regular mathematical intervals should not, however, mean that many of those events did not take place. The baby should not be thrown out with the bath water.

---

[2] During the 1920's and 1930's archaeologists unearthed the royal palace in Mari, a city which had existed at the time of Ur. Here among thousands of cuneiform tablets were religious as well as legal and other political records. These records include mention of the exodus of certain Semitic tribes at this time. They also provide insight into the religious practices and religious legends of the period.

[3] From the days of earliest recorded history, nomadic or migrating tribes have moved against and raided the homes and villages of settled people. The Habiru were no different, and some historians note that one translation of Habiru is "stranger" or "robber". One should not read into that the negative or criminal meaning of the word "robber" as it is used in the twenty-first century.

Like those of the Sumerians, Hebrew legends also listed kings for the idyllic world that supposedly existed before humankind was cleansed by the great flood. Whereas one Sumerian king of that mythical pre-flood world lived as long as 43,000 years, Hebrew kings before Noah lived only about 900 to a 1,000 years each. After Noah and until the time of Abraham they lived only 200 to 600 years.[4]

According to the bible Terah died at Harran when 205 years old and leadership of the Habiru (Hebrews) was assumed by his son Abraham. Even when disregarding the years these myths have assigned to the lives of Terah and his son Abraham, ancient records do indicate a lengthy stay in the area of Harran with its religions and customs somewhat similar to those of Ur.

According to *Genesis*, Abraham led the Hebrews from Harran at the age of 75. Harran lay near the northern edge of that extension of the Arabian Desert now known as the Syrian Desert. The Arabian Desert stretched from what is today the southern part of Saudi Arabia to Turkey, a distance of more than 1,200 miles. It would be around 1400 BC when their wanderings eventually brought the Hebrews to Palestine. During the five hundred or more years from the time they left Harran until they reached Palestine they had lived with their flocks mostly in desert or semi-desert regions. Unlike the urban civilizations of the time, Hebrews as nomads had little access to minerals and did not produce bronze or later iron. However, through their contacts with the peoples of the areas through which they traveled, and where at times they would settle during those five hundred years, they were exposed to a variety of religions.

The people of each of these regions believed in several gods. Usually, however, they believed one god was superior to the others and was their particular god. Monolatry, this belief in several gods, but with one god being superior and protector of his people, was an early step toward the monotheism the Hebrews would come to adopt slowly over the centuries after reaching Canaan.

Those centuries of wandering in the desert and on its fringes had by 1400 BC led the Hebrews to Palestine, the home of the Canaanites. The Hebrew were still a small tribe and were only one of the Semitic peoples populating the Near East, but unlike most other Semites they had not built cities and an urban culture. For the most

---

[4]   The years each of those early Hebrew kings is supposed to have lived are taken from the fifth chapter of *Genesis*.

part they had kept apart from everyone except fellow tribesmen. Whereas Canaanites had developed villages and cities with houses and shops the Hebrews, still semi-nomadic, lived in brush huts or tents. Despite this deliberate separation, Hebrews did recognize the Canaanite gods, especially El, the superior god.[5]

It may have been this common adoption of the same god at that point in history, and probably intermarriage, which led some Canaanites and others to become part of the Hebrew community. Hebrew archeologists, such as Ze'ev Herzog and Israel Finklestein of Tel Aviv University, not only cast doubts that there had ever been a presence in or an exodus from Egypt; they also support earlier historians who have described the "magnificent" biblical kingdom of Solomon and later David as a gross exaggeration of later centuries. It is now recognized that Hebrew tribes later grew to the size they eventually reached, some eight hundred years after their entry into Palestine, in large part because of the large number of Canaanites and others who became part of the Hebrew extended families.

Having no written language in those earlier years, Hebrew history, as recorded by Hebrew writers some 800 years after their entry into Palestine, was that which had been passed down by word of mouth at campfires and in rituals over the centuries.[6] It would not be until Josiah, king of Judah (c. 640-609 BC) directed that the myths, legends, religious rituals, travels, trials and tribulations of the Israelites be recorded that the early books of the *Old Testament* came into being.[7] Over the next four centuries further books would be added to the *Old Testament*; the last being written about two hundred years before Jesus.

---

[5]   Despite writings of the *Old Testament* aiming to trace the Hebrew's belief in only one God from the time of Adam, Joshua notes, "They served other Gods."

[6]   Hebrew, the spoken language gave way after 300 BC to Aramaic which became the language spoken by most Jews. It was the language spoken by Jesus. Although Hebrew was used in religious services and in liturgical poetry, it did not become the spoken language of most Jews again until modern Hebrew came into common use in the late 18th century AD.

[7]   After entering Palestine the Hebrews became known as Israelites and their land Israel. One of the twelve tribes settled in what became known as Judah, the southern part of the country. They became known as Jews. After the Babylonian exile in 538 BC, all who followed the religious teachings of Judaism would be called Jews.

Judah had been considered a vassal of the Assyrians for around eighty years when Josiah became king of Judah, but by then the Assyrian empire was on the verge of collapse. The Babylonians who had long been a part of the Assyrian empire were rising against their Assyrian monarchs and appeared about to take over the empire. Egypt, no longer the power she had once been, realized her future would be threatened by the rise of a new strong power. For her it was important that the Near East remain divided among weak powers, which meant a strong Babylonia could not be tolerated. Obviously, a preemptive invasion by Egypt would include Israel and Judah and would put an end to Josiah's hopes and plans for unifying the Jews.

Recent discoveries by Israeli scholars point to this threat as the reason for Josiah ordering that a history of the Hebrews, from Adam to what was then the present, be compiled. In what these Israeli scholars refer to as a part of Josiah's efforts to unify the squabbling tribes of Israel and Judah, writers of the *Old Testament* were to show that their current belief of one God and a chosen people stemmed from the days of Adam and Eve.

According to recent findings of these Israeli scholars Josiah was using the threatened invasion by Egypt as a means to instill what today we would refer to as a chauvinistic nationalism. Among other important points in this saga, was reference to a supposed captivity imposed upon them in Egypt and an escape followed by years of wandering in the desert where a leader, Moses, received the Ten Commandments from God.

Whether one accepts these new interpretations of King Josiah's role and purpose in recording these books that we refer to as the *Old Testament*, Egypt did become a symbol of potential invasion and captivity for the people of Israel and Judah. Under Josiah, the Jews did become a more unified and xenophobic nation.

EARLY RELIGIOUS INFLUENCES

In their early development all major religions have been influenced by religious, ethical, and other social beliefs of neighboring peoples. Early Judaism was no exception. Babylonian religious stories of Creation, the Great Flood, and the Tower of Babel had influenced Abraham's people in Sumer as early as 2,000 B.C. The laws of Hammurabi, supposed to have been written on stone tablets given him by a God, had been part of the Sumerian legacy which the descendants of Abraham carried with them for four hundred years before the heart of those laws appeared in commandments attributed to Moses.

Under the reign of Amenhotep (1375-1350 B.C.), the people of Egypt were ordered to adopt monotheism. Later pharaohs would return to belief in several gods, but the belief in resurrection remained constant over the thousands of years.[8] Over the centuries Jews had become well aware of Egypt and its traditions. We have already noted the years spent in Canaan, and the influence of monalatry.

Around 600 B.C. Zarathustra brought reform to the Persians in the form of a new religion, Zoroastrianism. It was only fourteen years later that Jews were swept into captivity in Babylonia where Zoroastrianism was by then flourishing. So, for a second time Babylonian beliefs impacted and influenced the religion of the Jews. Surrounded by Babylonians, the exiles soon became familiar with new religious rituals, such as baptism. Biblical scholars now acknowledge the great influence Zoroastrianism had on Judaism, particularly during the period in which much of the Jewish scriptures was being written after the reign of King Josiah of Judea.

Among the more familiar of the Zoroastrian beliefs which would find their way into Jewish scriptures and would thereby eventually influence Christianity and Islam were the ideas of an evil Satan, a hell and a heaven, and an eventual Armageddon with a final judgment as the world came to an end.[9] But, before the end, Zoroasterians believed a Messiah would appear to lead the way into a new age for true believers. Only in the past century have biblical scholars and historians come to recognize just how deeply precepts of Zoroastrianism became embedded in Jewish scriptures. The book of Job, for example, appears to be either an adaptation or a crude translation of a Zoroastrian work.

The religion of the Jews would grow and be refined by the influences of the religions of their neighbors until it was the religion into which Jesus was born. It had not been a stagnant religion rejecting new ideas. It was the product of two thousand years of developing religious thought.

---

[8] Embalming of mummies and burial beneath pyramids with treasures to be used in the hereafter had long been practiced.

[9] Zoroastrians believed the first man had two sons; one evil and one good; a Cain and Abel as it were.

PALESTINE, THE LAND AND THE PEOPLE OF JESUS' TIME

Palestine was never a land of milk and honey, never a land of plenty, but often a land of hardship. In the north "The Great Plain (Esdraelon)" separated the hill country of Galilee from the hills of Samaria and Judea. It was one of the few fertile spots in Palestine and though only twenty-five miles long seemed "great" in the relatively tiny country.

Northern Galilee was an area of low rugged mountains and high hills cut by gorges and often barren.[10] Walking down from those hills toward the south of Galilee one would find the hills becoming smaller; but it was still hill country. The largest town in those lower hills was Nazareth. Jews living in those hills of Galilee, being relatively isolated in those northern reaches of Israel, were all too often looked down upon by those living elsewhere in Israel. The manner in which urban Americans of the first half of the twentieth century often looked down their noses at the people of Appalachia as "hillbillies" might well be considered an apt comparison with the manner in which Jews in Jerusalem looked at Galileans in the days of Jesus.

Israel and Judah were not easy places for a rural population to eke out a living. Hillsides, or as some would see them, mountain sides, and rock strewn valleys forced shepherds to move frequently to find graze for their sheep. After rains, angry torrents swept down the rough gullies, while at other times the earth baked under the Near East sun. Life was a trying time in which the Twenty Third Psalm carried practical meaning, a vision bringing hope.

The Lord is my shepherd,
I shall not want,
He makes me lie down in green pastures;
He leads me beside still waters.

A good teacher tries to draw examples from the lives of his or her pupils. The *Old Testament*, the bible of Jesus in his youth, is replete with such examples.

---

[10] In comparison, the Allegheny mountains of New York and Pennsylvania are roughly the same height though tree covered whereas the mountains of Palestine were mostly barren. The highest peak of the Appalachian chain is roughly a third higher than the highest of those Palestinian mountains.

To the east of the Galilean hills the earth dropped to a lake thirteen miles long and seven miles wide, which in Jesus' time had become known as the Sea of Galilee. Along streams flowing into and out of the "sea" there was another narrow area of fertile fields. Here, in contrast to the hills of Galilee, were prosperous farms and villages. Such sharp contrast between those eking out a living in the hill country and those living in the fertile areas could not help but create resentment. If anything it would emphasize the remoteness and relative isolation of the hill country Galileans.

Jesus was born at a time of considerable political unrest, a time when Jews agitated to rid their nation of foreign rule. Some, like the Zealots, were even organizing armed resistance. There was almost universal belief that the Messiah was about to appear to lead them to victory over their Roman occupiers and to restore a glory that existed only in myth. The meaning given to the title Messiah by most readers of the *New Testament* is not that which most of the people of Judah and Israel meant by the term.

Over a period of four hundred years, from roughly 200 BC to 200AD prophets predicted that God would intervene on behalf of his "chosen" people. A savior would be sent who would deliver Israel from Roman rule.[11] This savior, or Messiah, would establish a kingdom of God with peace and justice for his chosen people. For the most part the people of Israel were not thinking of a spiritual (heavenly) kingdom, but rather of a kingdom on earth in which all who had adopted Yahweh as their god would live in peace while non-believers would be consigned to subservience under the Jews and their Messiah.[12]

It is not surprising that this expectation resulted in the appearance of numerous false Messiahs from 200 BC to the time of Jesus. However, the prophets of an apocalypse insisted that the true Messiah would have to be a descendant of David, who had lived almost

---

[11]   Such divine intervention on behalf of a persecuted people would, according to the belief of the time, result in a period of chaos and tremendous physical, social, and political upheavals. Such a period, would be known as an apocalypse (from the Greek word meaning "revelation"). See the book of *Daniel* in the Old Testament and the *Revelation to John* in the New Testament.

[12]   This was not an uncommon belief among the religions of the world. Mahayana Buddhism and Zoroastrianism, for example, fostered the belief that a Buddha or a son of Zoroaster would descend from heaven to cleanse the world and resurrect the dead.

a thousand years before the time of Jesus; a crucial point upon which the Pharisees insisted. Although anyone claiming to be the Messiah would realize this and would need to claim this lineage, none were able to prove it. This lack of proof had prevented those claiming to be the Messiah from assuming the throne, and assured the continuing power and influence of the Sadducees and the Pharisees.[13]

By this time the roles of the Sadducees and the Pharisees were clearly defined. Not too unlike today - when protestant denominations have proliferated and there are Roman, Greek Orthodox, and Russian Orthodox Catholic churches in the Christian community - Jews of the First Century BC supported various sects. Sadducees had, over two centuries, developed as a priestly sect supporting the government. This gave them status similar to the higher members of the aristocracy. They claimed that the "Law", the sacred scriptures now found in the first five books of the *Old Testament*, was the complete account of God's revelation to his chosen people. Therefore they denied the possibility of resurrection of the body and the existence of an immortal soul.

Whereas the Sadducees were a "priestly" body, the Pharisees were laymen, sometimes referred to as a community of scholars, who worked closely with scribes in spreading their teachings. They recognized the Torah as Mosaic Law, but also believed this "Law" should include oral traditions handed down over the centuries.

The Sadducees had every reason to perpetuate the government which, in turn, assured them of support by the Roman governors; thereby making them part of the political hierarchy. They not only accepted Roman occupation, but maintained friendly relations with the Romans. The Pharisees, instead, leaned heavily on scholarship. They spent lifetimes seeking new interpretations of the Law in their conviction that oral law had become a part of Mosaic Law. Their work was largely responsible for a growing body of religious wisdom that drew Jews closer together, keeping their religion "pure" and thereby separating them from the Romans, Greeks, and other Gentiles.

---

[13] "Messiah" is the English translation of the Hebrew word meaning "the anointed one"; the Greek translation is "Christos." David is supposed to have been anointed king by Samuel acting as an agent for the divine. This strengthened the belief that a Messiah would need to be a direct descendant of David, a lineage each claimant tried to prove. Though the messiah would be called "the anointed one, he was not to be thought of as divine; that would conflict with the commandment ordaining "One God."

14

The Sadducees, who centered their life and work in the temple, had little contact with other Jews. From their position of wealth and friendship with the Romans they adopted an arrogant attitude of superiority toward all other Jews which made them a class hated by most other Jews. In contrast the Pharisees, as laymen, established synagogues where rabbis could teach people meeting therein.[14]

Not everyone was willing to wait for a Messiah, and it was amid this political turmoil that Jesus grew from infancy to the time he began his years of teaching. In Galilee, where there was fierce resentment of the Romans and disgruntlement over the Jewish establishment's cooperation with the Romans, the Zealots were born. They were the most extreme of the major Jewish political elements in their fierce insistence on strict adherence to the Law. As this sect grew, so grew its hatred for the multi-god religion of the Romans. They believed it was their duty to remove all obstacles the coming Messiah might otherwise face in making Israel the Kingdom of God.

Jesus was about twelve years old when the Romans sent officials to take a census in Galilee. It was the last straw. The Zealots ordered the Galileans to refuse to participate. Anyone who participated was considered to have accepted Rome's right to govern the Jews as a colony. So extreme were the Zealots that in their fanaticism many became terrorists. Jews known to have cooperated with the Romans were cut down wherever they were found, preferably where the public would witness the murder and thereby be warned of the fate awaiting any who worked with the Romans.[15] Jesus would grow up in the midst of this hatred and violence.

In sharp contrast to the Zealots were the Essenes who lived in monastic communities in or at the edge of the "wilderness." The "Law of Moses" was the center of their lives. Deeply religious, they lived a puritanical existence in which they believed God would punish them, if they sinned. Though they preached peace they were firm in their belief

---

[14] Synagogues are thought to have been first established during the Babylonian Exile, when for the Jews in exile there was no temple; the Temple having been destroyed in 596 BC. Historians believe services were then held in private homes until the first synagogues were built. For Jews, after the second destruction of the Temple in 70 AD, the synagogue became the important community center for worship and the teaching of their religion.
[15] The Zealots would eventually (forty-three years after the death of Jesus) lead an open revolt against the Romans which would end with their mass suicide when the Romans defeated them at Masada seven years after their open revolt had begun.

that anyone who used the name of Moses or God in vain should be put to death. Except for their monastic existence, their interpretation of the law did not differ greatly from that of the Pharisees. However, one difference should be noted. Essenes believed in immortality of the soul, though not in resurrection of the physical body.

Although he may not have been an Essene, John the Baptist had lived in the same desert area the Essenes populated before beginning his years of preaching. His message was simple. The world would soon come to an end and God would judge all who lived therein. Those who repented their sins would be saved. Baptism by John, unlike later baptism in Christian churches, was a necessary cleansing of the individual which would save that repentant person from the cleansing fire God would bring on his day of judgment. And, John preached, that day was fast approaching.

Jesus, who had grown to manhood in a Galilee in which the Zealots were growing as a sect, would move to live for a while with the disciples of John. This exposed him to an almost opposite approach to life than that of the Zealots. By the time Jesus was thirty-three years old he had lived among Galileans who had to struggle for their daily existence. He had walked among the farms of the fertile valleys of the streams feeding the Sea of Galilee, and visited prosperous towns along its shores. He had lived in the wilderness among the disciples of John and was familiar with the beliefs of the Essenes, and he had accepted baptism from John. It would be only then that he would step out into the world as the teacher whose message would become the foundation upon which Christianity would become a world religion not merely a cult or sect of one people.

* * * * * * * * * * * *

So, the *Old Testament* was not meant to be an accurate chronological journal or a history. So, some of its earliest "history" was partially a product of the myths of the Sumerians, the Assyrians, the Canaanites and others. So, the ancient Hebrews may have believed in other Gods for thousands of years. So there may never have been an exodus from Egypt or a wandering in the wilderness where a Moses received tablets from God. Does this mean the *Old Testament* is unimportant, or even something to discard as little more than a collection of stories? Are the Psalms any less beautiful or meaningful because they were composed over centuries instead of all being the works of David?

Absolutely not! The *Old Testament* is a wonderful account of a people whose thoughts evolved from primitive beliefs in multiple gods into monolatry, the belief in one superior god among other gods. It is a saga that shows how the "chosen people" eventually came to accept a single creative power. It lets us see how important that God became to them, so important that they called for "him" to bring his rule to them on earth.

Without those thousands of years of growing there would never have been the belief in one creative God that became the basis for Jesus' life and teachings. Never set aside the *Old Testament* as having little importance just because it is not an accurate chronicle of the year by year or century by century development of humankind, for it is far more important than any chronicle and is a part of history.

Remember, the scriptures of the *Old Testament* were the bible Jesus knew as a boy and a man.

CHAPTER 2

TWO DIFFERENT WAYS

The human mind is not a blackboard on which whatever one sees, hears, or reads is recorded just as it is recorded in the mind of any other person. A human brain can never be replicated, even in the most fantastic dreams of high technology; no two human brains are ever alike. Each of us is a unique individual.[16] Furthermore, this marvelously complex mind never records what it sees, hears, or otherwise senses exactly as does the mind of any other individual for, on a much less complex level, no two minds have received the same input in the past. Even in the last twenty-four hours each individual has seen, read, or heard something different from what his friends or family saw, read, or heard, and it is within this unique background that new input is perceived and interpreted.

Whether the reader of the bible is a creationist, or is one who believes humans have adapted (evolved) to meet changing conditions as this planet has changed over the millennia, there is general agreement that each individual is unique. The Christian minister or priest looking out over his or her congregation should recognize that no two minds will record his sermon in exactly the same manner.

As a shortcut to thinking, minds develop concepts built from information the mind receives throughout one's life. An individual

---

[16] Neuroscientists like Dr. Gerald Edelman point out that the cortex of the human brain consists of 30,000,000,000 neurons which have a million billion synapses (connections), each of which can work in a variety of ways.

seeing or hearing the word "horse" does not need a detailed description of a four legged animal. Instead, he or she immediately pictures a four-legged animal; but what first came to mind – a palomino, a snow white Arab, a roan mustang, a sturdy plodding Percheron, or a pony? A dozen people, if asked what first came to their minds when the word "horse" was mentioned, will offer a dozen different descriptions.

So it is when reading the bible. However, even though there will be differences in what each reader of the bible sees, in general readers fall into two categories. One group accepts the old and new testaments as factual chronicles of events and of acts of individuals. These readers accept the bible as literally true.

Readers of the second category may be equally faithful in their relationship to their religion. These readers, however, look upon the accounts in the bible not as literal truth, but rather as stories or parables in which a moral or lesson is brought to the reader.

It is with these two general categories of readers in mind that *Can Religion Survive Worship* concentrates on the message of the gospels.

Those who read the bible as an accurate history believe prophets and writers were literally writing what God was saying through them. Thus, to them, the bible becomes the word of God. Just as our modern thinking has been molded in large part by the "factual" approach of the scientific revolution, the manner in which the old and new testaments were written reflects the time and the people of that age. People did not preach, teach, or relate campfire stories as though they were facts. That was an age of symbols; when people expressed important ideas in terms of symbols. To understand the old and new testaments we need to step into the sandals of the writers and learn to interpret the message they have passed on in their symbolic writings.

No matter which way you read the bible, you should remember to put yourself in the sandals of the writers. Try to understand the world in which the writers lived. Remember that writings we call the *Old Testament* were the "bible" of Jesus and of his fellow countrymen living at that time. Two thousand years ago most people believed the world to be no larger than the lands they had explored. They could believe a "ceiling", in which the stars, moon, and sun were located, lay just above the clouds. They could believe heaven was located just above that ceiling from which, as in Jacob's dream, angels might even descend by a long ladder.

These were not stupid people. Readers should never fall into the trap of thinking that just because two thousand years ago technology had not evolved to the point where the universe could be explored as it is now being explored by scientists and astronauts of the twenty-first century, that the wisdom of that time has nothing to offer us today. We do not ignore the philosophies of Plato and Aristotle who lived centuries before Jesus. We find wisdom in the writings of Confucius and Lao Tzu, in Hindu and Buddhist teachings, and in the Koran. We respect the work of early scientists like Copernicus and Galileo and of those Arab scholars who gave us the Arabic numerals making modern mathematics possible and who opened doors for astronomers and surgeons.

It is the lessons those early prophets and writers of the bible were trying to bring to their listeners and readers that are important. Regardless of how you read the bible, literally or figuratively, try to discover what its writers were trying to teach.

HOW THE BIBLE WAS WRITTEN

The order in which the books of the *New Testament* appear in our bibles is not the order in which they were written. For example, Paul wrote his first letter (the one we now know as First Thessalonians) to a congregation practicing an early form of Christianity some eighteen to twenty years before the first Gospel was written. There are twenty-seven parts to the *New Testament*. Only the first four are Gospels about the life and teachings of Jesus.

The writers of the *Old Testament* used a style or method known as midrash. In writing of the lives and preachings of the prophets, those writers were teaching in a manner that required the listener or reader to study or search for the real meaning of the scriptures. During the six hundred and fifty years before Jesus began his teaching, these "scriptures" were not being written to be read as an accurate history, and most readers understood that. Instead of taking every story as historical fact, early followers and readers of the prophets searched for a deeper meaning in the stories, and they in turn wrote their own stories with a deeper meaning to be *discovered* by their readers.

There are few people today who have not read at least one of the *Fables* told by the Greek moralist Aesop some three hundred to four hundred years before Jesus was born. What we read today are those stories as they were remembered by men who wrote them down four or five hundred years after Aesop's death. We all know there was no race between a hare and a tortoise, but we do know there was a "moral" in that fable. We are supposed to look for what the writer wanted us to learn from his fables.

Those early writers knew that people forgot all too soon that which they heard. They knew nothing of the complex workings of the human brain, but believed people tended to have a better memory for things they saw, including that which they read. Those who taught in a midrashic manner understood that even that which people see is too often forgotten.[17] On the other hand, those early teachers and prophets believed that what one discovers, one tends to remember.[18]

It would be a grave mistake to assume because of the above illustration that the writings of the old and new testaments are fables. The only similarity is in the authors' inclusion of a moral or lesson to be discovered. Writings of the old and new testament are considerably more complex than the fables of Aesop. There is far more to be discovered.

Two thousand years ago, while Jesus lived, teaching by parables was the accepted way of getting a lesson across to a listener, and was the method of writing employed by the "wisdom writers." Psalm 78 begins with the explanation:

> Give ear, O my people, to my teaching;
> incline your ears to the words of my mouth.
> I will open my mouth in a parable.

Webster's Dictionary defines a parable as a "short fictitious story that illustrates a moral attitude or religious principle." Others add that parables have a sense of reality; that they use a situation with which the listener or reader is familiar. It is a way of getting people to use their imagination. If Aesop had only said, "the winner in life is not always the

---

[17] "Midrash" may be more literally interpreted to mean digging – as in digging up a hidden truth.

[18] Socrates on the other hand spoke out against written texts. He believed one had a better chance of retaining what one had discovered, if one had to rely upon his memory rather than a written text. Retaining as a memory what one discovered made it a permanent part of the mind which was constantly receiving new ideas.

fastest, but often is the one who keeps working steadily," how many people would remember? On the other hand, 2,400 years after the first telling of the tale of the Hare and the Tortoise we still retell the story to get across its moral.

Keep in mind that the *Old Testament* was the "bible", the collection of religious teachings that Jesus read. It was from those scriptures that he would have learned much about the method of teaching employed by early prophets and wisdom writers. We should also remember that Jesus considered himself a devout follower of the religion of the Jews. He sought to bring about reforms in the religion in which he had grown to manhood; reforms he believed necessary to bring people to live as he believed God wanted them to live. It was not until years after his death that followers of his teachings were in a sense "excommunicated" by fellow Jews, and no longer considered themselves or were no longer considered by others to be merely a reform sect of Judaism. Only then did they assume a separate identity as Christians.

THE GOSPELS

We have not found anything written about Jesus during his lifetime. It was around forty years after the death of Jesus that Mark wrote the first of the gospels. Mark had been an associate of Peter and Paul, and as we have noted his gospel was written some eighteen to twenty years after Paul's message to the Thessalonians, the first of Paul's letters. It was for those early churches that Paul had helped bring into being, that Mark was providing the first written collection of the material available about Jesus. By then churches were scattered through Anatolia, Greece, Egypt and what is today Italy; and some carried on practices definitely unacceptable to other Christian churches.[19]

Mark's gospel is the first written material that has been discovered that could have been used to bring a degree of conformity to all these young Christian churches. However, the reader should remember that in those days there was no good way to preserve

---

[19]   Some sects or cults had sprung up calling themselves Christians but seemed unaware of Jesus' teachings. Some even involved sexual orgies in their services. Paul needed to create a common awareness of the teachings of Jesus as a basis of belief and worship in all Christian churches. Mark's gospel, written shortly after Paul's death, provided this common ground for the development of each church.

writings over a long period of time. We do know that in copying the writings in what are today our old and new testaments, changes were made. Copying a book of the *Old Testament* could take months when done with a quill pen. Mistakes were bound to happen. There is also evidence that some scribes made changes to insert their own ideas.

The oldest copies of the gospels of the *New Testament* that have been found were made by scribes some 200 to 300 years after Jesus died. We know there were considerably more than four "gospels," but we are not certain how many of those writings were "biographical" as well as being a record of Jesus' teachings. We only know that the four gospels in the *New Testament* were those chosen to be included in the bible by church leaders putting the *New Testament* together in Rome more than two hundred years after Jesus died, and that these reflect what those leaders considered necessary to unite a religion under their leadership.

TEACHING BY PARABLES

Shortly after Jesus began teaching, his disciples asked him about parables. He told them that for other people than the disciples "everything comes in parables," (Mark 4:10-11). He had just finished speaking to people who had gathered around him to whom he had said:

Listen, A sower went out to sow, And it happened that as he sowed, some seed fell along the footpath; and the birds came and ate it up. Some seed fell on rocky ground, where it had little soil, and it sprouted quickly because it had no depth of earth; but when the sun rose the young corn was scorched, and as it had no root, it withered away. Some seed fell among thistles, and the thistles shot up and choked the corn, and it yielded no crop. And some of the seed fell into good soil, where it came up and grew, and bore fruit; and the yield was thirtyfold, sixtyfold, even a hundredfold.

Mark: 4.3-9

Then Jesus said to his disciples: "If you have ears to hear, *then hear.*" When the disciples asked what he meant by that he said to them:

> You do not understand this parable? How then will
> you understand any parable? The sower sows the
> word. Those along the footpath are people in whom
> the word is sown, but no sooner have they heard it
> than Satan comes and carries off the word which has
> been sown in them. It is the same with those who
> receive the word on rocky ground; as soon as they
> hear the word, they accept it with joy, but it strikes
> no root in them; they have no staying-power; then,
> when there is trouble or persecution on account of
> the word, they fall away at once.
>
> Others again receive the seed among the thistles;
> they hear the word, but worldly cares and the false
> glamour of wealth and all kinds of evil desire come
> in and choke the word, and it proves barren. And
> there are those who receive the seed in good soil;
> they hear the word and welcome it; and they bear
> the fruit thirtyfold, sixtyfold, or a hundredfold
>
> Mark: 4.13-20

As we shall see when we have read further, Jesus did not speak of Satan as a person. If we think of Satan as someone with superhuman power we are talking of more than one god, a god of good and a god of evil. To Jesus there was only one god. He personified in an image of Satan all the temptations of the world that could draw people from the way of God.

The *New Oxford Bible* notes that: "the devil, tempter, and Satan are names for evil." These were words Jesus used when speaking of a person's will or desire to live in a way he saw as being against God's will. He spoke of people being so interested in such things as gaining a political position, finding wealth, seeking praise and prestige, or seeking pleasure that these things became more important than trying to live according to the way he believed God wanted them to live.

The *"Word"* was the message Jesus was trying to bring to people; a message in which he described how God wanted people to live. Some speak of the "*Word*" as being the truth. Greek was the language in which the Gospels were first written. The Greek word *logos* translates into English as "*word*", but it means far more than what "word" means in English. The *New Oxford Bible* notes: "The *Word* of God is more than speech; it is God in action, creating, revealing, redeeming."

As used in the Gospel According to John, "Jesus is the *Word*." (John: 1. 1-2). The *New English Bible* explains that John used *Word* to describe Jesus as the messenger who would show us the God we could not see.

Parables require us to use our imagination. Suppose Jesus had just said, "People can be told about the way God wants them to live, but if they have other things to do that they think are more important they will not pay attention. They may hear, but when other people ridicule their belief, or if in some parts of the world they are punished for their belief, they will turn away from that belief."

Would those words have been remembered by those who listened to him? Would anyone have passed those words down to us 2,000 years later? However, people remembered the parable of the sower because it made them use their imagination. They had to *discover* the meaning for themselves.

When the disciples asked Jesus why he spoke to the people in parables he explained that he spoke to them in parables because, "….they look *without seeing*, and listen *without hearing* or understanding." They had to discover the truth for themselves.

USING THE DISCIPLES

If the disciples had not been unable to understand the parable of the sower, Mark would not have had a reason for providing an explanation; an explanation that in turn provided an introduction to the way of teaching by parable. When reading the gospels a reader finds Jesus usually speaking to, or at least in the presence of, his disciples. Mark uses the disciples' lack of understanding, mistakes made by them, and lack of their faith as the target for Jesus' teachings. Mark's gospel would have been very dull, if it had merely been written as a long list of things Jesus stood for and wanted people to practice in their daily lives.

The disciples of the gospels provide a reason for Jesus to offer his teachings. When Matthew and Luke used Mark's gospel as the core of their gospels they retained the use of the disciples as the target for Jesus' lessons. As readers move on in their reading of the gospels, they will note the need for the presence of disciples in the parable in which Jesus calms the storm threatening their boat. This provides a reason for Jesus to offer a discourse on faith. In the parable in which a rich man seeks to enter the kingdom of heaven it is to the disciples that Jesus explains what is required for entrance into that kingdom. It is to the disciples at the Last Supper that Jesus explains the need for his death. A doubting Thomas provides a gospel writer an opportunity to discuss faith as it is related to spiritual resurrection.

Throughout the gospels the disciples repeatedly provide an audience which fails to understand the role of faith, or whose mistakes need correcting, or whose questions call for answers. Without this role of the disciples as targets for Jesus' teachings the gospel writers would have had little success in providing the basis for two thousand years of Christian thought. If readers were to remove every parable or teaching of Jesus that involves disciples as his audience, what would be left for them to read? And would there then have been any basis for the later writings of letters and epistles? The disciples were the absolutely essential sounding board for Mark, Matthew, and Luke.

RESPECT TWO WAYS OF READING THE BIBLE

To his disciples, Jesus was a teacher (rabbi). His use of parables demonstrates his effectiveness as that teacher. Whereas there is little disagreement about Jesus' parables between those reading the bible literally or figuratively, it is when reading what the writers of the Gospels wrote about Jesus that the differences between the two ways of reading the *New Testament* become a gulf.

It is here that literalists believe that what Matthew, Mark, Luke, and John wrote is an accurate chronicle of all that took place in Jesus' life and of all he said as a teacher. Figurativists, on the other hand, believe the Gospel writers were not recording history when writing about Jesus' life, but were writing in the form of parables just as Jesus had taught them. It is important to remember that the writers of the Gospels were also trying to teach.

If a new reader considers the Bible to be merely a collection of historical facts, it is easy to become confused when he or she finds contradictions within a gospel, or when two gospels describe something so differently that it appears that they are contradicting each other. The reader will not be confused, if he or she realizes each gospel writer is trying to get across Jesus' message, but that each is using some parables and stories that are different than those of other gospels in order to do this. Learn to dig into these parables and stories to find the beauty and the treasure of their real meaning.

Figurativists who do not accept the bible as literally accurate read the bible for what they consider is its "real" message. Within the midrash of the time when Jesus lived they seek a deeper meaning in what they consider to be parables about Jesus' life.

So, herein lies your challenge. Regardless of whether you read the bible as literal truth or as figurative writings with a deeper message, the challenge is for you to discover the message the writers of the gospels intended for you to find. No matter which way you read the bible, always remember those who read it differently than you are also seeking the truth; and do not doubt their faith because of your differences.

CHAPTER 3

THE FIRST GOSPEL

It was a rare individual in rural Israel who could read or write when Jesus lived. Even if such an individual had happened to know Jesus during his childhood or during the adult years before Jesus met John the Baptist, there would have been no reason to write about a fellow Nazarene.

Without the food and medical care we take for granted in the twenty-first century, few people in Jesus' lifetime lived past the age of forty-five. Most adults who had heard Jesus preach when they were twenty or thirty years old had died well before Mark picked up his quill to begin the first Gospel. His sources were oral traditions passed down through two generations; and biblical scholars believe that being close to Peter and Paul he was quoting much of what they had preached.

Forty years had passed since the crucifixion by the time Mark had collected what was then known of Jesus' life and teachings and had given them to Christians as the first Gospel. As there was no written record, and apparently no oral account, of Jesus life before he walked into the camp of John the Baptist, Mark would begin his gospel with the introduction of a thirty-three year old Jesus about to begin his teaching.

The English word *Apostle* stems from the Greek word meaning "people sent"; and from his many disciples Jesus is said to have selected twelve, who after he was crucified were to be sent on missions to preach his message.[20] Later, feeling he had been sent by God to carry the word of Jesus, Paul would also assume the title apostle.

The *New Oxford Bible* describes Mark's gospel as "the earliest attempt" to bring together, in written form, the oral traditions and teachings of the apostles. Thus, 'The Gospel According to Mark' becomes "a collection of traditions about Jesus". But, as pointed out in *New English Bible,* we should not let the term collection "mislead one to suppose that the material is presented haphazardly."

MARK – THE FORERUNNER

Later, Mark's gospel would provide Matthew and Luke with their major source of information about the teachings of Jesus as well as an outline for their gospels.[21] It would not be until roughly fifty-five or sixty years after the death of Jesus, about twenty years after Mark had written his gospel, that Matthew and Luke would write theirs.

As "The Gospel According to Mark" is the earliest written account we have of the life and teachings of Jesus, readers of the *New Testament* are well advised to read Mark as the "first book" of the *New Testament.*[22] As is the case with most biblical writings, no one is certain who wrote "The Gospel According to Mark." However, most biblical scholars attribute the gospel to John Mark who had traveled with Paul during years of the early development of the Christian church, and consider his gospel to be based largely on material drawn from Peter's sermons.[23]

---

[20] By the time Jesus entered Jerusalem he was being followed by a band of disciples considerably larger than the twelve named in the Gospels.

[21] Matthew and Luke appear to have also used another source from which they drew material. Biblical historians refer to that source as "Q", from the German *Quelle,* meaning source.

[22] Although Paul's letters were written before Mark wrote his gospel, Paul did not discuss Jesus' life, sermons, or travels. His correspondence dealt primarily with the affairs of the churches he had founded, and his personal theology as it developed.

[23] We too find John Mark's background such as to make him the author of this gospel. Biblical scholars have commented that Mark has more or less recorded Peter's sermons.

From certain references in his gospel, scholars place Mark in Rome at a time of his writing. Both Peter and Paul were living in Rome giving Mark the opportunity to spend much time with them. Peter died in 64 A.D. and Paul in 67 A.D. It was a time when Christians were still being persecuted by Nero, who for political purposes had accused them of setting the fire that had wiped out much of Rome in 64 A.D. It was also shortly before Jerusalem was destroyed by the Romans in 70 A.D.; Mark's gospel being written shortly before the destruction of the temple.

Mark knew well the land, customs, beliefs, and language (Aramaic) of the Jews. However, by the time he wrote, Christians were no longer just a reform sect of Judaism, but were to be found in the growing church in Greece, Anatolia, Egypt, and what is today Italy. It was for those expanding Gentile congregations, and for Jews who were being ostracized for adhering to the teachings of Jesus that Mark prepared his gospel; bringing together the stories and preaching comprising the oral traditions of the apostles.

So, let us start where Mark started his gospel, which he made available to Christians forty years after Jesus was crucified.

JESUS ARRIVES

Keeping in mind the background of the times and the role of John the Baptist, Mark's opening passage provides a smooth segue into the works of Jesus.

> In the prophet Isaiah it stands written: 'Here is my herald whom I send on ahead of you, and he shall prepare your way. A voice crying aloud in the wilderness, "Prepare a way for the Lord; clear a straight path for him." And so it was that John the Baptist appeared in the wilderness proclaiming a baptism in token of repentance, for the forgiveness of sins; and they flocked to him from the whole Judean country-side and the city of Jerusalem, and were baptized by him in the River Jordan, confessing their sins.
>
> His proclamations ran: "After me comes one who is mightier than I. I am not fit to unfasten his shoes. I have

> baptized you with water; he will baptize you with the
> Holy Spirit."
>
> It happened at this time that Jesus came from
> Nazareth in Galilee and was baptized in the Jordan by
> John. At the moment he came out of the water, he saw
> the heavens torn open and the Spirit, Like a dove,
> descending upon him. And a voice spoke from heaven:
> "Thou art my Son, my Beloved; on thee my favor rests."
>
> Thereupon the Spirit sent him away into the
> wilderness, and there he remained for forty days
> tempted by Satan.....
>
> Mark: 1. 2-13

Was there anything Mark wanted the reader to grasp from this introduction beyond a literal reading of the passage? Was the Spirit something people could see? Mark indicates others were present, because he has John telling them about Jesus. But by speaking of the "Spirit" John is implying something that could not be seen. What then is the purpose of this introduction that Mark prepared for this Gospel?

Writers of the gospels wrote concisely. They did not waste words. There was meaning in every paragraph of their writings. Serious readers of the *New Testament* should seek that meaning - should discover whatever Mark hoped and intended that his readers would discover.

As we have noted, Jesus spent some time, probably months, with John and John's disciples. He did not arrive at the river Jordan, stop only long enough to be baptized, and then move on into the wilderness. Several important points are being made by Mark in these few lines of introduction.

First, Mark says Jesus is from Nazareth in Galilee. Nothing more is said of Jesus' past. It is as though Mark is rebutting those who would say: "What good can possibly come out of the hills of Galilee?" Mark is saying that whatever Jesus did in the years from his birth until he was baptized at the age of thirty-three is unimportant; that Jesus should be judged only by what he did and said from that point on until his death; not by his humble origins; nor by anything he might have done or not done before he left the hills of Galilee.

Second, Mark uses the word "beloved." In the context of the time and circumstances that was not a term used to describe an emotional feeling. "Beloved" meant the "chosen one." Therefore, Mark is introducing Jesus as being revealed, at the time of his baptism, as the chosen messenger of God.

Third, by introducing Jesus as he is being baptized by John, Mark has placed Jesus in a specific time period recognized by those who knew of John. Remember, Mark is introducing Jesus to Gentiles, as well as to a new generation of Jews, forty years after the crucifixion. He has given Christians a starting place in time, a point from which to build.

Fourth, Mark has given reason for Jesus' departure from John. Historians note that Jesus had favorably impressed most of John's disciples. Upon his departure John's followers were divided. Some wished to leave and accompany Jesus, others remained loyal to John. The line "Thereupon, the Spirit sent him away into the wilderness" gives reason for Jesus to depart alone, which was necessary if he were to be able to meditate in the wilderness and to find the strength to defeat the temptations now facing him.

Mark tells us that during those forty days Jesus was "tempted by Satan." Twenty years later Matthew and Luke elaborated on those temptations. Mark assumes his readers will understand that Jesus is being tempted to use his talent for persuading listeners, and his ability to attract loyal followers, to attain the material power with which to become the king of Israel; but that Jesus will reject the material for the spiritual. Mark does not see the need to go into the detail that Matthew and Luke do in their fourth chapters.

INTRODUCING THE TEACHER

Apparently with no further knowledge of Jesus' activities until he began his teaching in Galilee, Mark jumps to the beginning of Jesus' ministry by taking his readers directly to Galilee.

> After John had been arrested, Jesus came into Galilee proclaiming the Gospel of God: "The time has come; the Kingdom of God is upon you; repent, and believe the Gospel."
>
> Mark: 1.14-15

Jesus is next seen walking beside the Sea where he sees Simon, Andrew, James, and John to whom he says: "Come with me and I will make you fishers of men." Though Mark does not indicate what Jesus may have done or preached from the time he returned to Galilee until he met these men, whatever he had done or said was such as to make these fishermen follow him with confidence. They just did not pick up and leave with a complete stranger.

Artists' versions of the disciples, painted centuries later, depict mature men. Considering the life expectancy during Jesus' lifetime, his disciples were undoubtedly young adults, who with the exception of Simon (Peter) were yet without families of their own.[24] In empathizing with Jesus and his followers, readers should keep in mind that Jesus is still only thirty-three years old and his disciples are younger. This is a relatively youthful band of enthusiastic disciples, still young enough to challenge the settled ways and traditions of the communities in which they lived.

With his new companions Jesus entered Capernaum, a town at the Northern end of the Sea of Galilee, the most prosperous area of Galilee. Here we find our first conflict between those who read the New Testament literally and those who read it figuratively.

> ...on the Sabbath he went to the synagogue and began to teach. The people were astounded at his teaching, for, unlike the doctors of law, he taught with a note of authority. Now there was a man in the synagogue possessed by an unclean spirit. He shrieked: "What do you want with us, Jesus of Nazareth? Have you come to destroy us? I know who you are - the Holy One of God." Jesus rebuked him :
>
> 'Be silent,' he said, 'and come out of him.' And the unclean spirit threw the man into convulsions and with a loud cry left him...
>
> Mark: 1.21-27

The congregation was impressed. They were used to speakers who quoted from the prophets or from familiar religious authorities. Here before them was a stranger who was speaking with authority; but

---

[24]   Mark and Matthew refer to Jesus' visit to Simon's mother-in-law.

not authority based upon those religious sources with which they were familiar. A literal reading of this passage has a man possessed by demons, and Jesus performing the miracle of casting out those unclean spirits.

A figurative approach to this passage notes the shrieking man's questions, "What do you want with us, Jesus of Nazareth? Have you come to destroy us?" These are not surprising questions coming from a deeply religious man. Jesus' message is not that expected of a rabbi on the Sabbath. It might even appear blasphemous in its non-conformity when compared with traditional services.

You have come down from the hills of Galilee, from Nazareth to tell us how we should change our way of worship. What do you want of us here in Capernaum? Have you come to destroy our faith?

Demons were credited as those forces and temptations associated with the idea of Satan. Keep in mind that "Satan" was not meant to be an evil god, but rather was a representation of all those material things in the world that would draw people from the way God would have them live. The shrieking man may be seen as a symbol of all those who feared losing the comfortable security they had long felt through regularly attending the synagogue to listen to reassuring repetitions of ritual readings. One who reads this passage looking for a message beyond the mere description of a shrieking man may find it in Mark's description of the positive effect Jesus' message had in overcoming even the strongest doubts of his most critical listener. Mark's description of the congregation's reaction immediately following the above passage is important in this context.

> They were all dumbfounded and began to ask one another, "What is this? A new kind of teaching! He speaks with authority. When he gives orders, even the unclean spirits submit."
>
> Mark: 1.27-28

Mark has introduced a Jesus whose message is so important that it successfully challenges even the security listeners had long derived from formalistic and traditional practices. His first chapter has introduced Jesus through John the Baptist. The chapter continues by introducing Jesus as the leader-teacher who attracted disciples. The teacher is further introduced as the messenger whose message is so powerful that it overcomes the fears of the man most afraid to let go of that security to which he has clung for so long. But Mark is not finished with introducing Jesus. Until he has, he will not begin to pass on to us the teachings of Jesus.

Mark describes Jesus' departure from the synagogue and his visit to the home of Simon and Andrew. It is here in his introduction of Jesus that Mark describes a series of miraculous healings. Interpretation of these passages by figurative readers will differ considerably from readers who accept Mark's description of the miracles as literal history.

Two things stand out in this early description of miracles. First is the very reference to miracles, which were by legend performed by gods and heroes throughout the Mediterranean world. In that sense Mark has given Jesus the same credentials of authority as those mythical heroes so his literal readers will not dismiss the teachings of Jesus as mere opinions of an ordinary man. But there is more to these verses than merely the establishment of Jesus' authority.

As in later descriptions of Jesus healing those who were brought to him, there was the belief that illness was the result of the victim having sinned. This linkage of sin and illness was common in those days, and Jesus is shown here as offering a forgiveness which, if the sick person had faith, would heal. Faith is the key in these passages. Mark shows his readers a Jesus who is calling for people to be forgiven their past transgressions, if they will but turn away from their old ways and have faith in the way of God. Jesus' emphasis on faith and on belief in his message is illustrated in the story of the leper.

> A leper came to him begging him, and kneeling he said to him, "If you choose, you can make me clean." Moved with pity. Jesus stretched out his hand and touched him, and said to him, "I do choose. Be made clean!" Immediately the leprosy left him. And he was made clean. After sternly warning him he sent him away at once, saying to him, "See that you say nothing to anyone, and offer for your cleansing what Moses commanded, as a testimony to them."
>
> Mark 1. 40-44

A footnote in the *New Oxford Bible* notes: "Jesus wished the healing to carry with it a spiritual obligation. He apparently feared that rumors of miracles would gather the curious and foster cries for help only in physical terms, thus hindering his message."[25] Using a leper in this illustration is important. Lepers were considered unclean. Mark leaves it to the reader to decide whether the cleansing of the leper was a symbolic cleansing of a sinner for his sins before setting him on a new path. Most important though is Mark's warning that his use of miracles in introducing Jesus should not become the reason for worship of the messenger, worship that could blind people to the message borne by the messenger.

JESUS' MINISTRY

Here again readers of the *New Testament* will differ in their reading of the gospel according to Mark. Some will read the stories of the miracles and the introduction of Jesus by Mark as literal history. Others will point out that Jesus had taught his disciples to teach with parables, just as he taught. It was not easy to write as Mark wrote. It required great skill for a teacher to convey two messages, one for those who would read his passages literally and one for those who, as Jesus put it, would have eyes to see and ears to hear the message wrapped within a parable.

Following his introduction of Jesus, Mark moves on to the beginning of Jesus' ministry with a description of his visit to the home of Levi, a tax collector. Tax collectors symbolized Rome's hold over Israel, and as such were held in contempt by most Jews, yet as Mark wrote:

> When Jesus was at table in his (Levi's) house, many bad characters - tax collectors and others were seated with him and his disciples; for there were many who followed him. Some doctors of the law who were Pharisees noticed him eating in this bad company, and said to his disciples, "He eats with tax collectors and sinners!" Jesus heard it and said to them, "It is not the healthy that need a doctor, but the sick; I did not come to invite

---

[25] *The New Oxford Bible*, Oxford University Press, New York, 1991, p. 49 NT.

> virtuous people, but sinners."
>
> Mark: 2.15-17

Deeply religious Jews considered anyone who did not conform to religious laws, such as the dietary laws, to be sinners. This passage, as do several which follow, emphasizes Jesus' insistence that religious laws are man-made, and must never prevent one from doing good. Mark expands this emphasis in this following passage:

> Once when John's disciples and the Pharisees were keeping a fast, some people came to him and said, "Why is it that John's disciples and the disciples of the Pharisees are fasting, but yours are not?" Jesus said to them, "Can you expect the bridegroom's friends to fast while the bridegroom is with them? As long as they have the bridegroom with them there can be no fasting. But the time will come when the bridegroom will be taken away from them, and on that day they will fast."
>
> "No one sews a patch of unshrunk cloth on to an old cloak; if he does, the patch tears away from it , the new from the old, and a worse tear is made. And no one puts new wine into old wine skins; otherwise, the wine will burst the skins and the wine is lost, and so are the skins; but one puts new wine into fresh wine skins."[26]
>
> Mark: 2.18-22

Mark's emphasis is on the inevitable conflict between Jesus' message and the "old" traditional and ritualistic religion. Jesus' message of personal responsibility and faith could be accepted by new believers, but as in the case of the shrieking man, could tear apart one's security, if that security was based only on traditional authority and ritual.

That shrieking man represents those whose religion was based entirely on the law and the teachings of the Pharisees. Jesus, in this

---

[26] A patch of new unshrunken cloth would shrink when first washed or caught in the rain, and in shrinking would tear the old cloth to which it was sewn. New wine, still fermenting, could rupture an old wine bag.

passage, is saying I have not come to try to patch up the doctrine of the Pharisees. I have not come to try to add new laws to the religion preached by the Pharisees. If I were to try to patch the holes in their thinking or to pour new content into their doctrine, it would only hasten the complete collapse of our religion. No, I have come to show you an entirely new way to the Kingdom of God. Jesus is trying to preserve what he sees as the good in the religion in which he had been brought up. His aim is to show new ways within that religion. He seeks to reform, not destroy, the faith of his fellow Jews.

Mark continues to tell of a Jesus who was teaching that personal behavior, following the path God would have one follow, was far more important than any man-made formalities of religion.

> One Sabbath he was going through the cornfields; and his disciples, as they went, began to pluck ears of corn. The Pharisees said to him, "Look, why are they doing what is forbidden on the Sabbath?" He answered, "Have you never read what David did when he and his men were hungry and had nothing to eat? He went into the House of God, in the time of Abiathar the High Priest, and ate the sacred bread, though no one but a priest was allowed to eat it, and even gave it to his men."
>
> He also said to them, "The Sabbath was made for humankind and not humankind for the Sabbath: therefore the Son of Man is sovereign even over the Sabbath."
>
> Mark: 2.23-26

Mark has again pressed the point that religious rules and regulations, such as those pertaining to the Sabbath, were supposed to be made *for the benefit of the believers*. This was in sharp contrast to traditions going back to the Sumerian priests who taught that man was created to worship God. He follows this passage with the story of Jesus healing a man with a withered arm, in a synagogue, on the Sabbath.[27]

Was there really a man there with a withered arm? Did Jesus miraculously heal that man? When reading figuratively a reader seeks

---

[27] Mark: 3. 1-6

the purpose of this parable. To that reader the man with the withered arm need not to have existed. Instead, for him or her the parable is seen as providing the means for Mark to put the question: "Is it permitted to do good or to do evil on the Sabbath, to save life or to kill?"

To the twenty-first century reader the answer is obvious, but in the days of Jesus respecting the Sabbath was one of the most important of religious laws. His comments about the Sabbath were obviously blasphemy to most ears.

With this parable Mark has introduced the plotting of the Pharisees. Eliminating Jesus would eliminate this new threat to the established and traditional. At this point Mark's readers realize why, during the rest of his years of teaching, Jesus will be confronted with attempts to discredit him.

It is also at this point that Mark tells his readers that Jesus chose twelve of his followers to go forth as apostles carrying his message and casting out demons. This reference to apostles also having the power to cast out demons would, if demons and devils were to be taken literally, mean that there were now thirteen men who could literally perform miracles. This again emphasizes that Mark did not mean actual demons and devils exorcised through miracles.

It is very important that Mark decided that it was at this point that he should insert the parable of the sower in which Jesus said: "Do you not understand this parable? Then how will you understand all the parables?" The placement of this parable and Jesus' comment on understanding parables is a message from Mark that what he has been writing and is continuing to write must also be searched for its deeper meaning. Mark immediately follows the parable of the sower with Jesus' further words,

> "Is a lamp brought in to be put under a bushel basket, or under the bed, and not on the lampstand? For there is nothing hidden, except to be disclosed; nor anything secret except to be disclosed. If you have ears to hear, then hear,"
>
> Mark 4.21-22

Readers should keep in mind that Christian churches at the time of Mark's writing had no common written basis for their teachings. Some churches had been established by apostles who had then moved on. Others were opened by wandering "preachers". After a few years churches frequently differed from other churches in their basic beliefs and teachings. In some churches rival points of view were splitting the congregations. Paul's letters to churches show his concern over these rival interpretations of Jesus and his teachings.

If, as biblical scholars believe, the author of the "Gospel According to Mark" was the John Mark who had earlier accompanied Paul and had worked closely with him, then undoubtedly Paul contributed to Mark's thinking and influenced his gospel. As Mark was writing either at a time when Paul was in deep need of a gospel which could be sent to all churches, or shortly after Paul's death, Mark's reference to the lamp and "secrets" that would be disclosed to those who sought the real meaning of Jesus' teachings was most timely. He was saying, "You will be taught by parables, 'Let anyone with ears listen."

Mark follows this group of parables noting:

> With many such parables he (Jesus) would give them his message, *so far as they were able to receive it*. He never spoke to them except in parables, but privately to his disciples he explained everything.
>
> Mark: 4.33

Note particularly Mark's words: *"He never spoke to them except in parables."* Whether reading Mark literally or figuratively the reader should keep in mind that Mark's gospel will be the first written basis for a common belief among all those new Christian churches that had come into being in the forty years since Jesus died. Those churches were located in what is today Italy, Greece, Turkey, Lebanon, Israel, and Egypt. Seldom, and often never, could one of these churches contact another lying a hundred miles distant. By the time Mark wrote, members of Gentile congregations then in existence had been born after Jesus had been crucified, had never been in Israel, did not speak the same language, and had no knowledge of Jesus except that carried to them by word of mouth.

Mark had a gigantic task. He was creating a common source of information about Jesus and Jesus' message to help bring unity to the churches Paul had shepherded to that point in time.

WHY MIRACLES ?

At this point Mark presents further accounts of miracles performed by Jesus. A key to the recounting of these miracles may be found in the passage about Jesus and his disciples crossing the lake.

> A great windstorm arose, and the waves beat into the boat, so that the boat was already being swamped. But he was in the stern, asleep on the cushion; and they woke him up and said to him, "Teacher, do you not care that we are perishing?" He woke up and rebuked the wind, and said to the sea, "Peace! Be still!" Then the wind ceased and there was dead calm. He said to them "Why are you afraid? Have you still no faith?" And they were filled with great awe and said to one another, "Who then is this, that even the wind and the sea obey him."
>
> Mark. 4.37-41

Reading literally, one sees an immediate calming of the storm; truly a miracle. For these literal readers Mark provided further reason for them to be in awe of Jesus. For those of his readers who sought deeper meaning in his parables Mark has highlighted Jesus' insistence that all is possible to those who have faith. To them it is not important whether forty years later someone actually knew what the disciples may have said. They see Jesus' giving the disciples faith before which the storm no longer is something with which they can not cope. It is his disciples, not the storm, that are calmed through faith. The all-important point of the story is not a miraculous calming of a raging storm but rather Jesus' insistence on the need for faith.

Here again the use of a parable is important. The *New English Bible* notes that, "a *parable* is a realistic story or true-to-experience observation which points beyond the every day situation it describes. The parable is to be contrasted to the allegory, which is a puzzle whose meaning is discovered by unlocking the symbolic significance of each detail of the story. The parable's message is found by letting the metaphor stimulate the imagination to see things (God's kingdom, human relations, life) in a new way."[28]

When the reader realizes the purpose of a parable she or he will not worry about inaccuracies. For example, Mark follows the story of the storm struck boat with the parable of the demented man possessed of thousands of unclean spirits that were ordered by Jesus to leave the man. In that parable a herd of two thousand pigs were feeding on a hillside nearby and the unclean spirits were ordered into them. A skeptic could point out that Jewish dietary laws prohibited the use of pigs for food. Why then was there a herd of pigs, especially two thousand? And, the critic would note pigs do not feed like sheep on the grasses on a hillside. But, those who see these inconsistencies merely as part of the setting for the parable look further. Again they see a "madman" cured through faith.

Following the parable of the madman with an even more direct reference to faith as Jesus passes through a crowd, Mark writes:

> Among them was a woman who had suffered from hemorrhages for twelve years; and in spite of long treatment by many doctors, on which she had spent all she had, there had been no improvement; on the contrary she had grown worse. She had heard what people were saying about Jesus, so she came up behind in the crowd and touched his cloak; for she said to herself, "If I touch even his clothes, I shall be cured." And there and then the source of her hemorrhages dried up and she knew herself that she was cured of her trouble. At the same time Jesus, aware that power had gone out of him turned round in the crowd and asked, "Who touched my clothes?" His disciples said to him, "You see this crowd pressing around you and yet you ask, 'Who touched me?'" Meanwhile he was looking round to see who had done it. And the woman trembling with fear when she grasped what had happened to her, came and fell at his feet and told him the whole truth. He said to her, "My daughter, your faith has cured you. Go in peace, free for ever from this trouble."
>
> Mark. 5.25-34

---

[28] *The New English Bible*, New Testament, footnote p. 46.

A literal reading of this passage carries the limited message of an ill individual being made well again. Other readers see a deeper message. They ask whether the woman symbolizes all those who face the end, the Day of Judgment, with fear of an impending doomsday as their inner strength is eroding. If so, faith has removed that fear and replaced it with inner peace. Is Mark saying those who have "touched" and been "touched by" Jesus are saved? "Your faith has cured (saved) you. Go in peace …."

In Mark's gospel Jairus, president of a synagogue, has asked Jesus to come to his house to save his daughter who was dying. But Jesus has been interrupted by the woman he had just healed; and while speaking to her he overhears a messenger telling Jairus not to bother the rabbi further as the young girl has just died. Turning to Jairus he says, "Do not be afraid, only have faith." Upon arriving at the home of the president Jesus finds weeping relatives and mourners to whom he says, "Why this crying and commotion? The child is not dead; she is asleep." Writing at least twenty years after Mark, Luke has Jesus telling the president, "Do not be afraid, only show faith and she will be well again."

In this story of healing, Mark notes that when they came to the president's house, "they found great a commotion with loud crying and wailing." This added detail indicates that in this case Mark is speaking of a daughter who is actually physically dead, not merely figuratively dead. Jesus tells the father, "The child is not dead: she is asleep." Sleep, in Mark's account, is seen as that state when her physical life has ceased but her new spiritual life has yet to begin.

Mark, as the recorder of the gospel as it had been preached by Peter, Paul and other early founders of the young Christian church, is making the distinction between physical resurrection and resurrection of the spirit (soul). In this, as readers will later note when reading Paul, Mark is presenting Paul's teaching that resurrection is spiritual, not physical (First Corinthians: 15. 35-58). There are two bodies, Paul tells the Corinthians. One is physical, which is left behind. The other is the spiritual body.

Curing of the seriously ill had for centuries been a common element in miracle stories involving heroes and gods. There is, however, a notable difference in the parables where the emphasis is on cure by faith, not by magic. Mark follows the story of Jairus' daughter with Jesus' return to his home town of Nazareth.

> When the Sabbath came he began to teach in the synagogue; and the large congregation who heard him were amazed and said, "Where does he get it from?", and "What wisdom is this that has been given him?" and "How does he work such miracles? Is not this the carpenter, the son of Mary, the brother of James and Joseph and Judas and Simon? And are not his sisters here with us?" So they fell foul of him. Jesus said to them, "A prophet will always be held in honor except in his home town, and among kinsmen and family." He could work no miracle there, except that he put his hands on a few sick people and healed them; and he was taken aback by their want of faith.
>
> Mark. 6.1-6

In summing up his recital of miracles Mark has emphasized once more Jesus' insistence that faith was the vital ingredient by which one was healed (saved). Time and again, in one way or another, Mark puts forth the point that Jesus is not claiming to be anything other than a prophet. Instead, the faith Jesus calls for is not faith in him but in the truth of his message. He has repeatedly told the beneficiaries of his "miracles" not to tell others about him, but rather about how they were restored by faith.

This use of miracle stories to get across this point was important two thousand years ago. Throughout Rome, Greece, Egypt, all of Anatolia, and even through the lands to the East in which in religions already several centuries old and in new religions that would eventually blossom, miracles were attributed to hundreds of heroes, priests, and gods. People might ignore a prophet as they did in Jesus' home town where they could not believe a neighbor could perform miracles. And so it was that there, where Jesus was in the eyes of his neighbors just another ordinary man; that he could not expect his listeners to have faith in anything he said. Forty years after Jesus' death Mark gives the messenger the status of other heroes and gods, thereby assuring that from such a messenger the message would by heard and remembered.

It can not be noted too often that Jesus warned against being revered as the messenger for he knew all too well that could blind the people to the message.

CHAPTER 4

JESUS, THE THREAT

John the Baptist was not the only target of Herodias' hate. As the wife of Herod she carried considerable influence, and was feared as a potential political threat to those who had found privileged positions under the Roman occupiers of Israel. In a land where the vast majority of the people lived in poverty, John's potential appeal to the masses could not be easily accepted by the authorities.

Jesus had come from Galilee, that poor land that was breeding Zealot terrorists. Later he had lived with John and John's disciples. Already, early in his travels and teachings, he was attracting crowds of potential followers. He was someone the Roman governors, the Sadducees who had hitched their privileged position to the Romans, and the Pharisees who controlled the synagogues were bound to view with suspicion.

Was it his intention to stir up the masses? Was he a revolutionary? Was he going to try to use the poverty of the masses to wipe out the privileged? Roman governors, knowing they had the backing of Roman Legions, may not have been greatly disturbed. But the Sadducees were of the elite, and it was through their control of the temple and their support of the Roman occupiers that they cemented their elite status. Then too, this Jesus had challenged religious laws held dear by the Pharisees. Where among the authorities could Jesus ever expect other than suspicion as to his real purpose?

JESUS' INFLUENCE GROWS

In such a small country Jesus could not help but become aware of the concern he was causing and the reaction it was stirring. The influence he was gaining by attracting more and more people to the preaching of his message is illustrated in Mark's story of Jesus speaking to the "five thousand." Here Mark notes that weary apostles whom Jesus had earlier sent out to spread his message had just returned and reported to him.

He said to them, "Come with me, by yourselves, to some lonely place where you can rest quietly." (For they had no leisure even to eat, so many were coming and going.) Accordingly, they set off privately by boat for a lonely place. But many saw them and came round by land, hurrying from all the towns towards the place, and arrived there first.

When he came ashore, he saw a great crowd; and his heart went out to them, because they were like sheep without a shepherd; and he had much to teach them.

As the day wore on his disciples came up to him and said, "This is a lonely place and it is getting very late; send the people off to the farms and villages round about, to buy themselves something to eat."

"Give them something to eat yourselves," he answered. They replied, "Are we to spend twenty pounds on bread to give them a meal?"

"How many loaves have you?" he asked; "go and see." They found out and told him, "Five, and two fishes also." He ordered them to make the people sit down in groups on the green grass, and they sat down in rows, a hundred rows of fifty each. Then, taking the five loaves and two fishes, he looked up to heaven, said the blessing, broke the loaves, and gave them to the disciples to distribute. He also divided the two fishes among them.

> They all ate to their heart's content; and twelve great basketfuls of scraps were picked up, with what was left of the fish. Those who ate the loaves numbered five thousand men.
>
> Mark: 6.31-44

As night fell the disciples left by boat while Jesus remained on shore to pray. It is here that Mark tells of Jesus walking out on the lake toward the boat. The disciples "all saw him and were terrified."

> But at once he spoke to them: "Take heart! It is I; do not be afraid." Then he climbed into the boat beside them, and the wind dropped. At this they were completely dumbfounded, for they had had not understood the incident of the loaves; their minds were closed.
>
> Mark: 6.50 -52

At this point it is wise for the reader of Mark to skip a couple of pages and to read Mark. 8: 1-21, after which the reader should return to read the pages skipped. This second story is about a crowd of four thousand. This time there were seven loaves among the disciples, which when broken by Jesus fed the four thousand. Again after feeding the crowd Jesus and his disciples left in their boat.

Matthew, using Mark's Gospel as a basis for his own Gospel, tells the story of the feeding of the five thousand (Mt: 14. 13-21). He also repeats the story of the feeding of four thousand in his next chapter (Mt: 15. 32-39). Biblical scholars note that in both of these gospels the stories of the feeding of the five thousand and the feeding of the four thousand are two versions of the same event. Why then is this story repeated? What is the point that is so important that both Mark and Matthew believe it too important to be missed? Recalling that these gospel writers were trying to teach by parables, just as Jesus had taught his disciples to teach, a reader is challenged to search for the light beneath the bushel, the "hidden" truth waiting to be discovered.

A reader may read this as being a literally true account of what happened on a slope near a lake two thousand years ago. However, there is the danger that such a reading can leave this passage as little more than a rather shallow story that does little other than show Jesus as one more of the many legendary miracle workers of the time. This is why skeptics may immediately raise three questions.

First, they may ask: "There being no means of amplifying sound, how could Jesus be heard?" One hundred rows of fifty seated men would stretch from front to rear about the length of one and a half football fields, and from side to side roughly the width of a football field.

Second, they may also ask: "Where did the five thousand come from?" Mark notes only men were there. Matthew says five thousand men but adds that women and children were also there with the men. Even if every shepherd in the area abandoned his flock, every shopkeeper closed his shop, and every farmer dropped his work there would not have been anywhere near five thousand men available within walking distance in the remaining daylight hours. Neither could word have been spread far enough to attract five thousand men in a single day to say nothing of the short time they would have had to reach the hillside where Jesus was headed before he was able to get there.

Third, the skeptic may further ask: "If there were only as many disciples as could fit in the boat with Jesus, and if each took no more than thirty seconds to hand bread and fish to a man before moving on to the next man, would it not take more than four hours to feed the crowd? Yet it was approaching dusk and 'growing late' when they arrived."

The reader who seeks something beyond the literal surface of this story will particularly note Jesus' words in the boat after leaving the four thousand. The disciples had forgotten to bring the remaining bread with them. Jesus understanding what they were thinking warned them:

> "Beware," he said, "be on your guard against the leaven of the Pharisees and the leaven of Herod." They said among themselves, "It is because we have no bread." Knowing what was in their minds, he asked them, "Why do you talk about having no bread? Have you no inkling yet? Do you still not understand? Are your minds closed? You have eyes: can you not see? You have ears; can you not hear? Have you forgotten? When I broke the five loaves among five thousand, how many basketfuls of scraps did you pick up?" "Twelve", they said. "And how many when I broke the seven loaves among the four thousand?" They answered, "Seven." He said, "Do you still not understand?"
>
> Mark: 8.14-21

This parable is one of the most important of the entire New Testament, perhaps in some ways the most important. After the "feeding of the five thousand" Mark tells us of the terrified disciples in the boat. He describes them as "completely dumbfounded, for they had not understood the incident of the loaves; their minds were closed."

After explaining the meaning of the parable of the sower, Jesus had said:

> "To you the secret of the Kingdom of God has been given; but to those who are *outside* everything comes by way of parables, so that (as Scripture says) they may look and look, but see nothing; they may hear and hear, but understand nothing; otherwise they might turn to God and be forgiven."[29]
>
> Mark: 4.11-12

Mark has stressed the point that those who fail to find the deeper lesson of a parable are the outsiders. He is showing his own

---

[29] This reference to the scriptures is to Isaiah: 6. 9-10. "You may listen and listen, but you will not understand. You may look and look again, but you will never know. This people's wits are dulled, their ears are deafened and their eyes blinded so that they cannot see with their eyes nor listen with their ears nor understand with their wits, so that they may turn and be healed (saved)."

fear that people will fail to discover lessons hidden within these parables. It is not enough for him to have described the disciples as failing to "understand the incident of the loaves." Repeating the parable, the second time as a feeding of four thousand, provides an opportunity for Mark and for Matthew to drive home this point by describing Jesus' berating of the disciples for not understanding the feeding of the five thousand and then the four thousand.

"Do you still not understand?" A reader can almost feel Mark's frustration.

Mark has described the reaction of the disciples who watched Jesus walk across the lake to their boat. Matthew goes a step further, writing twenty years after Mark. He adds further explanation and lifts the bushel a bit for others to see. He adds a story of Peter stepping out onto the lake to meet Jesus, but then sinking after a few steps. "Why did you hesitate?" Jesus asked, "How little faith you have!"

Faith is the heart of the parable of the feeding of thousands, and Matthew apparently felt it necessary to make that more apparent to his readers than did Mark to his. Jesus has warned his disciples after the feeding of the four thousand. "Beware, be on your guard against the leaven of the Pharisees and the leaven of Herod." *The New English Bible* notes that "leaven was a conventional symbol for an evil influence. *The New Oxford Bible* notes that yeast, the translation it uses instead of leaven, "refers to a settled conviction which affects all life as yeast raises dough. Yeast of the Pharisees is hypocrisy which spreads its influence by means of their teaching. The leaven of Herod is worldliness and irreligion"

In Mark's gospel Jesus is warning his disciples not to limit their thinking to the material. Don't you see, he is asking, that you should not be thinking of *loaves* of bread? Those people on the hillside were hungry for the Word. They needed something in which to believe that would make their lives have meaning. They needed faith. My message filled their need, satisfied their hunger.

Bread, as in the Lord's Prayer, referred to more than sustenance supporting physical life. Jesus is criticizing his disciples for not realizing that people also needed "food" that would sustain them spiritually.

Between the two stories of feeding thousands, lie the pages we just skipped. In them Mark tells of a group of Pharisees and doctors of law who had come from Jerusalem. In that passage the hypocrisy, the leaven, of the Pharisees is highlighted.

A group of Pharisees and doctors of law who had come
from Jerusalem, met him and noticed that some of the
disciples were eating their food with 'defiled' hands – in
other words, without washing them. (For the Pharisees
and the Jews in general never eat without washing the
hands, in obedience to an old established tradition; and
on coming from the marketplace they never eat without
first washing. And there are many other points on which
they have a traditional rule to maintain, for example,
washing of cups and jugs and copper bowls.)
Accordingly, these Pharisees and the lawyers asked him,
"Why do your disciples not conform to the ancient
tradition, but eat their food with defiled hands?" He
answered, "Isaiah was right when he prophesied about
you hypocrites in these words: 'This people pays me lip-
service, but their heart is far from me: their worship of
me is in vain, for they teach as doctrines the
commandments of men.' You neglect the commandment
of God, in order to maintain the tradition of men."

He also said to them, "How well you set aside the
commandment of God in order to maintain your
tradition! Thus by your own tradition handed down
among you, you make God's word null and void. And
many other things you do are just like that."

Mark. 7.1-13

By placing this passage between the two descriptions of the
feeding of thousands Mark has described the hypocrisy of the Pharisees
before he has described Jesus' scolding of his disciples for not being
aware of the true meaning of the satisfying the hunger of the five
thousand. Twenty years later Matthew seems to believe the point of the
parable is too deeply hidden to be discovered by those for whom Mark
wrote it. He adds to Jesus' words to the disciples in the boat.

> "Why do you talk about bringing no bread? Where is your faith? Do you not understand even yet? Do you not remember the five loaves for the five thousand, and how many basketfuls you picked up? Or the seven loaves for the four thousand, and how many basketfuls you picked up? *How can you fail to see I was not speaking about bread?*[30] 'Be on your guard,' I said, 'against the leaven of the Pharisees and the Sadducees.' Then they understood; they were to be on their guard, not against the baker's leaven, but against the teaching of the Pharisees and the Sadducees."
>
> Matthew. 16.8-12

Jesus has identified the Pharisees with tradition and man-made religious restrictions and laws. He has identified the Sadducees with material possessions and social position. Mark is saying the people on the hillside have listened all their lives to Pharisees sermonize and lecture about the man made commandments that bound them to those traditions so sacred to the Pharisees. Then came Jesus, who spoke not of the law or tradition, but gave the people a message about God's purpose and how important each of them was in fulfilling that purpose rather than merely abiding unquestioningly by the man-made laws of the Pharisees.

MARK'S CONTRIBUTION

To fully grasp Mark's role in uniting Christian thought it is essential that a reader appreciate Mark's relationship to the early founders of Christianity. He had been a disciple of Peter whose teachings had been instrumental in forming Mark's early religious philosophy. Furthermore, he was the cousin of Barnabas.

---

[30] Mark, and especially Matthew, wherever possible presented to their fellow Jews a Jesus whose acts were in line with the Scriptures. They knew fellow Jews would be familiar with verses 42-44 of 2nd Kings in which a man brought a sack containing loaves of barley and ears of corn and Elisha had said: "Give it to the people and let them eat. But the servant said, "How can I set this before a hundred people?" Elisha replied, "Give it to the people and let them eat, for thus says the Lord, 'They shall eat and have some left.' He set it before them, they ate, and has some left, according to the word of the Lord."

Barnabas was one of the earliest missionaries to spread the teachings of Jesus. He had become a member of the newly organized church in Jerusalem shortly after Jesus' death. Selling all he owned and giving the proceeds to the new Christian community he left for Antioch, at that time the third largest city in the Roman Empire. There he organized a church. His work among Gentiles was so successful that, having heard of Paul, he went to Tarsus seeking to enlist Paul as his assistant. Barnabas' work had by then made Antioch the core of the new efforts to expand Christianity. Paul would spend a year working with Barnabas, and of course Mark would be in close contact with Paul during that time. Barnabas and Paul worked so well as a team that they set out together in 48 AD as missionaries.

At one point, Mark, who had accompanied them, left for Jerusalem. Later, when Paul and Barnabas were to leave on another missionary trip Barnabas insisted on bringing Mark. Paul, who had accused Mark of deserting them on their earlier trip, refused to let Mark accompany them. It was this difference that drove a wedge between Barnabas and Paul and sent them on their different ways, never again to work together.

It would be later in Rome that Mark would again be in contact with both Peter and Paul. When did Mark write his gospel? Remember, Peter died in Rome in 64 AD, Paul died in Rome in 67AD. Rome had burned in 64AD. Mark's gospel was written sometime after the burning of Rome and before Jerusalem was destroyed in 70AD. As we have already noted, Mark's gospel is a collection of stories and teachings about Jesus, but until this point in time no one had brought this traditional material together in written form.

Peter had been the unchallenged leader of the Jewish Christian congregation in Jerusalem at the time he had visited Barnabas' church in Antioch. During that visit he ate with Gentiles of Barnabas' congregation. When James, the brother of Jesus and a founder of the church in Jerusalem, heard of this practice he sent representatives to Antioch to warn Peter that eating with Gentiles was absolutely forbidden. The Jerusalem church insisted that Jewish law and traditions were to be observed at all times. Therefore, dietary laws and circumcision were required of all who would be a part of this new church.

Peter, bowing to the will of James, then stood apart from the Gentiles in Antioch. At this point Paul returned to Antioch and berated Peter for his backing away from union with Gentiles. It was

54

here, in Antioch, that the name Christianity was given to this new religion that adhered to the message of Jesus.[31] Paul was a Jew, a rabbi, a Pharisee by training, and now highly respected for his missionary work and his organizing of Christian churches throughout the Middle East. The church could not afford to lose either Peter or Paul. It was, therefore, in 49 or 50 AD that the Jerusalem Council was convened and determined that henceforth Peter would be responsible for bringing the gospel to the circumcised and Paul for the missions to the uncircumcised.

Paul describes this distinction in his letter to the Galatians. That letter, as we will see later, emphasized the need to be *free,* free from man-made religious legalisms. In it Paul writes:

> "Next, fourteen years later I went again to Jerusalem with Barnabas, taking Titus with us. I went up because it had been revealed by God that I should do so. I laid before them - but at a private interview with the men of repute - the gospel which I am accustomed to preach to the Gentiles, to make sure that the race that I had run, and was running, should not be run in vain. Yet even my companion Titus, Greek though he is, was not compelled to be circumcised. That course was urged only as a concession to certain sham- Christians, interlopers who had stolen in to spy upon the liberty we enjoy in the fellowship of Christ Jesus. These men wanted to bring us into bondage, but not for one moment did I yield to their dictation; I was determined that the full truth of the Gospel should be maintained for you.
>
> "But as for the men of high reputation (not that their importance matters to me: God does not recognize these personal distinctions) - these men of repute, I say did not prolong the consultation, but on the contrary acknowledged that I had been entrusted with the Gospel

---

[31] He (Barnabas) "went off to Tarsus to look for Saul; and when he had found him, he brought him to Anticoch . For a whole year the two of them lived in fellowship with the congregation there, and gave instruction to large numbers. It was in Antioch that the disciples first got the name Christians."

Acts: 11. 25-26

> for Gentiles as surely as Peter had been entrusted with the Gospel for Jews. For God whose action made Peter an apostle to the Jews, also made me an apostle to the Gentiles."
>
> Galatians: 2.1-8

Mark could not help but be aware of Paul's concerns in the ensuing years. Paul had envisioned a church embracing people of all races, nationalities, and former religions; a universal church that could unite the disparate units of the Roman Empire. By the time Mark would bring together the traditions of this new religion in his Gospel, there were so many Christian churches spread throughout the Roman Empire and elsewhere in the Middle East and North Africa that, as we have already noted, they were all too often going their own way. Practices in some of those churches were actually contrary to the teachings of Jesus.

By collecting the important elements of Peter's beliefs, of Paul's philosophy of embracing Gentiles, and of the deeper message of Jesus as passed down orally for more than thirty-five years, Mark is providing a common core for all Christian churches. He is trying for that unity Paul had felt essential for the survival of the Christianity he had striven to make an all-embracing religion within a universal church.

Mark wrote with a message for those who would lead the congregations, a message that one needed to discover. At the same time he wrote for the *outsiders*, those who would only read his parables literally, in order to show them Jesus as a teacher and "miracle worker" to whose message they should listen. This was no easy task.

Mark wrote nothing of Jesus' life before Jesus met John the Baptist. Repeatedly Mark emphasized Jesus' insistence that he not be spoken of as *the* Messiah. He describes Jesus' humility and unwillingness to be praised. For those who would seek the light beneath the bushel Mark is downplaying the messenger and is emphasizing the importance of the message.

THE TEACHER

Mark ended his parable about the feeding of the four thousand with Jesus and the disciples in the boat. Jesus has just admonished them for not *seeing*. "Why do you talk of having no bread? Have you no inkling yet?" And then he concludes this passage with the words, "Do you still not understand?" This, Mark immediately follows with the parable of the blind man.

> They arrived at Bethsaida. There the people brought a
> blind man to Jesus and begged him to touch him. He
> took the blind man by the hand and led him away out of
> the village. Then he spat on his eyes, laid his hands upon
> him, and asked whether he could see anything. The
> man's sight began to come back, and he said, "I see men;
> they look like trees, but they are walking about." Jesus
> laid his hands on his eyes again; he looked hard, and now
> he was cured so that he saw everything clearly.
>
> Mark: 8.22-26

Mark has described the failure of the disciples to see Jesus real message and purpose. They have been thinking of the material, and Jesus has scolded them for not seeing the spiritual. "You have eyes: can you not see?" Immediately thereafter, Mark offers the parable of Jesus meeting a man who is blind to the way of God. This man without faith has his eyes opened and understands Jesus' message. The old American hymn "Amazing Grace" sums up this parable in the two brief lines: "I once was lost, but now am found. I once was blind, but now I see."

Mark uses this parable as a lead in to his next passages in which bit by bit the disciples' eyes are also opened. From there, Mark takes Jesus and his disciples on to the villages of Caesarea Philippi. This is not just a simple mention of a place where Jesus would stop. Caesarea Philippi was a border region between Jews and Gentiles, an area populated by pagan (Gentile) worshippers. Mark is making special note of the fact that Jesus will not limit his ministry to Jews.

> On the way he asked his disciples, "Who do people say
> that I am?" And they answered him, "John the Baptist";
> and others, "Elijah"; and still others, "one of the
> prophets." He asked them, "But who do you say that I
> am?" Peter answered him, "You are the Messiah." Then
> he gave them strict orders not to tell anyone about him.
>   Then he began to teach them that the Son of Man
> must undergo great suffering, and be rejected by the

> elders, the chief priests, and the scribes, and be killed, and after three days rise again. He said this quite openly. And Peter took him aside and began to rebuke him. But turning and looking at his disciples, he rebuked Peter and said, "Get behind me, Satan! For you are setting your mind not on divine things but on human things." (or as the *New English Bible translates* "Away with you Satan, you think as men think, not as God thinks.")
>
> Mark: 8.27-33

The disciples were not only telling Jesus what others thought of him, but also what they believed. Two points stand out in this passage. Mark has Peter offering what Jesus had rejected when tempted in the wilderness, namely worldly power. "You are the Messiah." And in the context of the times the Messiah would be a worldly leader, a king as it were, sent to rule Israel and make it the leader among nations. The disciples, if that were the case, would be sitting in prized positions in the royal court. Again Jesus is rebuking them for thinking in worldly terms, not as "God thinks." Slowly, ever so slowly, the disciple's eyes are being opened. "You have eyes; can you not see?"

The second point of importance is Jesus' repetition of his early orders that they were not to tell anyone about him. Over and over Mark emphasizes Jesus insistence that he be seen as a messenger of God's word, not as a divine potential Messiah. This could be a very confusing part of Mark's gospel; picturing Jesus as a miracle worker for the "outsider" while at the same time having him repeatedly deny that he is to be seen as anything more than a messenger.

Jesus will later repeat his warning that he must suffer. No one living when Mark wrote could have known the private conversations between Jesus and his disciples. *The New English Bible* footnotes an explanation supported by many biblical scholars. It notes: "This is the first of three predictions of the suffering of the *Son of Man*. These predictions probably reflect the way the cross and resurrection were preached by early missionaries, so that their present form may have been influenced by that preaching. From this point the story of Mark moves forward with the cross clearly in view."

There is also here a repudiation of Peter's insistence that Jesus is the long awaited Messiah, for by Jewish tradition the Messiah would be exalted and could never suffer. Mark then adds:

> Then he called the people to him, as well as his disciples, and said to them, "Anyone who wishes to be a follower of mine must leave self behind; he must take up his cross, and come with me. Whoever cares for his own safety is lost; but if a man let himself be lost for my sake and for the Gospel, that man is safe. What does a man gain by winning the whole world at the cost of his true self?" (or as the *New Oxford Bible* translates, 'For what will it profit them to gain the whole World and forfeit their life?")
>
> Mark: 8.34-37

For those who prefer a literal reading of the bible, taking up the cross can be seen as assuming the burdens of being a Christian. That could mean giving up one's worldly possessions and living each day not knowing from whence would come one's food or lodging. But Mark was going further. He had Jesus warning that by following him one might well lose his life. The reader should remember that much of Rome had burned to the ground a few years before Mark wrote. Christians were still the scapegoats and were being persecuted, often killed, by those who were being told Christians were responsible for the tragedy.

Readers of the *New Testament* are familiar with Jesus' parable about how a wealthy man will find it as impossible to enter the kingdom of heaven as it is for a camel to pass through the eye of a needle. In speaking of taking up one's cross and leaving behind material belongings Mark shows Jesus choosing as his followers, with few exceptions, those who have no wealth to lose. It would be the rare exception among the Sadducees, scribes, Pharisees, well-to-do merchants and farmers, and Roman officials who would not feel threatened as the band of followers around this man from the hills of Galilee continued to grow. Mark wants his readers to realize that Jesus was well aware that suffering and probably death would be the fate of one who taught as he did. His disdain for the material; his insistence that the Kingdom of God was spiritual, and not of material political or military power, was contrary to all that was a part of what Jews had been taught to expect of a Messiah. It tore at the very roots of the "law" of the Pharisees and the traditions of the Sadducees. It could have made Jesus appear even more a dangerous threat to those who preached of a powerful material kingdom when he also said:

> "I tell you this: there are some of those standing here who will not taste death before they have seen the kingdom of God already come to power."
>
> Mark: 9.1

CHAPTER 5

THE ROAD TO CALVARY

Israel was a land torn by political conflict. With Sadducees at one extreme of the religious-political spectrum; Zealots at the other; and Pharisees, Essenes and others in between; there was a continual struggle to determine the direction in which Israel should go. Violence and death were all too often the price paid by those perceived as a threat to one or another of the emerging political-religious parties.

Jesus had grown up in the heart of this struggle. By the time he left John the Baptist to begin his life as a teacher of God's will he would have been well aware of the dangers he would be facing by teaching his version of the Kingdom of God.

Pharisees and Sadducees could not help but fear the teachings of this man Jesus. However, readers should not imagine this to be like a plot out of a twenty-first century novel or motion picture where corrupt men of position plot to eliminate a threat only to their personal power and position. Pharisees were scholars who believed deeply in the Law. The threat they felt was a threat to the religion to which they were devoting their lives. They watched this threat grow ever greater as larger and larger crowds gathered to hear Jesus tell them to think beyond blind adherence to the Law and tradition. He spoke about a Kingdom of God on earth which was not at all like the long expected kingdom a true Messiah was supposed to bring into being.

Sadducees saw their entire way of life threatened. Zealots saw a threat to their impossible dream of an Israel so militarily strong that it could defeat the legions of the Roman Empire. There was not a religious sect or political-religious party that did not believe Jesus was urging people to go against what those sects and parties believed was the will of God. Theirs were honest fears. Remember the man in the synagogue in Capernaum who shrieked in panic: "What do you want with us, Jesus of Nazareth. Have you come to destroy us?" And those who react to an honest fear can be the most terrifying and ruthless in their attempts to combat what they fear.

A TIME OF TESTING

Mark continues to use miraculous healings to drive home Jesus' emphasis on the need for faith to open eyes and ears and drive out "evil" that corrupted and crippled one's life. Once more faith becomes the centerpiece of a parable when Mark describes an attempt by the disciples to cast out evil spirits. Jesus, Peter, James, and John had just come down from a mountain described by Mark as the scene of the Transfiguration.

When they came back to the disciples they saw a large crowd surrounding them and lawyers arguing with them. As soon as they saw Jesus the whole crowd were overcome with awe, and they ran forward to welcome him. He asked them, "What is this argument about?" A man in the crowd spoke up: "Master, I brought my son to you. He is possessed by a spirit which makes him speechless. Whenever it attacks him, it dashes him to the ground, and he foams at the mouth, grinds his teeth, and goes rigid. I asked your disciples to cast it out, but they failed." Jesus answered: "What an unbelieving and perverse generation! How long shall I be with you? How long must I endure you? Bring the boy to me."
"So they brought the boy to him and as soon as the spirit saw him it threw the boy into convulsions, and he fell on the ground and rolled about foaming at the mouth. Jesus asked his father, "How long has he been like this?"
"From childhood," he replied; "often it has tried to make an end of him by throwing him into the fire or into water. But if it is at all possible for you, take pity upon us and help us."

"If it is possible!" said Jesus. "Everything is possible to
one who has faith." "I have faith," cried the boy's father;
"help me where faith falls short."

Jesus saw then that the crowd was closing in upon them,
so he rebuked the unclean spirit. "Deaf and dumb
spirit," he said, "I command you, come out of him and
never go back!" After crying aloud and racking him
fiercely, it came out; and the boy looked like a corpse; in
fact, many said, "He is dead." But Jesus took his hand
and raised him to his feet, and he stood up.

Then Jesus went indoors, and his disciples asked him
privately, "Why could we not cast it out?" He said,
"There is no means of casting out this sort but prayer."

Mark: 9.14-29

One who reads this passage as a literal account of what
happened will see only a miraculous curing of an epileptic child, but
unfortunately no lesson. For those who read this passage figuratively
this is a parable with two important lessons. A figurative reading does
not assume an actual healing of an epileptic. Mark has chosen an
example of an illness which people knew had never been cured. So,
when the disciples are shown to have failed, and the father's faith has
not been enough, Jesus makes a most important statement.

Your faith, Jesus says to his disciples, is not sufficient. You
argued with the lawyers and the crowd and insisted that *your* faith could
heal. But the fact that *you* have faith is not enough. When faced with
eyes that refuse to open or ears that remain deaf when you present the
truth, your faith alone will never be enough. Only God can heal in such
cases and you must use your faith in God to pray for him to open the
eyes and ears and cast out evil.

Faith is still the key to all these miracle parables, but Jesus is
adding that it must be the faith that the one to be cured has in God's
power, and that it is God's Word that heals, not the words or even the
faith of the disciples. It is not the faith of the disciples that will open
the eyes of the blind. Only when the blind man himself has faith will
he see the truth. It is the task of the disciple to generate this faith in

those who are blind and deaf to the Word, and in those crippled by corruption.

Mark then moves a step further in this parable. He makes it clear that Jesus is saying that it is not in him that the disciples should have faith; nor does Mark have Jesus claim that even he has the power to cure. Instead Jesus says, "There is no means of casting out this sort but prayer."

As a note in the *New English Bible* interprets this statement, "Only *prayer* succeeds in the difficult situation because only God's power is adequate."[32] A note in the *New Oxford Bible* interprets Mark's use of this ending of the parable as indicating, "Prayer to God *is faith in God*, and contrasts with the argumentative attitude (which Jesus witnessed at the beginning of this passage). The potency in faith rests with God and is not under the believer's control."[33] It is not prayer itself that heals, says Jesus. When one prays sincerely, it is the faith one has that his prayer will be answered that will heal; *"Prayer to God is faith in God."* Throughout the four gospels and the letters of Paul, this emphasis on faith will be at the heart of each writer's message.

＊ ＊ ＊ ＊ ＊ ＊ ＊ ＊ ＊ ＊ ＊ ＊

Once more Jesus returns to Galilee, and once more he tells his disciples, "The Son is now to be given up into the power of men, and they will kill him, and three days after being killed, he will rise again." These repeated references of Jesus' prediction of his death are considered by most biblical scholars as a product of Christology. Such references are not to be seen as history, not as something Jesus said, but as theological interpretation inserted by Christian writers decades after the death of Jesus. This is not unlike such use of interpretations found in the writings of the Old Testament. Years or even centuries later, a writer, knowing what had happened, could weave that happening into his writing as a prophecy or prediction by the one about whom he was writing.

In this case Mark knows of the crucifixion that happened almost forty years before and of a spiritual resurrection as described by Paul. These predictions Jesus is described as making are Mark's attempt to make those known events fit in with Jesus' awareness that if

---

32   The New Testament, p.54, *The New English Bible,* 1970 Edition.
33   The New Testament, p. 61, *The New Oxford Bible*, 1991 Edition.

he continued his teachings, he would be courting arrest and execution. This is quite in line with the manner of writing in the Old Testament.

Early books of the Old Testament describe events which took place or quote prophets who were supposed to have spoken from the time of Adam and Eve until sometime after 640 BC. These books were written when King Josiah (640BC-609BC) ordered that the oral history, traditions, and religious beliefs of the Jews be written for the people of Israel. They were written according to theological interpretations current in each writer's lifetime, but about events and prophecies that took place as much as a thousand years earlier. So it also was when the gospels were written. Writers, knowing what had actually taken place, were thus able to add what they had learned to explain "theologically" some events in the life and in the works of Jesus. The gospels are not a biography of Jesus. They are the interpretation made from a Christian point of view two and three generations after the crucifixion. They provide a base on which the new Christian churches could build; a firm foundation for a lasting religion.

Does the fact that Jesus did not actually utter some of the words that are attributed to him by the Gospels mean they are of no religious value? Absolutely not! The way of life Jesus taught men and women to follow had spread after his death until churches were springing up throughout North Africa and the lands bordering the Eastern Mediterranean. The essence of his teachings were best preserved and passed on to succeeding generations by explaining his beliefs and teachings as actual conversations with his disciples and others. This does not mean that what Jesus taught was distorted or made up by these writers of the Gospels. This way of telling people what Jesus believed actually lent more credibility to his message when it was being presented to the generations following his death. Throughout two thousand years it has preserved the message of the teacher, which is still of such great importance in the twenty-first century.

* * * * * * * * * * * *

On the way to Galilee Jesus noted that the disciples were arguing. Arriving once again in Capernaum Jesus waits until all are indoors and then asks them:

> "What were you arguing about on the way?" They were silent, because on the way they were discussing who was the greatest. He sat down, called the Twelve, and said to them, "If anyone wants to be first, he must make himself last and servant to all." Then he took a child, set him in front of them, and put his arm around him. "Whoever receives one of these children in my name," he said, "receives me; and whoever receives me, receives not me but the One who sent me."
>
> Mark: 9.33-37

Once more Mark has highlighted the difference between the Kingdom of God anticipated by the Pharisees and other devout Jews, and the Kingdom of God which Jesus preached. In this case, even the expectations of his young disciples included positions they would occupy and other rewards they would receive in the court of a Messiah sent by God to be a king of Israel.

This parable concludes with Jesus picking up the child, a symbol of purity - of lack of greed and other worldly weaknesses of adults - a symbol which the gospels use on other occasions. Jesus then says that whoever accepts his teachings is not accepting them because of the teacher, but rather because what he is teaching is the Word of God.

* * * * * * * * * * * *

Having later passed into Judea and Transjordan, Jesus is surrounded by a crowd where "he followed his usual practice and taught them." He was asked whether divorce was lawful. The question was put to him by those who were hoping they might catch him making a statement contradicting the Law of Moses. In this test they did indeed hear him take a position differing from the Law which permitted men to divorce their wives. This parable is not just about divorce. It is an opportunity to present Jesus' view of all the Law. Jesus is asking why there was such permission in the Law. And then answers his own questions.

66

> "It was because your minds were closed that he (Moses) made this rule for you."
>
> Mark. 10.5

As when the disciples picked and ate corn on the Sabbath, and when they ate with unwashed hands, Jesus is saying the Law was made by men for men, and you are hypocrites for putting it above the welfare of God's people. Remember when he said, "You neglect the commandment of God, in order to maintain the tradition of men." Mark could not have made it clearer that Jesus was, with full awareness of what he was doing, taking a strong stand against the very basic values and traditions of the Pharisees.

Mark's next passage again deals with children as a symbol of purity.

> They brought children for him to touch. The disciples rebuked them, but when Jesus saw this he was indignant, and said to them, "Let the little children come to me; do not stop them; for it is to such as these that the kingdom of God belongs. Truly I tell you, whoever does not receive the kingdom of God as a little child will never enter it."
>
> Mark: 10.13-15

Whether this parable about the children is read literally or figuratively it should be read as the first part of a two parable message. The second part deals with the rich man seeking eternal life.

> As he was starting out on a journey, a stranger ran up, "Good Master, what must I do to win eternal life?" Jesus said to him, "Why do you call me good? No one is good except God alone. You know the commandments: Do not murder; do not commit adultery, do not steal; do not give false evidence; do not defraud; honor your father and mother." "But, Master," he replied, "I have kept these since I was a boy." Jesus looked straight at him; his heart warmed to him, and he said, "One thing you lack:

> go sell everything you have, and give it to the poor, and you will have riches in heaven; and come, follow me." At these words his face fell and he went away with heavy heart; for he was a man of great wealth.
>
> Jesus looked round at his disciples and said to them, "How hard it will be for the wealthy to enter the kingdom of God!" They were amazed that he should say this, but Jesus insisted, "Children, how hard it is to enter the kingdom of God!" It is easier for a camel to pass through the eye of a needle than for a rich man to enter the kingdom of God." They were more astonished than ever, and said to one another, "Then who can be saved?" Jesus looked at them and said, "For men it is impossible, but not for God; everything is possible for God'."
>
> Mark: 10.17-27

"Truly I tell you, whoever does not receive the kingdom of God as little child will never enter it." Just as a little child turns to its mother or father for solace and has complete faith that the parent will protect and care for him, Jesus is saying, so one should have such complete trust in God. Furthermore, the little child has not yet taken on the burden of material possessions. The child is not yet devoting most of his or her life to gaining possessions and then protecting those possessions; nor is that child's mind clouded with envy, jealousy, lust, greed, hate, or self-righteousness. Only with the simple purity and trust of a child can one enter the Kingdom of God. The point has been made, but it is so important, so much a key to the peace of the Kingdom of God preached by Jesus, that Mark has followed it immediately with the parable of the rich man.

Jesus is kind and has sympathy for this young man of wealth. But, he is saying, you will never attain that peace of the spiritual Kingdom of God until your mind is free of concern about your possessions. They are a burden from which your mind needs to be freed. While your mind is filled with these material thoughts it has no room for the blessings of the Kingdom of Heaven. No matter that you keep the commandments every day of your life; no matter how much you try to do good; you can never free your mind of concerns about the material world in which you live. You can never find room for that total trust found in an innocent little child, so the peace of the Kingdom of God will elude you.

"It is easier for a camel to pass through the eye of a needle than for a rich man to enter the kingdom of God." But, as the disciples asked, "Then who can be saved?" Jesus' answer is clear: "For men it is impossible." And the reader should not forget that Jesus had said to the young man, "Why do you call me good? No one is good except God alone." Is Jesus setting the goal of entry into the Kingdom of God as something no human, including himself, could ever reach, but for which all humans should strive?

Jesus' implication is that no matter that the rich man might use much of his wealth to support religious causes it would not bring him entry into the Kingdom of God. This, however, is not restricted to the rich man. A life of good deeds is not sufficient for anyone to enter that kingdom.

Too often readers slip across this parable retaining only the thought that it is a rich man who is unable to enter the Kingdom of God. But, Jesus has said no one can ever so completely cut his or her ties to the material world that he or she can enter the completely spiritual Kingdom of God. That kingdom where one can experience complete peace, a realm of no worries, no concerns for loved ones and no thoughts of what tomorrow will bring, lies beyond the reach of humans. All one can do is strive toward that complete trust of a child. There is a deeper sense to "giving away everything." Jesus is saying that just as a cup already filled can hold no more,[34] a mind and heart when filled with material desires and concerns has no room to receive what the Kingdom of God has to offer.

There is another interpretation of the parable of the rich man offered by biblical scholars. They point to the word "difficult" when Jesus says, "How difficult it will be for the wealthy to enter the kingdom of God." Jesus did not say impossible. This leads some interpreters to point out that the small postern gate called a needle's eye was the only gate in a city's walls that was left open at night. For a

---

[34] Lao Tzu (circa 604-524 BC) wrote in the *Tao Tê Ching* that: "Thirty spokes will converge in the hub of a wheel; but the use of the cart will depend on the part of the hub that is void (the empty spot where the axle must fit). Mould clay into a vessel; from its not-being (its empty hollowness) arises the utility of the vessel. Cut the doors and the windows in the walls of the house; from their not-being (empty space) arises their utility." Jesus' words are not unlike that in their deeper meaning.

camel to pass through that small gate it would be necessary to strip it of all it carried from bundles of possessions to adornments of the owners rank or position. Then with much shoving from behind and pulling from in front the camel might be brought through the gate. In this interpretation it no longer is *impossible* to enter the kingdom of God, but very *difficult*.

Regardless of which interpretation a reader assumes the lesson is that entry into the kingdom of God requires giving all. That means not just worshiping and preaching and following the commandments, but giving fully one's mind and strength, what we so often speak of as heart and soul. Certainly, Jesus was concerned with this type of giving when he said one must give all. It would be difficult to imagine him advocating giving everything one owned when he was so concerned with alleviating poverty. We must remember that one without anything, one in poverty, is pressed by his or her circumstance to concentrate on scraping out enough for his or her family and himself or herself to live. There are material strings tied to a poor man's struggle to exist just as there are for the rich man with concerns about his property. For both it becomes an impossible struggle to think only of the spiritual.

* * * * * * * * * * * *

Once more on the road to Jerusalem the disciples argued about their position in the coming kingdom they still assumed Jesus would head as king. James and John approached Jesus and said:

> "'Master, we should like you to do us a favor." "What is it you want me to do?" he asked. They answered, "Grant us the right to sit in state with you, one at your right and the other at your left." Jesus said to them, "You do not understand what you are asking. Can you drink the cup that I drink, or be baptized with the baptism I am baptized with?" "We can," they answered. Jesus said, "The cup that I drink you shall drink, and the baptism I am baptized with shall be your baptism; but to sit on my right or left is not for me to grant; it is for those to whom it has already been assigned."'
>
> Mark: 10.35-40

70

The *cup* as a figure of speech in the Old Testament and the New Testament means "experiencing trouble."[35] *Baptism* as Jesus uses the term here means accepting as God's will the persecution he will experience.[36]

When the other disciples heard James and John (sons of Zebedee) make this request of Jesus they were indignant.

> Jesus called them to him and said, "You know that in the world the recognized rulers lord it over their subjects, and their great men make them feel the weight of authority. That is not the way with you; among you, whoever wants to be great must be your servant, and whoever wants to be first must be the willing slave of all. For even the Son of Man did not come to be served but to serve, and to give up his life as a ransom for many."
>
> Mark: 10.41-45

Even in the material world of the twenty-first century one who would lead - not direct - but lead, must be the servant of those he or she would lead. True leadership, as Jesus was telling his disciples, means serving the welfare of those one leads. He is forever trying to get his disciples to raise their sights above the material and toward the spiritual.

* * * * * * * * * * * *

> They came to Jericho; and as he was leaving town, with his disciples and a large crowd Bartimeus son Timaeus, a blind beggar, was seated at the roadside. Hearing that it was Jesus of Nazareth, he began to shout, "Son of David. Jesus have pity on me!" Many of the people told him to hold his tongue; but he shouted all the more, "Son of

---

[35] See footnote for Mark. 10.38 in the *New English Bible* for further comment.
[36] See footnotes for Mark 10.38 in both the *New Oxford Bible* and the *New English Bible*. There is some question among biblical scholars as to whether the baptism phrase was added by Mark who forty years later had witnessed in Rome the persecution and execution of Christian martyrs.

> David, have pity on me." Jesus stopped and said, "Call him"; so they called the blind man and said, "Take heart; stand up; he is calling you." At that he threw off his cloak, sprang up and came to Jesus. Jesus said to him, "What do you want me to do for you?" "Master," the blind man answered, "I want my sight back." Jesus said to him "Go your faith has cured you." And at once he recovered his sight and followed him on the Road.
>
> Mark: 10.46-52

This is more than just another miracle story, although like the others it emphasizes faith. In this case the beggar has been calling Jesus the Son of David, a term used for one who would be the Messiah. He was told to be quiet, but he continued to shout that Jesus was the Messiah. He was proclaiming Jesus as David's descendent, therefore King of the Jews. There had just been a violent outbreak in Jerusalem and a rebel named Barabas had been imprisoned for murder committed during this rioting.[37] Proclaiming Jesus as the Son of David was to call him King of the Jews, which was not only dangerous for Jesus, but also for the one who proclaimed him to be the Messiah.

Readers should note that when Luke repeats this story he uses the word *saved* instead of *cured*. Further faith is shown by the beggar who when "saved" immediately joined Jesus' followers on the road to Jerusalem, which in view of Mark's reference to an insurrection in Jerusalem was indeed an act of courage. By now, knowing what awaited so-called rebels in Jerusalem, the disciples were committing themselves and showing their faith in Jesus, who was at odds one way or another with part or all of the thinking of each of the political/religious parties of Israel. Entering Jerusalem as a perceived rebel was courting death.

* * * * * * * * * * * *

---

[37] Mark refers to this "insurrection" (Mark 15. 6-7), although it does not appear in historical records. However, with all the unrest of the time one more outbreak of violence might not have seemed important enough to be officially recorded by the Roman governor's scribes.

Arriving at Bethany, just East of Jerusalem, Jesus used the Mount of Olives as the base for his visits to Jerusalem and the temple; it being but a short walk to the temple. Mark has shown us a Jesus who had earlier been reluctant to be called Messiah in public, but now Jesus appears to believe he could be the Messiah; someone to awaken Israel to its chosen role to carry God's light to the rest of the world. That, of course would be a far different Messiah than the popularly expected Messiah.

Jesus knew he would be rejected by the Romans, the Pharisees, and the Sadducees. He also knew that when it became apparent that he was not the long-expected Messiah who would make Israel the greatest of nations, but instead was trying to bring about a spiritual Kingdom of God on earth, he would be rejected not only by the Zealots but also by many of the poorer Jews. He knew that if he stayed his course he could suffer far more than just rejection.

Jesus had molded much of his life to fit his belief in the teachings of Deutro-Isaiah.[38] Remember Mark's opening verses.

> The beginning of the good news of Jesus Christ, the Son of God. As it is written in the prophet Isaiah, 'See, I am sending my messenger ahead of you, who will prepare your way; the voice of one crying out in the wilderness; "Prepare the way of the Lord, make his path straight."'
>
> Mark: 1.1-3

Luke tells of a Jesus teaching from the scroll of Isaiah during that first time he spoke in Nazareth after returning from the wilderness. And it is here in our reading of Mark that we should pause to look for a moment on those verses of Isaiah that meant so much to Jesus (Isaiah. 40-55). Isaiah speaks of God's servant and messenger, and to Isaiah the servant and the messenger are Israel which as God's chosen people was to carry God's word to the rest of the world. Passages of Isaiah such as verses in the forty-second chapter are reflected throughout the Gospels. For example :

---

[38]   Of the several authors of the book of Isaiah, Duetro Isaiah (the second writer) is credited with authoring chapters 40-55 (some credit Second Isaiah with chapters 40-66). These are chapters differing from those Old Testament writers whose God is a god of vengeance in that here God is seen as a god of love and justice.

> Thus says God, the Lord, who created the heavens and stretched them out, who spread out the earth and what comes from it, who gives breath to the people upon it and spirit to those who walk on it: I am the Lord, I have called you in righteousness, I have taken you by the hand and kept you; I have given you as a covenant to the people, and a light to the nations, to open the eyes that are blind, to bring out the prisoners from the dungeon, from the prison those who sit in darkness."
>
> * * * * * * * * * * * *
>
> "Listen, you that are deaf; and you that are blind, look up and see! Who is blind but my servant, or deaf like my messenger whom I send? Who is blind like my dedicated one, or blind like the servant of the Lord? He sees many things but does not observe them; his ears are open, but he does not hear."
>
> Isaiah: 42.5-8,18-20

The *New Oxford Bible* notes that, according to the Second Isaiah, to be *blind* to God's will and way is Israel's chief sin. Jesus of the Gospels sees himself as one sent to open those eyes and ears and to restore Israel to its role as the loyal servant of God and messenger of his Word. Some biblical scholars have pointed to this time in his life as the point where Jesus believed that the true Messiah had to suffer in order to be the Messiah; in order to have his message accepted by the people; in order to open their eyes and ears. He could have continued to preach in Galilee, or in some isolated community, and avoided the cross. But, he knew his message would also have remained isolated, unheard, and unseen. He chose the sacrifice that he believed to be the only way to open Israel's eyes and ears. [39]

The Second Isaiah continues to speak of Israel as God's witness on earth:

---

[39] Without paying the price (death) would the messages of Socrates, Jean d'Arc, and Abraham Lincoln among others have been burned so indelibly into our history? But in those cases, death was not a deliberately chosen sacrifice for the purpose of opening the minds (eyes and ears) of those they hoped their message would benefit.

74

> "Bring out this people, a people who have eyes but are blind, who have ears but are deaf. All the nations are gathered together and the peoples assembled. Who amongst them can expound this thing and interpret for us all that has gone before? Let them produce witnesses to prove their case, or let them listen and say, 'That is the truth.' "My witnesses," says the Lord, "are you, my servants, you whom I have chosen to know me and put your faith in me and understand that I am He. Before me there was no god fashioned nor shall there be after me."
>
> Isaiah: 43.8-10

Mark's repeated stories of the blind and the deaf being healed (saved) and the dead (lost) being brought back to life (being born again) show a Jesus, who like Isaiah, looked upon his fellow Jews as the servants, messengers, and witnesses of God. But, like Isaiah he sees them as blind to their role; deaf to the Word of God; and therefore incapable of standing before all nations as witnesses of the true God. He sees his role as that of God's witness who must open those eyes and ears and bring back all of Israel as God's witness. He needs to show all Israel the road to the Kingdom of God. This is the role of the true Messiah as Jesus envisions it.

This Messiah can not be a king riding into Jerusalem in royal splendor. This Messiah must demonstrate the humility of one who is truly the servant of God. No chariots. No trumpets. Just a colt.

> When they were approaching Jerusalem, at Bethpage and Bethany, near the Mount of Olives, he sent two of his disciples and said to them, "Go into the village ahead of you, and immediately as you enter it, you will find tied there a colt that has never been ridden; untie it and bring it. If anyone says to you, 'Why are you doing this?' just say this, "The Lord needs it and will send it back immediately.'"
>
> Mark: 11.1-3

The disciples did as Jesus had directed. When the people heard what the disciples had been told to say they followed the disciples.

> Many people spread their cloaks on the road, and others spread leafy branches they had cut in the fields. Then those who went ahead and those who followed were shouting, "Hosanna! Blessed is the one who comes in the name of the Lord! Blessed is the coming kingdom of our ancestor David! Hosanna in the highest heaven!"
>
> Mark: 11.8-10

Once more Mark has Jesus fulfilling an earlier prophecy. At least a century and a half before Jesus was born Zechariah wrote:[40]

> Rejoice, rejoice, daughter of Zion (Israel), shout aloud, daughter of Jerusalem; for see, your king is coming to you, his cause won, his victory gained, humble and mounted on an ass. He shall banish chariots from Ephraim and war horses from Jerusalem; the warriors bow shall be banished, He shall speak peaceably to every nation, and his rule shall extend from sea to sea, from the River to the ends of the earth.
>
> Zechariah: 9.9-10

Mark tells us that, after his humble entry into Jerusalem, Jesus went into the temple where he "looked around at everything." As it was late he then returned to his base with his disciples. He had, therefore, all night to consider what he would do the next day to fulfill his responsibility to God in opening the eyes and ears of God's chosen witnesses, the people of Israel.

---

[40] The first eight chapters of Zechariah were authored by someone other than the author of the remainder of the book.

CHAPTER 6

JERUSALEM

And The Cross

There could be no doubt in Jesus' mind when he set out the next morning for the temple. He would be confronting both the Law and "sacred" traditions, a confrontation with all that the political-religious parties held dear. The gauntlet was to be thrown at their feet. The differences between two concepts of the Kingdom of God were to be spelled out clearly for the people of Israel. There was no way other than by such a public confrontation that large masses of "God's chosen people" could ever have been made so aware of the message of Jesus. No other way could ever have opened so many eyes and ears.

Jesus had never remained long in one place. It had been difficult to pin him down as a "trouble maker", or "heretic", or "blasphemer" who was creating a rebellious spirit in any one town. When he came for his last visit to Jerusalem he knew his message had popular support among the masses, no matter how unpopular it might be with the political/religious powers of Israel and Judah. Had crowds not paved his way with leafy branches and accompanied him with shouts of Hosanna? He would have hoped that there would be enough of a public display of popular support that he would be able to bring about some degree of reform here in the religious capital of Judaism.

Whatever the cost, Jesus knew he had to pay for this chance to make the people "see" the true "Kingdom of God." He realized the cost could be his life. So it is that Jesus is committed to that ultimate sacrifice by his decision to enter the temple to confront Sadducees and Pharisees in order to save "God's chosen servants", and to make those chosen servants witnesses to God's purpose.

THE ROAD OF NO RETURN

Mark now brings the reader to the temple.

> Then they came to Jerusalem. And he entered the temple and began to drive out those who were selling and those who were buying in the temple, and he overturned the tables of the money changers and the seats of those who sold doves; and he would not allow anyone to carry anything through the temple. He was teaching and saying, "'Is it not written, My house shall be called a house of prayer for all the nations? But you have made it a den of robbers."
>
> Mark: 11.17

Once again Mark has noted Jesus' reference to Isaiah who had used the phrase, "For my house shall be called a house of prayer." Further reference to the temple some six hundred years before Jesus was born had been made by the prophet Jeremiah who said:

> Has this house, which is called by my name, become a den of robbers in your sight? You know, I too am watching, says the Lord. Go now to my place that was in Shiloh, where I made my name dwell at first, and see what I did to it for the wickedness of my people Israel. And now, because you have done all these things, says the Lord, and when I spoke to you persistently, you did not listen, and when I called you, you did not answer, therefore I will do to the house that is called by my name,

78

> in which you trust, and to the place that I gave to you
> and to your ancestors, just what I did to Shiloh.[41]
>
> Jeremiah: 7. 11-15

It had long been the custom to permit the sale of sacrificial animals and birds, and the changing money for offerings, in the outer court of the temple. Roman money, the common currency used to pay for services and goods purchased by the Roman occupiers, had to be changed for Jewish money by which worshipers paid the temple tax. Like the priests of the Sumerian temple two thousand years earlier, the priests of the temple in Jerusalem could dispose of the sacrificed animals and birds as they wished, and also were the recipients of the money given to the temple. This went far toward maintaining the privileged level of life of the Sadducees for it was only at the Temple that sacrifices could be made. Sacrifices were not permitted at synagogues.

Jesus deplores the obvious hypocrisy involved in this material use of the temple which was supposed to be the house where God's servants could be witness to the spirituality of the Kingdom of God. He is not so much venting his wrath on the money changers and the sellers of sacrificial doves, who were there legally, as he is figuratively cleansing the temple of the spiritual contamination resulting from its misuse. That misuse included the tax the Sadducees demanded of even the poorest before they could worship at the temple. This was the plainest possible challenge to the Sadducees, and lesser priests, and lawyers. This is not a Jesus trying to destroy the religion in which he had grown to manhood, but a Jesus seeking to reform and strengthen that religion

> And when the chief priests and the scribes heard it, they
> kept looking for ways to kill him; for they were afraid of
> him, because the whole crowd was spellbound by his

---

[41] Shiloh, though a Canaanite town, was a headquarters for the early confederacy of Israeli tribes (1200-1100 BC). Eventually the Israelites conquered Canaan, and Shiloh became the site of the tabernacle in which the Arc of the Covenant was located. Around 1050 BC the Philistines defeated the Israelites, captured the Arc and razed Shiloh. Jeremiah is saying God permitted this defeat of his chosen people, destruction of Shiloh, and the loss of the Arc because of their wickedness and refusal to "listen".

> teaching. And when evening came, Jesus and his disciples went out of the city.
>
> Mark: 11. 18-19

* * * * * * * * * * * *

Whether one reads Mark literally or figuratively one finds the parable of the fig tree puzzling. Mark's version of this parable notes that on the way to Jerusalem on the day Jesus would drive out the money changers, Jesus and the disciples saw a fig tree in the distance. They saw that it was in leaf, and Jesus being hungry went to see whether there were any figs on it. Obviously, even from a distance one could tell that there would be no figs because the leaves of the fig trees of Israel do not appear until after the tree has borne its fruit. As Mark writes, "When he came to it, he found nothing but leaves, for *it was not the season for figs.*"

Jesus then says to the tree, "May no one ever eat fruit from you again." The next day when returning to Jerusalem the disciples saw that the fig tree had completely withered away overnight.

Matthew appears to have been trying to make the meaning of this parable clearer by having Jesus see the fig tree on the morning after he had cleansed the temple. Jesus then tells the fig tree, "May no fruit ever come from you again!" and Matthew then has the tree withering away immediately while the disciples watched. It is agreed among most biblical scholars that this may be seen as another example similar to the healing of the beggar where Jesus explains that faith is not enough, that only God can accomplish such "miracles."

> When the disciples saw it they were amazed saying, "How did the fig tree wither at once?" Jesus answered them, "Truly I tell you, if you have faith and do not doubt, not only will you do what has been done to the fig tree, but even if you say to this mountain, 'Be lifted up and thrown into the sea,' it will be done.
>
> "So I tell you, whatever you ask for in prayer, believe that you have received it, and it will be yours'"
>
> Matthew: 21.21-22

But, why did Mark insert this parable at this point? What does it have to do with the purpose of Jesus' visit to Jerusalem and the cleansing of the temple? Those who read the bible figuratively see in this parable a rejection of Israel for its straying from God's way and, therefore, relate the parable to Jesus' condemnation of the despoilers of the temple. With this interpretation one sees the fig tree representing Israel, and no matter how much faith Jesus had he could not bring about the reform he believed God wanted. Because Israel would not listen, God then would see Israel wither away.

This is one parable that escapes universal interpretation. Yet, no matter how the reader may interpret the parable, he or she should remember that it was obvious that fig trees did not bear figs at that time of the year. Therefore, this was not meant to be read literally, as though Jesus did not realize there would be no figs and cursed the tree because of his displeasure at finding none. Even if Jesus could have called for the withering of the tree merely because there were no figs at that time of the year, would he have so abused his power to call upon God for such a trivial matter? Mark intended the parable to have a deeper meaning, and we are still arguing about it today. The *New Testament* is not a simple document. It needs to be read with great care by one seeking to discover all its secrets.

Often overlooked is Jesus' concluding comment above: "...whatever you ask in prayer, believe that you have received it, and it will be yours." Though this part of Jesus' response may be short, we must not underestimate its importance. At this point in his gospel, Mark has already made two things clear through various parables. One, Jesus has insisted that the Kingdom of God is within each individual, but can only grow when one makes room for it by emptying himself or herself of material concerns and desires. Two, he has repeatedly insisted that an absolute requirement for entering the Kingdom of God was faith. Therefore, his disciples were to realize that one did not ask in prayer for worldly rewards or material gifts. Prayer was for such purposes as asking for strength to meet life's problems or to do what was right. Therefore, if individuals pray for such purposes and have complete faith in God, then through prayer they will receive that for which they ask.

Believing that one receives what one asks for in prayer places the responsibility on the one who is praying. If that person has complete faith in God, then his or her prayer is answered when that person, through faith, believes it is answered. Mark is saying that Jesus has described prayer not as something that would be answered by God's direct intervention, but rather as a means by which one's faith in God made it possible for one to gain the strength to meet whatever problems one faced. It could heal one who was plagued by fear. It could give one the strength to resist temptation. It could remove doubts as to which path should be followed. It could bring one closer to that peace beyond all understanding, the Kingdom of God. It placed the responsibility for a positive response to prayer directly on the individual who was praying.

Jesus then added the words later gospel writers would include in what we now refer to as the Lord's Prayer.

> "Whenever you stand praying, forgive, if you have anything against anyone; so your Father in heaven may also forgive you your trespasses."
>
> Mark: 11.25

This is akin to the spirit of Yom Kippur, the Jewish Day of Atonement, when purification is sought by forgiving those who have sinned against you, a necessary prerequisite to asking God's forgiveness of one's own sins. Jesus is not in any way seeking to undermine Judaism. He is trying to bring about the reforms he believes necessary to make Israel once more God's witness and messenger. It is the materialistic wall between Israel and the Kingdom of God that Jesus is trying to tear down.

If Jesus had been proclaiming a new religion or had been calling for conversion to one of the many religions of the region, he would probably have been ignored by the Sadducees and Pharisees. The crowds of sincerely religious Jews would have paid him little attention. But, he was calling for reform of their religion, and they were hungry for that which he preached; and what he preached was seen by the Sadducees and Pharisees as a direct threat to them and to what they believed. Their role in the religion of the Jews would no longer be needed. Jesus was saying the Kingdom of God could be reached by individuals without the need for temple authorities as intermediaries.[42]

* * * * * * * * * * * *

> They came once more to Jerusalem. And as he was walking in the temple court the chief priests, lawyers, and elders came to him and said, "By what authority are you acting like this? Who gave you authority to act in this way?" Jesus said to them, "I have a question to ask you too; and if you give me an answer I will tell you by what authority I act. The baptism of John: was it from God, or from men? Answer me." This set them arguing among themselves: "What shall we say? If we say from God, he will say, 'Then why did you not believe him?' Shall we say from men?" – but they were afraid of the people, for all held that John was in fact a prophet. So they answered, "We do not know." and Jesus said to them, "Then neither will I tell you by what authority I act."
>
> Mark: 11.27-32

The fear authorities felt when seeing those crowds following Jesus could not be more evident than in the manner by which those questioners equivocated when pinned down by Jesus. This was no trivial game being played here. On one side was Jesus' influence over the crowds he had taught, and on the other side the religious-political powers in Jerusalem. The stakes were the highest: Jesus' life against the resistance to reform; two versions of the Kingdom of God in conflict.

Jesus did not settle for a stalemate at this point. He continued the confrontation by "speaking to them in parables."

---

[42] 1,500 years later, the Protestant reformation appeared to threaten what church leaders in Rome believed to be the necessary intermediary structure of Christianity, and resulted in reformers being burned at the stake or otherwise executed. Reformers within a faith or an organizations may often appear to be a greater threat to established beliefs and traditions than an outsider trying to establish a completely new belief. Outsiders may be ignored, but not reformers.

> "A man planted a vineyard and put a wall around it,
> hewed out a winepress, and built a watch-tower; then he
> let it out to vine-growers and went abroad. When the
> season came, he sent a servant to the tenants to collect
> from them his share of the produce, But they took him,
> thrashed him, and sent him away empty handed. Again,
> he sent them another servant, whom they beat about the
> head and treated outrageously. So he sent another, and
> that one they killed; and many more besides, of whom
> they beat some, and killed the others. He now had only
> one left to send, his own dear son. In the end he sent
> him. 'They will respect my son', he said. But the tenants
> said to one another, 'This is the heir; come on, let us kill
> him, and then the property will be ours.' So they seized
> him and killed him and flung his body out of the
> vineyard. What will the owner of the vineyard do?" They
> said to him, "He will come and put the tenants to death
> and give the vineyard to others."
>
> Mark: 12.1-9

Jesus indicates his agreement with the answer of the priests, and then adds:

> "Can it be that you have never read this text: 'The stone
> which the builders rejected has become the main
> cornerstone. This is the Lord's doing, and it is wonderful
> in our eyes."
>
> Then they began to look for a way to arrest him, for they
> saw the parable was aimed at them; but they were afraid
> of the people, so they left him alone and went away.
>
> Mark: 12.1-12

The priests and doctors of law understood that, as in the Old Testament, the vineyard referred to Israel. The owner, God, had created the vineyard. In Isaiah he is dissatisfied with the quality of the produce of the vineyards. In Jesus' parable the Master has sent prophet after prophet to no avail. Now he has sent his son and the priests are confronted with the dilemma of accepting the son or killing him.

Then Jesus has added the reference to the corner-stone. The corner-stone was essential for a firm foundation. He was telling the priests that they and other political/religious groups might reject him, even eliminate him, but they could not wipe out his message. He and his message were to become the corner-stone of a new religious structure that would replace them and their tradition bound doctrine and practices.

Let us go back now to a passage we left unread until this point. Jesus is describing the Kingdom of God in response to questions from his disciples.

> He also said, "With what can we compare the kingdom of God, or what parable will we use for it? It is like the mustard seed, which, when sown upon the ground, is the smallest of all seeds on earth; yet when it is sown it grows up and becomes the greatest of all shrubs, and puts forth large branches, so that the birds of the air can make nests in its shade."
>
> Mark: 4.30-32

Some see in this parable a description of the manner in which God's kingdom will come into the world some time in the future and how it will then grow. Others, pointing to a passage in Luke when Jesus is being questioned by Pharisees, see the Kingdom of God already here in the present.

> The Pharisees asked him, "'When will the Kingdom of God come?" He said, "You cannot tell by observation when the kingdom of God comes. There will be no saying, 'Look here it is!' or 'there it is!' ; for in fact the kingdom of God is among (within) you.'"
>
> Luke: 17.20-21

He or she who spends a lifetime watching and waiting for the "coming" of the Kingdom of Heaven, a kingdom to be brought to the world by some outside power, has wasted his or her life. Even though it is only a tiny seed within each individual, it can grow when one has emptied himself or herself sufficiently to give it room to grow. Then it shall take over one's life as it becomes greater than any other thought, desire, or problem.

How different this was from the material Kingdom of God in which the Sadducees saw themselves becoming privileged members of a worldly Messiah's court. The contrast could not be greater. And, there would be no role for the Sadducees, if the people believed they could find the Kingdom of God without need of a temple, or priests, or religious laws, or sacrifices. This was more than "blasphemy." This was a revolution in making, one that presaged an imminent and complete destruction of the world of the Sadducees -and Jesus was also challenging "the law" of the Pharisees.

Unrest among the general populace was already a major concern of the Romans. Pilate might at any moment intervene to suppress demonstrations of support for Jesus as he saw growing crowds filling the streets in support of this man who they were proclaiming as the Messiah. If that were to happen, not only the Sadducees but also the lawyers and the Pharisees could very well find Pilate curtailing their role. It had been the Roman custom to let local religious authorities play a major part in civil government. While this made allies of these local religious leaders it also enhanced the political power of these religious authorities. All this could be lost.

The Sadducees concern was not wholly one of retaining personal privileges. There were sincere priests among them who appreciated the fact that the Romans were permitting them to maintain their religion. Jews strongly supported monotheism, whereas the Romans worshipped several Gods. The Sadducees saw in Jesus, and in the crowds he was drawing, something that might so alarm the Roman governors that they would close the temple and the synagogues of the Jews and outlaw their religion.

Whether Jesus actually confronted his questioners with the parable of the corner- stone or whether Mark used it to demonstrate Jesus' stand before the Sadducees and doctors of law is not clear. The reader can be certain, however, that both Mark and Jesus would be familiar with Isaiah's parable of a vineyard, and of the passage in the118[th] Psalm which reads:

> The stone which the builders rejected has become the chief corner-stone. This is the Lord's doing; it is marvelous in our eyes. This is the day on which the Lord has acted.
>
> Psalm: 118.22-24

Is Mark further establishing Jesus' credentials in this confrontation with the keepers of the temple by this use of Psalms and writings of prophets which were such important parts of the Judaism preached by the high priests? The priests and lawyers had asked by what authority Jesus acted. Mark is showing a Jesus who can find roots for his authority in the teachings of the *Old Testament* with which the priests would obviously be familiar. Why not otherwise have Jesus say something original rather than have him repeating passages with which the priests were familiar?

Jesus is challenging the very authority of the Sadducees even as he is establishing his own authority.

* * * * * * * * * * * *

Pharisees now joined the Sadducees in their efforts to trap Jesus. Those sent to do this began by flattering him, and then appearing to ask his advice. They asked:

> "Are we or are we not permitted to pay taxes to the Roman Emperor? Shall we pay or not?" He saw how crafty their question was, and said, "Why are you trying to catch me out? Fetch me a silver piece, and let me look at it." They brought one, and he said to them, "Whose head is this, and whose inscription?" "The emperor's," they answered. Then Jesus said, "Give to the emperor the things that are the emperors, and to God the things that are God's." And they were utterly amazed at him.
>
> Mark: 12.14-17

The Pharisees having failed to trap him, the Sadducees again undertook to catch Jesus in contradiction of the scriptures. The reader should keep in mind that whereas the Pharisees believed in resurrection the Sadducees did not. Quoting the law from Deuteronomy they said:

> "Teacher, Moses wrote for us that 'if a man's brother dies, leaving a wife but no child, the man shall marry the widow and raise up children for his brother.' There were seven brothers; the first married, and when he died, left no children; and the second married her and died, leaving no children; and the third likewise; none of the seven left children. Last of all the woman herself died. In the resurrection whose wife will she be? For the seven had married her."
>
> Jesus said to them, "Is not this the reason you are wrong, that you know neither the scriptures nor the power of God? For when they rise from the dead, they will neither marry nor be given in marriage, but are like the angels in heaven. And as for the dead being raised, have you not read in the book of Moses, in the story about the burning bush, how God said to him, 'I am the God of Abraham, the God of Isaac, and the God of Jacob?' He is God not of the dead, but of the living; you are quite wrong."
>
> Mark: 12.19-27

Mark's report of Jesus' comments on resurrection are in line with Paul's interpretation of resurrection when Jesus says that those with faith, though physically dead, are resurrected in other than the physical sense of life on earth. Matthew and Luke will go further with this passage. This is another example of Matthew and Luke feeling the need to make clearer the intent of Mark's words. Luke will add:

> "And the fact that the dead are raised Moses himself showed, in the story about the bush, where he speaks of the Lord as the God of Abraham, the God of Isaac, and the God of Jacob. Now He is God not of the dead, but of the living; *for to him all are alive.*"
>
> Luke: 20.37-38

88

A pertinent footnote in *The New Oxford Bible* referring to the last sentence of the above passage by Luke notes: "Luke makes the same point as Matthew and Mark, but in somewhat different language: human relations in the home do not exist in the same way beyond death. Jesus distinguishes two ages and kinds of existence. Mortals are part of this age by the fact of physical birth, and of the age to come by resurrection." Luke is the only one of the four gospel writers to carry the story beyond the life of and the days immediately following the death of Jesus. In the book of *Acts* he will describe the works of Paul, the apostle, building the Christian church among the Gentiles.[43] He is familiar with Paul's thinking in this matter.

We must remember that Mark completed his gospel about two years after Paul had died in Rome. This is important because Paul insisted that resurrection was spiritual, not physical. Thus Mark and the other three gospel writers are making the point here that according to Jesus there is a difference between the physical lives of mortals here on earth and a spiritual life or consciousness after resurrection.

This point, whether there is physical resurrection of the mortal body or resurrection of the spirit (soul) would remain a divisive topic over the centuries. Although presented as a creed developed by the twelve apostles, the *Apostle's Creed* actually was produced by the bishops in Rome some two hundred years after Jesus death and completed in its present form in France during the late 600s or early 700s AD. This includes the phrase, "I believe in….the resurrection of the body," and this emphasis on physical resurrection continued to grow through the centuries. For the careful reader of the gospels this early reference by Jesus of the difference between the mortal life on earth and existence after resurrection becomes important, whether one believes these passages should be accepted literally or are designed to be read figuratively.

When after further questions the Pharisees, Sadducees, and Scribes finally gave up questioning him, Jesus said:

> "How can the teachers of the law maintain that the Messiah is 'Son of David'? David himself said, when inspired by the Holy Spirit, 'The Lord said to my Lord,

---

[43] This assumes that the same person authored both *The Gospel According To Luke* and *Acts*. The question of authorship is discussed in later chapters about Luke's gospel.

> Sit at my right hand until I put your enemies under your feet.' David himself calls him Lord.; how can he also be David's son?"
>
> Mark: 12.35-37

David's first uses the word "Lord" to refer to God. The second time he uses the word "Lord" it is a reference to the Messiah. As biblical scholars note, Jesus' point is that when God speaks to the Messiah it makes clear that the Messiah is the agent of God. As David looks to the Messiah as his Lord, how could the Messiah also be David's son?

Mark has highlighted the problem for the Sadducees and Pharisees. For centuries they had taught that the Messiah would have to be a descendant of David. Now a thousand years after the death of David, they treated David as a Messiah and refused to accept any claimant to the role of Messiah who was not a direct descendant of David. Jesus has posed a question, which as Matthew will later write, completely stumped the Pharisees. Matthew says that when Jesus had concluded his question about David's comment on the Messiah: "No one was able to give him an answer, nor from that day did anyone dare to ask him more questions" (Matthew 22. 43-45).

While still at the temple Jesus continued to be the teacher.

> There was a great crowd and they listened eagerly. He said as he taught them, "Beware of the doctors of law, who love to walk up and down in long robes, receiving respectful greetings in the street; and to have the chief seats in the synagogues, and places of honor at feasts. These are the men who eat up the property of widows, while they say long prayers for appearance' sake, and they will receive the severest sentence."
>
> Mark: 12.38-40

With this last statement Jesus has assured the enmity of the scribes. Mark continues with a contrasting example from Jesus' teaching to his disciples that day in the temple.

> He sat down opposite the treasury, and watched the crowd putting money into the treasury. Many rich

> people put in large sums. A poor widow came and put in two small copper coins, which are worth a penny. Then he called his disciples and said to them, "Truly I tell you, this poor widow has put in more than all those who are contributing to the treasury. For all of them have contributed out of their abundance; but she out of her poverty has put in everything she had, all she had to live on."
>
> Mark: 12.41-44

This contrast between the wealthy and often pompous and arrogant scribes and priests on the one hand and this deeply religious poor widow was bound to appeal to the masses crowding about the gates of the temple. There they thronged to see and hear this new teacher, this man who might be the long-awaited Messiah. From the Sadducees' point of view it was well past the time when they should have gotten rid of this "agitator".

> As he was leaving the temple, one of his disciples exclaimed, "Look Master, what huge stones! What fine buildings!" Jesus said to him, "You see these great buildings? Not one stone will left upon another; all will be thrown down."
>
> When they were sitting on the Mount of Olives facing the temple, he was questioned privately by Peter, James, John, and Andrew. "Tell us," they said, "when will this happen? What will be the sign when the fulfillment of this is at hand?"
>
> Mark: 13.1-4

In a later passage Jesus speaks of the destruction of the temple which would be rebuilt in three days. This has been interpreted as meaning Jesus spoke of himself as the temple which would be resurrected after three days. In contrast, the reference quoted above about the destruction of the temple has been interpreted by some as meaning Jesus would personally destroy the temple. Most biblical scholars, however, see it intended as a warning that the world was about to come to an end.

Jesus then continues with a list of warnings for his disciples. Whether read literally or figuratively, the meaning is the same. The disciples are warned to be on guard against those who, after Jesus was gone, would claim to be the Messiah. He again warns the disciples that they will be persecuted; and that families would be split between those who believe and those who will not accept the word of the Holy Spirit when spoken through you.

When Mark wrote, it was a time when there was great concern about the coming end of the world. He concludes this chapter with Jesus meeting this concern in his response to the disciples.

"But in those days, after that distress, the sun will be darkened, the moon will not give her light; the stars will come falling from the sky, the celestial powers will be shaken. Then they will see the Son of Man coming in the clouds with great power and glory, and he will send out the angels and gather his chosen from the four winds, from the farthest bounds of the earth to the farthest bounds of heaven.

"Learn a lesson from the fig tree. When its tender shoots appear and are breaking into leaf, you know that summer is near. In the same way when you see all this happening, you may know the end is near, at the very door. I tell you this: the present generation will live to see it all. Heaven and earth will pass away; my words will never pass away.

"But about that day or that hour no one knows, not even the angels in heaven, not even the Son; only the Father.

"Be alert, be wakeful. You do not know when the moment comes. It is like a man away from home: he has left his house and put his   servants in charge, each with his own work to do, and he has ordered the door-keeper to stay awake. Keep awake, then, for you do not know when the master of the house is coming. Evening or midnight, cock-crow or early dawn – if he comes

> suddenly, he must not find you asleep. And what I say to
> you, I say to everyone: Keep awake."
>
> Mark: 13.24-37

In his 24th chapter Matthew will repeat these same warnings, sometimes word for word, that appear here in this 13th chapter of Mark. Reference to a generation meant twenty to thirty years, but what Jesus meant here is not clear.

PREPARING FOR THE END

> Now the festival of Passover and Unleavened Bread was
> only two days off; and the chief priests and the doctors
> of the law were trying to devise some cunning plan to
> seize him and put him to death. "It must not be during
> the festival," they said, "or we should have rioting among
> the people."
>
> Mark: 14.1-2

There was among the disciples one named Judas Iscariot. Although Greek was the language used by scholars and writers in Israel, Latin was the language of Roman occupiers and was, therefore, frequently used in the markets and on the streets. It is believed by many biblical scholars that the surname Iscariot was derived from the Latin word "sicarius". Translated, "sicarius" means assassin. One of the extreme radical groups in Israel at that time was the Sicarii. As with the Zealots, there were among the Sicarii many terrorists seeking to rid Israel of the Romans in order to make way for the Messiah, who would make Israel a great power among nations.

If Judas did indeed come to Jesus from the Sicarii, it would explain his acts. Like the Zealots, the Sicarii would be as fearful of Jesus' influence as were the Sadducees, Scribes, and Pharisees, but for a different reason. Whereas the Sadducees feared that Jesus' influence among the people would cause the Romans to reduce the authority and privileges of the Sadducees, the Sicarii and Zealots would be concerned that Jesus' message of a non-material Kingdom of God would wipe out all chance of a violent revolution supported by the people. Even if

Judas were not active in the Sicarii, he did come from the region in which sentiment against Roman rule ran high, and which was home to the Sicarii.

Obviously, Judas wished to get rid of Jesus. If ever he had believed Jesus could be recognized as the Messiah, he would have been attracted by the vision of a Messiah who could lead the people in a successful revolt against the Romans. In that respect he would now have become disillusioned and fearful of this new leader who preached peace. "Give to the Romans what is Roman and to God what is God's." At the same time, like the Sadducees, Judas would not wish to have the people rise against him and those he supported. This could easily happen, if the people tied the death of Jesus to any movement with which Judas might be associated. Get rid of Jesus, but let the Sadducees get the blame. That would serve two purposes. It would get rid of Jesus and could rouse the people to violence against the Roman supported Sadducees.

> Then Judas Iscariot, one of the Twelve, went to the chief priests to betray him to them. When they heard what he had come for, they were greatly pleased, and promised him money; and he began to look for an opportunity to betray him.
>
> Mark: 14.10-11

Mark now takes us to the upper room where Jesus is having the Passover supper with his disciples. Jesus could well have left Jerusalem at this time and returned to his role as a traveling teacher showing the way to the Kingdom of God. He knew remaining in Jerusalem after his confrontation with the leaders of the political/religious parties that he would be arrested and no doubt executed. He speaks of betrayal by one of the twelve, but this could well be Christology, Mark's insertion of knowledge attained after the fact. However, Mark notes Jesus also saying:

> "The Son of Man is going in the way appointed for him in the scriptures."
>
> Mark: 14.21

Here again is an indication not only that Jesus knew he would be put to death, but why he had to be put to death. He believes this is the only way his message will resonate among the people and last beyond the moment. This is a deliberate sacrifice; a knowing sacrifice. As in the parable of the vineyard, he will be the last messenger.

> During the supper he took bread, and having said the blessing he broke it and gave it to them, with the words: "Take this; this is my body." Then he took the cup, and having offered thanks to God he gave it to them; and they all drank from it. And he said, "This is my blood, the blood of the covenant, shed for many."
>
> Mark: 14.22-24

One should not pass over this passage too lightly. Remember, Jesus knows he will be sacrificing his life within the next day or two. As soon as he will be arrested he will be separated from his disciples. By definition a covenant is a formal, solemn, and binding agreement, usually under seal. In *Exodus* the people have gathered to hear Moses.

> He then sent the young men of Israel and they sacrificed bulls to the Lord as whole offerings and shared offerings. Moses took half the blood and put it in basins and the other half he flung upon the altar. Then he took the book of the covenant and read it aloud for all the people to hear. They said, "We will obey, and do all that the Lord has said." Moses then took the blood and flung it over the people, saying, This is the blood of the covenant which the Lord has made with you on the terms of this book."
>
> Exodus: 24.5-8

In *Exodus* God's covenant with the people is, by Moses' action, sealed in blood. All covenants were supposed to be solemnly sealed. In Mark's description of this symbolism Jesus is using the wine to represent the blood he *will* be shedding. The actual shedding of his blood when he is put to death will be Jesus' sealing of a covenant with not only the disciples, but with all believers. With this action he is saying he is the connecting link between God and the people. God is a forgiving God, and he will forgive those who live according to his word. The covenant of which Jesus speaks, "This is my blood, the blood of the covenant, shed for many," is a new covenant with God. In this he is speaking much as had Moses. The *New Oxford Bible* notes: "Jesus speaks of his blood as being the mediating reality in the new relationship between God and humankind." He is pledging his life as his part of the covenant. He will not be going to his death unknowingly, but deliberately as his part of the covenant.[44]

In sealing this new covenant with God, Jesus is symbolically fulfilling the Old Testament prophecy of Jeremiah.

> "The days are surely coming," says the Lord, "when I will make a new covenant with the house of Israel and the house of Judah. It will not be like the covenant that I made with their ancestors when I took them by hand to bring them out of Egypt – a covenant that they broke, though I was their husband, says the Lord. But this is the covenant I will make with the house of Israel after those days, says the Lord: I will put my law within them, and I will write it on their hearts; and I will be their God, and they shall be my people. No longer shall they teach one another, or say to each other, 'Know the Lord,' for they shall know me, from the least of them to the greatest, says the Lord; for I will forgive their iniquity, and remember their sin no more."
>
> Jeremiah: 31.31-34

After that last supper with his disciples Jesus led them to Gethsemane, a garden spot on the slope of the Mount of Olives overlooking the temple in the distance.[45] On their way Jesus told these

---

[44] Sealing with blood was a solemn promise to keep an agreement used by people around the globe throughout thousands of years. Even among primitives the symbolism of blood brothers had a most solemn meaning. This was a promise that could not be broken.

young men that when he was arrested, they would out of fear desert him. Of course they insisted they would never abandon him. But, Jesus knew that though he was willingly sacrificing his life to carry his message to the people he could not expect his disciples to do the same. They had not the same motive for sacrifice.

No one could know what Jesus said or thought during his prayers for according to Mark he left his disciples sleeping while he walked a short way from them to pray. It is therefore up to Mark to put in Jesus' mouth the words that would best describe how he must have felt at that time. Mark describes the moment thusly:

> ...he said to his disciples, "Sit here while I pray." And he took Peter and James and John with him. Horror and dismay came over him, and he said to them, "My heart is ready to break with grief; stop here, and stay awake." Then he went forward and threw himself on the ground, and prayed that, if it were possible, this hour might pass him by. "Abba, Father," he said, "all things are possible to thee, take this cup away from me. Yet not what I will, but what thou wilt.'."
>
> Mark: 14.32-36

Mark shows us Jesus' humanity in this passage. He does not present Jesus as a divine being above physical and mental suffering. He shows us a mortal Jesus who prays that he might not need to go through with his sacrifice, but who will not back away from making that sacrifice; if it is the only way to make the people remember the word of God.

This is important. It is another point at which those who read the bible literally and those who read it figuratively find their paths diverging. The reader who has accepted the stories of healing the blind, the lepers (unclean), the deaf, and the epileptic as literal miracles, now faces a question from critics of Christianity. How, they are asked, could Jesus really suffer pain on the cross, if he had the miraculous power to relieve pain? Those who have read as parables those passages

---

[45] The name Gethsemane is taken from the Hebrew words meaning "oil press". This leads researchers to believe the place where the disciples slept while Jesus prayed was in an olive grove.

concerning miracles, through which Mark and Jesus try to convey "God's Word", are at this point more likely to appreciate the fullness of the sacrifice Jesus is making.

Throughout Jesus' praying his disciples slept. He repeatedly asked them to stay awake, but each time they again fell asleep; they were so tired. Jesus understood and even as he told them to pray that they would not be put to the test he added: "The spirit is willing, but the flesh is weak."

It was then that Judas arrived, having guided to this spot a contingent of armed men sent by the chief priests, lawyers, and elders. He kissed Jesus, the signal that this was the man to be arrested.

> Then Jesus spoke: "Do you take me for a bandit, that you come out with swords and cudgels to arrest me? Day after day I was within your reach as I taught in the temple, and you did not lay hands on me. But, let the scriptures be fulfilled.' Then the disciples all deserted him and ran away."
>
> Mark: 14.48-50

Jesus understands that he could have been arrested at the temple, but that the Sadducees were afraid of the reaction of the people crowding around the temple to hear him. By quickly turning him over to the Romans and insisting that the Romans make the final judgment and carry out the sentence of death, the chief priests, lawyers, and elders could divert the wrath of the crowds from themselves and onto the Romans who were already hated by most Jews.

Therefore, immediately upon being arrested Jesus was taken to the home of the high priest where the chief priests, doctors of law, and elders had gathered to await his arrival. No time was wasted. They needed to complete their "trial" before daylight. Over and over they questioned Jesus.

> The chief priests and the whole Council tried to find some evidence against Jesus to warrant a death sentence, but failed to find any. Many gave false evidence against him, but their statements did not tally. Some stood up and gave false evidence to this effect: "We heard him say, 'I will pull down this temple, made with human hands,

98

> and in three days I will build another, not made with
> hands.'" But even on this point their evidence did not
> agree.
>
> Again the High Priest stood up in his place and
> questioned Jesus: "Have you no answer to the charges
> that these witnesses bring against you?" But he kept his
> silence; he made no reply.
>
> Again the High Priest questioned him: "Are you the
> Messiah, the Son of the Blessed One?" Jesus said, "I am;
> and you will see the Son of Man seated at the right hand
> of God and coming with the clouds of heaven." Then
> the High Priest tore his robes and said, "Need we call
> further witnesses? You have heard the blasphemy. What
> is your opinion?" Their judgment was unanimous: that
> he was guilty and should be put to death.
>
> Mark: 14.55-64

As there were no written records of the all-night trial of Jesus, Mark has used this occasion to have Jesus proclaim himself as the Messiah, but to refuse to dignify any of the other charges by answering them. Mark, thereby, is saying that the killing of Jesus is because he is believed to be falsely claiming to be the long awaited Messiah. This is complete blasphemy in the eyes of the Council. To them Jesus is not only one more imposter, but one to be feared. Theirs is a firm belief that the true Messiah will be one who comes in royal glory to raise Israel to great heights; not one who preached that the Kingdom of God was within and would grow like the mustard seed described by Jesus. Yet, Jesus' message has resonated through the streets of Jerusalem and the villages from Galilee to Bethany. Jesus must be out of their hands and turned over to the Romans as soon as possible the next morning.

> As soon as it was morning the chief priests held a
> consultation with the elders and scribes and the whole
> council. They bound Jesus, led him away, and handed
> him over to Pilate. Pilate asked Him, "Are you the King
> of the Jews?" He answered him, "You say so." Then the
> chief priests accused him of many things. Pilate asked

> him again, "Have you no answer? See how many charges they bring against you." But Jesus made no further reply, so that Pilate was amazed.
>
> Now at the festival he used to release a prisoner for them, anyone whom they asked. Now a man called Barabbas was in prison with the rebels who had committed murder during the insurrection. So the crowd came and began to ask Pilate to do for them according to his custom. Then he answered them, "Do you want me to release for you the King of the Jews?" For he realized that it was out of jealousy that the chief priests had handed him over. But the chief priests stirred up the crowd to have him release Barabbas for them instead. Pilate spoke to them again, "Then what do you want me to do with the man you call the King of the Jews?" They shouted back, "Crucify him!" Pilate asked them, "Why, what evil has he done?"
>
> But they shouted all the more, "Crucify him!" So Pilate, wishing to satisfy the crowd, released Barabbas for them; and after flogging Jesus, he handed him over to be crucified.
>
> Mark: 15.1-15

The high priests knew there was one charge that Pilate could not ignore, incitement to a rebellion. There could be no independent king of the Jews in Israel without an overthrow of their Roman occupiers. Any one who would claim to be King of the Jews would obviously be considered a rebel, an instigator of a revolt.

Mark could not have appreciated what his use of the word crowd would come to mean over the centuries. In English, for example, crowd can mean a group of people with a common interest. One often hears the expression that someone and "his crowd" (a dozen friends) did something or believed something. Even in Greek the word could not in this case refer to a huge gathering.

The high priests had brought with them the scribes and elders of the Council. They had intentionally arrested Jesus in the dark of the night and had tried him immediately during that same night. They then rushed him to Pilate in the early morning, a time when fewer people would be out and about than later in the day. ("As soon as morning came, the chief priests, having made their plan with the elders and lawyers in full council, put Jesus in chains; then led him away and handed him over to Pilate." Mark 15. 1)

Everything was being done to keep the people of Jerusalem from rising in support of the man they had been thronging to see and hear. Furthermore, there would have been no room for a large crowd at Pilate's palace. Palaces for local Roman governors were not the grand residences that one associates with post-medieval Europe. Some biblical scholars believe it would be unlikely that the crowd numbered more than a couple of dozen priests, lawyers, and elders chosen to bring Jesus before Pilate and to bring charges against him. As their purpose was to have Jesus executed, but executed by the Romans, there would have been no cry from them other than to demand his crucifixion.

However, from pulpits over the centuries, and in modern day motion pictures and novels, the impression is given of a huge mob of Jews filling the streets and shouting for Jesus to be crucified. For almost two thousand years people have lost sight of the fact that the disciples, and the crowds whose support of Jesus had frightened the high priests, and the writers of the gospels, and the founders and organizers of the first Christian churches were Jews.

Crucifixion was a form of punishment in effect in Rome and the Middle East for about a thousand years beginning in the 6th century BC. Mark was writing in Rome. By then crucifixion in Rome was carried out at a particular site set aside for that purpose. Poles were permanently implanted at that site, about four or five feet of the pole being in the ground. The pole extended another fifteen to eighteen feet above the ground. The criminal was sometimes forced to carry the short cross beam to the place of execution.[46] Upon reaching the upright pole the one to be executed was tied by the wrists to the crossbeam which was then hauled up to a point about three feet below the top of the pole. At the top of the upright a board was placed bearing the criminal's name and the crime for which he was being executed.

---

[46] Unlike depictions in paintings and motion pictures the one to be executed did not carry the full upright and cross beam. That would have been a physical impossibility as it would take several men just to lift the upright pole.

The means of death was asphyxiation. The man being crucified hung by his extended arms and the weight of his body slowly caused the muscles of his upper body to weaken until he could no longer breathe. It was meant to be a slow death. Sometimes a victim was nailed to the short crossbeam with nails through the wrists. This, however, was not as common as binding because the shock and the loss of blood defeated the purpose of a slow death.

It is important to note these details because Mark was able to witness crucifixions in Rome. However, in the provinces executions were less formal. Often the victim's extended arms were tied to a tree at the place where executions were carried out. As there were no witnesses of Jesus' crucifixion still living, and in Rome, at the time Mark wrote, there are many who believe Jesus was most likely tied to a tree. If that be the case, the question facing the reader is whether or not the carrying of the cross by Jesus is meant to be a symbolic reference to the "cross" Jesus has chosen to bear, especially as he could only have carried the short crossbeam. It is a question no one can answer. We do know, however, that Jesus was crucified, died, and was buried.

> It was nine o'clock in the morning when they crucified him, The inscription of the charge against him read, "The King of The Jews." And with him they crucified two bandits, one on the right and one on the left."
>
> Mark: 15.25-27

The arrest and trial had been rushed through at night. Sentence was passed quickly at Pilate's palace. Jesus was then rushed to Golgotha, the site for crucifixions, while most people were still not about on the streets, and Mark says it was only nine o'clock by the time they had either raised the crossbeam into place on the upright pole or bound him high on a tree. Chief priests, elders, and lawyers stood around mocking him. But for the presence of some Roman soldiers they were, according to this reading, the "crowd" that was present. They were still able to proceed without the presence of or even the awareness of the crowds that had supported Jesus. According to Mark,

Jesus died at three o'clock in the afternoon after six hours on the cross.[47]

> Then Jesus gave a loud cry and breathed his last. And the curtain of the temple was torn in two, from top to bottom.
>
> Mark: 15.37-38

This passage may be read literally as another miracle in which the curtain was actually rent from top to bottom. The curtain to which this passage referred closed off the inner sanctum of the temple. In the inner sanctum God's presence was symbolized much as later Christian churches taught of God's presence at the altar. The curtain was the barrier which kept all but the priests from entering this Holy of Holies where priests were supposed to be the peoples' mediators with God. Knowing that Mark used parables for much of his presentation readers may also see this as a symbolic rending of the curtain.

In a figurative reading Jesus' death made certain his message would be with the people forever, and the curtain which symbolized a bar against direct access to God by the people would be gone forever. No longer would it be necessary for believers of Jesus' message to go through the priests. His death had removed the barrier between the people and God.

Normally, the bodies of crucified criminals could not be buried where the rest of the community buried their dead. Instead, bodies of the crucified were usually thrown into a pit, a common grave. Mark describes for us a different situation.

> When evening had come, and since it was the day of Preparation, that is, the day before the Sabbath, Joseph of Arimathea, a respected member of the Council, who was himself waiting expectantly for the Kingdom of

---

[47] The evidence is strong that Jesus was crucified by having his wrists bound to a tree with no support for his feet. The lack of support was necessary in order that the victim's weight would be supported only by his wrists, thus causing the slow asphyxiation as the muscles of the chest could no longer make it possible for the victim to breathe. This mitigates against the long held belief that Jesus' hands and feet were nailed to a cross. Loss of blood and shock would have resulted in a much quicker death.

> God, went boldly to Pilate and asked for the body of
> Jesus. Then Pilate wondered if he were already dead; and
> summoning the centurion, he asked him whether he had
> been dead for some time. When he learned from the
> centurion that he was dead, he granted the body to
> Joseph. Then Joseph bought a linen cloth, and taking
> down the body, wrapped it in the linen cloth, and laid it
> in a tomb that had been hewn out of the rock. He then
> rolled a stone against the door of the tomb.
>
> Mark: 15.42-46

The haste with which the high priests, elders, and lawyers had acted in order to avoid the wrath of the people is highlighted by Pilate's unawareness that the execution had already taken place. It had been early morning when Pilate had agreed to the crucifixion, and here was Joseph of Arimathea asking for Jesus' body in the early evening of the same day. There had been no imprisonment during which those crowds feared by the high priests could have gathered demanding that Jesus be released.

> When the Sabbath was over, Mary Magdalene, and Mary
> the mother of James, and Salome bought spices, so they
> might go and anoint him. And very early on the first day
> of the week, when the sun had risen, they went to the
> tomb. They had been saying to one another, "Who will
> roll away the stone for us from the entrance of the
> tomb?" When they looked up, they saw that the stone,
> which was very large, had already been rolled back. As
> they entered the tomb, they saw a young man, dressed in
> a white robe, sitting on the right side; and they were
> alarmed. But he said to them, "Do not be alarmed; you
> are looking for Jesus of Nazareth, who was crucified. He
> has been raised; he is not here. Look, there is the place
> they laid him. But go tell his disciples and Peter that he is
> going ahead of you to Galilee; there you will see him, just
> as he told you." So they went out and fled from the
> tomb, for terror and amazement had seized them; and
> they said nothing to anyone, for they were afraid.

104

> And all that had been commanded them they told briefly
> to those around Peter. And afterward Jesus himself sent
> out through them, from east to west, the sacred and
> imperishable proclamation of eternal salvation.
>
> Mark: 16.1-8

Biblical scholars know this is the last of Mark's version. The two oldest of ancient manuscripts of the *Gospel According to Mark* end at this point. Verses after this point were written by one or more other authors whose form of writing differs considerably from that of Mark. Although in those oldest available versions Mark's gospel ends at this point, it is quite unlike Mark to have concluded his gospel that abruptly. Another ancient source includes this additional verse:

> And all that had been commanded them they told briefly
> to those around Peter. And afterward Jesus himself sent
> out through them , from east to west, the sacred and
> imperishable proclamation of eternal salvation.

This addition provides an explanation for the work of apostles and missionaries whereby they carried Jesus' teachings to all peoples, including Gentiles. Later, apparently sometime in the second century A.D., eleven more verses were added by other writers in place of the brief ending that had earlier been added.

Mark's ending is so abrupt that biblical scholars believe he probably wrote further verses which did not fit in with later interpretations being put forth by leaders of the church. These may, therefore, have been removed, and the eleven verses written by others substituted by early church officials to fit with later resurrection doctrine.

A literal reading of those added verses indicates a physical resurrection after which Jesus joined his disciples.

> Later he appeared to the eleven themselves as they were
> sitting at the table; and he upbraided them for their lack
> of faith and stubbornness, because they had not believed
> those who saw him after he had risen. And he said to
> them, "go into the world and proclaim the good news

> (gospel) to the whole creation."
>
> * * * * * * * * * * * *
>
> So then the Lord Jesus, after he had spoken to them, was taken into heaven and sat at the right hand of God. And they went out and proclaimed the good news everywhere, while the Lord worked with them and confirmed the message by the signs that accompanied it.
>
> Mark: 16.14-15,19-20

For the past two thousand years so much emphasis has been placed on the physical resurrection of Jesus that Mark's last chapter has been largely ignored. Yet, the reader of the *New Testament* should remember that the *Gospel According to Mark* was based on what was known about Jesus forty years after his death. It reports what was the basic belief of the churches organized and nurtured by Paul. So, what was Mark saying in the last of those verses he wrote?

A literal reading has the women arriving at the tomb to find the circular slab rolled to one side. They find the body of Jesus is gone. A man in white tells the women, "He has been raised; he is not here." Therefore Jesus has been physically resurrected and has walked away.

A different message is received by readers who remember that Mark used Jesus' method of teaching by parables. A figurative reading has Jesus spiritually resurrected. The disciples will return to their native Galilee where they first joined Jesus. There, after three days of mourning and despondency, they see the light. They understand Jesus' sacrifice and his teachings, and this new understanding sends them out to spread his word.

> And afterward Jesus himself *sent out through them*, from east to west, the sacred and imperishable proclamation of eternal salvation."
>
> Mark: 16.1-8

This then has been the Gospel according to Mark.

CHAPTER 7

THE GOSPEL ACCORDING TO MARK

.   *The Gospel According to Mark* was written shortly before 70 AD.
The Gospels according to Matthew and Luke were written almost
twenty years later, and the Gospel according to John about ten years
after Matthew's and Luke's versions.
        Why?

        Why did Matthew and Luke feel the need to write when Mark's
Gospel was already available? Why did they use Mark as an outline and
repeat so much that he had written, but then add material that no one
had apparently heard of twenty years earlier? What was this new
material? Where did it come from? For what readers were they
writing? Why did John write still another version ten years after
Matthew and Luke?

* * * * * * * * * * * *

        Mark had been a disciple of Peter and had worked closely with
Paul. Why does he not mention the birth of Jesus, which Matthew and
Luke so emphasized? A child prodigy who could sit with elders in the
synagogue and discuss the prophets was certainly worthy of mention.
A Jesus risen from the tomb and walking and talking with the women
who were mourning his death and later talking at length with his
disciples was certainly good news. Yet, Mark says nothing of these
things later reported by Matthew and Luke.

It is obvious that these happenings were not known by the earliest Christians. Why were they then later added by Matthew and Luke? It is time for the reader once more to step back in time. What ideas, philosophies, and theological contributions of the time would influence those later Gospel writers? At this point it behooves the reader to examine those influences in order to interpret and understand what was happening to Christianity during those years between Mark's Gospel and the later Gospels.

Readers should keep in mind that Paul, Barnabas, and others had built the church among the Gentiles. Mark who is providing the first written basis for a common foundation among those churches is writing for those Gentiles, especially for those in Rome among whom he was living. We have noted the physical environment in which Jesus was born and lived. We have touched upon the political-religious parties and the social structure built by the Jews. But, Paul is building the church outside Israel, among Gentiles without the religious heritage of the Jews. It is in this different philosophical and theological environment that Christianity will grow and in which Matthew, Luke, and John will write. Before the reader can further attempt to empathize with these early developers of Christianity as a religion the reader needs to be aware of that environment.

INFLUENCING EARLY CHRISTIANITY

The world in which Gospel writers and early Christian churches emerged was not a philosophical or religious vacuum. Socrates had been born about 464 years before Jesus, Plato about 414 years before Jesus, and Aristotle about 378 years before Jesus. Even though that great age of Greek philosophy was declining during the years when Alexander the Great and Julius Caesar were building their great empires, there still were continuing philosophical contributions.

Whether reading the bible figuratively or as literal history one should remember that Christianity did not spring full blown into the world at the moment Jesus was being lifted from the cross. As a philosophy, a religion, and a conception of Christ it would develop over centuries, although never as rapidly as during the century immediately following his death, the century during which the gospels were being written.

A history of the decisions about what to include in the New Testament, how to organize and edit that which would be included, and which interpretations of that material should prevail would require several volumes in itself. Even though we are concentrating on the contents of the New Testament, it is wise to note some of the contributions to the changing nature of Christianity, and therefore of influences, that led to changes in interpretations between the time Mark wrote and when the later gospels were written.

* * * * * * * * * * *

The Roman Empire extended from the Caspian Sea in the East to the Atlantic coast of Spain and along the coast of Northern Africa from the Strait of Gibraltar to the Nile by the time Mark wrote his Gospel. It was home to growing concerns among its many peoples about their lives and their futures. It was a region rife with vying and overlapping religious and non-religious philosophies. Gnosticism, Epicureanism, Neo-Platonism, Stoicism, Hellenistic Judaism, mystery religions, and new Pauline interpretations among other influences were no longer confined to small groups of intellectuals. From the lowest to the highest, people were seeking answers.

Who am I? What is the relationship between creation and a god? What is my relationship to a god or gods? And most important, what happens to me after death? Each of the above philosophies and religions struggled with these questions. It was in that world that Paul struggled to establish churches that would bring Jesus' teachings to the people. It was the world in which Mark felt it important to try to draw together the emerging and widely divergent Christian churches by providing a common understanding of Jesus and a basis for Jesus' teachings.

* * * * * * * * * * *

New religions, promising something other than a bleak eternity in an underworld of the dead, found ready acceptance among the Greeks. Even earlier Egyptian religions offered this promise of a brighter existence after death on earth. Because these religions usually included secret rituals known only to believers, historians have given them the label, "Mystery Religions." Even as the popularity of these mystery cults increased among the Greeks they began to sweep through the Mediterranean world.

In each of these mystery religions the god, or one of the gods, was killed and then resurrected. This usually symbolized the fight between good and evil, with good eventually triumphing. To the general populace these religions gave promise of life after death. Some promised spiritual resurrection, others physical resurrection. Often these religions existed side by side with or even merged with earlier religions. However, there was a major difference between them and the earlier worshipping of the Greek gods on Mount Olympus or the pantheon of Roman gods.

Mystery religions taught that *the* truth had been revealed to man by a teacher or leader. Because he had revealed the long hidden truth this leader was revered and often became the object of worship instead of the god whose word he had revealed. Amid this steadily growing attraction of the mystery religions Paul and later missionaries strove to hold the new Christian churches to their acceptance of the teachings of Jesus.

Early converts were often drawn to Christianity by the recognition Jesus had given to the worth of each individual. To him they were each important. However, they also yearned for salvation after physical death, and thus the early Christian church was faced with the conflicting promises of the mystery religions. Was this salvation to be in the form of spiritual resurrection or physical resurrection?

* * * * * * * * * * * *

Those early churches might see and hear a visitor like Paul only once in several years, if at all. There was no telephone, no radio, no television communication. There were no newspapers or magazines. Only the larger congregations received letters from Paul. Bringing unity to these far flung congregations was a gigantic task. Already congregations were splitting over differing theological interpretations. Peter had died. Paul had died. Mark was left to provide the only written basis for this new Christianity struggling for survival in a sea of disparate religions.

What has Mark given us?

He has given us the "Gospel According to Mark."

He has given us a window into the beliefs of the earliest of Christians. He has shown us what was believed by Peter, Paul, and other early fathers of the church. He has given us a base from which to examine the later gospels with their additions of teachings apparently unknown to Peter and Paul and the earlier founders of the religion that would become known as Christianity.

He should be read with great care.

CHAPTER 8

PAUL

Four hundred years after Jesus' death on the cross, Church Fathers were still arguing over what to include in what we now call the *New Testament*. Another eleven centuries later, with the advent of the Reformation, there were new arguments; this time about what should be included in the new Protestant bible.

As we have already noted, the earliest writings available about Jesus, the church, and Christianity were Paul's letters. However, if read alone, these would have left later generations of readers confused and with little understanding as to what Christianity was. Paul worked with congregations at a time when it was safe for him to assume they were abiding by oral traditions about Jesus that were then current.[48] There would have been no need to retell the stories of Jesus' life and teachings in his letters to those congregations. Paul either did not write anything about Jesus' life or, if he did, nothing was preserved. Instead, he concentrated on the meaning of Jesus' teachings. Wherever he went, whether to establish or to support a church, he relied solely upon oral traditions. In a letter to the church in Corinth he said:

> "I commend you for always keeping me in mind, and maintaining the tradition I handed on to you. For the

---

[48] As noted earlier, Mark's Gospel was the first attempt to collect those oral traditions about Jesus and oral accounts of his teachings as related by apostles and others.

> tradition which I handed on to you came to me from
> the Lord himself."
>
> 1 Corinthians: 11.2 and 23

Some one hundred and fifty years after Paul's death, when leaders of the church began organizing the *New Testament*, they realized that readers would need some knowledge of the life and teachings of Jesus in order to understand Paul's concerns and the reason for his letters. The obvious solution was to open the *New Testament* with gospels describing the life and works of Jesus, even though the first of these was not written until after Paul had died. That early work of canonizing what would become the New Testament would continue for another two hundred and fifty years.

Because Mark had lived and worked with Peter and especially with Paul, and had collected in written form the oral traditions about Jesus less than three years after Paul's death, we suggested that one should begin reading the *New Testament* by turning first to the "Gospel According to Mark." By doing this the reader gains a basis for understanding Paul, his work, and his writings.

Among the more than a billion and a quarter people in the twenty-first century who profess to be Christians, hundreds of millions have some knowledge of the four gospels. However, those who have read the writings of Paul are but a small percent of those hundreds of millions. So, why should we bother to read Paul? The Christmas story and the celebration of Easter find their roots in the gospels, not in Paul. The oft quoted parables are found in the gospels. Why read Paul?

Whether reading the New Testament literally or figuratively, what the reader is reading is the heart of Christianity. *But*, it is commonly agreed among historians and church scholars that there would be no Christianity were it not for the work of Paul. Without Paul's years of organizing and holding together the early Gentile churches, Christianity would in all likelihood have been just one more mystery religion to pass into oblivion in the ancient world.

Having read Mark's collection of traditions about Jesus and thereby having an awareness of what those early congregations believed, let us now step into the sandals of Paul who preached so effectively of those traditions.

PAUL – THE MAN, THE APOSTLE

Paul was about forty-one years old when he wrote the first of his letters, his letter to the Thessalonians. In his letters his is a voice of authority. How did he come to be so respected by congregations throughout so much of the Roman Empire? Just who was he?

Born in Tarsus around 10 AD, Paul was a Jew who also held Roman citizenship. In Jewish communities he used his Jewish name Saul, elsewhere his Roman name Paul. What little biographical material we have about him comes mostly from the *New Testament*, primarily from the book of "Acts". As "Acts" was written at least thirty-five years, and some scholars believe as much as fifty years, after Paul began his missionary work and well after Paul's death, this remains a very thin and sometimes questionable biography.[49]

Our limited information indicates that Paul, having been born into a well-to-do family of some influence, received a good education. Although a frail man suffering from a physical infirmity, he appears to have been a tireless worker when faced with any task to which he was dedicated. There is no indication in historical records that any other missionary or teacher in the Christian community, who may have been physically stronger and healthier, ever matched Paul in his efforts to build this new religion.

Living in Tarsus, he had a much better understanding of the "world" of that time than did most people. Not only was Tarsus a major city through which caravans heading East or West would travel, it was also a center where Stoic philosophers had gathered over the years. Having become an ardent Pharisee, Paul later traveled to Jerusalem for formal training as a rabbi.[50] By then he already had a far

---

[49] Acts was written sometime after the bloody revolt of the Jews in Israel had been put down by the Romans. That revolt ended in 70 AD. "The Gospel According to Luke" is dated at somewhere around 90 AD; leading some biblical historians to believe "Acts" may have been written before the Gospel by Luke was written. Questions have arisen as to whether the long held belief that the same author wrote both "Acts" and the "Gospel According to Luke" is valid.

[50] As already noted, much of the material we have on Paul, such as his training to become a rabbi, is drawn from "Acts". However "Acts" includes so many errors in chronology, geography, relationship of events to people and to other events, and in descriptions of Paul's actions that contradict what Paul himself says in his letters, as to lead the reader to realize that the description of Paul's early life

114

more sophisticated and cosmopolitan outlook than most of the leaders of the early Christian movement.

Among Jerusalem's better educated Jews were the Hellenistic Jews; Jews who spoke Greek and had adopted Greek customs; a necessity for anyone dealing with traders from the rest of the Mediterranean world. They were among the most active in attempts to reform Judaism in the manner prescribed by Jesus. Among these activists were scholarly Pharisees who accepted Jesus as the long awaited Messiah; claiming his crucifixion was a sacrifice making worship through the temple no longer necessary; thereby strengthening their influence as leaders of the synagogues. Some went so far as to say Jesus' teachings and his sacrifice had precedent over the Law.

According to the Law[51] anyone crucified was cursed and anyone who defied the Law was likewise cursed. As an ardent Pharisee, Saul had great respect for the Law of Moses. Pronouncements and actions of those who Saul considered to be Hellenistic Jewish rebels within Judaism led him to devote his energy toward cleansing his religion of these accursed rebels.

Paul's version of his conversion to Christianity is definitely at odds with the description of that conversion in "Acts".

> Meanwhile Saul was still breathing murderous threats against the disciples of the Lord. He went to the High Priest and applied for letters to the synagogues at Damascus authorizing him to arrest anyone he found, men or women. who followed the new way, and bring them to Jerusalem. While he was still on the road and nearing Damascus, suddenly a light flashed from the sky all around him. He fell to the ground and heard a voice saying, "Saul, Saul, why do you persecute me?"
>
> "Tell me, Lord," he said, "who are you." The voice answered, "I am Jesus, whom you are persecuting. But

may be seriously flawed. The author/s of "The Gospel According to Luke" and of the "Acts" is/are unknown. Traditionally, Luke, a young physician who had traveled with Paul was credited with authorship. However, it is noteworthy that the author of "Acts", appears to have had little or no awareness of the content of Paul's letters written when Luke supposedly was traveling with him.

[51] Deuteronomy 21. 23 and 27. 26.

> get up and go into the city, and you will be told what to do." Meanwhile the men who were traveling with him stood speechless; they heard the voice but could see no one. Saul got up from the ground, but when he opened his eyes he could not see; so they led him by the hand and brought him into Damascus. He was blind for three days, and took no food or drink.
>
> Acts: 9.1-9

Paul's quite different version of what happened is seldom mentioned. The account in *Acts* is far too dramatic to have taken second place among congregations over the past 2,000 years. Paul says only:

> "You have heard what my manner of life was when I was still a practicing Jew: how savagely I persecuted the church of God, and tried to destroy it; and how in the practice of our national religion I was outstripping many of my Jewish contemporaries in my boundless devotion to the traditions of my ancestors. But then in his good pleasure God, who had set me apart from birth and called me through his grace, chose to reveal his Son to me and through me, in order that I might proclaim him among the Gentiles. When that happened, without consulting any human being, without going up to Jerusalem to see those who were apostles before me, I went off at once to Arabia, and afterwards returned to Damascus."
>
> Paul's Letter to the Galatians: 1.13-17

Paul's conversion, according to his own account, was an experience within himself. He did not consider it necessary to dramatize the conversion as though it were brought on by a miraculous outward experience. In "Acts", however, the writer will repeat his dramatic conversion story three times, apparently believing such emphasis necessary to lend authority to Paul's work. He even quotes word for word the voice no one heard but Paul.

Paul emphasized that his conversion was in no way influenced by any individual human being. He makes a point of never having been in contact with any of the apostles in Jerusalem before his conversion. He does not want to be mistaken as one of the "Jerusalem Christians." After being baptized in Damascus he left for Arabia. It would not be until after his stay in Arabia and three more years in Damascus that he would travel to Jerusalem to meet any of the disciples or apostles. He had, therefore, about four years before that meeting in which to develop a more mature understanding of what Jesus meant to the world and what this new religion could be – should be.

There is no record of the date of Paul's conversion. We can, however, add the years of his work, his time in prison, and his years in Arabia and Damascus before he became a missionary, and subtract these from the date of his death.[52] This would make Paul a young man, about 28 years of age at the time of his conversion.

The religion of the Jews declared them to be the chosen people of God. The Messiah, when he came, would be God's agent sent to lead his chosen people to their rightful place as the leader among all nations. Some historians point to Paul's broader cosmopolitan view of the world, and find reason to believe Paul saw the limits of a religion that limited God's grace to one small nation. No other nation would accept a God who chose only the small Jewish nation to rule over all other nations. If a religion was to be universal; if it were to encompass all peoples of all nations; it could not preach of a national Messiah sent by God to lead a "chosen people" to reign over all nations.

We do know from Paul's letters and from his years of work establishing churches among the Gentiles that he could not accept the idea of a Jewish national Messiah. We also know that as a Roman citizen with a world-view he would have been deeply disturbed by the frequent outbreaks within the empire as nations and tribes sought either to break from the empire or to increase their power in relation to their neighbors within the empire. A universal religion might well bring peace and unity to the empire.

---

[52] Paul was born in 10 AD. He died in 67 AD at the age of 57. He arrived in Rome, under arrest in 60 AD, and spent much of the rest of his life under house arrest. He had before that, 58-60 AD been in prison in Caesarea. He spent 14 years traveling as a missionary and organizer of churches prior to 58 AD. Earlier he had been in Jerusalem long enough to be considered a potential successor as a member of the "Seven" (the deacons of the church in Jerusalem) after Stephen had been stoned to death. Before that he had spent about 4 years in Arabia and Damascus.

Jews living throughout the Roman Empire, but outside Palestine, strongly supported the imperial system. It maintained peace and provided a common currency, both essential for business, especially for traders. As a Jew in Tarsus, Paul was quite familiar with these advantages of living within the Empire. Furthermore, the leader among the Stoic philosophers in their well known center in Tarsus was Athenodorus. Although a Greek, he had been the tutor of Octavius, and became a leader in establishing policy for the Empire.

Athenodorus was later ordered by emperor Augustus to draft a constitution for Tarsus and to take a major role in governing the city. It has been pointed out by many historians that Paul's views on the necessity of maintaining a strong united empire were similar to those of Seneca because both were well acquainted with Athenodorous' teachings.[53]

Paul's early enthusiasm for strengthening the religion of the Jews so that it might become a uniting factor within the empire may be traced to this background. However, living in Gentile lands where Jews were a small minority would have made him keenly aware that the messianic vision of the Jews with a Jewish messiah ruling over all could never be accepted. Historians note that in Christianity, which Paul had a major role in molding, it was possible to retain the morality and much else of the Jewish religion, while freeing Gentiles from the yoke of the Law. In this he could see the desirable unity of all peoples.

Paul was deeply religious, and according to his own writings had become convinced that Jesus was bringing God's word to the people. Because he believed Jesus message correctly interpreted the will of God, he came to believe Jesus' crucifixion had been wrong. Jesus had not been guilty of those things with which the Sadducees had charged him. Therefore, for Paul, the crucifixion could not carry with it the curse described in Deuteronomy as being required by the Law.

For fourteen years after his stay in Arabia and his time in Damascus and Jerusalem, Paul's life was devoted to organizing churches and revisiting them when they required strengthening. We earlier noted Paul's work with Barnabas and his early dedication to working with Gentiles.[54] It was during this period, when numerous philosophies and miracle religions were spreading throughout the

---

[53]   Joseph W. Swain, *The Ancient World, Vol.* 2, Harper & Brothers, New York, 1950. See fn. p 485.
[54]   See Chapter 4.

Mediterranean world, that some Christian congregations founded by Paul began to adopt non-Christian practices and beliefs.

Pagan religions did not emphasize personal morality as did the religion of the Jews. In that time of turmoil and struggle for identity within the Roman Empire, growing numbers of Gentiles were impressed by the moral code of the Jews. The idea of one creator God, before whom all humans were responsible for their own moral behavior, was drawing Gentiles to synagogues throughout the Empire. However, Jewish leaders refused to permit those Gentiles to participate in the Jewish religion unless they adhered strictly to the Law, including circumcision and dietary rules. Unwittingly they were erecting the very barrier that made Paul's concept of a universal church become reality.

Without this wall created by hard-line Jewish religious leaders it is quite possible there would today be no religion known as Christianity. It was the missionary teaching of Paul and his coworkers that gave those Gentiles the monotheism and morality they sought without binding them with the exclusive restrictions and requirements of Jewish Law that would make them Jews. Gentiles of all races and nations could become Christians without giving up their national identity or their ties to other Gentiles.

PAUL AND THE GENTILES

Mystery religions abounded in the Gentile world. Within those Jewish communities where reform sects had adopted Jesus and most of his teachings there was complete distrust of the new "Christian" churches springing up among the Gentiles. Jesus could be accepted as a prophet in most Jewish "Christian" sects, but only as a prophet. Gentiles were, on the other hand, often quick to adopt this new religion as another mystery religion.

The problem facing Paul as he began his work with the Gentiles was that many Gentiles were not only attracted by Jesus' teachings, but were worshiping Jesus as a god. This was a complete contradiction of the monotheism of the Jews. They could never accept these Gentile churches as being "Christian" because they could not accept a mystery religion that believed in a Jesus being crucified and then rising from the dead to hold the position of a god.

When he first began his work Paul found this worship of Jesus threatening to dominate the Gentile churches. He could have tried to discourage this worship, but it was bringing new worshipers into the church and was holding those already in the church. As members of this rapidly expanding religion these congregants were being shown the way Jesus said humans should live. Paul had to consider which was more important. Should the Gentiles be disillusioned? Should they be compelled to look at Jesus as other than a divine being to be worshipped? If that happened would most drift off into other mystery religions? On the other hand, if they remained in the church because of their worship of Jesus, could they not be taught the way of life that Jesus had said reflected the will of God?

Paul was not a hypocrite. He would not have just "gone along with" the majority. What he would have seen was a strong force that could lead these Gentile worshipers to follow the path Jesus called for all humans to follow. His letters at times reflect his concern that there was the danger that people would eventually spend so much time worshiping the messenger that they would have little time for hearing and learning the message. As long as he was alive Paul would have had reason to believe he could assure a balance between worshiping Jesus and learning to live according to Jesus teachings.

Biblical scholars believe that the longer Paul worked with these churches, the more he accepted what he saw as good within their approach. Most mystery religions taught redemption, freeing one of the bondage of sin. This was not in conflict with Paul's concept of Jesus as the redeemer. He could see a Jesus, who not only died on the cross to free humans from man-made religious restrictions and to rend the priestly barrier between the people and God, but also as the redeemer giving his life to redeem all from the sins of man. However, Paul made a sharp distinction between other mystery religions and Christianity by condemning their reliance on magical rites and religious sacraments rather than on living according to the word of God. Paul always stressed morality as contrasted to those stressing ritual.

Paul's earliest letter, and therefore the earliest of all the documents of the *New Testament*, is the first letter to the Thessalonians. It is a prime example of the differences between descriptions of Paul's activities in "Acts" and Paul's own versions as found in his letters.

At this point it is well for us to note that most biblical scholars and historians believe Paul was the author of only the first letter to the Thessalonians, the first letter to the Corinthians and the first nine chapters of Second Corinthians, and the letters to the Romans, Galatians, and Philippians. A century and a half later, and for another two centuries after that, men who were putting together the *New Testament* incorrectly ascribed other letters to Paul, perhaps by mistake; perhaps to give authority to the words of unknown or lesser known writers whose writings supported and defended the growing church.

CHAPTER 9

PAUL'S LETTERS TO THE THESSALONIANS

At the head of a sheltered bay in northern Greece, Thessalonica was a thriving commercial center where Paul's friend and one-time traveling companion Gaius had been named bishop. Luke's version of Paul's missionary visits to Thessalonica has him preaching in synagogues and declaring Jesus the Messiah.[55] Unlike Luke's account, Paul's letter indicates he had been teaching and working with Gentiles who were recent converts from pagan religions, and who were the members of the church in Thessalonica. His letter obviously was written for Gentile Christians. Readers should note the contrasting versions at this point to better understand Luke's motivation forty years later. Luke says:

> They now traveled by way of Amphipolis and Apollonia and came to Thesalonica, where there was a Jewish synagogue. Following his usual practice Paul went to their meetings; argued with them, quoting texts of the Scripture, which he expounded and applied to show that the Messiah had to suffer and rise from the dead. "And this," he said, "whom I am proclaiming to you, is the Messiah." Some of them were convinced and joined

---

[55] To avoid confusion, whenever referring to "Acts" we shall refer to Luke as the author.

> Paul and Silas; so did a great number of godfearing
> Gentiles and a good many influential women."
>
> Acts: 17.1-4

This is followed by Luke's description of the "rabble" of the city being roused by Jews to create a riot. Luke has Paul fleeing the city at night to escape the "mob". This is a most improbable tale. Paul had only a year or two earlier made his trip to Jerusalem to confront Peter. It was then that the church fathers in Jerusalem gave Paul complete charge of bringing the church to the Gentiles, while Peter would have responsibility for Jewish congregations. As we have seen, Paul did not want the term Messiah used among the Gentiles. Why would he go into a Greek city, seek out the synagogue, and try to force upon a Jewish congregation the belief that Jesus was the Messiah? It would have negated the very victory he had won in Jerusalem in receiving authority over Gentile churches in which Jewish law, circumcision, and dietary restrictions were not to become an issue. It would have undone the work he had already undertaken to downplay the idea of Jesus being the Jewish Messiah; a belief that would alienate the Gentiles.

Paul's own version has him not only not fleeing Thessalonica, but remaining for an extended visit during which time he taught in a Gentile church to a congregation composed largely of former pagans. This first letter to the Thessalonians is to that congregation. At the time of writing, around 51 AD, Paul was about 41 years old, with about thirteen years of maturing Christian theology in his background.

Paul has learned that members of the church in Thessalonica have been harassed for being different than the rest of the community in which they lived. This was Greece, not Palestine, and citizens of the community outside the church were pushing members of the church to return to their former pagan religion. Some of that community saw the new Christian church as a threat, and harassment of the Christians was having its effect.

There was a still greater problem; one not entirely separate from the concerns of those outside the church. This involved the belief and fear that the world was coming to an end in a very short time. Members of the church had accepted Paul's teaching that Jesus had promised resurrection of the dead. That was fine for those already dead, but, what would happen to those still living when the world came to this fiery end? Other mystery religions were promising salvation.

What, Christians in Thessalonica were asking, could Paul promise? Were they included in Jesus' promise of resurrection? After all, most had joined the church because like other mystery religions it had promised life after death.

Paul having been unable to make another trip to Thessalonica had sent Timothy in his stead. The news Timothy brought to Paul on his return was apparently good news, and Paul then responded with his letter. As with all letters, except that to the Galatians whom he would be scolding, Paul opens with a rather flowery and lengthy greeting. The letter then moves on to the matter of "persecution" supposedly reported to him.

> "We call you to witness, yes and God himself, how devout and blameless was our behavior towards you who are believers. As you well know, we dealt with you one by one, as a father deals with his children, appealing to you by encouragement, as by solemn injunctions, to live lives worthy of the God who calls you into his kingdom and glory.
>
> "This is why we thank God continually, because when we handed on God's message, you received it, not as the word of men, but what it truly is, the very word of God at work in you who hold the faith. You have fared like the congregations in Judaea, God's people in Christ Jesus. You have been treated by your countrymen as they are treated by the Jews, who killed the Lord Jesus and the prophets and drove us out , the Jews who are heedless of God's will and enemies of their fellow-men, hindering us from speaking to the Gentiles to lead them to salvation. All this time they have been making up the full measure of their guilt, and now retribution has overtaken them for good and all."
>
> First Thessalonians: 2.10-16

Most biblical scholars and historians do not believe Paul wrote that above passage. They point to the reference to retribution having overtaken the Jews as referring "to the Roman destruction of the temple in 70 A.D."[56] The temple was destroyed three years after Paul's death. There is little doubt but that this passage was added long after Paul's death.[57]

Scholars of the bible also point to the first paragraph of the above passage. This is a typical "thanksgiving" which writers of letters such as Paul used as an introductory greeting to those to whom the letter was written. Why, is there a second greeting inserted at the point where this passage begins?[58]

Paul would have no reason to write that the Jews were: "...hindering us from speaking to the Gentiles to lead them to salvation." The early church fathers in Jerusalem had already placed Paul in charge of all Gentile churches, and Peter in charge of those Jewish congregations that had adopted Jesus teachings. He was being praised for his work with Gentiles. Furthermore, Paul never uses such anti-Jewish comments in any of his other writings. This is so atypical of Paul's teachings, and of the writings of Mark, as to indicate this passage was not only added after the death of Paul and Mark, but long after.

Readers should also note that elsewhere in this same letter Paul has expressed his pleasure with the report Timothy has brought to him. Nowhere does he indicate that Timothy witnessed any persecution by Jews, or by fellow Greeks. Paul at this time in his teaching has accepted the concern sweeping through not only Christian churches, but pagan mystery religions as well, that the world would be coming to an end within the lifetime of the members of the church. Some historians note Paul's references to hardships faced by members of the Thessalonica church as normal for believers preparing for the end. Others note that most religious groups, other than those involved in Emperor Worship, suffered some degree of harassment.

---

[56]   See note in the *New English Bible*, p. 255, New Testament, 1976 edition.

[57]   The question arises as to whether a writer adding this passage years later was influenced by having read Luke's story in which Luke has Paul barely escaping with his life when Jews rose against him in Thessalonica. Obviously, it was written so long after Paul's death that the writer was ignorant of the fact that the temple was destroyed after Paul had died. It may have been written by church 'fathers' in Rome a century and a half or two centuries later when gospels, Paul's letters, and other materials were being collected and decisions were being made as to what should be included in the *New Testament*.

[58]   See Introduction to "First Letter of Paul to the Thessalonians", *The New Oxford Bible, p. 291,* 1991 edition.

> "So when we could bear it no longer we decided to remain alone at Athens and sent Timothy, our brother and God's fellow worker in the service of the gospel of Christ, to encourage you to stand firm for the faith and, under all these hardships, not to be shaken; for you know that this is our appointed lot. When we were with you we warned you that we were bound to suffer hardship; and so it has turned out, as you know. And thus it was that when I could bear it no longer, I sent to find out about your faith, fearing that the tempter might have tempted you and my labor might be lost.
>
> But now Timothy has just arrived from Thessalonica, bringing good news of your faith and love."
>
> First Thessalonians: 3.1-6

Paul then moves on to remind the Thessalonians "that we live to please God. You are indeed already following it, but we beg you to do so yet more thoroughly." After listing those things from which the members must abstain and those things they should do, he comes to the question of resurrection.

> "We wish you not to remain in ignorance, brothers, about those who sleep in death; you should not grieve like the rest of men, who have no hope. We believe that Jesus died and rose again; and so it will be for those who died as Christians; God will bring them to life with Jesus.
> "For this we tell you as the Lord's word: we shall not forestall those who have died; because at the word of command, at the sound of the archangel's voice and God's trumpet-call, the Lord himself will descend from heaven; first the Christian dead will rise, then we who are left alive shall join them, caught up in clouds to meet the Lord in the air. Thus we shall always be with the Lord. Console one another, then, with these words.
> "About dates and times, my friends, we need not write to you, for you know perfectly well that the Day of the Lord comes like a thief in the night. While they are

> talking of peace and security, all at once calamity is upon
> them, sudden as the pangs that come upon a woman with
> child; and there will be no escape. But you, my friends,
> are not in the dark, that the day should overtake you like
> a thief. You are the children of light, children of day.
> We do not belong to light or darkness, and we must not
> sleep like the rest, but keep awake and sober. Sleepers
> sleep at night and drunkards are drunk at night, but we,
> who belong to the daylight, must keep sober, armed with
> faith and love for coat of mail, and the hope of salvation
> for helmet. For God has not destined us to the terrors of
> judgment, but to full attainment of salvation through our
> Lord Jesus Christ. He died for us so that we, awake or
> asleep, might live in company with him. Therefore
> hearten one another, fortify one another – as indeed you
> do."
>
> 1 Thessalonians: 4.13-18,5.1-11

Did Paul mean physical resurrection, or spiritual resurrection – resurrection of the soul, of consciousness? This question faces both those who read Paul's letter literally and those who read it figuratively. Read literally, this passage would indicate that no one who died before Jesus once more returned to earth would be resurrected until Jesus returned. Paul sent this letter to the Thessalonians only about twenty-one years after Jesus had been put to death. The wait for those who had died since the crucifixion would not have been more than a generation. Combined with the belief that very shortly the world would be coming to an end, this might not seem an unreasonable wait.

If generations were to pass, even centuries, would the skies be filled with the physical bodies of those who had lain dead for all those years; all rising at once to a heaven just above the star and cloud studded ceiling? Readers should consider whether it was likely that most Thessalonians would believe Paul's words described such a physical resurrection? In his later letter to the Corinthians Paul will speak at more length about the difference between the physical body and the "spiritual body".

A literal reading may lead a reader to believe Paul meant that the physical body would be resurrected. However, those reading figuratively note that Paul's congregations (Thessalonians, Corinthians,

Philippians) consisted of Greeks living in Greece. For several centuries Greek philosophers had spoken of the soul, and pagan religions often adopted the Greek concept of the soul. Paul having lived among these people, and having received much of his early training from them, knew of their respect for the soul. Resurrection of the soul was a promise they could accept and would long to receive. Would Paul have ever attempted to press a concept of a complete physical resurrection of the body on these Greeks, when as a missionary he was seeking to convert them, and later to hold them to faith in Jesus? If he did, he would have had to face the possibility of losing his credibility before these congregations.

It is important in reading Paul's later letters that one observe how he increasingly emphasizes the spiritual   He was only about twenty-eight years old at the time of his conversion. That was only eight years after the crucifixion of Jesus. The reform movement by "Christians" within the Jewish religion was in its infancy. There were no Gospels. There was no fixed Christian doctrine. The church and Christianity was still to be developed.

Paul would be forty-one years old when he wrote his letter to the Thessalonians. It would be about six years later that he would write to the Romans. He was fifty-seven when he died in Rome, where Mark would bring together the collection of oral traditions which would in large part have been used by Paul in his teaching. Just as there had been a maturing of his religious thought during his time in Arabia after being converted to Christianity, so there was continual growth in Paul's thinking and development of religious concepts in his later years, as is demonstrated in his letters. - Watch for this as you read Paul.

CHAPTER 10

PAUL AND THE CORINTHIANS

Over on the Greek Peloponnesus, about fifty miles west of Athens, lay the city of Corinth. Humans had lived at that site since the end of the stone-age more than three thousand years earlier. Being favorably located, it had, for the last eight hundred years before the birth of Jesus, been thriving as a trading center. Like Thessalonica it was a logical location for founding a church. From there word would spread with the constant flow of traders passing through on their way to other Middle-Eastern trading centers.

Paul had arrived in Corinth in 50 AD, a year before he had written his first letter to the Thessalonians.[59] He had personally founded the church at Corinth as he had churches in other strategic trading centers. By the time Paul left for Ephesus the church in Corinth had become an important hub for churches of the region. As

---

[59] If Luke's account in "Acts" is accepted as accurate, Paul was brought into court in Corinth by a body of Jews. Gallio, governor of Achaia, was an older brother of the famous philosopher Seneca. He exhibits some of the same wisdom with which Seneca has been credited. Before Paul could even speak Gallio, according to Luke, said to the Jews who had brought Paul to court: "If it had been a question of crime or grave misdemeanor, I should, of course, have given you Jews a patient hearing, but if it is bickering about words and names and your Jewish law, you may see to it yourselves; I have no mind to be a judge in these matters. And he had them ejected from the court." Acts: 18. 14-16. This incident would date Paul's presence in Corinth. Gallio took office in 51 AD.

he did with all "his" churches, he continued to keep himself informed of the progress and problems of the church in Corinth. It was while teaching in Ephesus, in what is today Turkey, that disturbing news reached him about rivalries threatening to split the Corinthian church into squabbling factions.

Being then on the far side of the Aegean, Paul could not undertake a sea and land trip to Corinth without breaking off his missionary work with the Ephesians. Instead he sent a letter, referred to in First Corinthians, but since lost. His second letter, which is better known today as "The First Letter of Paul to the Corinthians," deals with a potential splintering of the church in Corinth. Of more importance, however, are his detailed comments on resurrection and his exposition on what being a Christian really meant. Readers of his letters should keep in mind Paul's deep feeling that he was the father of the Christian communities he had founded and developed. They were his children. Sometimes they were praised. Sometimes they were helped to find the way. Sometimes they were scolded.

ONE CHURCH UNITED AND UNBROKEN

After the usual flowery greeting of those times Paul wastes no time in getting to the heart of the problem of church authority.

"Now I appeal to you, brothers and sisters, by the name of our Lord Jesus Christ, that all of you be in agreement and that there be no divisions among you, but that you be united in the same mind and purpose. For it has been reported to me by Chloe's people that there are quarrels among you, my brothers and sisters. What I mean is that each of you says, 'I belong to Paul,' or 'I belong to Apollos,' or 'I belong to Cephas,' or 'I belong to Christ.' Has Christ been divided? Was Paul crucified for you? Or were you baptized in the name of Paul? I thank God that I baptized none of you except Crispus and Gaius, so no one can say that you were baptized in my name. (I did baptize also the household of Stephanas; beyond that, I do not know whether I baptized anyone else.) For Christ did not send me to baptize but to proclaim the gospel, and not with eloquent wisdom, so that the cross of Christ might not be emptied of its power.

"For the message about the cross is foolishness to those who are perishing, but to us who are being saved it is the power of God. For it is written,

> 'I will destroy the wisdom of the wise, and the discernment of the discerning I will thwart.'

Where is the one who is wise? Where is the scribe? Where is the debater of this age? Has not God made foolish the wisdom of the world? For since, in the wisdom of God, the world did not know God through wisdom, God decided through the foolishness of our proclamation, to save those who believe. For Jews demand signs and Greeks desire wisdom, but we proclaim Christ crucified, a stumbling block to Jews and foolishness to Gentiles, but to those who are the called, both Jews and Greeks, Christ the power of God and the wisdom of God. For God's foolishness is wiser than human wisdom, and God's weakness is stronger than human strength.

"Consider your own call, brothers and sisters: not many of you were wise by human standards, not many were powerful, not many were of noble birth.[60] But God chose what is foolish in the world to shame the wise; God chose what is low and despised in the world, things that are not, to reduce to nothing things that are, so that no one might boast in the presence of God. He is the source of your life in Christ Jesus, who became for us wisdom from God, and righteousness and sanctification and redemption, in order that, as it is written, 'Let the one who boasts, boast in the Lord'."

First Corinthians: 1.10-31

---

[60] A rather interesting insight into the make-up of early congregations.

Paul's reference to Apollos, Cephas, and himself indicates that no fewer than three factions were threatening to divide the church.[61] This church, he points out, is the church of Christ, not a church of one of its leaders. Was Jesus divided, he asks? Was I crucified, or for that matter were any of the other leaders in your church? You who have been baptized have been cleansed and committed to a new life in the name of Jesus. Just because Apollos, or Cephas, or even I baptized you does not mean you are now baptized in our name. You are committed to Jesus and through him to God, not to one of us humans who merely went through the act of baptizing you.

Reading figuratively it appears, from Paul's comments, that some of those rivaling to take over leadership of the church in Corinth had their eyes on more than spiritual leadership. Egos had become involved, and Paul does not hesitate to take to task those who would seek to gain power and prestige in the church by parading their so-called wisdom. This, he charges, is in sharp contrast with the simplicity and straightforwardness of the gospel he had been sent forth to carry to the people.

At this point Paul uses a tactic not uncommon in today's world of politics. Consider yourself, he tells the majority of the congregation, as the common man. "Consider your own call", he says, "not many of you were wise by human standards." This tends to open a gap between those who accept the word of God as true wisdom as contrasted to those who would appear to be seeking praise and recognition for their worldly (but inferior) wisdom. "Let the one who boasts, boast in the Lord."

Paul continues:

> "As for me brothers, when I came to you, I declared the attested truth of God without display of fine words or wisdom. I resolved that while I was with you I would think of nothing but Jesus Christ – Christ nailed to the cross. I came before you weak, nervous, and shaking with fear. The word I spoke, the gospel I proclaimed, did not sway you with subtle arguments; it carried conviction by spiritual power, so that your faith might be built not upon human wisdom but upon the power of God.

---

[61] Cephas, meaning "the rock", was the name given Peter by Jesus.

"And yet I do speak words of wisdom to those who are ripe for it, not a wisdom belonging to this passing age, nor to any of its governing powers, which are declining to their end; I speak God's hidden wisdom, his secret purpose framed from the very beginning to bring us to our full glory. The powers that rule the world have never known it; if they had they would not have crucified the Lord of Glory. But, in the words of the Scripture, 'Things beyond our seeing, things beyond our seeing, things beyond our hearing, things beyond our imagining, all prepared by God for those who love him,' these it is that God has revealed to us through the Spirit.

"For the Spirit explores everything, even the depths of God's own nature. Among men, who knows what man is but the man's own spirit within him? In the same way, only the Spirit of God knows what God is. This is the Spirit we have received from God, and not the spirit of the world, so that we may know all That God of his own grace has given us; and because we are Interpreting spiritual truths to those who have the Spirit, we speak of these gifts of God in words found for us not in by our human wisdom but by the Spirit. A man who is unspiritual refuses what belongs to the Spirit of God; it is folly to him: he cannot grasp it, because it needs to be judged in the light of the Spirit. A man gifted with the Spirit can judge the worth of everything, but is not himself subject to judgment by his fellow-men. For (in the words of the Scripture) 'who knows the mind of the Lord? Who can advise him?' We, however, possess the mind of Christ."

First Corinthians: 2.1-11

As becomes apparent a few paragraphs later in Paul's letter, those seeking to take over the church in Corinth have been belittling Paul's preaching. *The New Oxford Bible* notes "Paul has apparently been criticized at Corinth for preaching too simple a gospel."[62] Paul is now saying, when I first came to you I did not try to impress you with speeches filled with philosophical jargon. I did not try to impress you with my importance in order to get you to listen to the message I brought. I wanted your faith to be based on the power of God, not on what you might accept as human wisdom.

Readers should remember Paul's description of the Corinthian congregation. Did he deliberately present an over-simplified message when he first arrived as a missionary to establish a church? We do not know. We do know, however, that he is now indicating that that is what he did, and does not want it mistakenly believed that the so-called wisdom of Greek masters and scholars was something above and beyond the wisdom of Jesus or his messengers. Wisdom of humans, Paul notes, is shallow. Its roots are insufficient to keep it from being swept away by changing human thought. Paul challenges this human wisdom of his detractors, and of the challengers of the message upon which the church at Corinth was founded, by saying only "the ripe (mature)" can understand the wisdom of God.

> "For my part, my brothers, I could not speak to you as I should speak to people who have the Spirit. I had to deal with you on the merely natural plane, as infants in Christ. And so I gave you milk to drink, instead of solid food, for you are still not ready for it, for you are still on the merely natural plane. Can you not see that while there is jealously and strife among you, you are living on the purely human level of your lower nature? When one says, 'I am for Apollos,' are you not all too human?
>
> "After all, what is Apollos? What is Paul? We are simply God's agents in bringing you the faith. Each of us performed the task which the Lord allotted to him: I planted the seed, and Apollos watered it; but God made it grow. Thus it is not the gardeners with their planting and watering who count, but God, who makes it grow. Whether they plant or water, they work as a team, though each will get his own pay for his own labor. We are

---

[62] First Corinthians, *The New Oxford Bible*, New Testament, footnote, p. 232, 1991 Edition.

> God's fellow workers; and you are God's garden."
>
> First Corinthians: 3.1-9

Paul continues in this letter, to the Corinthians:

> "Or again, you are God's building. I am like a skilled
> master-builder who by God's grace laid the foundation,
> and someone else is putting up the building. Let each take
> care how he builds. There can be no other foundation
> beyond that which is laid; I mean Jesus Christ himself. If
> anyone builds on that foundation with gold, silver, and
> fine stone, or with wood, hay, and straw, the work that
> each man does will at last be brought to light; the day of
> judgment will expose it . For the day that dawns in fire,
> and the fire will test each man's work. If a man's building
> stands, he will be rewarded; if it burns, he will have to bear
> the loss; and yet he will escape with his life, as one might
> from a fire. Surely you know that you are God's temple,
> where the Spirit of God dwells. Anyone who destroys
> God's temple will himself be destroyed by God, because
> the temple of God is holy, and the temple you are."
>
> First Corinthians: 3.10-17

This letter is not addressed to an individual, but to the entire Corinthian church. You, the Christians of Corinth, Paul warns, are God's temple, and anyone who causes it to splinter faces God's judgment.

From here Paul moves on to comment further on the "wisdom" of critics who were calling for change in this new religion's message.

> "Make no mistake about this: if there is anyone among
> you who fancies himself wise – wise I mean, by standards
> of this passing age – he must become a fool to gain true
> wisdom. For the wisdom of the world is folly in God's
> sight. Scripture says, 'He traps the wise in their own
> cunning', and again, 'The Lord knows that the arguments

> of the wise are futile.' So never make mere men a cause
> for pride. For though everything belongs to you – Paul,
> Apollos, and Cephas, the world, life, and death, the
> present and the future, all of them belong to you - yet you
> belong to Christ, and Christ to God.
>
> "We must be regarded as Christ's subordinates and as
> stewards of the secrets of God. Well then, stewards are
> expected to show themselves trustworthy."
>
> First Corinthians: 4.1-2

After further comment on changeable wisdom and the role of missionaries like himself, Paul moves to a straight forward discourse on questions of personal morality and religious practices raised by members of the Christian community in Corinth. He notes the temptations and harassments that were to be expected when living amid neighbors practicing pagan religions.

Whether reading literally or seeking a message through a figurative reading it is important that the reader remember the historical period in which Paul lived. His comments on such matters as relations between spouses, the length of a man's hair, and the covering of a woman's head are made in the light of what was considered socially and morally correct in the Mediterranean culture of 50 A.D. He was trying to prevent the Corinthian church from splitting over what he considered non-religious issues, by telling the Corinthians to stick to what was considered the correct social code of that time. He elaborates; don't insist on being a social rebel for the temporary satisfaction it may give, and thereby cause dissension within the congregation. And don't let such non-religious acts of rebellion against the current social code cause the rest of you to over-react. Such matters should not be considered religious issues. There are enough major points of dissension without being side-tracked by non-church matters.

Then, having completed his instructions on living a moral life and avoiding idolatry, he once more discusses the Spirit.

GIFTS OF THE SPIRIT

"About gifts of the Spirit, there are some things of which I do not wish you to remain ignorant.

"You know how, in the days when you were still pagan, you were swept off to those dumb heathen gods, however you happened to be led. For this reason I must impress upon you that no one who says 'A curse on Jesus!' can be speaking under the influence of the Spirit of God. And no one can say 'Jesus is Lord!' except under the influence of the Holy Spirit.

"There are varieties of gifts, but the same Spirit. There are varieties of service, but the same Lord. There are many forms of work, but all of them, in all men, are the work of the same God. In each of us the Spirit is manifested in one particular way, for some useful purpose. One man through the Spirit has the gift of wise speech, while another, by the power of the same Spirit, can put the deepest knowledge into words. Another, by the same Spirit, is granted faith; yet another, by the one Spirit, gifts of healing, and another miraculous powers; another has the gift of prophecy, and another the ability to distinguish true spirits from false; yet another has the gift of ecstatic utterance of different kinds, and another the ability to interpret it. But all these gifts are the work of one and the same Spirit, distributing them separately to each individual at will.

"For Christ is like a single body with its many limbs and organs, which, many as they are, together make up one body. For indeed we were all brought into one body by baptism, in the one Spirit, whether we are Jews or Greeks, whether slaves or free men, and that one Holy Spirit was poured out for all of us to drink.

"A body is not a single organ, but many. Suppose the foot should say, 'Because I am not a hand, I do not

> belong to the body', it does belong to the body none the
> less."
>
> First Corinthians: 12. 1-16

Paul acknowledges a wide variety of gifts and, he points out, these are not limited to Christians. Pagans also possessed certain gifts. Certainly, he says, their displays of ecstasy through loud utterances and physical display of emotion could be considered gifts. Remember how, "in the days when you were still pagan, you were swept off to those dumb heathen gods." But now you must realize that the only gifts that count are those that come from God and make you a part of the whole body in which God has "combined the various parts" (First Corinthians 12. 24).

Paul continues with reference to other organs of the body, as an illustration of how, "God has combined the various parts of the body, giving special honor to the humbler parts."

> "Now you are Christ's body, and each of you a limb or organ of it. Within our community God has appointed, in the first place apostles, in the second place prophets, thirdly teachers; the miracle-workers, then those who have the gift of healing, or ability to help others or power to guide them, or the gift of ecstatic utterance of various kinds. Are all apostles? All prophets? All teachers? Do all work miracles? Have all the gift of healing? Do all speak in tongues of ecstasy? Can all interpret them? The higher gifts are those you should aim at.
>
> "And now I will show you the best way of all."
>
> First Corinthians: 12.27-31

> "If I speak in the tongues of mortals and of angels, but do not have love, I am a noisy gong of a clanging cymbal. And if I have prophetic powers, and understand all mysteries and all knowledge, and I have all faith, so as to remove mountains, but do not have love, I am nothing. If I give away all my possessions, and if I hand over my

> body so that I may boast (be burned), but do not have love , I gain nothing.
>
> "Love is patient; love is kind; love is not envious or boastful or arrogant or rude. It does not insist on its own way; it is not irritable or resentful; it does not rejoice in wrongdoing, but rejoices in truth. It bears all things, believes all things, hopes all things, endures all things.
>
> "Love never ends. But as for prophecies, they will come to an end; as for tongues, they will cease; as for knowledge, it will come to an end. For we know only in part, and we prophecy only in part; but when the complete comes, the partial will come to an end. When I was a child, I spoke like a child, I thought like a child, I reasoned like a child; when I became an adult I put an end to childish ways. For now we see in a mirror, dimly, but then we will see face to face. Now I know only in part; then I will know fully, even as I have been fully known. And now faith, hope, and love abide, these three; and the greatest of these is love."
>
> First Corinthians: 13.1-13

Earlier in his letter Paul had written:

> "When we bless 'the cup of blessing', is it not a means of sharing in the blood of Christ? When we break the bread, is it not a means of sharing in the body of Christ? Because there is one loaf, we, many as we are, are one body, for it is one loaf of which we partake."
>
> First Corinthians: 10.16-17

Reading figuratively, as Paul would have his readers do, one realizes Paul is again using the word "you" to speak of *the* church. This is not limited to the church in Corinth. He is speaking of all Christian churches. You, *the* church, are the body of Christ. You are what Jesus was and is. *You are now the messenger.* You are now responsible for carrying God's Word to all the world.

Individuals within a church are the various limbs or organs, just as are the various churches within *the* church. You are nothing alone. You are a part of a body which must act as one. No one individual, or group of individuals, or single church can act alone anymore than a foot or a hand can act without being a part of a whole body. Those who are church leaders are merely limbs appointed to that task by God, as are teachers, prophets, or any others within the church.

There were no glass mirrors at that time. People used a shiny piece of metal or some other reflecting surface as a mirror. Always the face one saw when looking into the mirror would be foggy or distorted, just as a child's conception of the world was limited and distorted. - One must grow. Some day you will see things clearly, not as though they are a hazy reflection from a mirror.

Paul is driving home his point that there is no way one can possibly know God's purpose. There is no way one can have but a partial knowledge of the world about us, of the Spirit, and of God's intentions for us. But, the time will come when our knowledge will be complete.

This is a lead in to Paul's famous passage on love. Love, he tells the Corinthians, is not only another of the gifts of the Spirit. It is the greatest gift without which other gifts are of little avail. Few passages of the bible have been quoted more often than these poetic lines about the importance of love. However, readers do not always appreciate that it is part of Paul's description of the gifts of the Spirit. Just as Jesus showed us God's love, Paul is saying, so we must let the Holy Spirit work through us to show love for others. We must grow.

RESURRECTION

When Paul has completed his instructions for the Christian community in Corinth, he turns to the subject he had been told was troubling Corinthians – the question of resurrection. How were they to be resurrected? Once again those who accept the bible literally and those who read it figuratively will find it difficult to reconcile their differences.

"And now, my brothers, I must remind you of the gospel that I preached to you: the gospel which you received, on which you have taken your stand, and which is now bringing you salvation. Do you still hold fast the Gospel as I preached it to you? If not, your conversion was in vain.

"First and foremost, I handed on to you the facts which had been imparted to me: that Christ died for our sins, in accordance with the scriptures; that he was buried; that he was raised to life on the third day, according to the scriptures; and that he appeared to Cephas, and afterwards to the Twelve. Then he appeared to over five hundred of our brothers at once, most of whom are still alive, though some have died. Then he appeared to James, and afterwards to all the apostles.

"In the end he appeared even to me. It was like an abnormal birth; I had persecuted the church of God and am therefore inferior to all other apostles – indeed not fit to be called an apostle. However, by God's grace I am what I am, nor has his grace been given me in vain; on the contrary, in my labors I have outdone them all – not I indeed, but the grace of God working with me. But what matter, I or they? This is what we all proclaim, and this is what you believed.

"Now, if this is what we proclaim, that Christ was raised from the dead, how can some of you say there is no resurrection of the dead? If there be no resurrection, then Christ was not raised; and if Christ was not raised, then our gospel is null and void, and so is your faith; and we turn out to be lying witnesses for God, because we bore witness that he raised Christ to life, whereas, if the dead are not raised, he did not raise him. For if the dead are not raised, it follows that Christ was not raised; and if Christ was not raised, your faith has nothing in it and you are still in your old state of sin. It follows also that

> those who have died within Christ's fellowship are utterly
> lost. If it is for this life only that Christ has given us
> hope, we of all men are most to be pitied.
>
> "But the truth is, Christ was raised to life – the first fruits
> of the harvest of the dead….."
>
> First Corinthians: 15.1-20

Paul has made it clear that he not only believes in resurrection of the dead, but that it is a key component of his religion. A literal interpretation would have the body of Jesus resurrected, and Jesus then appearing physically before crowds of people. Keep in mind Paul's introductory comment that, "First and foremost, I handed on to you the facts which had been imparted to me." I was not witness to this, he is saying. Rather, this is the oral tradition passed on to me. We should keep in mind that Paul was twenty years old when Jesus was crucified, and that this letter is being written about twenty-five years later.

Paul is not casting doubt on the version that was handed down to him, but those who read the *New Testament* figuratively will at this point question whether Paul meant actual physical resurrection or spiritual resurrection. Did Jesus appear before his disciples in person, or did they become aware that what he had taught them by example and in words would always be with them? Was it a physical Jesus, or was it Jesus' beliefs that were resurrected in the eyes of the disciples and others?

Paul says, "In the end he appeared even to me;" yet even in Luke's dramatic account of Paul's conversion in "Acts" no one saw a physically resurrected Jesus, and in Paul's version of his conversion no such physical resurrection occurred. The Christians of Corinth have been asking whether they are supposed to believe in resurrection of the physical body. For them this is a most important question for they are Greeks, and Greeks had for centuries believed in a soul; a soul that would survive after death of the physical body. Having been born in and having grown to adulthood in a culture that did not believe in physical resurrection, the Greeks of Corinth were balking at that idea of resurrection of the body. Paul next addresses this question.

> "But, you may ask, how are the dead raised? In what
> kind of body? How foolish! The seed you sow does not

come to life unless it has first died; and what you sow is not the body that shall be, but the naked grain, perhaps of wheat, or of some other kind; and God clothes it with the body of his choice, each seed with its own particular body. All flesh is not the same flesh; there is the flesh of men, flesh of beasts, of birds, and of fishes — all different. There are heavenly bodies and earthly bodies; and the splendor of the earthly, another. The sun has a splendor of its own, the moon another splendor, and the stars another, for star differs from star in brightness. So it is with the resurrection of the dead. What is sown in the earth as a perishable thing is raised imperishable. Sown in humiliation, it is raised in glory; sown in weakness it is raised in power; sown as an animal body, it is raised as a spiritual body.

"If there is such a thing as an animal body, there is also a spiritual body. It is in this sense that Scripture says, 'The first man Adam, became an animate being', whereas the last Adam has become a life-giving spirit. Observe, the spiritual does not come first; the animal body comes first, and then the spiritual. The first man was made 'of the dust of the earth'; the second man is from heaven. The man made of dust, and the heavenly man is the pattern of all the heavenly. As we have worn the likeness of man made of dust, so we shall wear the likeness of the heavenly man.

"What I mean, my brothers, is this: flesh and blood can never possess the kingdom of God, and the perishable cannot possess immortality. Listen! I will unfold a mystery: we shall not all die, but we shall all be changed in a flash, in a twinkling of an eye, at the last trumpet-call. For the trumpet will sound, and the dead will rise immortal, and we shall be changed. This perishable being must be clothed with the imperishable, and what is mortal must be clothed with immortality. And when our mortality has been clothed with immortality, then the saying of the Scripture will come true: "Death is swallowed up; victory is won.' 'O Death, where is your

> victory? O Death, where is your sting? The sting of
> death is sin, and sin gains its power from the law; but
> God be praised, he gives us the victory through our Lord
> Jesus Christ.
>
> "Therefore, my beloved brothers, stand firm and
> immovable, and work for the Lord always, work without
> limit, since you know that in the Lord your labor cannot
> be lost."
>
> First Corinthians: 15.35-58

Shorn of all its examples and parabolic descriptions Paul has told the Corinthians that resurrection is resurrection of the soul, not the physical body. The much later Apostle's Creed grew out of questions put to those about to baptized around 200 AD and its wording, as readers now know it, was developed in France during the sixth and seventh centuries. In its final wording it says "We (I) believe in the resurrection of the body." Paul's message to the Corinthians can satisfy both those who believe they are pledging belief in a literal resurrection of the physical body, and those who believe in resurrection of the soul; for Paul has made clear his belief that there are two bodies – one physical and the other spiritual.

SECOND CORINTHIANS

Troubles continued to plague the church at Corinth. It had become the religious center for the Christian churches of much of what is today Greece and Turkey. As such it had become a tempting target for outsiders who saw leadership in the church at Corinth as a means to control, and to set policy for, all the churches of the region. The obvious first step was to find ways to encourage an erosion of Paul's authority.

Paul was not only working in Ephesus, but had been establishing new churches in several new areas where he worked with and trained local missionaries. This time the crisis in Corinth was so serious that he dropped what he was doing in Ephesus and rushed to Corinth. Despite this personal intervention he appears to have been unable to regain the confidence of the Corinthians. Returning to

Ephesus after what he describes as his "painful visit" to Corinth (2 Corinthians 2.1), Paul wrote a most severe letter to that church. He could not again leave his work at Ephesus, nor does he apparently believe it would be any more effective than the trip from which he had just returned. The letter had to suffice.

That letter was given to Paul's trusted colleague, Titus, to carry to Corinth. Unfortunately, no copy of that letter has ever been found. The Corinthian church was far too important as a center for the churches of that region for it to fall into the hands of those who would undermine all that Paul had done to bring this new Christianity to the Gentile world. He could not wait for an answer. One who empathizes with Paul can feel his deep concern and inability to sit in Ephesus waiting for a reply. He was about to begin new work in Troas, but instead left there for Macedonia to meet the returning Titus.

By now Paul appears to have feared that he had made a mistake in sending such a severe letter to the Corinthians. It was this deeply concerned Paul who intercepted Titus in Macedonia. The news; how bad would it be?

Only one who has donned the sandals of Paul can imagine his relief when Titus told him the severe letter had restored the Corinthian's confidence in him, and that once more all was well. It would be a most grateful and relieved Paul who would then sit down to write "The Second Letter of Paul To The Corinthians."

Biblical historians believe Paul wrote only chapters 1-9 of Second Corinthians. The complete change of tone; the insertion of charges that the intruders who tried to undermine him in Corinth had been Jewish-Christians; and the somewhat boastful autobiographical inserts just do not fit with Paul's first nine chapters of reconciliation and gratitude.

CHAPTER 11

PAUL'S LETTER TO THE GALATIANS

After years in Babylonian exile the majority of the exiled Jews chose to remain in Babylon or to move from there to other lands where there were more opportunities for a prosperous life than could be found in Israel. More than 550 years had elapsed since the end of that Babylonian exile by the time Paul began organizing churches among the Gentiles. By then Jews were living throughout the Mediterranean world in lands populated by Gentile majorities. Some of these Jewish congregations had, as we have noted established synagogue-churches which taught about Jesus, but required adherence to all Jewish dietary laws, circumcision, and obedience to all other Jewish religious law. However, their insistence that the congregations of Paul's Gentile Christian churches also be required to abide by the Law was having a serious impact upon those churches.

At the heart of early church services, referred to by some historians as primitive Christianity, was a meal usually including a celebration of communion (Eucharist). It was here that Jews, especially Pharisees who had joined these churches, insisted that those who observed the Law could not sit or share the meal with those who did not observe the Law. Such obedience to the Law required Gentile men to be circumcised, if they were to share these acts of worship. Hard-line Judaizers insisted that only by Gentile observance of the Law could the "church" be held together.

A reader who has stepped into Paul's sandals cannot help but feel the anguish in Paul's letter to the Galatians. Had his race been run in vain? At the heart of his teaching, and of his life's work of creating Christian churches, was his insistence that Jesus had taught that being pure of heart was more important than spending one's life seeking some form of salvation by adhering to a set of regulations. This, he had preached, was what Jesus taught. Now he learns that churches he had founded had, in the years since he had last visited them, been slipping back into what he saw as the very "slavery" from which Jesus had lifted them. Was the all embracing universal religion he had been building about to slip back into being a national religion for a tiny national group?

Paul's response to these threats to the religion he had been preaching and to the churches he had organized was through letters he dispatched to various congregations. As we have noted, Paul looked upon the churches he had established as his children. Sometimes his letters praised his children; sometimes they helped them find their way; and sometimes he scolded. The church in Galatia was about to be scolded.

PAUL'S LETTER TO THE GALATIANS

Paul had already argued with Peter over such matters as Jewish Christians abiding by the Law forbidding them to eat with Gentiles. There had also been the earlier dispute over whether circumcision could be required of Gentile Christian men. With these troubles threatening to split the church in Galatia Paul wrote:

> "....I went again to Jerusalem with Barnabas, taking Titus with us. I went up because it had been revealed by God that I should do so. I laid before them – but at a private interview with men of repute – the gospel which I am accustomed to preach to the Gentiles, to make sure that the race I had run, and was running, should not be run in vain. Yet even my companion Titus, Greek though he was, was not compelled to be circumcised. That course was urged only as a concession to certain sham-Christians, interlopers who had stolen in to spy upon the liberty we enjoy in the fellowship of Christ

Jesus. These men wanted to bring us into bondage, but not for one moment did I yield to their dictation; I was determined that the full truth of the Gospel should be maintained for you.

"But as for the men of high reputation (not that their importance matters to me: God does not recognize these personal distinctions) - these men of repute, I say , did not prolong the consultation, but on the contrary acknowledged that I had been entrusted with the Gospel for Gentiles as surely as Peter had been entrusted with the Gospel for the Jews. For God whose action made Peter an apostle to the Jews, also made me an apostle to the Gentiles."

Paul's Letter to the Galatians: 2.1-8

Paul makes it crystal clear that he has been given the authority to preach and interpret the Gospel (good news) to Gentile congregations, and that he is not required to interpret the Gospel in the same manner as those apostles in Jerusalem who were treating Christianity as nothing more than a reform movement within Judaism. Titus was a close colleague of Paul. Although he was a Gentile, extreme Judaizers (those who would make all practices Jewish) had demanded that he be circumcised, if he were to be able to practice this new religion. However, Paul had dug in his heels and the Jerusalem apostles had backed away from enforcing the Law in this case. Paul now points to this as further proof that the Jerusalem apostles had agreed to approve his role as the founder and organizer of Gentile churches. It also highlights the clout Paul carried now that the Gentile churches outnumbered the Jewish Christian congregations. Paul continues:

"Recognizing, then, the favor thus bestowed upon me, those reputed pillars of our society, James, Cephas,[63] and John, accepted Barnabas and myself as partners, and shook hands upon it, agreeing we should go to the Gentiles while they went to the Jews. All that was asked

---

[63] Paul continues to use the name Cephas when referring to Peter.

148

> was that we keep their poor in mind, which I had made it
> my business to do."
>
> Paul's Letter to the Galatians: 2.9-10

Don't skim over this passage for you may miss an important clue as to just what kind of man Paul was. If this had been done in the twenty-first century we would be commenting on Paul's ability as a CEO to win a major corporate battle. Paul has driven a hard bargain. In a sense he has said that the church among the Gentile Christians is rapidly becoming a universal religion. Do you want to be a part of it – or do we leave you and go our own way alone? He has obtained freedom to develop Christianity among Gentiles who will not be required to abide by Judaic Law. Like Jesus, he is insisting that the Law was made for man, not man for the Law. He also makes the point that this is a religion that will reach far beyond the people of any one nation. He is proving to be a strong and intelligent leader who will not compromise his principles, no matter the cost.

Readers should also note reference to the poor of the Jewish Christian churches. Jesus' message had attracted cosmopolitan congregations among the Gentiles; traders, intellectuals, and others of the Hellenistic world. In Jerusalem, Jesus' message had attracted many of the poor, while Jews who felt more secure tended to remain worshipers in the established temple and synagogues. Paul's agreement with the Jerusalem elders promised aid for the poor in those Jerusalem churches whose needs were beyond what the Jerusalem churches could provide. The Jerusalem churches were becoming increasingly dependent on aid from the growing Gentile churches.

> "But when Cephas came to Antioch I opposed him to his face, because he was clearly in the wrong. For until certain persons came from James he was taking his meals with gentile Christians; but when they came he drew back and began to hold aloof, because he was afraid of the advocates of circumcision. The other Jewish Christians showed the same lack of principle; even Barnabas was carried away and played false like the rest. But when I saw that their conduct did not square with the truth of the Gospel, I said to Cephas, before the whole congregation, 'If you, a Jew born and bred, live like a

> Gentile, and not like a Jew, how can you insist that
> Gentiles must live like Jews?'
>
> "We ourselves are Jews by birth, not Gentiles and
> sinners. But we know that no man is ever justified by
> doing what the law demands, but only through faith in
> Christ Jesus; so we too have put our faith in Jesus Christ,
> in order that we might be justified through his faith, and
> not through deeds dictated by law; for by such deeds,
> Scripture says, no mortal man shall be justified.
>
> "If now, in seeking to be justified in Christ, we ourselves
> no less than Gentiles turn out to be sinners against the
> law, does that mean that Christ is an abettor to sin? No,
> never! No, if I start building up again a system which I
> have pulled down, then it is that I show myself up as a
> transgressor of the law. For through the law I died to
> law – to live for God. I have been crucified with Christ:
> the life I now live is not my life, but the life which Christ
> lives in me; and my present bodily life is lived by faith in
> the Son of God, who loved me and gave himself up for
> me. I will not nullify the grace of God; if righteousness
> comes by law, then Christ died for nothing."
>
> Paul's Letter to the Galatians: 2.11-21

Paul is mincing no words. He is on the attack. He is not wasting words trying to be diplomatic. He is drawing a sharp line between the new Gentile Christian churches and congregations treating "Christianity" merely as a reform movement within Judaism. He demands that the churches of Galatia defend their freedom as churches recognizing Jesus as the messenger from God, rather than as churches recognizing the rule of the Law. He is verbally chastising any church that would treat the Law as superior to the teachings of Jesus when he writes:

> "You stupid Galatians! You must have been bewitched –
> you before whose eyes Jesus Christ was openly displayed
> upon his cross! Answer me one question: did you receive

150

> the Spirit by keeping the law or by believing the gospel message? Can it be that you are so stupid? You started with the spiritual; do you now look to the material to make you perfect? Have all your great experiences been in vain – if vain indeed they should be? I ask then: when God gives you the Spirit and works miracles among you, why is this? Is it because you keep the law, or is it because you have faith in the gospel message? Look at Abraham: he put his faith in God, and that faith was counted to him as righteousness.
>
> "You may take it, then, that it is the men of faith who are Abraham's sons. And Scripture foreseeing that God would justify the Gentiles through faith declared the Gospel to Abraham beforehand: 'In you all nations shall find blessing.' Thus it is the men of faith who share the blessing with faithful Abraham.
>
> "On the other hand those who rely on obedience to the law are under a curse; for Scripture says, 'A curse is on all who do not persevere in doing everything that is written in the Book of the Law.' It is evident that no one is ever justified before God in terms of law; because we read, 'he shall gain life who is justified through faith'. Now the law is not at all a matter of having faith: we read,' he who does this shall gain life by what he does'."
>
> Paul's Letter to the Galatians: 3.1-12

Paul has gone further than just drawing a line between the two approaches to the teachings of Jesus. He is here making a clear-cut break with churches treating Christianity as a reform sect of Judaism. Keep in mind that those churches were not only in Israel. They were operating in Jewish communities throughout the Mediterranean world, and they were under Peter's control. Paul is demanding that Gentile Christians base their behavior on faith in the message Jesus brought to them, and must never, in any way, accept the law as superior to faith. Where the law and faith differed in the direction man should follow, faith was always the guide to righteous living.

Paul goes further. He now saw the law as a yoke people had been forced to bear; a yoke from which Jesus had freed them when he died upon the cross. They had been prisoners of the law, and were now to be free.

> "Christ bought us freedom from the curse of the law by becoming for our sake an accursed thing; for the Scripture says, 'A curse is on everyone who is hanged on a gibbet.' And the purpose of it all was that the blessing of Abraham should in Jesus Christ be extended to the Gentiles, so that we might receive the promised Spirit through faith.
>
> "My brothers, let me give you an illustration. Even in ordinary life, when a man's will and testament has been duly executed, no one else can set it aside or add a codicil. Now the promises were pronounced to Abraham and to his 'issue'. It does not say 'issues' in the plural, but in the singular, 'and to your issue'; and the 'issue' intended is Christ. What I am saying is this: a testament, or covenant, had already been validated by God; it cannot be invalidated, and its promises rendered ineffective by a law made four hundred and thirty years later. If the inheritance is by legal right, then it is not by promise; but it was by promise that God bestowed it as a free gift on Abraham.
>
> "Then what is the law? It was added to make wrongdoing a legal offence. It was a temporary measure pending the arrival of the 'issue' to whom the promise was made. It was promulgated through angels, and, there was an intermediary; but the intermediary is not needed for one party acting alone, and God is one."
>
> Paul's Letter to the Galatians: 3.13-20

Paul is turning the law on itself. He is making a case that even the ancient Law of Judaism was only a temporary measure until God's messenger arrived. On this point he is careful not to refer to Jesus as the Messiah, a king sent by God to lead only a chosen nation.

Unfortunately, over the next two thousand years far too many Christians would interpret this conflict as being Jews versus Jesus. But Paul's attacks on the orthodoxy of the Law and its extreme advocates were not attacks, or even an accusation, against Jews. Paul, like Jesus, was a Jew, as were most of Paul's early assistants, and they belonged to Paul's churches in Gentile communities.

His opposition was to legalistic restrictions tending to hold Jews of that time in a religious straight jacket. It is not Jews as a people, not the prophets of the Scriptures, but the religion of the temple that he is attacking. Never make the mistake of assuming this was a fight between Christians and Jews.

Paul continues:

"Does the law, then, contradict the promises? No, never! If a law had been given which had power to bestow life, then indeed righteousness would have come from keeping the law. But Scripture has declared the whole world to be prisoners in subjection to sin, so that faith in Jesus Christ may be the ground on which the promised blessing is given to those who have such faith.

"Before this faith came, we were close prisoners to the custody of law, pending the revelation of faith. Thus the law was a kind of tutor in charge of us until Christ should come, when we should be justified through faith; and now that faith has come, the tutor's charge is at an end.

"For through faith you are all sons of God in union with Christ Jesus. Baptized into union with him, you have all put on Christ as a garment. There is no such thing as Jew and Greek, slave and freeman, male and female; for you are all one person in Christ Jesus. But if you thus belong to Christ, you are the 'issue' of Abraham, and so heirs by promise."

Paul's Letter to the Galatians: 3.21-29

Paul further draws on the comparison of one who is a slave to law and one who is free. We are free because "God sent his own Son, born of a woman, born under law, to purchase freedom for the subjects of the law, in order that we might attain the status of sons."

Paul repeatedly reminds his readers that he has built a church in which members based their religion on faith in God, and in Jesus' teachings about God. He continually contrasts this with a religion in which members worshiped through rituals and restrictions prescribed by the Law. He despairs for his congregations who he looks upon as his children, and now, as Jesus did, and the writers of the gospels would later do, he teaches by a parable.

"For my children you are, and I am in travail[64] with you over and over again until you take the shape of Christ. I wish I could be with you now; then I could modify my tone; as it is, I am at my wits' end about you. "Tell me now, you who are so anxious to be under law, will you not listen to what the Law says? It is written there that Abraham had two sons, one by his slave and the other by his freeborn wife. The slave woman's son was born in the course of nature, the free woman's through God's promise. This is an allegory. The two women stand for two covenants. The one bearing children into slavery is the covenant that comes from Mount Sinai: that is Hagar. Sinai is a mountain in Arabia and it represents the Jerusalem of today, for she and her children are in slavery. But the heavenly Jerusalem is the free woman she is our mother. For Scripture says, 'Rejoice, O barren woman who never bore a child; break into a shout of joy, you who never knew a mother's pangs; for the deserted wife shall have more children than she who lives with the husband.

"And you, my brothers, like Isaac, are children of God's promise. But just as in those days the natural born son persecuted the spiritual son, so it is today. But what does Scripture say? 'Drive out the slave- woman and her son, for the son of the slave shall not share the inheritance with the free woman's son.' You see, then, my brothers, we are no slave-woman's children; our mother is the free

---

[64] "Travail," labor pains in giving birth.

154

woman. Christ set us free, to be free men. Stand firm,
then, and refuse to be tied to the yoke of slavery again.

"Mark my words: I, Paul, say to you that if you receive
circumcision Christ will do you no good at all. Once
again, you can take it from me that every man who
receives circumcision is under obligation to keep the
entire law. When you seek to be justified by way of the
law, your relation with Christ is completely severed: you
have fallen out of the domain of God's grace. For to us,
our hope of attaining that righteousness which we eagerly
await is the work of the Spirit through faith. If we are in
union with Christ Jesus circumcision makes no difference
at all, nor does the want of it; the only thing that counts
is faith active in love."

"You were running well; who was it
hindered you from following the truth? Whatever
persuasion he used, it did not come from God who is
calling you; 'a little leaven', remember, 'leavens all the
dough'. United with you in the Lord, I am confident that
you will not take the wrong view; but the man who is
unsettling your minds, whoever he may be, must bear
Gods judgment."

Paul's Letter to the Galatians: 4.19-31 and 5.1-10

Paul repeatedly uses circumcision as an example because it was
a demand being made repeatedly by Judaizers. However, it is only an
example of the major concern he is trying to communicate to the
Galatians. That concern is over their teetering on the edge of becoming
a religion of worship and obedience according to the Law. As his
words imply, he is desperately trying to make them see that blind
adherence to the Law was in no way a substitute for their faith in God
and the way of life Jesus preached as God's way. The church he had
been organizing, the religion it represented, called for people to live
their lives according to what their faith in Jesus' message told them was
right, not by following a set of rules and regulations made by fallible
men. It came down to a confrontation between living according to

faith in one's own freedom to interpret what God would want him or her to do, or to living according to rules made by men.

At the same time, Paul is aware that *this* freedom is freedom to follow the way of life taught by Jesus as the way God would have man live, but is not freedom to throw over all regard for anything but one's self. He warned:

> "You, my friends, were called to be free men, only do not turn your freedom into license for your lower nature, but to be servants to one another in love. For the whole law can be summed up in a single commandment: 'Love your neighbor as yourself.' But if you go on fighting one another, tooth and nail, all you can expect is mutual destruction.
>
> "I mean this: if you are guided by the Spirit you will not fulfill the desires of your lower nature. That nature sets its desires against the Spirit, while the Spirit fights against it. They are in conflict with one another so what you will to do you cannot do. But if you are led by the Spirit, you are not under law.
>
> "Anyone can see the kind of behavior that belongs to the lower nature: fornication, impurity, and indecency; idolatry and sorcery; quarrels, a contentious temper, envy, fits of rage, selfish ambitions, dissensions, party intrigues, and jealousies; drinking bouts, orgies and the like. I warn you, as I warned you before, that those who behave in such ways will never inherit the kingdom of God.
>
> "But the harvest of the Spirit is love, joy, peace, patience, kindness, fidelity, gentleness, and self-control. There is no law dealing with such things as these. And those who belong to Christ Jesus have crucified the lower nature with its passions and desires. If the Spirit is the source of our life, let the Spirit also direct our course."
>
> Paul's Letter to the Galatians: 5.13-25

Paul makes it clear that some hard-liners demand circumcision because it is part of the Law, but that at the same time they ignore other parts of the Law which would restrict other aspects of their behavior.

"Make no mistake about this: God is not to be fooled; a man reaps what he sows. If he sows seed in the field of his lower nature, he will reap from it a harvest of corruption, but if he sows in the field of the Spirit, the Spirit will bring him a harvest of eternal life. So let us never tire of doing good, for if we do not slacken our efforts we shall in due time reap our harvest. Therefore, as opportunity offers, let us work for the good of all, especially members of the household of the faith.

"....It is all those who want to make a fair outward and bodily show who are trying to force circumcision upon you; their sole object is to escape persecution for the cross of Christ. For even those who do receive circumcision are not thoroughgoing observers of the law; they only want you to be circumcised in order to boast of your having submitted to that outward rite. But God forbid that I should boast of anything but the cross of Lord Jesus Christ, through which the world is crucified to me and I to the world! Circumcision is nothing; uncircumcision is nothing; the only thing that counts is new creation! Whoever they are who take this principle for their guide, peace and mercy upon them, and upon the whole Israel of God.

Paul's Letter to the Galatians: 6.12-16

The letter to the Galatians was written at a time when Paul was most active, some say at the peak of his career, around 55 A.D. It is important to note that in keeping with the teachings of Jesus, Paul is insisting that man-made law was blinding and deafening man to the Word, which was the will of God. For Paul this constant struggle to keep his "children" from slipping back became a crusade to which he gave his all.

Combined with this continual confrontation with the Judaizers were the temptations to adopt the promises of physical resurrection offered by the mystery religions and the salvation sought by the Gnostics. This is why it was so important to read Mark before reading the other gospels. Mark is reflecting the beliefs Paul was fighting so hard to preserve at the time he died. In Mark we see the gospel as it was being taught by Paul in the early church, which makes it easier to understand the battle Paul has been waging through his letters.

This is a most critical time. Christianity is being molded. Unless one steps into the sandals of Paul and his listeners there is the danger of being confused by the use of the term "church". Readers, both literal and figurative, should realize that the church as we know it is the result of centuries of growth. There is no *New Testament*, no written gospel during Paul's lifetime. Paul is fighting to keep these early congregations on one track. His struggle will fill the gap between the death of Jesus and the unifying of the church through the acceptance of the gospels yet to be written.

Readers moving on to Matthew and Luke should keep in mind that, during the twenty years following Paul's death, the need to retain that freedom from the Law for which Jesus gave his life required constant vigilance. But, something else would become as great, if not a greater concern. The mystery religions with their promises of physical resurrection, the licentiousness and unrestrained pleasures of some pagan religions, the new Emperor worship, and the challenges of Gnosticism continually threatened to erode the foundations of this early Christianity. These were threats that would bring to the fore a new generation of defenders of Christianity. Among them would be Matthew, Luke, and John seeking with their new versions of the gospel to combat the competing religions and to bring new converts into the fold.

When reading the gospels according to Matthew, Luke, and John, one should never lose sight of Mark. In Mark the reader finds the basis for Christianity as the early church was being born. In moving on to the later gospels the reader should not only be aware of the additions made by Matthew, Luke, and John, but should also try to understand the reasons for those additions.

CHAPTER 12

PAUL'S LETTER TO THE ROMANS

Part One - Chapters 1-8

When recalling that at the time of Jesus' death Paul was only twenty years old, the age of most American college sophomores, and that he lived in Tarsus more than four hundred and fifty miles by land from Jerusalem, we realize why it was unlikely that he had ever heard of Jesus by the time of the crucifixion. If, as the author of "Acts" writes, Paul had become an ardent Pharisee, and then had traveled to Jerusalem to study to become a rabbi, it is likely that would have been his first acquaintance with the teachings of Jesus. He would then have been the age of seniors in our university graduating classes.

Keeping in mind Paul's knowledge of and his strict observance of the Law, one can understand how a young man's ardor would lead him to react ruthlessly upon learning of Hellenistic Jews trying to reform synagogues in Jesus' name. Over the next six years he would throw himself enthusiastically into the battle against those "blasphemers".

* * * * * * * * * * * *

It is well to recall several other points as we move on to what is considered the best exposition of the theology of Paul, the man without whom there would in all likelihood not be a Christian church.

Obviously there was no Christianity while Jesus was alive. There was no Christian church. There were no gospels or other writings that would later be known as the *New Testament.*

Christianity, like all other religions, is a man-made religion. The church had to be created and developed by men like Paul and Barnabas. There was no body of written material about Jesus or his teachings for congregations to read; and Jesus had not established a new church or a new religion.

The founders and early ministers of the first Gentile Christian churches[65] were men who had never met Jesus, never heard him speak, never observed him with his disciples, and never witnessed any of the miracles or other acts of which they preached. Their preaching and their work with the churches they were founding were based on oral tradition. However, that does not mean that those oral reports handed down over the preceding generation were nothing but myth.

As we noted earlier Mark would not write the first gospel until almost forty years after Jesus' death, and then he based what he wrote upon what was being taught in the Gentile Christian churches at that time. That would be after Paul and fellow missionaries had spent almost twenty years developing the message they were carrying to the people; the message that would become Christianity.

Remember, when *The New Testament* was being compiled two hundred years later it was not intended to be a history or a biography, but rather as a witness to this new faith. It would include only those writings chosen by the men charged with the task of creating the *New Testament.* This means they selected from all the gospels and epistles written throughout a century or more following Jesus' death only those they considered relevant to the new Christianity they were consolidating in Rome; and these were then arranged, not in chronological order, but rather as a narrative bearing witness to the faith.

Those gospels and epistles which were chosen were the work of the founders and leaders of this new religion during the century after

---

65   As we have previously noted, the congregations established in Jerusalem by James and Peter were not Christian churches like those created among the Gentiles. They were more a reform movement within the synagogues which adopted certain of Jesus' teachings. The reader should always keep in mind that Jesus never called for a new religion or an abandonment of the Jewish religion in which he had been reared. He made it clear that he had come, not to destroy, but to strengthen that religion.

Jesus' death. This is why Paul, his theology, and his work with the churches being created among the Gentiles are so important.

Keep in mind that Paul was only twenty-eight years old at the time of his conversion. From that time until his death twenty-nine years later, his own theological and philosophical beliefs would continue to mature. He was not frozen in time. He grew; and as he grew so did his concept of what this new religion should be.

The reform movement under way in synagogues which had accepted parts of Jesus' message was quite limited. Over the past two thousand years religious leaders and some historians have spoken of this as "the early Christian church." Although it preached some of Jesus' message, it still considered itself a religion whose membership was restricted to Jews and to others abiding by the Law. Outside those congregations there was no new religion devoted to Jesus' teachings, no Christianity as we know it; that was still to be brought into being by missionaries like Barnabas [66]and Paul.

Christianity just did not spring full bloom onto the world stage. It grew as its founders grew. From the earliest preachings of a few it grew, even as their theological concepts grew. And Paul's theology continued to mature. As a well traveled Pharisee Paul would have held the hope, as did other Pharisees, that the religion of the Jews would become the religion of the world. The Roman Empire at that time was beset with revolts and wars among the various peoples who had been swept into that rather loosely controlled empire. A universal religion could heal many wounds; unite diverse ethnic groups; and reach beyond nationalistic barriers. However, trying to foist on all those peoples a national religion of one of the smallest nations within the empire, based on the coming of that nation's Messiah, would be far more divisive than unifying.

* * * * * * * * * * * *

The letter known as "Romans" was written around 57 AD, when Paul was about forty-seven years old. By then his theological

---

[66] Barnabas, a Hellenized Jew had joined the church in Jerusalem not long after the crucifixion. Selling all he owned and contributing the money thus earned to the Jerusalem church, he moved on to join fellow Cypriots in founding the Antioch church. It was from there that he called Paul to join him.

concepts reflected some nineteen years of experience, thought, and growth as a Christian, and it is at this point that biblical historians consider him to be at the peak of his career. This letter is considered the most mature, the most complete, and the "most balanced statement of his theology."[67]   Several years had passed since his letter to the Corinthians; time for Paul's theology to mature still further before penning this letter to the Romans.

Being written so soon after his letter to the Galatians, the letter to the Romans should be read with care, for it is the best exposition of what Christianity had become by then; not what it is today, but what it was just twenty seven years after Jesus' death.   It would become the basis for the Christianity Mark would present in the first gospel to be written; and that gospel would become the outline for the gospels of Matthew and Luke.

WHY THE LETTER ?

Paul's letters to this point had been written to churches he had founded. Why now was he writing to Roman Christians with whom he had never had any personal contact?

When the decision had been made to give Paul control of the rising Gentile churches, and to give Peter the "churches" organized as reform movements of the Jewish religion, Paul was asked to remember the poor in the Jerusalem "church".[68] For several years he had gathered collections from Gentile churches to be eventually taken to Jerusalem. It was hoped this would provide an important bridge between the Jerusalem churches and the Gentile churches; a bridge between Paul and the leaders in Jerusalem.

The ethical and moral code of the Jewish religion appealed to many Gentiles.   As they did not abide by Jewish religious law (circumcision, diet, etc.) they could not become members. Despite this they were attracted to the synagogues by the teachings therein. Among these Gentiles Paul, and other early founders of churches, found ready

---

[67]   *The New English Bible*, p. 183, Introduction to "The Letter of Paul to the Romans."

[68]   Aside from Hellenistic Jews who had accepted some of Jesus' teaching, congregations of the Jerusalem churches consisted largely of the poor. For the most part those who were economically secure continued to practice their Jewish religion.

listeners as they preached their message. Still, despite the authority granted Paul to develop and organize Gentile churches, Judaizers continued to infiltrate these new Gentile churches with the aim of turning them back into congregations requiring slavish adherence to the Law, and with a Jewish identity. As they made it increasingly difficult for Paul to continue his work in Anatolia and Greece, he began looking to the West. Southern France and Spain appeared to be fertile ground for the development of Christian churches. He could go to Jerusalem, deliver the collection for the poor, and then head for Rome.

While Paul's letter was a means of introducing himself and his theology to those Christians whom others had organized in Rome, it could at the same time develop support for missionary work in the West. However, he first needed to make clear to the Roman congregations his version of the gospel and of this newly emerging Christianity.

Although "Romans" is more an essay than a letter, going more into depth on certain subjects than in his shorter "letters," there are several important theological points not covered. Paul does not discuss the controversial subject of the resurrection of Jesus, nor of what occurs at the time of human death. Likewise it is notable that he does not speak of the Eucharist as a spiritual communion with God. Why?

Paul was in Corinth when he wrote this letter to the Romans. He indicates his concern that he will not only be unwelcome in Jerusalem, but actually may be in grave danger. Although presented as a letter to introduce himself and his ideas for establishing churches as far west as Spain, this letter is actually aimed to gain support of the Roman Christians in resisting further intrusion by Judaizers, especially in Rome.

As he makes clear in his introduction, he is not opposed to fellow Jews. His concern is over Judaizers who would prevent the spread of Jesus' message through their insistence that non-Jews adhere to the Law. In this regard he reveals his vision of the Gentile church growing so rapidly that its influence upon the Jewish (Jerusalem) church would once more open the eyes and ears of Israel thereby making it the messenger God had intended it to be in carrying the Word to the rest of the world.

> "For there is deep truth here, my brothers, of which I want you to take account, so that you may not be complacent about your own discernment: this partial

> blindness has come upon Israel only until the Gentiles
> have been admitted in full strength; when that has
> happened, the whole of Israel will be saved, in agreement
> with the text of the scripture:"
>
> Romans: 11.25-26

PAUL INTRODUCES HIMSELF TO THE ROMANS

Following the first flowery paragraphs of greeting Paul writes:

> "But I should like you to know, my brothers, that I have
> often planned to come, though so far without success, in
> the hope of achieving something among you, as I have in
> other parts of world. I am under obligation to Greek and
> non-Greek, to learned and simple; hence my eagerness to
> declare the Gospel to you in Rome as to others. For I am
> not ashamed of the Gospel. It is the saving power of
> God for everyone who has faith - the Jew first, but the
> Greek also — because here is revealed God's way of
> righting wrong, a way that starts from faith and ends in
> faith; as Scripture says, 'he shall gain life who is justified
> through faith'."
>
> Romans: 1.13-17

Paul has introduced what becomes the theme of his entire letter
– faith; and its role will be woven throughout this letter. According to
Paul, God rights wrong because by his very divinity he is righteous.
God's gift to humans is life and, through faith, the ability to be
righteous. Men and women, therefore, have been given the key to
salvation - faith. With this, Paul has placed a great responsibility on
each individual. Salvation, as stressed in his earlier letter to the
Galatians, could only be achieved by putting aside a life devoted to the
satisfactions of the flesh (Galatians 5. 16-26 and 6. 1-10).[69] This, he
now emphasizes, each individual had to do by and for himself.

---

[69] The manner in which the subject matter is handled in each letter and the
problems being addressed lead biblical historians to believe the time (continued)

164

* * * * * * * * * * * *

Platonic tradition had called for a life in which devotion to the spiritual transcended physical desires. This ideal, conceived centuries before the birth of Jesus, was still prominent in Greek thinking during Paul's lifetime. Furthermore, the Gnostic's emphasis on the spiritual and the intellectual was at the center of numerous mystery religions. Gnosticism had even influenced the ongoing development of the Jewish religion.

Gnosticism, in part an offspring of Platonism, had become a combination of philosophy and religion. It not only absorbed religious elements of Platonism, but drew also from Egyptian mysticism, the myths of the Babylonians, the basics of Persian (Iranian) dualism, the religion of the Jews, and from Greek philosophers other than Platonists. But, it not only drew from these sources; it also in turn influenced them.

Gnosticism, like the mystery religions springing up throughout the region, was seeking a way of life that would lead to salvation. Gnostics believed in a single God. To them the world was evil and chaotic. This chaos and evil was not a product of God, but of a Demiurge that was the creator of the material world. Salvation was the freeing of the spiritual being from the physical body which was always beset with temptations of the evil world.

Early Christians could no more completely accept the Gnostics' path to salvation than could the Gnostics totally accept the Christian way. However, readers of Paul's teachings, and of the gospels which followed in the decades after Paul's death, will recognize Gnosticism's influence on the founders of Christianity.

Our knowledge of Jesus is drawn almost entirely from the descriptions of him and his works as found in the writings of Paul and the authors of the gospels. Those sources portray a Jesus who fills a role which could in part be accepted by Gnostics. In the parables that gospel writers wrote and added to supplement those passed down to them as Jesus' parables, readers can see the influence of Gnostics in the words those writers attributed to Jesus. The need to separate the spiritual being from the physical body as the way to salvation is apparent.

---

between Paul's writing to the Galatians and his letter to the Romans was relatively short, and his concerns similar.

Even in those parables which were Jesus' own, such as that about the rich man seeking to enter the kingdom of heaven, the reader sees a reflection of both the Platonist and Gnostic belief that physical and material desires (the flesh) were evil and in constant conflict with the spirit (the good). The disciples had asked, "Then who can be saved?" Jesus had replied, "For men it is impossible." In both Platonic and Gnostic philosophies salvation was achieved by the defeat of the flesh in this continuing battle.[70] Paul has also insisted that salvation was won by the spirit's victory over flesh but -through faith - not through mystic rituals as practiced in mystery religions.

* * * * * * * * * * * *

Religions, at the time when the early Christian religion and its churches were being formed, were also influenced by the philosophy of the Stoics. Stoicism had been a major philosophical movement for at least three hundred years before the birth of Jesus, and would continue to influence religious development in Greece and Rome for another two hundred years after Jesus' death.

For the reader who reads the gospels and the letters of Paul as literal history, these influences may not be apparent. However, for one seeing these as figurative presentations, the continuing influence of both Gnosticism and Stoicism is seen in the development of Christianity from the earliest letters of Paul to the latest of the gospels. For that reason, it is important for the reader of Paul to have an awareness of the philosophies of both the Gnostics and the Stoics.

For the Stoics nature had no favorites; it was neutral. Most importantly, nature was rational. God and nature are inseparable. As God is rational, so nature must be rational. Nature, therefore, was more than just the material world in which humans found themselves. *Being rational meant there must be purpose.* As a part of this rational and purposive world each human had a bit of that divine rationalism, a bit of God, within him or her. Therefore, each man and woman has through this inborn God been given rationality, the ability to determine the virtuous path.

---

[70] Flesh, as in Mark, refers to all things material and physical as contrasted to the purely spiritual. It includes desires for material "rewards" such as those Jesus referred to in the wilderness as Satan's temptations.

166

Because each individual in this world has a bit of that divine rationality within him or her, everyone on earth is a brother or sister of everyone else. Everyone is a son or daughter of the Father, God. Therefore, all humans should live as part of a world brotherhood. A woman or a man can determine good and evil. For the completely rational man or woman everything is good. However, for one who has not become completely rational there will always be room to perceive evil. Thus, man can control all that is good or evil. Everything that humans cannot control is "indifferent". It is neither good nor evil.[71]

* * * * * * * * * * * *

What we know of John the Baptist's values and his teachings resembles the Gnostic values prevalent in the Middle East during his lifetime. Paul's theology definitely reflects both Gnostic and Stoic philosophies with which he would have been quite familiar. Remember, he had been born and reared in Tarsus, the center of Stoicism, and he was surrounded by mystery religions heavily influenced by Greek Gnostics.

Most of Jesus' teachings, as passed on to congregations of those early churches, were sufficiently similar to Gnostic and Stoic beliefs as to attract followers of those philosophical/religious combinations. Salvation through the eventual freeing of the spiritual from the physical body; belief that a bit of the Kingdom of Heaven lay like a seed within each individual; the strong ethical code; the need for faith; and a good God calling for individuals to fight the evil found in worldly temptations were aspects of the new Christianity that could easily be accepted by many Gnostics and Stoics.

* * * * * * * * * * * *

Paul continues by describing sinners and the fate that is reserved for them.

---

[71] The above descriptions of Gnosticism and Stoicism are so abbreviated as to do an injustice to both philosophies/religions. They may, however, provide a glimpse into the philosophical/religious world into which Paul was born and reared, and which could not help but have some influence on his theological thoughts as they developed over the years before and after his conversion.

> "For we see divine retribution revealed from the heaven and falling upon all the godless wickedness of men. In their wickedness they are stifling the truth. For all that might be known of God by men lies plain before their eyes; indeed God himself has disclosed it to them. His invisible attributes, that is to say his everlasting power and deity, have been visible, ever since the world began, to the eye of reason, in the things he has made. There is therefore no possible defense for their conduct; knowing God, they have refused to honor him as God, or to render him thanks. Hence, all their thinking has ended in futility, and their misguided minds are plunged in darkness. They boast of their wisdom, but they have made fools of themselves, exchanging the splendor of immortal God for an image shaped like mortal man, even images like birds, beasts, and creeping things."
>
> Romans: 1.18-23

According to Paul, Jews and all those who by then were following the teachings of Jesus (Christians) had a special knowledge of God and his will through what God had revealed to them. However, Paul adds, all others still have had the opportunity to recognize God through all creation that lies before their eyes.

> "For this reason God has given them up to the vileness of their own desires, and the consequent degradation of their bodies, because they have bartered away the true God for a false one, and have offered reverence and worship to created things instead of to the Creator, who is blessed forever, amen.
>
> "In consequence I say God has given them up to shameful passions. Their women have exchanged natural intercourse for the unnatural, and their men in turn, giving up natural relations with women, burn with lust for one another; males behave indecently with males, and are paid in their own persons the fitting wage of such perversion.

168

> "Thus because they have not seen fit to acknowledge
> God, he has given them up to their own depraved reason.
> This leads them to break all rules of conduct. They are
> filled with every kind of injustice, mischief, rapacity, and
> malice; they are one mass of envy, murder, rivalry,
> treachery, and malevolence; whisperers and scandal-
> mongers, hateful to God, insolent, arrogant, and boastful;
> they invent new kinds of mischief, they show no loyalty
> to parents, no conscience, no fidelity to their plighted
> word; they are without natural affection and without pity.
> They know well enough the just decree of God, that
> those who behave like this deserve to die, and yet they do
> it; not only so, they actually applaud such practices."
>
> Romans: 1.24-32

These verses are part of the greeting and introduction that were
found in most letters of this period. They should be read as such. This,
however, raises some questions. Paul knows he is a stranger to the
Romans. Why does he feel it necessary to expound on sin while he is
introducing himself?

In these passages Paul has listed what he sees as the sins of non-
Christian Gentiles. A reader may wonder at the breadth of this
accusation; perhaps even its logic. Romans reading this letter could not
help but gain the impression that Paul is saying injustice, mischief,
malice, envy, rivalry, treachery, malevolence, whispering and scandal-
mongering, insolence, boastfulness, inventing mischief, and lack of
loyalty to parents is to be found among those who had committed the
"sins" he had described in his preceding paragraph. Thus, the Romans
to whom the letter was addressed might assume that those who spread
false rumors, or rivaled for church leadership, or otherwise were
involved in undermining Paul and his churches could not be considered
reliable. After all, were they not supposed to be the same individuals or
groups that had indulged in the "shameful" sins Paul listed in that
preceding paragraph?

Paul is leaving Anatolia and Greece where he feels his work is
being undermined not only by Judaizers, but also by envious local
leaders seeking to grab control of churches he has fathered. In his
earlier letter to the Corinthians he had criticized these local leaders and

intruders from other churches for rivaling to take over leadership of that church. In his letter to the Galatians his deep frustration is even more evident. He has repeatedly likened himself to a father, and his churches as his children. Now he feels his "children" may be forsaking him and his teaching. His reference to whisperings, false accusations (scandal-mongering), treachery, mischief making, and lack of loyalty (to Paul the father of the churches) might, therefore, be read as an attempt to refute those rumors or accusations that may already have reached Roman ears, and which impugned Paul and his work. Such tales, he is making clear, come from Judaizers and others who would change the course of the church as it continued to grow, and would make it subservient to the Law.

JUSTIFYING THE GENTILE CHURCH

Paul is about to go to Jerusalem on his way to Rome, and in this letter he first attempts to assure his credibility with the Romans, especially important, if he were to be seized and imprisoned or threatened with death while in Jerusalem. Having done so in his introduction and greeting (Chapter 1, Romans), he now moves on to his major concern.

Paul desperately needs support in his struggle to keep the new Christian church from being taken over by Judaizers. Among biblical historians there seems little doubt that in this letter he is making the strongest possible presentation of that threat, and is combining it with a plea for support in this struggle.

> "You therefore have no defense- you who sit in judgment, whoever you may be – for in judging your fellow-man you condemn yourself, since you, the judge, are equally guilty. It is admitted that God's judgment is rightly passed upon all who commit such crimes as these; and do you imagine – you who pass judgment on the guilty while committing the same crimes yourself – do you imagine that you, any more than they, will escape the judgment of God? Or do you think lightly of his wealth of kindness, of tolerance, and of patience, without recognizing that God's kindness is meant to lead you to a

change of heart? In the rigid obstinacy of your heart you are laying up for yourself a store of retribution for the day of retribution, when God's just judgment will be revealed, and he will pay every man for what he has done. To those who pursue glory, honor, and immortality by steady persistence in well-doing, he will give eternal life but for those who are governed by selfish ambition, who refuse obedience to the truth and take the wrong for their guide, there will be the fury of retribution. There will be trouble and distress for every human being who is an evil-doer, for the Jew first and for the Greek also, and for every well-doer there will be glory, honor, and peace, for the Jew first and also for the Greek.

"For God has no favorites: those who have sinned outside the pale of the Law of Moses will perish outside the pale, and those who have sinned under that law will be judged by the law. It is not by hearing the law, but by doing it, that men will be justified before God. When Gentiles who do not possess the law carry out its precepts by the light of nature, then, although they have no law, they are in their own law, for they display the effect of the law inscribed on their hearts. Their conscience is called as a witness, and their own thoughts argue the case on either side, against them or even for them, on the day when God judges the secrets of human hearts through Christ Jesus. So my gospel declares."

Romans: 2.1-16

Paul is developing a basis for his ultimate argument. All humans, he emphasizes, will be judged according to the way they have lived. Just because a person believes in the Law of Moses, or insists that it be followed, does not assure escape from the judgment of God. It is living according to the Law that is important, not the advocating or preaching of the Law. Jews were given the Law by Moses at the time of their covenant with God, so they cannot plead ignorance of the way God would have them live. They are to be held far more accountable for living according to the Law than are those who know nothing of the Law. Gentiles who may know nothing of the Law of Moses but, by their recognition of right and wrong, live the way God would have men and women live are living by the "law inscribed on their hearts."

"But as for you - you may bear the name of Jew; you rely upon the law and are proud of your God; you know his will; instructed by the law, you know right from wrong; you are confident that you are the one to guide the blind, to enlighten the benighted, to train the stupid, and to teach the immature, because in the law you see the very shape of knowledge and truth. You, then, who teach your fellow-man, do you fail to teach yourself? You proclaim, 'Do not steal'; but are you yourself a thief? You say, 'Do not commit adultery'; but are you an adulterer? You abominate false gods; but do you rob their shrines? While you take pride in the law, you dishonor God by breaking it. For as the Scripture says, 'Because of you the name of God is dishonored among the Gentiles.'

"Circumcision has value, provided you keep the law; but if you break the law, then your circumcision is as if it had never been. Equally, if an uncircumcised man keeps the precepts of the law, will he not count as circumcised? He may be uncircumcised in his natural state, but by fulfilling the law he will pass judgment on you who break it, for all your written code and your circumcision. The true Jew is not he who is such in externals, neither is the true circumcision the external mark in the flesh. The true Jew is he who is such inwardly, and the true circumcision is of the heart, directed not by written precepts but by the Spirit; such a man receives his commendation not from men but from God."

Romans: 2.17-29

This continuing emphasis on circumcision is not on its physical aspect, but rather as an act representing the covenant God made with his people, the covenant sealed with blood by Moses at Sinai.[72] Paul uses it to contrast those who are partners in that covenant with those who are not aware of the covenant and the Law of Moses. He continues:

> "Then what advantage has the Jew? What is the value of circumcision? Great, in every way. In the first place Jews were entrusted with the oracles of God. What if some of them were unfaithful? Will their faithlessness cancel the faithfulness of God? Certainly not! God must be true though every man living were a liar; for we read in Scripture, 'When thou speakest thou shalt be vindicated, and win the verdict when thou art on trial.'"
>
> Romans: 3.1-4

Paul further stresses the point that Jews, being favored by God, became the people with whom God chose to make his covenant. Among other things he gave his favored people the Scriptures (oracles) which included the promises he made to them as partners of the covenant. If Jews do not abide by their promises as partners of the covenant, that does not mean God will then not keep his promises. But, Paul makes it clear, Jews cannot claim that because God is just and faithful, and because his word will be kept, that they can sin as much as they want and that that will bring even more honor to God as he acts to forgive his people.

> "Another question: if our injustice serves to bring God's justice, what are we to say? Is it unjust of God (I speak of him in human terms) to bring retribution upon us? Certainly not! If God were unjust, how could he judge the world?
>
> "Again if the truth of God brings him all the greater honor because of my falsehood, why should I any longer

---

[72] "God said to Abraham, 'For your part, you must keep my covenant, you and your descendants after you, generation by generation. This is how you shall keep my covenant between myself and you and your descendents after you; circumcise yourselves, every male among you. You shall circumcise the flesh of your foreskin, and it shall be the sign of the covenant between us. (Genesis: 17. 9-11)

> be condemned as a sinner? Why not indeed 'do evil that
> good may come', as some libelously report me as saying?
> To condemn such men as these is surely no injustice."
>
> Romans: 3.5-8

Only twenty four to twenty eight years had passed since Jesus had been crucified, and the earliest Christian churches founded by Paul and Barnabas were only ten or twelve years old; yet already political infighting for leadership and control of those churches was threatening to tear them apart. Some of those who would undermine Paul have accused him of being antinomian, one who believed faith alone could assure one of salvation; that one's own personal behavior was unimportant as long as one has faith. This accusation could be an effective instrument in the hands of Judaizers insisting on the need to bring the church back under the Law. Paul is putting this accusation to rest in the above quoted verses.

At this point Paul adds passages from the Scriptures which he then follows with the comment:

> "Now all the words of the law are addressed, as we
> know, to those who are within the pale of the law, so that
> no one may have anything to say in self-defense, but the
> whole world may be exposed to the judgment of God.
> For (again from Scripture) 'no human being can be
> justified in the sight of God' for having kept the law; law
> brings only the consciousness of sin."
>
> Romans: 3.19-20

Here Paul has made an important point in his argument. He says it is not by being under the Law or even by keeping the Law that one's actions, one's life, will be "justified in the sight of God." The Law does not make a believer right or wrong. God gave the Law to humans so that they might realize just where they stood in relation to a perfect life. Thus, realizing their imperfections, humans can only be "justified in the sight of God" through faith in Jesus; which means faith in the Word he brought.

174

Paul is building his case that the church should encompass not only Jews, but also Gentiles. Justification (salvation) is not to be found through enslavement by the Law. Jesus liberated humans from such enslavement and now, Paul says, God's justice is available to all.

> "But now, quite independently of law, God's justice has been brought to light. The Law and the prophets both bear witness to it: it is God's way of righting wrong, effective through faith in Christ for all who have such faith – all, without distinction. For all alike have sinned, and are deprived of the divine splendor, and all are justified by God's free grace alone, through the act of liberation in the person of Christ Jesus. For God designed him to be the means of expiating sin by his sacrificial death, effective through faith. God meant by this to demonstrate his justice, because in his forbearance he had overlooked the sins of the past – to demonstrate his justice now in the present, showing that he is himself just and also justifies any man who puts faith in Jesus.
>
> "What room then is left for human pride? It is excluded. And on what principle? The keeping of the law would not exclude it, but faith does? For our argument is that a man is justified by faith apart from success in keeping the law.
>
> "Do you suppose God is the God of Jews alone? Is he not the God of the Gentiles also? Certainly, of Gentiles also, if it be true that God is one. And he will therefore justify both the circumcised in virtue of their faith, and the uncircumcised through their faith. Does this mean that we are using faith to undermine law? By no means: we are placing the law itself on a firmer footing."
>
> Romans: 3.21-31

Judaizers were insisting that Gentiles not under the Law (i.e. uncircumcised) could never be justified. Therefore, all Gentile churches must be brought under the Law of the Jews. This would give the Judaizers authority over all churches. By using the Scriptures (the Law, the prophets, and the writings) to support his point that God's justice is completely independent of the Law, Paul discredits this claim of the Judaizers.

Paul particularly emphasizes that there is no distinction between Jew and Gentile when God renders justice, because all have sinned and can only be justified by God. *The New English Bible* notes that Paul is saying: "God's way of dealing with sin (i.e. *righting wrong*) depends on the believer's trust (i.e. *faith*) in Christ."[73] Paul applies this to both Jew and Gentile.

ONLY THROUGH FAITH

Paul refers to those with faith as having been freed by Jesus "sacrificial death". This is the strongest reference made in any of his letters with regard to Jesus death and its role in demonstrating God's justice in forgiving the sins of those with faith in Jesus. Here again is a point at which the literal and figurative readings will differ.

Sacrifices made by figures in the Old Testament were made by placing the body, human or otherwise, on an altar and then killing the victim as a sacrifice to God. Literal reading of Paul's reference to Jesus' "sacrificial death" would have mankind's sins wiped out by the very act of dying. The slate was wiped clean.

Mark, collecting the oral traditions available at the time of Paul's death, describes Jesus' death as a sacrifice deliberately made by Jesus. With this in mind, a figurative reading of Paul's reference to the "sacrificial death" goes well beyond the idea of an immediate forgiveness of all the sins of humankind just because God has sacrificed his son. That kind of sacrifice would fall into the same category as the story of Abraham placing his son Isaac on an altar and preparing to make him a sacrifice to God. Such a sacrifice when offered was supposed to bring forth immediate results.

Paul's reference to the "sacrificial death" is later reflected in the Gospels of Mark and John in which Jesus knowingly gives his life because he believes it to be the only way for his message to resonate among the people beyond his lifetime. Like the parable of the vineyard, Jesus chose to be the "last messenger". A deliberate sacrifice of his life was made that the Word be not lost in time. "For God designed him to be the means of expiating sin by his sacrificial death, *effective through*

---

[73]   *The New English Bible, op. cit.* footnote p. 186.

faith." In those words a figurative reader sees Paul saying that all are justified "who put their faith in Jesus." *And Jesus was the messenger.* It is the message, the Word, in which people were to have faith through having faith in the messenger. Living by that Word, by the way of life taught by Jesus, would lead to justification. Again, Paul is insisting that faith is the key.[74]

Paul now adds still further arguments to support his thesis of justification through faith, rather than through the Law:

> "What, then, are we to say about Abraham, our ancestor in the natural line? If Abraham was justified by anything he had done, then he has a ground for pride. But he has no such ground before God; for what does the Scripture say? 'Abraham put his faith in God and that faith was counted to him as righteousness.' Now if a man does a piece of work, his wages are not 'counted' as a favor; they are paid as a debt. But if without any work to his credit he simply puts his faith in him who acquits the guilty, then his faith is indeed 'counted as righteousness'. In the same sense David speaks of the happiness of the man whom God 'counts' as just, apart from any specific acts of justice: 'Happy are they', he says, 'whose lawless deeds are forgiven, whose sins are buried away; happy is the man whose sins the Lord does not count against him.' Is this happiness confined to the circumcised, or is it for the uncircumcised also? Consider: we say, 'Abraham's faith was counted as righteousness'; in what circumstances was it so counted? Was he circumcised at the time, or not? He was not yet circumcised, but uncircumcised; and he later received the symbolic rite of circumcision as the hall-mark of the righteousness which faith had given him when he was still uncircumcised. Consequently, he is the father of all who have faith when uncircumcised, so that righteousness is 'counted' to them; and at the same time he is the father of such of the circumcised as do not rely upon their circumcision

---

[74] Centuries later, Paul's insistence that justification is through faith alone became the cornerstone of Martin Luther's theology, and thereby the foundation of the Reformation.

alone, but also walk in the footprints of the faith which our father Abraham had while he was uncircumcised.

"For it was not through law that Abraham, or his posterity, was given the promise that the world should be his inheritance, but through the righteousness that came from faith. For if those who hold by the law, and they alone are heirs, then faith is empty and the promise goes for nothing, because law can bring only retribution; but where there is no law there can be no breach of law. The promise was made on the ground of faith, in order that it might be a matter of sheer grace, and that it might be valid for all Abraham's posterity, not only for those who hold by the law, but for those who have the faith of Abraham. For he is the father of us all, as Scripture says: 'I have appointed you to be the father of many nations.' This promise, then, was valid before God, the God in whom he had put his faith, the God who makes the dead live and summons things that are not yet in existence as if they already were. When hope seemed hopeless, his faith was such that he became 'father of many nations', in agreement with the words which had spoken to him: 'Thus shall your descendants be.' Without any weakening of faith he contemplated his body, as good as dead (for he was about a hundred years old) and the deadness of Sarah's womb, and never doubted God's promise in unbelief, but, strong in faith, gave honor to God, in the firm conviction of his power to do what he had promised. And that is why Abraham's faith was 'counted to him as righteousness'.

"Those words were written, not for Abraham's sake alone, but for our sake too: it is to be 'counted' in the same way to us who have faith in the God who raised Jesus our Lord from the dead; for he was given up to death for our misdeeds, and raised to life to justify us."[75]

Romans: 4.1-25

---

[75]   Paul; has already explained in his earlier letters to other congregations that when he speaks of being raised from the dead, he is speaking of the "spiritual body" not the "physical body".

Paul has made the point that according to Scripture, Abraham, the father from whom all Jews were descendents, had been declared righteous by God after living a hundred years without having been circumcised. How then, the Romans are being asked, can Judaizers who are attacking Paul claim he is sinning by preaching that Gentiles not under the Law (uncircumcised) can attain salvation? *The New Oxford Bible* notes that Paul is telling the readers of his letter that: "The true descendants of Abraham are those who have faith in Christ, whether Jews or Gentiles. To them the benefits promised to Abraham belong."[76]   Paul, the well-educated former Pharisee is referring the readers of his letter to that passage in "Genesis" in which God credited Abraham with righteousness for believing in him (having faith) even though Abraham had no physical proof to justify that faith.

This fourth chapter of the Romans has concentrated on the one theme that justification is through faith, not deeds. In no way is justification dependent upon adherence to man-made rules; and that included rules made by churches. At the same time Paul is making certain that Romans reading his letter see that bringing the Gentile churches under the authority of the Law would be to deny that it is faith alone that can assure salvation. Such a move would negate the very teachings of Jesus who called for freedom from the slavery of the Law.

Paul is combining a theological lesson on faith with a plea for understanding how that supports a church for all those of faith. It lessens the impact of Paul's letter, if one sees only the call for faith or only the plea for understanding the need for this new religion to open its arms to all. Paul is melding the two. In a sense he is calling for his "gospel" to be practiced as well as learned.

Paul now moves further into his explanation of man's reconciliation with God through faith. A reader of Paul should never forget that Paul, like Jesus, has not rejected the scriptures of his people. Like Jesus he sees the need to move beyond the boundaries that were limiting the religion in which he was born and reared.

All humans have sinned. God is pure and righteous. God does not need to be reconciled to humans; it is they who need reconciliation with God. Yet through his love all are given the gift of the ability to achieve such reconciliation through faith. This becomes the opening theme of the fifth chapter of Paul's letter to the Roman

---

[76]   *The New Oxford Bible,* op. cit., footnote p. 213, New Testament

"Therefore, since we are justified by faith, we have peace with God through our Lord, Jesus Christ through whom we have obtained access to this grace in which we stand; and we boast (exult) in our hope of sharing the glory of God." And not only that, but we boast (exult) in our sufferings, knowing that suffering produces endurance, and character produces hope, and hope does not disappoint us, because God's love has been poured into our hearts through the Holy Spirit that has been given to us.

"For while we were still weak, at the right time Christ died for the ungodly. Indeed, rarely will anyone die for a righteous person – though perhaps for a good person someone might actually dare to die. But God proves his love for us in that while we still were sinners Christ died for us. Much more surely then, now that we have been justified by his blood, will we be saved through him from the wrath of God. For if while we were enemies, we were reconciled to God through the death of his Son, much more surely will we be saved by his life. But more than that, we even boast (exult) in God through whom we now have received reconciliation.

"Therefore, just as sin came into the world through one man, and death came through sin, and death spread to all because we have all sinned – sin was indeed in the world before the law, but sin is not reckoned when there is no law. Yet death exercised dominion from Adam to Moses, even over those whose sins were not like the transgressions of Adam, who is a type of the one who was to come."

Romans: 5.1-14

The stories of creation in the scriptures describe Adam and Eve as having been born "sinless." Read literally, their failure to obey is considered sin. In the perfect Eden, man and woman did not need to work. All they needed was at their fingertips. They could live *forever* in that paradise as long as they never ate the fruit of a certain tree. That fruit was the knowledge of good and evil. Knowing no evil they would live forever. When they took that forbidden fruit, and had knowledge of evil as well as good, they were expelled into the outer world where they lost their immortality, becoming mere mortals awaiting eventual death.

Read figuratively, all the tribulations that have beset humans from their first presence on earth are manmade. Knowing evil as well as good, humans have failed to live the life God had planned for them. They have failed God. Their lives are filled with problems and pain they have brought upon themselves.

It is through faith in Jesus and the word he carried that humans might once more achieve that all important inner peace. Sin existed long before Moses and the Law. Then came the Law, but sin did not disappear. The Law did not bring peace with God (reconciliation). It was Jesus, Paul says, who brought the means for that reconciliation. He died to make certain his message of the path to reconciliation with God was heard.

Continuing to use Adam and Eve to make his point Paul says that from the time of Adam and Eve until the coming of Jesus men and women have died a final and complete death. Now, through their faith in God's messenger, Jesus, and in the message he brought to them, men and women have become reconciled and the "dominion of death" can be brought to an end. Having laid the groundwork, Paul is now ready to explain the rewards a loving God is bestowing upon those with faith.

THE REWARDS

Death is final; as Paul uses the word, it is the end. The "dominion of death," he explains, had reigned since the expulsion from Eden. Through Jesus and faith in the message he brought, death was no longer the end. Men and women could be resurrected. At this point it is well to remember that Paul has in earlier letters pointed out that it is not the physical body, but the spiritual body that is resurrected.

"But God's act of grace is out of all proportion to Adam's wrongdoing. For if the wrongdoing of that one man brought death upon so many, its effect is vastly exceeded by the grace of God and the gift that came to so many by the grace of the one man, Jesus Christ. And again the gift of God is not to be compared in its effect with that of one man's sin; for the judicial action, following upon the one offence, issued in a verdict of condemnation, but the act of grace, following upon so many misdeeds, issued in a verdict of acquittal . For if by the wrongdoing of that one man death established its reign, through a single sinner, much more shall those receive in far greater measure God's grace, and his gift of righteousness, live and reign through the one man, Jesus Christ.

"It follows, then, that as the issue of one misdeed was condemnation for all men, so the issue of one just act is acquittal and life for all men. For as through the disobedience of the one man the many were made sinners, so through the obedience of the one man the many will be made righteous. "Law intruded into this process to multiply law-breaking. But where sin thus multiplied, grace immeasurably exceeded it, in order that, as sin established its reign by way of death, so God's grace might establish its reign of righteousness, and issue in eternal life through Jesus Christ our Lord."

Romans: 5.15-21

Paul refers to Adam as a man: "For as through the disobedience of the one man the many were made sinners." But he also refers to Jesus as a man; "…so through the obedience of the one man the many will be made righteous." Literally, this can be interpreted as a miracle. The coming of Jesus and his crucifixion were God's way of saving mankind.

A figurative interpretation of Paul's passage above sees all humans being made righteous (saved), not by the mere presence of Jesus, but by his obedience. He is obeying God in carrying God's Word to the people; opening their eyes and ears; and teaching them how to live according to the plan God had for humans. It is now the peoples' turn to be obedient, and to live according to the way of life described by Jesus in his teachings, and so to be reconciled with God. The

182

messenger has been sent. The message has been delivered. Salvation is now the responsibility of each recipient of the message.

In the preceding chapters of this letter to the Romans, Paul has pounded home the point that faith is the key to the Kingdom of Heaven, to inner peace - and to salvation. At this point, whether reading literally or figuratively, one should keep in mind that some of Paul's bitterest critics have been accusing him of antinomianism, that belief that an individual could sin as much as he or she wished as long as that individual had faith. Some even twisted his teaching to the point where he was being accused of saying one should sin as much as possible, because in this way she or he would be the recipient of more of God's grace. In opening the next part of his letter, now referred to as the sixth chapter, Paul firmly refutes those critics.

"What are we to say, then? Shall we persist in sin, so that there may be all the more grace? No, no! We died to sin: how can we live in it any longer? Have you forgotten that when we were baptized into union with Christ Jesus we were baptized into his death? By baptism we were buried with him, and lay dead, in order that, as Christ was raised from the dead in the splendor of the Father, so also we might set our feet on the new path of life.

"For if we have become incorporate with him in a death like his, we shall also be one with him in a resurrection like his. We know that the man we once were has been crucified with Christ, for the destruction of the sinful self so that we may no longer be the slaves of sin, since a dead man is no longer answerable for his sin. But if we thus died with Christ, we believe that we believe that we shall also come to life with him. We know that Christ, once raised from the dead, is never to die again: he is no longer under the dominion of death. For in dying as he died, he died in sin, once for all, and in living as he lives, he lives to God. In the same way you must regard yourselves as dead to sin and alive to God, in union with the Christ Jesus."

Romans: 6.1-11

The death to which Paul refers to at this point is the death of sin. Upon being baptized one becomes a partner of Christ. Sin dies at that time and one enters a new life, living as Jesus would live. Just as Jesus was "raised from the dead... so also we might set our feet on the new path of life."

Therefore, Paul continues, we must no longer let sin rule our lives. It is up to us to rule our bodies and not permit them to respond to the material temptations of the "flesh." But if humans are no longer under the Law, but under God's grace, can we not sin? Paul answers his own question:

> "By no means! Do you not know that if you present yourselves to anyone as obedient slaves, you are slaves of the one you obey, either of sin, which leads to death or of obedience, which leads to righteousness? But thanks be to God that you, having once been slaves of sin, have become obedient from the heart to the form of teaching to which you were entrusted, and that you, having been set free from sin have become slaves of righteousness."
>
> Romans: 6.15-18

Paul explains that he is speaking in terms that could be easily understood. Slavery was a bond so common at that time that everyone realized its implications. Everyone understood that a man or woman could not serve two masters.

Realizing that what he has said would be challenged by those who would ask why the new Christians were "no longer under the law, but under the grace of God" Paul opens his seventh chapter with an answer.

> "Do you not know, brothers and sisters – for I am speaking to those who know the law – that the law is binding on a person only during that person's lifetime? Thus a married woman is bound by the law to her husband as long as he lives; but if her husband dies, she is discharged from the law concerning the husband. Accordingly, she will be called an adulteress if she lives with another man while her husband is alive. But if her husband dies, she is free from that law, and if she marries another man, she is not an adulteress.

184

> "In the same way, my friends, you have died to the law
> through the body of Christ, so that you may belong to
> another, to him who has been raised from the dead in
> order that we may bear fruit for God. While we were
> living in the flesh, our sinful passions, aroused by the law,
> who were at work in our members to bear fruit for death.
> But now we are discharged from the law, dead to that
> which held us captive, so that we are slaves not under the
> old written code but in the new life of the Spirit."
>
> Romans: 7.1-6

Baptized, and following the path laid down by Jesus, Christians have died to the law (dead to that which held them captive). At this point Paul balances his criticism of the law. By no means, he says, is the law sin. It is holy, just, and good. However, sin uses whatever opportunity it finds, and though the law be good, sin uses it. People (he uses the example of himself) are the victims. Sin is defined by law, and becomes a temptation once it is recognized.[77] The law is good, but it is unfortunately used by sin as a means to enslave people. Just as the authors of the other gospels would later personify worldly temptations as Satan, so Paul has given the image of sin a personality. As a teaching method this makes it easier for him to enable the Roman recipients of his letter to see his point.

> "For we know that the law is spiritual; but I am of the
> flesh, sold into slavery under sin. I do not understand
> my own actions. For I do not do what I want, but I do
> the very thing I hate. Now if I do what I do not want, I
> agree that the law is good. But in fact it is no longer I that
> do it, but the sin that dwells within me. For I know
> nothing good dwells within me, that is, in my flesh. I can
> will what is right, but I cannot do it. For I do not do the
> good I want, but the evil I do not want is what I do.

---

[77] In Paul's earlier reference to Adam and Eve, he emphasized the complete purity of their lives until they took the fruit which gave them knowledge of good and evil. Only then, when aware of evil were they tempted by it. Here Paul is giving the law somewhat the same role as the forbidden fruit.

> Now if I do what I do not want, it is no longer I that do it, but the sin that dwells within me.
>
> "So I find it to be a law that when I want to do what is good, evil lies close at hand. For I delight in the law of God in my inmost self, but I see in my (bodily) members another law at war with the law of my mind, making me captive to the law of sin that dwells in my members. Wretched man that I am! Who will rescue me from this body of death? Thanks be to God through Jesus Christ our Lord!
>
> "So then, with my mind I am a slave to God, but in my flesh I am a slave to the law of sin."
>
> Romans: 7.14-25

Paul has portrayed himself as one who unwillingly sins. People may have sinned, but they resent and resist preaching that tells them they are wrong. By saying he himself is a captive of sin Paul is making his message acceptable. He is saying to the Romans that we all are sinners; I am no different than you. Sin is the dominion of death. Therefore the body that sins is already dead. But, there is a way to freedom from that slavery. It is by turning to God, through the message brought by Jesus.

Paul's earlier letters to the Corinthians made clear that he did not believe in physical resurrection. Readers will recall his description of the spiritual body as separate from the physical body. Now, at this point in his letter to the Romans, Paul refers to the body (physical) that sins and is therefore dead. However, as he explains, the spirit of those who have accepted the message carried by Jesus is saved. This is the means by which God gave life to the spirit through Jesus.

> "The conclusion of the matter is this: there is no condemnation for those who are united with Christ Jesus, because in Christ Jesus the life-giving law of the Spirit has set you free from the law of sin and death. What the law could never do, because our lower nature robbed it of all potency, God has done: by sending his

> own Son in a form like that of our own sinful nature, and as a sacrifice for sin, he has passed judgment against sin within that very nature, so that the commandment of the law may find fulfillment in us, whose conduct, no longer under the control of our lower nature, is directed by the Spirit.
>
> "Those who live on the level of our lower nature have their outlook formed by it, and that spells death; but those who live on the level of the Spirit have the spiritual outlook, and that is life and peace. For the outlook of the lower nature is enmity with God; it is not subject to the law of God; indeed it cannot be: those who live on such a level cannot possibly please God.
>
> "But that is not how you live. You are on the spiritual level, if only (since) God's Spirit dwells within you; and if a man does not possess the Spirit of Christ, he (does not belong to him) is no Christian.[78] But if Christ is dwelling within you, then although the body is a dead thing because you have sinned, yet the spirit is life itself because you have been justified. Moreover, if the Spirit of him who raised Jesus from the dead dwells within you, then the God who raised Christ Jesus from the dead will also give new life to your mortal bodies through his indwelling Spirit."
>
> Romans: 8.1-12

Paul uses his point that Jesus was resurrected spiritually, not physically, to explain that in like manner the spirit of each human who is justified will be resurrected. From Paul's perspective, Adam and Eve having lost their immortality when driven from Eden faced the eventual death of their physical bodies. As a result, the body of every human would thereafter be mortal. However, *The Spirit* (that bit of God within each individual) assures resurrection of the individual spirit of anyone who is saved, just as it did with Jesus. It is up to the individual to live

---

[78] This passage, "Romans: 8. 1-12," is drawn from *The New English Bible*. The wording in the parentheses is drawn from *The New Oxford Bible*.

either on the "spiritual level," by accepting Jesus' teachings, or to live entirely on the "level of our lower nature." For Paul nothing is automatic. The path to salvation is a path one may choose; or ignore, if one chooses the temptations of the "lower level." Paul wants his audience to accept what he considers a most important fact; namely that God leaves the choice up to each individual.

Paul is still in the process of introducing himself and his theology to the Romans at this point. He has had his problems with Judaizers and others who would place the religious Law of the Jews, or the rituals and practices of the new Christian churches, above the teachings of Jesus. The passages we have just read carry a second message. Paul has spoken of faith and of salvation through faith. He has said that only by living the spiritual life as Jesus taught can one be justified (saved). Therefore, the implication is that *the first priority of the church* is carrying that message to all people. That, quite simply, was the purpose of the church as Paul saw it. To him, Jesus died to keep his message alive; in no way expecting to be worshipped for carrying God's message.

Paul continues on this theme, speaking of those who are moved by *The Spirit* as thus becoming God's children and thereby "fellow-heirs" with Jesus. By giving up the lower nature we escape its slavery and become adopted "sons" of God. The entire universe, not just man, was created by God. Therefore, Paul says, the entire universe is awaiting liberation from the "shackles of mortality[79]."

Expanding further on this theme throughout the rest of the eighth chapter of "Romans", Paul concludes with a strong statement of his belief:

> "For I am convinced that there is nothing in death or life, in the realm of spirits or superhuman powers, in the world as it is or the world as it shall be, in the forces of the universe, in height or depths – nothing in all creation that can separate us from the love of God in Christ Jesus our Lord."
>
> Romans: 8.38-39

---

[79] The terminology in this paragraph is from *The New English Bible*.

CHAPTER 13

PAUL'S LETTER TO THE ROMANS

Part Two - Chapters 9-16

Matthew, Mark, and Luke wrote as though they were actually chronicling the teachings of Jesus and were describing them and the events surrounding him in an exact time frame. This may give the literal reader the impression that the gospels were meant to be an actual history of the short period of Jesus' ministry, even when gospel writers' inserted their own parables as though they were actually a part of that "history".

Whereas these writers of the gospels were presenting Jesus' teachings in the form of a chronicle, or brief history, Paul, writing well before the first gospel was penned makes no attempt to describe the life of Jesus. Yet, as we earlier noted, "Romans" is considered to be the best presentation of his theology. Some even refer to the first eight chapters as Paul's Gospel. He has been speaking of faith and the proper role of humans in God's plan and, by implication, the role of the church. With the opening of what is now known as the ninth chapter of the Letter to the Romans, Paul turns to the relationship of God to the Israelites. Who really are the people chosen by God?

* * * * * * * * * * * *

"I am speaking the truth in Christ – I am not lying; my conscience confirms it by the Holy Spirit – I have great sorrow and unceasing anguish in my heart. For I could wish that I myself were accursed and cut off from Christ for the sake of my people, my kindred according to the flesh. They are Israelites, and to them belong the adoption, the glory, the covenants, the giving of the law, the worship, and the promises; to them belong the patriarchs, and from them, according to the flesh, comes the Messiah, who is over all, God blessed forever. Amen

"It is not as though the word of God has failed. For not all Israelites truly belong to Israel, and not all of Abraham's children are his true descendants; but 'It is through Isaac that the descendants shall be named for you.' This means not all children of the flesh who are children of God, but the children of promise are counted as descendants."

Romans: 9.1-9

Having stressed that he is a fellow Israelite, Paul describes the relationship Israelites' had with God. They are, he says, by adoption the children of God who is always with them. However, not all Israelites are descendants covered by the promise made by God. The reader may recall Paul's earlier comment on this interpretation made in his letter to the Galatians.

"Tell me now, you who are so anxious to be under law, will you not listen to what the Law says? It is written there that Abraham had two sons, one by his slave and the other by his freeborn wife. The slave woman's son was born in the course of nature, the free woman's through God's promise. This is an allegory. The two women stand for two covenants. The one bearing children into slavery is the covenant that comes from Mount Sinai: that is Hagar. Sinai is a mountain in Arabia and it represents the Jerusalem of today, for she and her

190

> children are in slavery. But the heavenly Jerusalem is the
> free woman she is our mother. For Scripture says,
> 'Rejoice, O barren woman who never bore a child; break
> into a shout of joy, you who never knew a mother's
> pangs; for the deserted wife shall have more children
> than she who lives with the husband.
>
> "And you, my brothers, like Isaac, are children of
> God's promise. But just as in those days the natural born
> son persecuted the spiritual son, so it is today. But what
> does Scripture say? 'Drive out the slave-woman and her
> son, for the son of the slave shall not share the
> inheritance with the free woman's son.' You see, then,
> my brothers, we are no slave-woman's children; our
> mother is the free woman. Christ set us free, to be free
> men. Stand firm, then, and refuse to be tied to the yoke
> of slavery again.
>
> "Mark my words: I, Paul, say to you that if you receive
> circumcision Christ will do you no good at all. Once
> again, you can take it from me that every man who
> receives circumcision is under obligation to keep the
> entire law. When you seek to be justified by way of the
> law, your relation with Christ is completely severed: you
> have fallen out of the domain of God's grace. For to us,
> our hope of attaining that righteousness which we eagerly
> await is the work of the Spirit through faith. If we are in
> union with Christ Jesus circumcision makes no difference
> at all, nor does the want of it; the only thing that counts
> is faith active in love."
>
> Galatians: 4.19-31 and 5.1-6

So, Paul says, not all Israelites, not all descendants of Abraham are included in God's promise. Only those who are descendants of Abraham through Isaac are the remnant to be covered.[80] He then adds further quotes from the prophets to make his point.

---

[80] For further references to the Scriptures to which Paul is referring see footnotes in *The New English Bible,* p.193, New Testament; and (continued)

"Such vessels are we, whom he has called from among the Gentiles as well as Jews, as it says in the Book of Hosea: 'Those who are not my people I will call My People, and the unloved nation I will call My Beloved. For in the very place where they were told "you are no people of mine", they shall be called Sons of the living God.' But Isaiah makes this proclamation about Israel: 'Though the Israelites be countless as the sands of the sea, only a remnant shall be saved; for the Lord's sentence on the land will be summary and final"; as also he said previously, If the Lord of Hosts had not left us the mere germ of a nation, we should have become like Sodom, and no better than Gomorrah.

"Then what are we to say? That Gentiles who made no effort after righteousness, nevertheless achieved it, a righteousness based on faith; whereas Israel made great efforts after a law of righteousness, but never attained to it. Why was this? Because their efforts were not based on faith, but (as they supposed) on deeds. They fell over the 'stone' mentioned in Scripture: 'Here I lay in Zion a stone to trip over, a rock to stumble against; but he who has faith in him will not be put to shame'."

Romans: 9. 24-33

Thus, Paul explains for his readers in Rome, most of my kindred, my brother Jews, have been lost while Gentiles with faith will be saved. Even as he expresses great sorrow for his lost brothers, he deplores their lack of understanding of the role of faith in any relationship with God. To him they have substituted the Law for faith. He makes it quite clear that he has no quarrel with his fellow Jews, only pity and sorrow, for he does not wish to have the Romans believe he is carrying on some kind of vendetta against all Jews because of his problems with Judaizers that he described in the earlier chapters of his

---

The New Oxford Bible, p.219, New Testament.. We should not lose sight of the fact that Paul, as not only a well educated Pharisee, but also as one who studied the Scriptures at length while preparing to become a rabbi, would be far more familiar with them than were most of his fellow Jews.

letter. This tends to emphasize to his Roman readers that critics with whom he is in sharp disagreement, even within the Jewish community, are small in number.

Chapter Ten continues Paul's explanation that in God's eyes "there is no distinction between Jew and Greek, because the same Lord is Lord of all."

> "Brothers, my deepest desire and my prayer to God is for their salvation. To their zeal for God I can testify; but it is an ill-informed zeal. For they ignore God's way of righteousness, and try to set up their own, and therefore they have not submitted themselves to God's righteousness. For Christ ends the law and brings righteousness for everyone who has faith."
>
> Romans: 10.1-4

In continuing to contrast the Law of Moses with the righteousness that comes by faith, Paul once more lays emphasis on faith as the heart of the message brought by Jesus.

> "But not all have responded to the good news. For Isaiah says, 'Lord, who has believed our message?' We conclude that faith is awakened by the message, and that the message that awakens it comes through the word of Christ.
>
> "But, I ask, can it be that they never heard it? Of course they did: their voice has sounded all over the earth , and their words to the bounds of the inhabited world.' But, I ask again, can it be that Israel failed to recognize the message? In reply, I first cite Moses, who says, 'I will use a nation that is no nation to stir your envy, and a foolish nation to rouse your anger.' But Isaiah is still more daring: 'I was found', he says, 'by those who were not looking for me; I was clearly shown to those who never asked about me'; while to Israel he says, 'All day long I have stretched my hands to an unruly and defiant people."
>
> Romans: 10.18-21

While proceeding along this vein Paul assures his readers that God has not turned away from his people.

> "I ask then, has God rejected his people? I cannot believe it! I am an Israelite myself, of the stock of Abraham, of the tribe of Benjamin. No! God has not rejected the people which he acknowledged of old as his own."
>
> Romans: 11.1-2

Referring to the story of Elijah in the Scriptures, Paul further expands this theme.

> "What follows? What Israel sought, Israel has not achieved, but the selected few have achieved it. The rest were made blind to the truth, exactly as it stands written: God brought upon them a numbness of spirit; he gave them blind eyes and deaf ears, and so it is still."
>
> * * * * * * * * * * * *
>
> "Now I am speaking to you Gentiles. Inasmuch then as I am an apostle to the Gentiles. I glorify my ministry in order to make my people jealous, and thus to save some of them. For if their rejection is the reconciliation of the world, what will their acceptance be but life from the dead! If the part of the dough offered as first fruits is holy, then the whole batch is holy; and if the root is holy, then the branches are holy.
>
> "But if some of the branches were broken off, and you, a wild olive shoot, were grafted in their place to share each root of the olive tree, do not boast over the branches. If you do boast, remember that it is not you that support the root, but the root that supports you. You will say, 'Branches were broken off so that I might be grafted in.'

> That is true. They were broken off because of their
> unbelief, but you stand only through faith. So do not
> become proud, but stand in awe."
>
> Romans: 11.7-8, 13-20[81]

The reader finds here a passage important beyond its immediate message in which Paul has said rejection of the teachings of Jesus by Israelites is actually beneficial. "God has hardened their hearts for a loving purpose, namely, that the Gentiles have an opportunity to hear and receive the gospel."[82] Now that Gentiles are accepting the teachings of Jesus, Paul says, this may make Israelites "jealous" and thereby cause some to join Gentiles who have accepted the Word as brought by Jesus. This he follows with a warning to Gentiles that they in turn not believe themselves superior just because they have been given the opportunity to be grafted to the olive tree. You received that opportunity because of your faith, not because you have earned it through anything you have done.

That part of the message is self-explanatory. However, there is something further to be noted in this passage. Remember, Mark would write the first gospel after Paul died. Matthew and Luke would later build their gospels on what they drew from Mark. A literal reading of the stories in those gospels leaves a reader believing there was a series of physical miracles. But, here in Paul's letter to the Romans we find clues as to how Mark used miracles of healing and the story of the olive tree as parts of parables, not as historical fact.

Paul refers to those who are "blind" and "deaf" *to the truth*. He speaks of the acceptance of the message of Jesus as giving life to the *spiritually* dead. He speaks of the olive tree as being Israel; dead branches referring to Israelites who rejected the message. Mark will bring together these teachings of Paul and other early missionaries into written form for the first time. Mark and later Matthew and Luke, writing in parables, do not go into detail as to what they mean when in their parables they refer to blindness, deafness, death from which people rise, and the olive tree. After all these are parables. Paul, however, has offered an explanation of what he means by one being

---

[81]   Verses 7-8 of this quote are drawn from *The New English Bible;* verses 13-20 from *The New Oxford Bible.*

[82]   *The New Oxford Bible*, footnote, p. 222 New Testament.

blind, deaf, or dead, and his use of the figurative olive tree. He draws from the prophets and other passages of the Scriptures wherein these same terms were used, and which therefore were familiar to the people of his time. What was written in midrash style in the centuries before Jesus, or read as a New Testament parable two thousand years ago, has often been accepted as historical fact through the centuries that followed.

When Mark presents the parables of the healing of the blind, the deaf, the unclean, and the giving of life to the spiritually dead, he has the teachings of Paul upon which to draw. Here in "Romans" is a clear cut example of what Paul meant by those terms and what, therefore, they meant to Mark and later to those who drew from Mark to write their own gospels. We also see Paul's theology playing an important role in the framing of the parables of Mark, Matthew, and Luke.

CHRISTIANITY IN ACTION

With the beginning of the twelfth chapter of his letter to the Romans Paul shifts to a new theme, namely: How to live as a Christian.

> "Therefore, my brothers, I implore you by God's mercy to offer your very selves to him: a living sacrifice, dedicated and fit for his acceptance, the worship offered by mind and heart. Adapt yourselves no longer to the pattern of the present world, but let your minds be remade and your whole nature thus transformed. Then you will be able to discern the will of God, and to know what is good, acceptable, and perfect."
>
> Romans: 12.1-2

Whatever you do, Paul says, do it as God would have you do it. You have been given gifts of differing talents and abilities. Live as God would have you live and use those God-given abilities to create the world God would have you create.

> "The gifts we possess differ as they are allotted to us by God's grace, and must be exercised accordingly: the gift of inspired utterance, for example, in proportion to a man's faith; or the gift of administration, in administration. A teacher should employ his gift in teaching, and the one who has the gift of stirring speech should use it to stir his hearers. If you give to charity, give with all your heart; if you are a leader, exert yourself to lead; if you are helping others in distress, do it cheerfully."
>
> Romans: 12.6-8

The remainder of the twelfth chapter exhorts believers to love one another; to forego revenge; to "call down blessings – not curses" on those who would do you evil. It is a message of love; of a God of love rather than a God of vengeance. But, once more there is a shift in instructions as Paul begins his thirteenth chapter.

> "Let every person be subject to the governing authorities; for there is no authority except from God, and those authorities that exist have been instituted by God. Therefore, whoever resists authority resists what God has appointed, and those who resist will incur judgment. For rulers are not a terror to good conduct, but to bad. Do you wish to have no fear of the authority? Then do what is good, and you will receive its approval; for it is God's servant for your good."
>
> Romans: 13.1-4

Describing the role of authority in executing God's judgment on wrongdoers Paul adds the following:

> "Pay to all what is due them – taxes to whom taxes are due, revenue to whom revenue is due, respect to whom respect is due, honor to whom honor is due.
>
> "Owe no one anything, except love one another; for one who loves another has fulfilled the law. The

> commandments, 'You shall not commit adultery; You
> shall not murder; You shall not steal; You shall not
> covet'; and other commandments are summed up in this
> word, 'Love your neighbor as yourself. 'Love does no
> wrong to a neighbor; therefore, love is the fulfilling Of
> the law."
>
> Romans: 13.7-10

This is an interesting passage. Paul had great respect for the
Roman Empire. He admired the degree of orderliness it had brought
to society. Though a Jew, he took pride in having been granted Roman
citizenship, which stood him in good stead when arrested in Jerusalem
on false charges, and brought about his release from prison in
Caesarea.[83]

As a Pharisee, Paul would have been deeply concerned about
rebellions and warring between national groups that would threaten the
orderliness of the Empire. He could not help but be distressed by
general disorderliness, banditry, and abuse of neighbors. He believed
strongly in his religion, but also realized it could never be the unifying
force that could bring people to live together in peace and prosperity;
but as we have noted, he saw in Jesus' teachings something that could
unify disparate elements of the Roman world. This could not be done
in the name of a Messiah of a small nation. Yet, if all people could live
as Jesus taught was the way to achieve God's purpose, people could live
together in peace and be blessed with happiness.

An orderly state, governed by authorities whose duty it was to
assure that orderliness was, in Paul's opinion, a necessary component of
a peaceful unified world. People should realize it required revenues
(taxes) to fund such governing authority.

---

[83]   Falsely accused of bringing a Gentile into the inner court of the Temple, Paul
was arrested. To protect him from mobs threatening to drag him from the prison
he was sent to Caesarea where he spent two years in prison. When authorities were
about to send him back to Jerusalem for trial he appealed directly to Caesar, as was
the right of a Roman citizen, and was released. In all of his travels his Roman
citizenship stood him in good stead. Without the status and protection afforded
him as a Roman citizen there is little doubt that he could never have been able to
travel and preach to the point where he was able to become the father of the
Christian church.

Paul had said that there was one God; Lord not only of the Israelites, but of the Greeks and all other Gentiles. Having made the case for the necessity of an authority to assure the welfare of the good and the punishment of the bad, he then moved on to the role of love. Having concluded his argument in support of authority, he then added his strong statement that love assures that one has fulfilled the law. One who loves has no fear of authority because, if one loves his neighbors, he will be treating them with respect and will be living a righteous life. Only those who ignore love, and choose to relate to others in ways that hurt or take advantage of them, need to be kept in line by "governing authorities." If all people lived by the word, "Love your neighbor", authority would not be a burden; it might not even be needed, for the Law would be fulfilled.

Eight of the Ten Commandments are negative statements. They direct that one "Should not" worship another God, nor covet, nor steal, nor otherwise commit a sin. These are directives to remain neutral. "Do not" do certain things. They require no action, only abstention. In contrast, Paul emphasizes the positive in the directive "Love they neighbor" for it requires one *to do rather than to not do*.

Having pointed out that a Christian must love all fellow humans; Paul goes still further, stressing the need for Christians to refrain from judgment of other humans. The strong should never despise the weak. People are not to be judged by their habits or their customs, or by their failure to observe customs of others.

> "Let us therefore no longer pass judgment on one another, but resolve instead never to place a stumbling block or hindrance in the way of another. I know and am persuaded in the Lord Jesus that nothing is unclean in itself; but it is unclean for anyone who thinks it unclean."
> Romans: 14.13-14

Never cause another to stumble by what you do. "Let us then pursue what makes for peace and for mutual upbuilding." (Romans 14: 19) Hold always to what you believe. Keep your faith. Do not let others destroy it; but do not judge others who differ from you. Judge only yourself. "The faith you have, have as your own conviction before God." (14. 22)

As his letter begins to draw to a close, Paul will once more call upon Roman Christians to remember to serve others.

> "We who are strong ought to put up with the failings of the weak, and not to please ourselves. Each of us must please our neighbor for the good purpose of building up the neighbor. For Christ did not please himself; but as it is written, 'The insults of those who insult you have fallen on me.' For whatever was written in former days was written for our instruction, so that by steadfastness and by the encouragement of the scriptures we might have hope. May the God of stead-fastness and encouragement grant you to live in harmony with one another, in accordance with Christ Jesus, so that together you may with one voice glorify the God and Father of our Lord Jesus Christ.
>
> "Welcome one another, therefore, just as Christ has welcomed you, for the glory of God. For I tell you that Christ has become a servant of the circumcised on behalf of the truth of God in order that he might confirm the promises given to the patriarchs, and in order that the Gentiles might glorify God for his mercy."
>
> Romans: 15.1-9

Some ancient texts of Paul's letter to the Romans did not include the last two chapters (15-16) which appear in the *New Testament* as compiled later in Rome. We do not know the reason for this, although the last part of the fifteenth chapter offers no further theological insight. Instead, Paul explains to the Romans why he has been traveling and preaching as he has.

The last chapter is only an extended formal closing of his letter, and a closing benediction.

* * * * * * * * * * * *

It is unfortunate that Paul never left a written record of what he knew about the life of Jesus or that, if he did, it was not included by those charged with the task of creating the *New Testament*. Undoubtedly, having spent time with James, the brother of Jesus, and with Peter who had been Jesus' "rock", Paul would have been quite familiar with what they knew about Jesus. However, he may have seen no need to present a biography or a chronicle of Jesus' travels and teaching. After all, over the years he would have passed on to his congregations those "oral traditions" others had passed on to him. It would be left to Mark to put those oral traditions in written form as the first gospel to be written.

Paul's letters were written to "his" churches as instructions, warnings, and commendations, or as an introduction to his theology as in the case of the letter to the Romans. As these were churches he had founded, he would already have brought them the stories about Jesus as well as Jesus' message. He would have seen no reason to repeat in his letters what he had already taught them of the life of the messenger. His letters concentrated instead on his interpretation of the message.

PAUL'S LEGACY

As we have noted, Jesus never intended to start a new religion. His efforts were directed toward reforming the religion of the Jews. Repeatedly he referred to Israel as God's messenger; the messenger that had failed to carry out God's will. His frequent reference to eyes that did not see and ears that did not hear repeated the warnings of prophets in preceding centuries. His work, as he described it, was aimed to open the eyes and ears of the people of Israel, and to make Israel truly God's messenger carrying the Word to the rest of the world.

Jesus wanted to retain that high level of morality so important among Jews. As we have seen, even the Gentiles throughout pagan Greece and the Middle East were attracted to the high level of morality associated with Jewish congregations. Jesus strove to convince his countrymen that this moral strength would not be lost, if they freed themselves from man-made religious restrictions. In parable after parable he taught that the Kingdom of God could never be reached by even the most careful observance of the Law. It could only be achieved through faith, and living a life directed by that faith.

Like Jesus, Paul respected those high standards of morality that were such an important part of the Jewish religion. But, Paul wanted that morality to become a part of the life of the Gentiles, and needed to assure them and the Jews that this morality did not depend upon man-made rules. Paul is devoting the last half of his life to creating a church that would free its members from the yoke of man-made law and yet would retain all the good he saw in the religion of the Jews; while also adding Jesus' teachings about finding the peace of the Kingdom of Heaven. Gentiles and Jews would share much, but would part ways on these two crucial issues.

Paul could not help but hope that this new religion would unite its varied believers as it grew, until constant wars and revolts of various ethnic groups and clans no longer threatened to splinter the Roman Empire. This was to be a religion embracing all Gentiles and which, Paul hoped, would eventually draw Jews within that embrace. It might be described as a sort of reformed Jewish religion open to all non-Jews; the Jewish religion reformed as Jesus had tried to reform it.

Beginning from scratch, as it were, Paul, Barnabas and other early missionaries and preachers of the gospel created Christianity. Paul built the church, but that church would have been but a hollow vessel were it not for the new message which brought it into being and which became its *raison d'etre*. And that message was in large part molded by Paul and fellow preachers and passed down in what became known as the first Gospel, the Gospel According to Mark. It was a message they created based on salient points of Jesus' teaching.

The growth of the mystery religions, with their belief in the virgin birth and the physical resurrection of their messenger or founder, created a growing pressure on the new Christian churches. Local church leaders in responding to that pressure began turning Paul's churches into churches worshipping the messenger. Jesus, who saw himself as the humble servant of God, would have abhorred such worship. He could never have thought of himself or God as being some kind of oriental potentate seated, scepter in hand, on a throne overlooking a sea of worshippers.

Paul would preach of resurrection; though making it clear he was speaking of spiritual, not physical, resurrection. However, throughout his life he never left any evidence that he believed in a virgin birth. Mark, bringing together the oral traditions that had largely developed after the crucifixion and were the basis of Paul's teachings, shows no awareness or acceptance of the stories of a virgin birth in the early church. This would become a deep concern of the church in the years after Paul's death when the pressures and competition of the mystery religions threatened to overwhelm the new Christian congregations.

Christianity would develop after Paul into something considerably different than what Paul had intended when he began his missionary work. The beginnings of this dramatic change will be evident when the reader moves on to the Gospels of Matthew and Luke. But, when moving on to those Gospels, readers should not forget that those Gospels could never have been written were it not for the religion established by Paul and his co-workers almost a half century earlier.

CHAPTER 14

MATTHEW

We do not know who wrote *The Gospel According to Matthew*, nor do we know just why it was ascribed to Matthew. Some biblical historians suggest the author may have included sayings of Jesus supposedly collected by the disciple Matthew, and that this might account for a later anonymous author being called Matthew. In our reading of the *New Testament* we will refer to the author as Matthew.

We do know that the author who wrote this gospel was deeply concerned about the survival of the church. As a Jewish convert to Christianity, he was particularly alarmed by the threat posed by hard-line Judaizers within the church. By all indications in his writings he was well-educated and well-versed in the religion of the Jews. In his gospel his concern for the church's survival is obvious, although he never puts it in so many words.

Matthew's frequent reference to Pharisees indicates his concern that these scholarly laymen were, through their teachings, whittling away at the foundations of Christianity. He definitely was writing for Jews who had already joined the Christian church or who could become converts. He uses his knowledge of the prophets and the sacred writings of the Jews to demonstrate that Jesus fulfilled the role of the long-awaited Jewish Messiah. In this he contrasts sharply with Mark who, like Paul, down-played the label "Messiah".

As we have noted, Paul and Mark realized portraying Jesus as a Jewish Messiah would put an end to their hope of building a universal religion encompassing all nations. Matthew, on the other hand, knew he had to portray Jesus as all the *Old Testament* foretold about a Messiah, if he were to "open the ears and eyes" of Jewish congregations to the message of Jesus. Whether reading the *New Testament* literally or figuratively readers should always keep in mind the intended audience of each gospel writer, and how that would have influenced the nature of his message.

MATTHEW INTRODUCES JESUS

From Paul's teachings and Mark's gospel it is apparent that they were not aware of anything exceptional in Jesus' background before he joined John the Baptist when he was more than thirty years old. The description of Jesus' parents and his birth as described by Matthew is something new, for nothing has ever been discovered that would indicate this version had been preached prior to Mark's gospel. Readers should compare Mark's introduction of Jesus arriving at John the Baptist's camp to Matthew's introduction of Jesus.

An account of the genealogy of Jesus the Messiah, the son of David, the son of Abraham.

Abraham was the father of Isaac, and Isaac the father of Jacob, and Jacob the father of Judah the father of Perez and Zerah byTamar, and Perez the father of Hezron, and Hezron the father of Aram, and Aram the father of Aminadab, and Aminadab the Father of Nahshon, and Nahshon the father of Salmon, and Salmon the father of Boaz by Rahab, and Boaz the father of Obed by Ruth, and Obed the father of Jesse, and Jesse the father of King David.

And David was the father of Solomon by the wife of Uriah, and Solomon the father of Rehoboam the father of Abijah, and Abijah the father of Asaph, and Asaph the father of Jehoshaphat, and Jehoshaphat the father of Joram, and Joram the father of Uzziah, and Uzziah the father of Jotham, and Jotham the father of Ahaz, and Ahaz the father of Hezekiah, and Hezekiah the father of Manasseh, and Manasseh the father of Amos, and Amos the father of Josiah, and Josiah the father of Jechoniah and his brothers, at the time of the deportation to Babylon.

And after the deportation to Babylon: Jechoniah was the father of Salathiel, and Salathiel the father of Zerubbabel, and Zerubbabel the father of Abiud, and Abiud the father of Eliakim, and Eliakim the father of Azor, and Azor the father of Zadok, and Zadok the father of Achim, and Achim the father of Eliud, and Eliud the father of Eleazar, and Eleazar the father of Matthan, and Matthan the father of Jacob, and Jacob the father of Joseph the husband of Mary, of whom Jesus was born, who is called the Messiah.

So all the generations from Abraham to David are fourteen generations; and from David to the deportation to Babylon, fourteen generations, and from the deportation to Babylon to the Messiah, are fourteen generations.

Matthew: 1.1-17

Why did Matthew consider it important to introduce Jesus in this manner, especially as there is an obvious contradiction for critics to attack? How could Jesus be a descendent of David through his father Joseph and still be born of a virgin as described by Matthew in the verses immediately following the genealogy?

Remember Matthew's audience, and remember he shares the same deep concern of Paul and Mark before him; that deep concern over the attempts by hard-line Judaizers to bring members of the early church back under the Law.[84] However in sharp contrast with Paul and Mark, who avoided reference to Jesus as a Jewish Messiah, Matthew has

---

[84]   The bitterness and even violence that grew from the struggle by Judaizers to put an end to the independence of the new young Christian church and to bring it under control of Jewish religious authorities is in many ways similar to the long, bitter, and even bloody conflict between the newly created Protestant churches and Roman Catholic authorities.

206

opened with the line: "An account of the genealogy of *Jesus the Messiah.*" Whether reading literally or figuratively, readers should appreciate that Matthew will in his Gospel do his best to paint a picture of Jesus as a fulfillment of the prophecies of the Scriptures.

Matthew follows the tradition of early Jewish prophets and other authors of the books of the *Old Testament* by which only a descendent of David could become the Messiah sent to lead the chosen people; thus the need for the genealogy. However, Matthew also follows the traditional dating pattern of the early Jewish writers and prophets. Everything had to fit within neat mathematically exact dates; in this case three periods of fourteen generations each. Abraham had lived around 2000 BC; David roughly one thousand years later. With the life expectancy of that time, marriage at a young age, and the overlapping of generations; counting twenty-five years to a generation is generous. Fourteen generations would have covered no more than three hundred and fifty years.

The first deportation to Babylonia occurred in 598 BC. Thus the fourteen generations mentioned by Matthew in the period between David's rule and the deportation covered approximately four hundred and two years. The time lapse between the beginning of the Babylonian exile and the birth of Jesus was five hundred and ninety two years.

Luke also will compile a genealogy; one that traces Jesus ancestors back to Adam, but his list of names is quite different from those in Matthew's version.[85] Writing for Gentiles, and soft-peddling references that might claim Jesus as the Messiah of the chosen people of Israel, Luke includes David, but does not carry the lineage through Solomon or other royal descendants of David.

Once more readers are faced with the danger of throwing the baby out with the bath water. Because Matthew's mythical genealogy was so obviously designed to fit the prophecies of the *Old Testament* and is inaccurate, it does not mean that the message of Jesus as carried in Matthew's Gospel is also false. Matthew is establishing credentials for Jesus; credentials his Jewish audience can accept as being those prophesized for the Messiah who would be sent by God. This is not done with the intent of turning his Jewish compatriots into worshipers of Jesus, but rather to give authenticity to Jesus' teachings.

---

[85] Matthew has drawn some names from the *Old Testament* writing of *Ruth* who was the great- grandmother of David.

It is Jesus' message that Matthew wants to get across. If Jesus and his message are being rejected by Jews within the new church, then only by getting Jesus accepted as the Messiah does Matthew appear to believe Jesus' message will be accepted. The question of whether this too is the motive behind the story of Jesus' birth is also posed by biblical scholars and historians.

> Now the birth of Jesus the Messiah took place in this way. When his mother Mary had been engaged to Joseph, but before they lived together, she was found with child from the Holy Spirit. Her husband Joseph being a righteous man and unwilling to expose her to public disgrace, planned to dismiss her quietly. But just when he had resolved to do this, an angel of the Lord appeared to him in a dream and said, "Joseph, son of David, do not be afraid to take Mary as your wife, for the child conceived in her is from the Holy Spirit. She will bear a son, and you are to name him Jesus, for he will save his people from their sins. All this took place to fulfill what had been spoken by the Lord through the prophet. 'Look, the virgin shall conceive and bear a son, and they shall name him Emanuel,'[86] which means , 'God is with us.' When Joseph awoke from sleep he did as the angel of the Lord commanded him; he took her as his wife, but had no marital relations with her until she had borne a son; and he named him Jesus.
>
> Matthew: 1.18-25

Once more the reader sees Matthew pointing to a prophecy to lend credence to the Messiah who is born of a virgin. At the time of Matthew's writing, Mystery Religions and the more recently organized Emperor Worship were drawing Christians away from Christian churches, and were tempting still others to defect. Founders of these various Mystery Religions, as well as the Emperor, were being worshipped as divine characters born of virgins. A virgin birth not only

---

[86] Matthew draws from Isaiah: 7. 14 as evidence that his story of Jesus being born of a virgin fulfills a scriptural prediction of the birth of the messiah.

met the prophecy quoted by Matthew, but also matched the divinity credited to those born of virgins in the competing Mystery Religions.

Matthew had to be well-aware that descending from David through Joseph and being born of a virgin was a contradiction. Yet, these divine credentials would become accepted doctrine in Christian churches for the next two thousand years. These credentials, this authority, were intended to give credence to Jesus' message. It is most unlikely that Matthew could have foreseen that over the centuries it would lead billions to worship Jesus as a god to such an extent that most Christians would spend much more of their time in worshipping and praising Jesus than in listening to his message.

> Jesus was born at Bethlehem in Judaea during the reign of Herod. After his birth astrologers[87] from the east arrived in Jerusalem, asking, "Where is the child who is born to be king of the Jews? We observed the rising of his star, and we have come to pay him homage." King Herod was greatly perturbed when he heard this; and so was the whole of Jerusalem. He called a meeting of the chief priests and lawyers of the Jewish people, and put before them the question: "Where is it that the Messiah is to be born?" "At Bethlehem in Judaea," they replied; and they referred him to the prophecy which reads: "Bethlehem on the land of Judah, you are far from least in the eyes of the rulers of Judah; for out of you shall come a leader to be the shepherd of my people of Israel."
>
> Matthew: 2.1-6

Bethlehem was known as the "city" of David, and it had long been prophesized that when the Messiah came forth to lead the chosen people of God he would be a descendent of David born in the town of David. In a pastoral society such as that of Israel, "shepherd" often referred to a king; his subjects his sheep. At this point questions are once more raised about the accuracy of Matthew's account. This passage and the following verses describing Jesus' birth can be read as a literal account of what happened. However, those who do not read the *New Testament* as a literally accurate history, but as a vehicle designed to carry Jesus' message to the people, point to certain questions.

---

[87]   Astrologers, considered as Wise Men.

Why, they ask, did Mark never mention Jesus birthplace, the miracle of the virgin birth, or the visit of the astrologers? Peter had worked with Paul and Mark, and Peter had been a disciple close to Jesus and leader of the disciples after Jesus' death. Yet, nowhere is there any record of Peter having knowledge of these events. If he had such knowledge, why had he not taught and preached about it until it was widespread knowledge, especially knowledge passed on to Paul and Mark? Why is there no evidence that Jesus' mother and brother ever spoke of these matters? Why is it that almost sixty years pass after Jesus' death before a gospel reports these incidents and miracles?

This is but one of the additions Matthew made to the material found in the *Gospel According to Mark* that create problems for readers of Matthew's gospel. It is here that a reader can turn in any of three directions. The reader can accept all that Matthew has added as a literal chronicle of events. Or, as is increasingly the case, the reader may find the contradictions in the genealogy, the birth occurring in just the right location, and the miracle of a virgin birth make it impossible to accept anything in any of the gospels. Or, the reader may read Matthew figuratively and attribute Matthew's additions as an attempt to give Jesus such stature as a Jewish Messiah that his message would be accepted. In this latter case, those reading the bible figuratively will concentrate on trying to find Jesus' message.

This is the one of those forks in the road where some readers will find Matthew's story so compelling that Jesus rather than God becomes the main object of worship, while other readers believe the interpretation of "God's Word" as preached by Jesus should be the dominant theme of Christianity. Matthew continues:

Herod next called the astrologers to meet him in private, and ascertained from them the time when the star had appeared. He then sent them on to Bethlehem, and said, "Go and make a careful inquiry for the child. When you have found him, report to me, so that I may go myself and pay homage to him."

They set out at the king's bidding; and the star which they had seen at its rising went ahead of them until it stopped above the place where the child lay. At the sight of the star they were overjoyed, Entering the house they saw the child with Mary his mother, and bowed to the

> ground in homage to him; then they opened their
> treasures and offered him gifts: gold, frankincense, and
> myrrh. And being warned in a dream not to go back to
> Herod, they returned home another way.
>
> After they had gone, an angel of the Lord appeared to
> Joseph in a dream and said to him, "Rise up, take the
> child and his mother and escape with them to Egypt, and
> stay there until I tell you; for Herod is going to search for
> the child to do away with him." So Joseph rose from his
> sleep, and taking mother and child by night he went away
> with them to Egypt, and there he stayed till Herod's
> death. This was to fulfill what the Lord had declared
> through the prophet : "I called my son out of Egypt."
>
> Matthew: 2.7-15

Matthew continues to use the lengthy introduction to his gospel to present Jesus as fulfilling prophecy after prophecy relating to the coming of a Messiah. Here again critics challenge Matthew's story of the birth of Jesus. "How," they ask, "can Matthew, more than ninety years after the birth of Jesus, possibly know what was said in a "private" conversation between Herod and the astrologers?" Then too, there is the challenge of the story of the star. Stars, as these critics note, are suns millions of light years distant from the earth. They are not, as was believed two thousand years ago, a part of a ceiling between the earth and a heaven inhabited by angels immediately above that ceiling. Knowing what we know today of astronomy and outer space, critics ask, "How could a star move across the sky and stop over Bethlehem? Stars don't move; the earth rotates resulting in starts appearing to move across the sky each night."

Why, these critics ask, were Joseph and Mary in Bethlehem and not at home in Nazareth, especially when Mary was expecting a child and the trek on foot from Nazareth to Bethlehem was journey of several days. Luke says Joseph and Mary had to go to Bethlehem for the first registration ever to have been made in the Roman Empire, at a time "when Quirinius was governor of Syria." But, the registration under Quirinius actually took place more than twelve years after the birth of Jesus. However, Matthew never claims that Joseph and Mary were from Nazareth. Instead, unlike Luke, he will have Joseph move the family to Nazareth upon leaving Egypt. According to Matthew, Joseph and Mary would have been living in Bethlehem.

Luke will speak of Joseph and Mary traveling to Bethlehem where, upon finding there was no room left at the inn, they moved to the stable where Jesus would be born. There he would be found lying in a manger when the shepherds, sent by angels, arrived. Matthew, on the other hand, has Jesus born in a house where the wise men will find him.

> The time came that Herod died; and an angel of the Lord appeared in a dream to Joseph in Egypt and said to him, "Rise up, take the child and his mother, and go with them to the land of Israel, for the men who threatened the child's life are dead." So he rose, took mother and child with him, and came to the land of Israel. Hearing, however, that Archelaus had succeeded his father Herod as king of Judaea, he was afraid to go there. And being warned by a dream, he withdrew to the region of Galilee; there he settled in a town called Nazareth. This was to fulfill the words spoken through the prophets: "He shall be called a Nazarene."
>
> Matthew: 2.19-23

Only Matthew mentions the move from Egypt, and critics point to this as one more example of Matthew portraying fulfillment of prophecies. Hosea, in a short but rambling writing had chastised the people of Israel for their way of life, but he also preached of the love of God who looked upon them as a father upon his children. Matthew was referring to Hosea: 11. 1: "When Israel was a boy, I loved him; I called my son out of Egypt."

Herod was a harsh ruler, especially in his later years when, historians believe, he suffered from mental illness, yet there is no historical record of nor do any of the other writers of the gospels refer to a slaughter of children. However, having the child Jesus facing death at the hands of Romans made it easier for Jews to accept him as a fellow Jew who suffered under the Romans, and thus provided a reason for going to Egypt.

At this point in the *Gospel According to Matthew* the author jumps ahead 29 years to pick up Jesus as a thirty year old adult meeting John the Baptist. "Why," it is asked by critics, "if Matthew knew so much about the intimate details of Jesus' birth did he not find anything worth writing about in Jesus' life over the next thirty years? Why no mention of Jesus asking questions of the teachers in the temple when he was but twelve years old as in Luke 2. 45-47?

Critics who have found so many errors and have disputed so much of Matthew's first two chapters (his introduction of Jesus) are bound to clash with those who fiercely defend the Gospel as literal history. Readers who read Matthew figuratively see no need to become involved in that dispute. They are able to dismiss Matthew's two introductory chapters as unimportant, accepting them as merely Matthew's effort to counter the efforts of the Judaizers by convincing fellow Jews that Jesus fulfills all the requisites of the Messiah and that, therefore, his teachings should be accepted. Those involved in a figurative reading believe Matthew's introduction in no way affects Jesus' message for which this gospel was intended to be a vehicle. Instead they move on, seeking that message; and not allowing themselves to become entangled in the bitter dispute between the literalists and their critics.

Still strengthening his argument Matthew writes:

> In those days, John the Baptist appeared in the wilderness of Judaea, proclaiming, "Repent, for the kingdom of heaven has come near." This is the one of whom the prophet Isaiah spoke when he said, "The voice of one crying out in the wilderness: 'Prepare the way of the Lord, make his paths straight.'"
>
> Matthew: 3.1-3

In this short passage there are three things of note. In Hebrew "repent" can mean "turning back"; back to the ways of God which people had abandoned. A second point of note is Mark's frequent reference to the kingdom of *God*; but Matthew is writing for Jews, and among strict observers of the Jewish religion one did not use the word God. That could be interpreted as using God's name in vain. Instead, as he is writing for Jewish readers, especially hard-liners who had joined churches which they still considered to be reform sects of Judaism, he uses the term kingdom of *Heaven* throughout his gospel. A third point to be observed is Matthew's reference once more to an *Old Testament* prophet; this time the highly revered Isaiah.

Matthew moves on, drawing now from Mark as he describes the work of John the Baptist. However, in the twenty years since Mark had prepared his Gospel much had happened. The Mystery Religions' promise of resurrection after death was attracting more Jews and Gentiles. Jerusalem had fallen just after Mark had written his gospel. Since then Pharisees were, in much larger numbers, choosing to join Christian churches for their promise of resurrection; and Pharisees had long been respected for their knowledge of and their teaching of the Law. The difference they saw between the Mystery Religions and the new Christian church was that Christians had retained what we refer to now as the *Old Testament*. It is important that one not lose sight of the fact that these scriptures and wisdom writings had been the bible of Jesus; and that Jesus had not sought to build a new religion, but rather to bring about certain reforms in the religion of the Jews. It was only after his death that Christianity could be formed.

At this same time the Sadducees were holding fast to their belief that there was no such thing as resurrection. But, as the desire to believe in resurrection swept through Jewish communities throughout the Mediterranean world even as the Temple had been destroyed, the Sadducees' power and authority was seriously eroded. In contrast, those Pharisees who had joined the new churches were asserting their authority; seeking to retain the promise of resurrection while otherwise bringing the church back under the Law.

Matthew speaks of many Pharisees coming to John for baptism, and of John's berating them for seeking baptism only as a means of escaping from the harsh judgment (retribution) to be brought by he who is coming. As the strength of the hard-line Judaizers, enhanced by inclusion of scholarly Pharisees, had continued to grow in the twenty years since Mark's Gospel had been written, their role threatened the very existence of the young Christian church.[88] Matthew is reflecting

---

[88] One should not be surprised at how great and rapid were the changes in the new born religion. Look to the changes in Christianity in the short eighty years from the end of the First World War to the end of the 20th century. Especially note the rapid changes from the end of WW II to the end of the century. The ecumenical movement in the United States; the liberalization of restrictions and church leadership in the fight against racism; the ordination of women clergy; the move from Latin to the language of each country in Roman Catholic services. These are but a small sampling of the changes occurring in just 55 years; changes most worshipers never imagined would come about.

this fear when he adds John's verbal chastisement of the Pharisees to what had been Mark's earlier version.

Matthew is on the offensive. To those who read Matthew figuratively, it would appear he had decided that the best defense is attack. He is defending, trying to save, Christian churches by attacking those who would capture them. However, in his wisdom he does not directly attack those Pharisees who were calling themselves Christians even while they were urging a return to the Law from which Jesus had set Christians free.

Because these Pharisees were trying to return to the religion of the Jews, but with the addition of Jesus' promise of resurrection, Matthew has John the Baptist label them hypocrites. Moreover, he has John chastising them at a point in time when John had not yet met Jesus, and obviously when there was no Christian church for Pharisees to think of joining. This did, however, provide an opportunity for Matthew to introduce an accusation of hypocrisy made by the respected John the Baptist. Whether reading Matthew literally or figuratively, keep in mind the crisis facing the church, Matthew's devotion to that church, and how he would try to save it.

> Now John wore clothing of camel's hair with a leather belt around the waist, and his food was locusts and wild honey. Then the people of Jerusalem and all Judea were going out to him, and all the region along the Jordan, and they were baptized by him in the river Jordan, confessing their sins.
>
> But when he saw many Pharisees and Sadducees coming for baptism, he said to them, "You brood of vipers! Who warned you to flee the wrath to come? Bear fruit worthy of repentance. Do not presume to say to yourselves, 'We have Abraham as our ancestor'; for I tell you, God is able from these stones to raise up children to Abraham. Even now the ax is lying at the root of the trees; every tree therefore that does not bear good fruit is cut down and thrown into the fire.
>
> "I baptize you with water for repentance, but one who is more powerful than I is coming after me; I am not worthy to carry his sandals. He will baptize you with the

> Holy Spirit and fire. His winnowing fork is in his hand,
> and he will clear his threshing floor and will gather his
> wheat into the granary; but chaff he will burn with
> unquenchable fire.
>
> Matthew: 3.4-12

Note that Matthew, in using John to discredit Judaizing Pharisees who have joined the church and are trying to bring it back under the law, has added to John's words about the coming Jesus. Mark had said:

> "After me comes one who is mightier than I. I am not fit
> to unfasten his shoes. I have baptized you with water; he
> will baptize you with the Holy Spirit."
>
> Mark: 1.7-8

Matthew has added a threat of what will happen to the Pharisees, who would be the hard-line Judaizers of the church not yet born when Jesus arrives on the scene. At the same time, like Mark he is introducing Jesus through words of the respected John the Baptist. Because Matthew is writing roughly sixty years after Jesus arrived at John's camp, readers to whom this gospel was being addressed were not going to be aware that John could not at that time have known what Jesus would eventually be teaching. Remember, Jesus' message will actually draw disciples of John away from John. Never could John have anticipated the conflict between Jesus and the Pharisees that Matthew has him predicting, nor would John be chastising the Pharisees to the point of predicting what Jesus would do to them.

Once more we should remember that Matthew is using this introduction as part of his fight to save the church. This in no way will affect the message of Jesus which Matthew will then proceed to deliver in his following chapters. Readers, both literalists and figurativists, can only fully appreciate Matthew and his gospel by reading the gospel in the context of the time it was written. Once more, step into the sandals of the writer of a gospel.

CHAPTER 15

JESUS, ACCORDING TO MATTHEW

His introduction concluded; Matthew now moves quickly into following Jesus from the time he left John the Baptist until his death on the cross. Closely following Mark's gospel, but elaborating wherever it seems to appear to him to need strengthening or clarification, Matthew turns to a description of Jesus' forty days in the wilderness.

> Jesus was then led away by the Spirit into the wilderness, to be tempted by the devil.
>
> Matthew: 4.1

We have already noted the use of the terms Satan and devil when reading Mark. Whether reading Matthew literally or figuratively, keep in mind what the writer meant by those terms. A footnote in the *New Oxford Bible* notes: "The devil, tempter, and Satan are names for evil conceived as *personal will* actively hostile to God." There will be some who in reading the gospel as a historically accurate account will see Satan as an evil being existing throughout eternity. Critics will, as we have earlier noted, say that this means there is more than one god; a good god and an evil god. Then what becomes of monotheism? Those reading the Gospel figuratively may on the other hand see the devil as temptations existing within or facing each person. The struggle to do what a creator God would will one to do, as opposed to material temptations one feels within himself or herself, is personified by

Matthew's confrontation between Jesus and Satan in the forty days in the wilderness.[89]

> For forty days and nights he fasted, and at the end of them he was famished. The tempter approached him and said, "If you are the Son of God, tell these stones to become bread." Jesus answered, "Scripture says, man cannot live on bread alone; he lives on every word God utters. "
>
> Matthew: 4.2-4

Matthew, like Mark refers to forty days in the wilderness. This is another instance of a gospel writer adding an aside to strengthen his description of Jesus. Moses was supposed to have spent forty days with God.

> The Lord said to Moses: "Write these words; in accordance with these words I have made a covenant with you and with Israel." He was there with the Lord forty days and forty nights; he neither ate bread or drank water. And he wrote on the tablets the words of the covenant, the ten commandments.
>
> Exodus: 34.27-28

Here we see one of the advantages of having read Mark before reading the other gospels. In addition to his own considerable knowledge of the Scriptures and wisdom writers, Matthew has read Mark's gospel in which after feeding a huge crowd with seven loaves Jesus berated his disciples for failing to see that the crowd had been fed, not bread for the material body, but food for the spirit. This is an early example of Matthew paving the way for a better and easier understanding of Jesus' message by a new generation of congregations; congregations faced with promises made by competing religions, and with the arguments of dissidents within their own churches. Here we see Jesus being tempted with the vision of an enjoyable life of material

---

[89] Moses is portrayed in several books of the *Old Testament* as spending forty days and nights fasting.

218

comfort; instead of forsaking material wealth, as he did, in order to concentrate on spreading God's message.

> The devil then took him to the Holy City, and sat him on a parapet of the temple. "If you are the Son of God," he said, "throw yourself down; for the Scripture says, 'He will put his angels in charge of you and they will support you in their arms, for fear you should strike your foot against a stone.'" Jesus answered him, "Scripture says again, 'You are not to put the Lord your God to the test.'"
>
> Once again, the devil took him to a very high mountain, and showed him all the kingdoms of the world in their glory. "All these', he said, 'I will give you, if you do me homage. But Jesus said, "Begone Satan! Scripture says, 'You shall do homage to the Lord your God and worship him alone.'"
>
> Then the devil left him; and angels appeared and waited on him.
>
> Matthew: 4.5-11

These temptations are best described in a note in the *New English Bible*: "The devil, or Satan is properly defined as the tempter in the third verse; he is the personification of the evil force which opposes God." This should again remind readers that the gospel writers are using parables in the same manner that Jesus used them when teaching his disciples, and that forces such as evil or selfish temptations within us are described as the voice of an anti-God in the form of Satan.

In Matthew's parable the inner voice is telling Jesus that he has the ability to win whatever public support it would take to make him the ruler of the material world. He could use his powers of persuasion, his preaching, and the people's belief that he is the Son of God. That inner voice is telling him that he can become king; that he can be the Messiah and rule over all that he sees lying here before him. But, Jesus' response to these temptations is that he worships God, not riches or political power.

This refusal by Jesus to assume political power in order to rule as he would please does more than present Jesus as being above material temptations. Matthew is also denying that Jesus ever had any intention of seizing power from those who ruled in Jerusalem, which would include the Sadducees as well as the Roman governors. He is emphasizing the point that Jesus, though the Messiah, was concerned with his role as God's messenger and not with the material power most Jews associated with the coming Messiah. Therefore, Matthew is also telling his Jewish audience, just because Jesus in his humility appeared only as a penniless preacher does not mean he was not the Messiah. As the true Messiah he deliberately chose not to be a king ruling from a palace amidst a wealth of material possessions.

JESUS THE TEACHER

Matthew moves on to describe Jesus' wanderings through several areas of Palestine. In these accounts, Jesus' travels will match those described by ancient prophets in their prophecies about a coming messiah. Eventually his readers find Jesus walking by the sea where, as in Mark's Gospel, Jesus attracts disciples and preaches to an ever growing following. He drives out "devils" from the ill and possessed as he did in accounts by Mark; the devils being temptations to submit to evil. At last he arrives at a hill which he mounts to be able to seat himself where he could look out upon a crowd waiting to hear his words.

> Then he began to speak, and taught them saying:
> "Blessed are the poor in spirit, for theirs is the kingdom of heaven.
>
> "Blessed are those who mourn, for they will be comforted.
>
> "Blessed are the meek, for they will inherit the earth.
>
> "Blessed are those who hunger and thirst for righteousness, for they will be filled.

220

> "Blessed are the merciful, for they will receive mercy.
>
> "Blessed are the pure in heart, for they will see God.
>
> "Blessed are the peacemakers, for they will be called the children of God.
>
> "Blessed are those who are persecuted for righteousness' sake, for theirs is the kingdom of heaven
>
> "Blessed are you when people revile you and persecute you and utter all kinds of evil against you falsely on my account. Rejoice and be glad, for your reward is great in heaven, for in the same way they persecuted the prophets who were before you."
>
> Matthew: 5.2-11

There are two ways to interpret this Sermon on the Mount. One interpretation, the most common over the past two thousand years, is that an individual is being rewarded (blessed) for mourning, showing mercy, or acting as a peacemaker. A different interpretation sees "Blessed" as being the past tense. Reading "Blessed" as past tense means Jesus is not saying you *will be* blessed, if you mourn or show mercy. He is instead saying if you truly mourn and show mercy, it is an ability with which you *have been* blessed. Jesus knows mourning is a necessary part of healing after the tragic loss of a loved one. One who is blessed with the ability to love enough to mourn will thereby heal. One is blessed with the compassion that enables one to show mercy. One is not receiving a blessing as a reward for being a peacemaker or for hungering and thirsting for righteousness. Instead, in this second interpretation, such characteristics are blessings with which one has already been so blessed that it makes it possible for him or her to be able to be a peacemaker and to seek righteousness; something most individuals were unable to be or do.

At the time Matthew is writing, there were no Israeli armies confronting other nations. Why then does he give peacemakers such attention? Considering the audience for whom he is writing, and his concern over the hostility between the Judaizers and the Gentiles, it is far more likely that his reference to peacemakers is to those who would see beyond factions and would bring peace to a church whose survival was threatened by divisive quarrelling factions.

From where did Matthew pick up the beatitudes and other sermons which did not appear in writings of Mark or Paul? As we have noted, his writings demonstrate deep knowledge of the Scripture, and the wisdom writers. Looking back on them a reader will find a theme common with the Beatitudes.

> "Now, my sons, listen to me, listen to instruction and grow wise, do not reject it.
>
> "Happy (Blessed) is the man who keeps to my ways, happy the man who listens to me, watching daily at my threshold with his eyes on the doorway..."
>
> Proverbs: 8.32-34

> Happy (Blessed) is the man who does not take the wicked for a guide nor walk the road that sinners tread nor take his seat among the scornful; the law of the Lord is his delight, the law his meditation night and day.
>
> Psalms: 1.1-2

> "I can think of nine of whom I would call blessed, and a tenth my tongue proclaims: a man can rejoice in his children; a man who lives to see the downfall of his foes.
>
> "Happy (Blessed) the man who lives with a sensible wife, and the one who does not plow with ox and ass together.
>
> "Happy (Blessed) is the one who does not sin with his tongue, and the one who has not served an inferior.
>
> "Happy (Blessed) is the one who finds a friend, and one who speaks to attentive listeners.

> "How great is the one who finds wisdom! But none is
> superior to the one who fears the Lord."
>
> Sirach: 25.7-11

Those who read "Blessed" as being the past tense may see in these passages an individual already blessed with a characteristic that makes him or her able to mourn, or show mercy, or become a peacemaker. That these passages begin with the phrase "Happy is" or "Happy the man" become important as they strengthen the interpretation that a state of happiness (being blessed) existed before "the man" did the right thing. His deed may be seen as the result of his having been so blessed; this blessedness being a spiritual condition of the mind. It is not seen as a post-deed reward as in a literal reading; happiness being God's gift to those who are living as God would have them live.

This does not mean that for the figurativist there is no reward. For the figurative reader there still is a reward implicit in the beatitudes, it just is not a post-deed reward. Those who are blessed (a spiritual state of the mind) will enter the Kingdom of Heaven. That kingdom, Jesus has often reminded his disciples, is a peace which passes all understanding. Therefore entrance into that kingdom, which is already a seed within each individual, can only be achieved by those who are so blessed; those who do not put themselves and their desires first, but last. A "righteous" man or woman is "Happy" (blessed) in his or her complete faith; that very faith that results in their doing the right thing.

Critics will point out that Matthew has Jesus preaching on a mount where he "sits", as rabbis did when teaching. Luke, on the other hand, has Jesus "stand" on a level plain, with a "great multitude" coming to him from all over Palestine; from Sidon in the north to Jerusalem in the south, a span of more than one hundred and forty miles. Critics point to the number of days it would have taken for people to walk to that plain. They also note that Luke has Jesus saying things that Matthew does not note and *vice versa*.

These differences between the Sermon on the Mount and the Sermon on the Plain may cause distress when read literally, but are of little importance to those who read figuratively. Obviously the means for recording word for word what Jesus said during sermons did not exist at that time. Neither Mark nor Paul even refers to this sermon. Both were in Rome with Peter for several years. Peter, as a disciple, would have been present if such a gathering took place; yet does not seem to have mentioned it to Paul or Mark.

A figurative reading does not permit these contradictions to diminish the value of the Beatitudes. For one who reads the passage figuratively, the Beatitudes become a brief description of values Jesus held and taught to his disciples. They are in a sense a summary of much that Jesus believed and taught. Matthew has dramatized this collection and summary of Jesus' values as a sermon preached before a huge crowd. However, even with others present Jesus usually was directing his message at his disciples. The Sermon on the Mount, therefore, is important in its bringing together the essence of much of Jesus teaching in one short passage.

The New Testament is not an easy book to read.

I COME NOT TO DESTROY, BUT TO BUILD

> "Do not think that I have come to abolish the law or the prophets, I have come not to abolish but to fulfill. For truly I tell you, until heaven and earth pass away, not one letter, not one stroke of one letter, will pass from the law until all is accomplished. Therefore, whoever breaks one of the least of these commandments, and teaches others to do the same, will be called least in the kingdom of heaven; but whoever does them and teaches them will be called great in the kingdom of heaven. For I tell you, unless your righteousness exceeds that of the scribes and Pharisees, you will never enter the kingdom of heaven."
>
> Matthew: 5.17-20

Does a contradiction lie in these words? Paul and Mark have repeatedly emphasized Jesus' demand that the people be freed from the shackles of man-made Law. Yet, twenty years later Matthew has Jesus saying, "Do not think I have come to abolish the law or the prophets, I have come not to abolish but to fulfill."

Remember the audience for whom Matthew is writing. He has just completed his introduction of Jesus as the Jewish Messiah; and has introduced Jesus the teacher with his account of the Sermon on the

Mount. Within the young church things are moving rapidly, theology is developing, and changes take place frequently. Once more the reader should remember that Matthew is writing almost two generations after Paul has berated the Galatians and others for being tempted to give up the freedom they have won through faith, and are about to fall back into the comfortable "slavery" of the law. It was not only activist hard-line Judaizers within the Gentile churches who were deeply concerned that Jesus' teachings might be calling for abolishment of the Law. Most of those other Jews who had either organized or joined congregations around Jesus' teachings were likewise disturbed.

Paul had said all humans would be judged according to the way they lived. He said a person might believe in the Law, or insist that it be followed, but that would not remove her or him from the judgment of God. Instead it is living according to the standards outlined in the Law that is important. Mark likewise emphasized this point.

Matthew shows us a Jesus strongly declaring he is not attempting to abolish the Law. Instead he has come to teach people how to live the righteous life the creators of the Law would have them live; not because of those man-made rules, but because those with faith know it is the right way to live. It is not "knowing" the Law; after all the scribes and Pharisees were steeped in the Law. It is not advocating that others obey the Law, as was the want of the Pharisees. It is not even the very existence of the Law; which the Pharisees and Sadducees preach. It is by living the way God would have people live that one will be judged as righteous. "For I tell you, unless your righteousness exceeds that of the scribes and Pharisees you will never enter the kingdom of heaven. …unless you show yourselves far better individuals than the Pharisees and the doctors of law, you can never enter the kingdom of heaven."[90]

Jesus saw the good in the Law, but he goes much further. For him ethical behavior was not limited to man-made rules. It went far beyond the Law. For example, the Scripture was firm in its rules for the Sabbath.

> "You shall keep the Sabbath, because it is holy for you; everyone who profanes it shall be put to death; whoever does any work on it shall be cut off from among the

---

[90] The first quote is from the *New Oxford Bible*, p7 New Testament. The second quote is from the *New English Bible*, p7, New Testament.

> people. Six days shall work be done, but the seventh day is a Sabbath of solemn rest, holy to the Lord; whoever does any work on the Sabbath shall be put to death."
>
> Exodus: 31.14-15

> "Six days shall work be done, but on the seventh day you shall have a holy Sabbath of solemn rest to the Lord; whoever does work on it shall be put to death. You shall kindle no fire in all your dwellings on the Sabbath day."
>
> Exodus: 35.2-3

> When the Israelites were in the wilderness, they found a man gathering sticks of the Sabbath day. Those who found him gathering sticks brought him to Moses, Aaron, and to the whole congregation. They put him in custody, because it was not clear what should be done to him. Then the Lord said to Moses. "The man shall be put to death; all the congregation shall stone him outside the camp." The whole congregation brought him outside the camp and stoned him to death, just as the Lord had commanded Moses.
>
> Numbers: 15.32-36

These passages concerning the Sabbath were written during the period of religious reform under King Josiah, some four hundred years after Moses was supposed to have lived, and six hundred years before the birth of Jesus. According to the Scripture several prophets also declared that a person would incur God's lasting disfavor, if he or she failed to observe a Sabbath. Jesus could not have made it any clearer that he saw the Law as being made for the benefit of man, rather than the reverse, than in the story of the disciples picking and eating corn on the Sabbath. To those who criticized this "sin" against the Sabbath he had said: "The Sabbath was made for humankind, and not humankind for the Sabbath." This short story emphasizes that sharp contrast Jesus saw between the slavery of the Law and the freedom to live an ethical life above and beyond the confines of man-made rules, regulations, and rituals.

To drive home this relationship of the individual to the Law, Matthew continues; listing throughout the rest of this fifth chapter acts prohibited by the Law such as murder, adultery, divorce, and lying, (falsely swearing) In each case Jesus begins by saying: "You have heard that it was said…But I say to you." In this segment of the Sermon on the Mount Jesus tells his audience that they must look beyond the Law; they must go further. Matthew's Jesus has not come to abolish the Law, but to help people to live as God would have them live by going much further than the objectives of the written rules and regulations. A further emphasis of this passage highlights Jesus' belief in a God of love and forgiveness as opposed to the "Old Testament" God of vengeance given to frequent punishment of humans.

Matthew left for last what may be perceived as possibly the most important of these comments on the Law with the passage:

> "You have heard that it was said, 'You shall love your neighbor and hate your enemy.' But I say to you, Love your enemies and pray for those who would persecute you so that you may be children of your Father in heaven; for he makes his sun rise on the evil and on the good, and sends rain on the righteous and the unrighteous. For if you love those who love you, what reward do you have? Do not even the tax collectors do the same? And if you greet only our brothers and sisters, what more are you doing than others? Do not even the Gentiles do the same? Be perfect, therefore, as your heavenly Father is perfect."
>
> Matthew: 5.43-48

Loving one's enemy called for a drastic change for strict adherents of the Jewish faith. In Deuteronomy, considered the Second Law, and in Numbers and Exodus interpretation of the Law required that when an enemy had refused to surrender when besieged, all males were to be put to death, and women could be taken by the Israelite soldiers. If the resistance had been long and severe, women and children also were to be put to death. At this point in Matthew's account of the Sermon on the Mount, Jesus is actually contradicting a part of the Law.

The reader of Deuteronomy should remember that, as the written version of Jewish religious Law, it was written as a part of King Josiah's religious reforms in 621 AD. Just as it had been in the centuries prior to the Israelites entering Canaan, the term "neighbor" referred only to fellow Israelites. As with other ancient tribes, those outside the tribe with different gods were not included among those to be loved. "Love", as used in the Law, meant that each Israelite was to look upon all fellow Israelites as though they were one great family bound by close family ties.

Once more, keep in mind the audience for which each Gospel writer writes. Matthew is addressing Jews who are deeply disturbed by the claims of Judaizers and others that Jesus has come to abolish the Law. By then Gentile Christian churches greatly outnumbered those Jewish "Christian" churches founded by Jesus' brother James and shepherded by Peter. One who reads figuratively may interpret this passage as a command for fellow Jews to accept all non-Jews as "neighbors'. So interpreted, Matthew is saying: do not create a split in our growing church by treating all non-Jewish Christians as enemies (outsiders). His Jesus is telling Jewish "Christians" that all fellow Christians *and* other Gentiles are neighbors. *But* - remember there was no church or Christianity until after Jesus' death on the cross. In a figurative reading, one finds Matthew continuing to make his appeal to Jews through words he believes Jesus would have spoken were he present now when the church's survival was being threatened.

Matthew is trying to prevent a catastrophic split in the church. He is fighting for the church's survival in the best way he can. In these passages Matthew's Jesus is not saying the Law should be abolished. He is saying it should be expanded. "Do not think I have come to abolish the law or the prophets; I have come not to abolish but to fulfill." ...."You have heard that it was said....But I say to you..." go even further as our Father would have you do. Matthew handles this plea to his audience beautifully.

BE NOT HYPOCRITES

Matthew continues his account of the Sermon on the Mount:

> "Beware of practicing your piety before others in order to be seen by them: for then you have no reward from your Father in heaven.

228

"So whenever you give alms, do not sound a trumpet before you, as the hypocrites do in the synagogues and in the streets, so that thy may be praised by others. Truly I tell you, they have received their reward. But when you give alms, do not let your left hand know what your right hand is doing, so that your alms may be done in secret, and your Father who sees in secret will reward you.

"And whenever you pray, do not be like the hypocrites; for they love to stand and pray in the synagogues and at the street corners so they may be seen by others. Truly I tell you, they have received their reward. But whenever you pray, go into your room and shut the door and pray to your Father who is in secret; and your Father who sees in secret will reward you.

"When you are praying, do not heap up empty phrases as the Gentiles do; for they think that they will be heard because of their many words. Do not be like them, for your Father knows what you need before you ask him.
"Pray then in this way:
> Our Father in heaven
> hallowed be your name,
> Your kingdom come.
> Your will be done,
> on earth as it is in heaven.
> Give us this day our daily bread.
> And forgive us our debts as we
> have also forgiven or debtors.
> And do not bring us to the time of trial,
> but rescue us from the evil one.

"For if you forgive others their trespasses, your heavenly Father will also forgive you, but if you do not forgive others, neither will your Father forgive you."

Matthew: 6.1-15

Readers will recognize the similarity between Matthew's reference to hypocrites and that of Mark. However, instead of this being a part of a Sermon, Mark says Jesus was in the temple speaking to his disciples and a gathering crowd shortly before his crucifixion (Mark: 12. 37-44).

How important is it that the setting is different? It may cause confusion for one reading the bible literally; but for one reading the bible figuratively it is the message the writers are trying to pass on to their readers that is important. Matthew, Mark, and Luke have each sought the best way to get this message across to his particular audience. All three are saying that the hypocrite's reward is in the praise he receives from those around him. Those who do not parade their religion, but give quietly and pray in private receive their reward from the Father.

Paul, Mark and John do not mention the prayer which has come to be known as the Lord's Prayer. Luke does, but his version of the prayer is shorter, and is considered by biblical scholars as likely to be closest to the original prayer.

"Father, hallowed be your name.
Your kingdom come.
Give us each day our daily bread.
And forgive us our sins,
for we too forgive all who have done us wrong.
And do not bring us to the time of trial."

Luke: 11.2-4

Matthew added "And rescue us from the evil one" (deliver us from evil). The additional lines: "For thine is the kingdom and the power and the glory, forever were added much later; probably by church leaders in Rome when they were deciding upon, and were editing, material they would include in the bible they were creating. But, what is the meaning of certain segments of the original prayer? Obviously, the prayer reflects the Jewish background of both Jesus and Matthew. Its style and structure is that of Jewish prayers of that time. However, in trying to determine the intent of the prayer, biblical scholars are divided in their conclusions.

Some scholars, pointing out that life was difficult for the vast majority of Jews, see in the reference to daily bread a repetition of an age-old plea for the means of survival. Where was the next day's sustenance coming from? Others believe this is too simple an explanation. One who is reading the bible figuratively remembers Jesus' scolding his disciples: "Why do you talk about having no bread? Have you no inkling yet? Do you still not understand? Are your minds closed? You have eyes, can you not see? You have ears, can you not hear (Mark: 8. 17-18)?" In the earlier passage (Mark: 6. 51-52) when Mark described Jesus walking on the water of the storm lashed sea he emphasized the disciples' failure to understand Jesus' use of the word bread: "Then he climbed into the boat beside them, and the wind dropped. At this they were completely dumfounded, for they had not understood the incident of the loaves; their minds were closed."

In translating from the original Greek when creating the bible, the word "daily" was used as the adjective describing the bread. However, some biblical scholars point out that the Greek word which modified "bread" has not been used elsewhere, and should not be translated as "daily". By "daily", they point out, it meant not today but every day in the future. Thus asking for "daily bread" becomes a plea by the one praying for a chance to enjoy at least a foretaste of the "bread" that is waiting for him or her in the future. That future "bread" is thereby seen as a part of the Kingdom of Heaven.

Matthew has said, "Give us this day our daily bread." Luke has said, "Give us each day our daily bread." Luke's wording tends to support those who interpret this phrase as referring to the future.

"And forgive our debts as we have forgiven our debtors (Matthew)." Or according to other translations "Forgive us the wrong we have done, as we have forgiven those who have wronged us."[91] On the solemn Day of Atonement, Yom Kippur, Jews pray for God to forgive their sins even as they forgive the sins of others. The similarity of such prayers is in no way accidental.

Matthew told us earlier that Jesus said he had come not to abolish the Law, but to fulfill it. His Jesus was seeking to reform his people's religion; not to create an entirely new religion. The "Lord's Prayer" is one more illustration of Jesus' background as a deeply religious Jew who sought not only to save, but to strengthen, what he saw as good in the religion in which he had been reared since childhood. Whereas Paul and Mark did not mention the "Lord's

---

[91]   First quote is from the *New Oxford Bible*; the second from the *New English Bible*.

Prayer", Matthew gave it a prominent position in his account of the Sermon on the Mount. As a prayer that draws from the earlier prayers of the prophets, it could be accepted by Jews within the young church.

Although Mark made no mention of the Lord's Prayer, nor even of a Sermon on the Mount, readers will recall that he has Jesus saying, "Whenever you stand praying, forgive, if you have anything against anyone; so that your Father in heaven may also forgive you your trespasses." (Mark: 11. 25). Mark has Jesus telling this to his disciples as they pass the withered fig tree on their way to the temple. Twenty years after Mark, Matthew has Jesus saying as part of the Sermon on the Mount: "For if you forgive others their trespasses, your heavenly Father will also forgive you; but if you do not forgive others, neither will your father forgive your trespasses." (Matthew: 6. 14).

A literal reading of Mark and Matthew may lead to some confusion at this point. Just where and when did Jesus speak of forgiveness? Again, those reading the Gospels figuratively will see no problem in this. Mark's Gospel became the outline followed by Matthew and Luke. As we have noted, Mark's Gospel was a collection of oral traditions about Jesus and his teachings. Matthew is using the same collection of Jesus' teachings; about fifty percent of his material being drawn directly from Mark's Gospel. In so doing, Matthew has gathered together what Mark described as individual incidents and teachings of Jesus and has woven them into a single sermon. Remembering Matthew's intended audience, this was likely to be a more effective way of getting Jesus' message across to Matthew's readers. Once more, the figurative reader urges others to keep in mind that it is not when, or where, or how Jesus was supposed to have passed such messages along to his disciples that is important. It is his message that is all important.

By using his format of a single sermon, Matthew was able to bundle far more of Jesus' instructions into a written account of that sermon than could ever have been practically included in a single oral sermon. In his written version of a "sermon" he is, therefore, able to add still further instructions for the reader, whereas in Mark a reader finds these various unrelated instructions given to disciples at a variety of times and places. Matthew continues with his collection of these instructions.

Do not, Jesus says in this sermon, be a hypocrite when you fast. You are not fasting to impress others. Fast in secret and "…your Father who sees in secret will reward you." Matthew: 6. 16-18.

232

"Do not store up for yourselves treasure on earth, where it grows rusty and moth-eaten, and thieves will break in to steal it. Store up your treasure in heaven, where there is no moth and no rust to spoil it, no thieves to break in and steal. For where your treasure is, there will your heart be also." Matthew: 6. 19-21.

In Mark's parable about the young rich man Jesus says it is easier for a camel to pass through the eye of a needle than it is for a person to find complete inner peace, the Kingdom of God, while still clinging to material concerns (Mark:10. 17-27).   In Matthew, Jesus emphasizes that what an individual considers to be his treasure is where his or her heart will be. This point is at the heart of all Jesus' teaching, yet has been given relatively little attention except in monasteries and convents. But then, Jesus added, it really is impossible for humans ever to reach that perfect stage wherein they would have no attachments or material concerns (Mark: 10. 27).

Men and women could only achieve as much of the Kingdom of Heaven as they made room for in their heart. Jesus knew that entirely aside from concerns of wealth, men and women would still have deep attachments to their spouses, children, parents, and friends. Then who can find such peace the disciples asked. "For men it is impossible, but not for God; everything is possible for God." The disciples had left their homes. They had been chosen from those who had no families to support,[92] yet even they could never completely empty themselves of all other concerns.

Matthew continues:

> "The lamp of the body is the eye. If your eyes are sound, you will have light for your whole body; if the eyes are bad, your whole body will be in darkness. If then the only light you have is darkness, the darkness is double darkness."
>
> Matthew: 6.22-23

One of the difficulties in trying to understand what an author wrote two thousand years earlier in a drastically different physical and social environment is demonstrated in the above passage. Some biblical scholars and theologians see "sound" and "bad" as used by here by

---

[92]   Peter is the exception previously noted.

Matthew as referring to a probable contrast between "generosity" and "stinginess."[93] This interpretation is supported by the manner in which Luke and Mark handled this instruction given by Jesus

> "No one after lighting a lamp puts it in a cellar, but on a lamp stand so that those who enter may see the light. Your eye is the lamp of your body. If your eye is healthy, your whole body is full of light; but if it is not healthy, your body is full of darkness. Therefore, consider whether the light in you is not darkness. If then your whole body is full of light, with no part of it in darkness, it will be full of light as when a lamp gives you light with its rays."
>
> While he was speaking, a Pharisee invited him to dine with him; so he went in and took his place at the table. The Pharisee was amazed to see that he did not first wash for dinner. Then the Lord said to him, "Now you Pharisees clean the outside of the cup and of the dish, but inside you are full of greed, and wickedness. You fools! Did not the one who made the outside make the inside also? So give for alms those things that are within; and see, everything will be clean for you."
>
> Luke: 11.33-41

Mark, from whom both Matthew and Luke drew more than fifty percent of their material had earlier written:

> He said to them, "Is a lamp brought in to be put under the bushel basket, or under the bed? Surely it is brought to be put on the lamp-stand. For nothing is hidden unless it is to be disclosed, and nothing put under cover; unless it is to come into the open. If you have ears to hear, then hear."
>
> He also said, "Take note of what you hear; the measure you give is the measure you will receive, with something more besides. For the man who has will be given more,

[93] See note in *The New English Bible*, p.10 New Testament.

234

> and the man who has not will forfeit even what he has."
>
> Mark: 4.21-25

Continuing on this theme, Matthew adds Jesus' further warning:

> "No servant can be the slave of two masters; for either
> he will hate the first and love the second or he will be
> devoted to the first and think nothing of the second.
> You cannot serve God and Money."
>
> Matthew: 6.24

Once more Jesus is seen emphasizing his point that the seed of the Kingdom of God within each person can grow only if there is room for it to grow. Which will it be? Will you be so filled with material concerns that you can never experience the Kingdom of God, or will you make room for it? Do you have eyes that can see and ears that can hear what God would want you to hear, or are they so filled with worldly desires and concerns that the light can not penetrate, and therefore the seed cannot grow? Summarizing, Matthew adds as a quote from Jesus: "You cannot serve God and Money."

In his next eleven verses Matthew has Jesus listing material desires and anxieties such as the need for better clothing, food, and drink. Jesus concludes: "So do not be anxious about tomorrow; tomorrow will look after itself. Each day has troubles enough of its own" (Matthew: 6. 25-34). Once more the message: There is more to life than this; there is more than the material "bread"; there is also the other side of life to be fed with the bread of faith. If all your concern is for your material needs, you will have no time or space for the Kingdom of Heaven to grow within you.

As he changes the theme of Jesus' instructions, Matthew begins a new chapter.

> "Pass no judgment, and you will not be judged. For as
> you judge others so you will yourselves be judged, and
> whatever measure you deal out to others will be dealt
> back to you. Why do you look at the speck of sawdust in
> your brother's eye, with never a thought for the great
> plank in your own? Or how can you say to your brother,

> 'Let me take the speck out of your eye, when all the time
> there is a plank in your own? You hypocrite! First take
> the plank out of your own eye, and then you will see
> clearly to take the speck out of your brother's'."
>
> Matthew: 7.1-5

This hypocrisy which has plagued humans throughout the ages is as prevalent in the twenty-first century as it was in the time of Jesus. An individual's biases will always threaten to cloud his or her judgment of any other individual whose views (opinions and beliefs) differ from or agree with his or her own. One's own beliefs, opinions, and biases must not become the criteria by which others are judged.

With his emphasis on the "plank" in contrast with a speck of sawdust, Jesus makes clear that one whose judgment of another is based on his own opinions of right and wrong has much greater work ahead in removing his own biases than in removing those of the one he is judging. Only when you have cleared yourself of all your own biased ideas of right and wrong can you begin to judge another. Only God can be that free of bias and prejudgment. God's judgment of you, Jesus concludes, will be based on how fairly you have judged others.

Again, the emphasis is on emptying oneself. Such unbiased judgment requires ridding oneself of all personal opinions on what is politically, economically, socially, theologically, philosophically, or morally right for others. Twenty-first century humans, bombarded daily by news and entertainment media offerings drenched in judgment, find the temptation to participate in judging fellow humans to be no less today than it was two thousand years ago; if anything, the temptation appears to have grown as targets have multiplied.

Matthew adds still further instructions familiar to his Jewish readers. For instance, "Do not give what is holy to dogs;" (Matthew 7. 6) referring to meat left from holy sacrifices in the temple. Having continued with instructions encouraging prayer, he then adds what is one of the most important of Jesus' teachings.

> "In everything do to others as you would have them do
> to you; for this is the Law and the prophets."
>
> Matthew: 7.12

Up to this point the list of instructions was familiar to Jews, for these were instructions to be found in the Law and in the writings of prophets. It is here that Matthew now inserts this key point into his list of instructions. Esteemed Greek, Persian, Roman, Jewish, and Chinese philosophers for centuries instructed their followers and students on how to treat one's neighbors.[94] However, theirs had been the negative directive: "Do *not* do unto others what you would not have them do unto you." Even the Talmud of Judaism carries the instruction, "What is hateful to you, do not to your fellowman. That is the entire Law; all the rest is commentary."

> What I do not wish others to do unto me I also wish not to do to them.
> > The Sayings of Confucius; Kung-yeh Chang. 12

> Do not do to others what you would not desire yourself.
> > The Sayings of Confucius; Yen Hui. 2

> Tuan-mu Tz'u inquired. "Is there one word that will keep us on the path to the end of our days?" "Yes. Reciprocity What you do not wish for yourself, do not do unto others."
> > The Sayings of Confucius, Duke Ling of Wei. 2

> This is the sum of duty: Do naught unto others which would cause you pain if done to you.
> > From Brahmanism. Mahabharata. 5, 1517

> That nature alone is good which refrains from doing unto another what is not good for itself.
> > From Zoroastrianism. Dadistan-i-dinik, 94, 5

These admonitions require no action, no effort, no sacrifice, only a neutral stance. Jesus, on the other hand, is saying, "*Do* unto others what you would have them do to you." This requires positive

---

[94]   Plato (427-347 B,C.); Aristotle (384-322 B.C.); Seneca (4B.C.-A.D. 65); Confucius (551 B.C.-479 B.C.); Hillel (1st Century B.C.-1st Century A.D.); Philo (lived and taught during Jesus' lifetime); are notable among those offering this negative version.

action. *A Christian is supposed to "make an active contribution to the welfare and happiness of others."* [95] Matthew, making no point of this being different than Jewish Law or Scripture, has rather subtly inserted this key point of Jesus' teachings into his listing of instructions familiar to his Jewish readers. This fits neatly with Jesus' insistence that "I have not come to abolish the Law and the prophets; I did not come to abolish, but to complete."

* * * * * * * * * * * *

> "Beware of false prophets, men who come to you dressed up as sheep while underneath they are savage wolves. You will recognize them by the fruits they bear. Can grapes be picked from briars, or figs from thistles? In the same way, a good tree always yields good fruit, and a poor tree bad fruit. A good tree cannot bear bad fruit, or a poor tree good fruit. And when a tree does not yield good fruit it is cut down and burnt. That is why I say you will recognize them by their bad fruits.
>
> "Not everyone who calls me 'Lord, Lord' will enter the Kingdom of Heaven, but only those who do the will of my Heavenly Father. When that day comes, many will say to me, 'Lord, Lord, did we not prophesy in your name, cast out devils in your name, and in your name perform many miracles?' Then I tell them to their face, 'I never knew you and your wicked ways!'"
>
> Matthew: 7.15-23

Matthew has returned to his attack on those undermining the church from within. Beware of those who say they are preaching Jesus' gospel in Jesus' name, but are in truth splitting the young church with their attempts to take over its leadership. He then completes his account of the Sermon on the Mount with Jesus saying:

---

[95] See fn. p. 10, New Testament, *The New Oxford Bible*.

238

> "What then of the man who hears these words of mine and acts upon them? He is like the man who had the sense to build his house on a rock. The rain came down, the floods rose, the wind blew, and beat upon that house; but it did not fall, because its foundations were on rock. But what of the man who hears these words of mine and does not act upon them? He is like the man who was foolish enough to build his house on sand. The rain came down, the floods rose, the wind blew, and beat upon his house; down it fell with a great crash."
>
> Matthew: 7.24-27

* * * * * * * * * * * *

A long, long sermon, and a strong conclusion; believe what I have said and act upon my words, or fall by the wayside of life. Then, borrowing from Mark's description of the reaction of the people in the synagogue at Capernaum, Matthew adds one more verse. Only the place and time are different.

> When Jesus had finished this discourse the people were astonished at his teaching; unlike their own teachers he taught with a note of authority.
>
> Matthew: 7.28-29

> They were all dumbfounded and began to ask one another, "What is this? A new kind of teaching! He speaks with authority."
>
> Mark: 1.27

CHAPTER 16

MATTHEW AND THE TEACHER

In Matthew's account a "great crowd" met Jesus as he descended from the hill after his "Sermon on the Mount. While the crowd followed him, he performed miracles much as were described by Mark; and readers will find the same message in these stories as was found in reading "The Gospel According to Mark."

As did Mark, Matthew opened his account of miracles with the approach of a leper. In those days a variety of skin diseases were referred to as leprosy, not just the affliction we know today as leprosy. The actual disease is not important; it is not the point to be made. The important point is that one referred to as a leper was considered "unclean." That individual was not permitted to approach the "clean." He or she was someone who had become a social outcast; ostracized from society; unable to mingle with others or to participate in religious services in the synagogues or the temple.

> And now a leper approached him, bowed low, and said, "Sir, if only you will, you can cleanse me," Jesus stretched out his hand, touched him, and said, "Indeed I will; be clean again." And his leprosy was cured immediately. Then Jesus said to him, "Be sure to tell nobody; but go show yourself to the priest, and make the offering laid

> down by Moses for your cleansing; that will certify the
> cure.'"
>
> Matthew: 8.2-4

The leper, as in Mark, symbolizes one who has sinned and been lost. As in Mark, faith is the requirement for healing; but not faith in Jesus, as Jesus pointed out. It is faith in the word of God and in the commitment to live according to God's will that accompanies such faith. Being cured (saved) assures that the saved will no longer be an outcast. He is able to go immediately to the temple; present himself to the priest; and participate in worship by making "the offering laid down by Moses for cleansing; and that will certify the cure."

Further similarities between Mark and Matthew appear throughout the remaining accounts of miracles that make up Matthew's eighth chapter. Readers, having already sought the message in these stories when reading Mark, should continue to seek the message as before.

We should not forget that people of those times were convinced that diseases were the result of demons or devils entering a sinner. A literal reading of these healing miracles has Jesus casting out demons that existed only in the minds of the people of those days. A figurative reading, on the other hand, sees symbolism in leprosy, paralysis, blindness, deafness, apparent death, and other afflictions. When those who have been afflicted find faith through Jesus' teaching they are cured (saved) and made whole. They can now see and hear God's message. They are forgiven (cured) and able to move on in life. Those who had completely abandoned the path of righteousness (died) are shown the way and are "born again." Over and over both Mark and Matthew repeat the message: Faith; open your eyes and see; open your ears and hear; have faith and be "cured."

In his next chapter Matthew inserts several stories taken from Mark about Pharisees criticizing Jesus for eating with "sinners;" about friends of the bridegroom celebrating; and about the fallacy of sewing a new patch on old fabric or putting new wine in an old wineskin. He then returns to relating further miracles taken from Mark's Gospel.

THE TEACHER

> So Jesus went around all the towns and villages teaching
> in their synagogues, announcing the good news of the
> Kingdom, and curing every kind of ailment and disease.
> The sight of the people moved him to pity: they were like
> sheep without a shepherd, harassed and helpless; and he
> said to his disciples, "The crop is heavy, but laborers are
> scarce; you must therefore beg the owner to send
> laborers to harvest the crop."
> Matthew: 9.35-38

> Then he called his twelve disciples to him and gave them
> authority to cast out unclean spirits and to cure every
> kind of ailment and disease.
> Matthew: 10.1

> These twelve Jesus sent out with the following
> instructions: "Do not take the road to gentile lands, and
> do not enter any Samaritan town; but go rather to the
> lost sheep of the house of Israel. And as you go
> proclaim the message: 'The Kingdom of Heaven is upon
> you.' Heal the sick, raise the dead, cleanse the lepers, cast
> out the devils; You received without cost; give without
> charge."
> Matthew: 10.5-8

Do not burden yourselves with material possessions when you
set forth on this mission, Jesus tells his disciples. Do not worry about
extra clothes or money with which to buy food. In each town that you
enter look for a family with whom you can stay.

> "If anyone will not receive you or listen to what you say,
> then as you leave that house or that town shake the dust
> of it off your feet. I tell you this: on the day of judgment

242

> it will be more bearable for the land of Sodom and
> Gomorrah than for that town."
>
> Matthew: 10.14-15

Remember Matthew's audience. Once more the message: open your eyes and see, open your ears and hear. If you enter a town and no one there will accept the word you bring, they will be judged to be worse than Sodom or Gomorrah (cities which in "Genesis" were the epitome of sin). Those Bronze Age cities existed some 1,900 years before Jesus was born, so obviously his message had not been available to their citizens as they chose their way of life. Towns the disciples would enter as missionaries would have no such excuse. Theirs would be a conscious rejection of the message. They would be judged as worse than Sodom or Gomorrah.

> "Look, I send you out like sheep among wolves; be wary as serpents, innocent as doves.
>
> "And be on your guard, for men will hand you over to their courts, they will flog you in the synagogues, and you will be brought before governors and kings, for my sake, to testify before them and the heathen. But when you are arrested, do not worry about what you are to say; when the time comes, the words you need will be given you; for it is not you who will be speaking; it will be the Spirit of your Father speaking in you.
>
> "Brother will betray brother to death, and father his child; children will turn against their parents and send them to their death. All will hate you for your allegiance to me; but the man who holds out to the end will be saved. When you are persecuted in one town, take refuge in another; I tell you this: before you have gone through all the towns of Israel the Son of Man will have come."
>
> Matthew: 10.16-23

* * * * * * * * * * * *

The American Civil War too often set brother against brother over the question of whether to join the army of the Confederacy or the Union. Families were rent by arguments over which cause was just; states' rights or federal union. Three centuries earlier Christians had slaughtered hundreds of thousands of other Christians in defense of their beliefs as to who, Roman Catholics or Protestant reformers, correctly interpreted Jesus message. In some 19th century American protestant churches congregations split repeatedly and families stopped speaking to each other over disagreements as to how the words of Jesus should be interpreted.

Almost two thousand years earlier Jesus had insisted that he had come not to abolish the Law; not to destroy the religion of the Jews. He called for reforms to strengthen the religion in which he had grown to manhood. However, for many of his fellow Jews his call for reforms to strengthen their religion was blasphemy; even worse an attempt to destroy the religion in which they felt secure. Acceptance of Jesus' teaching by a son or daughter or parent or neighbor was all too often seen as an attempt to destroy sacred beliefs. For sixty years this had been splitting families. Jews who accepted Jesus' calls for reform were stoned to death or crucified. Judaizers within new Christian churches were strident in their calls for those Christian churches to return to the Law.

Matthew has witnessed this increasing split among his fellow Jews, and with his gospel he is trying to heal, even as at the same time he is proclaiming the message brought by Jesus. In these twin efforts he continues to make frequent reference to Old Testament prophecies and other traditional Jewish religious sources to strengthen his point that Jesus is fulfilling those prophecies and is speaking as the long awaited Messiah.

Now, three generations after Jesus' death, Matthew has Jesus predicting that wherever his disciples carried his message they will face arrest, floggings, and even death. Matthew is telling his audience that what *has* happened to Jesus, and to his disciples who carried the message which led to their persecution, *had* been predicted by Jesus. "You see," Matthew is saying, "they sought not to destroy your religion. They were so dedicated to the strengthening of it by the Messiah that they were willing to give their lives to carry out the prophecies of the Scriptures."

244

> "You must not think I have come to bring peace to the
> earth; I have not come to bring peace, but a sword. I
> have come to set a man against his father, a daughter
> against her mother, a son's wife against her mother in-
> law, and a man will find enemies under his own roof.
>
> "No man us worthy of me who cares more for his father
> or mother than me; no man is worthy of me who cares
> for son or daughter; no man is worthy of me who does
> not take up the cross and walk in my footsteps. By
> gaining his life a man will lose it; by losing his life for my
> sake, he will gain it."
>
> Matthew: 10.37-39

Matthew repeats this message in a later passage that may be
clearer to readers today. Again he will use the symbol of the cross as
did Mark (8: 34-37). As we have already noted, Roman execution by
crucifixion often required the condemned to carry the smaller
horizontal bar of the cross to his place of execution. In Matthew, Jesus
tells his disciples that those who followed him all the way could well
carry the burden of persecution throughout their lives, and their lives
might even be sacrificed. Again Matthew built upon one of Mark's
passages; this time concerning those who would follow Jesus.

> Jesus then said to his disciples, "If anyone wishes to be a
> follower of mine, he must leave self behind; he must take
> up his cross and come with me. Whoever cares for his
> own safety is lost; but if a man will let himself be lost for
> my sake, he will find his true self. What will man gain by
> winning the whole world, at the cost of his true self? Or
> what can he give that will buy that self back?"
>
> Matthew: 16.24-26

Another translation of those same verses reads:

> Jesus then said to his disciples, "If any want to become
> my followers, let them deny themselves and take up their
> cross and follow me. For those who want to save their
> life will lose it, and those who lose their life for my sake
> will find it. For what will it profit them if they gain the

> whole world but forfeit their life? Or what will they give
> in return for their life?"

Just as Paul, who in speaking of resurrection referred to two bodies, one physical and the other spiritual, so Matthew's reference to "losing life" or "true self" refers to one's spiritual life or self, not to one's physical life.

As a writer, Matthew is recognized in part for the careful organization of his gospel into five general discussions. Some scholars of the bible believe he "seems to have deliberately built his gospel around these five great discourses as though his object was especially to show the fullness of Jesus' teaching."[96] After the Sermon on the Mount, and the passages concerning the instructions he gave his disciples as he sent them out to begin their work as missionaries, we are now at a point of transition as Matthew turns to the parables concerning the Kingdom of Heaven.

Once more Jesus is saying that only by emptying one's self of all desires and concerns, even concerns for loved ones, can one achieve the Kingdom of Heaven. Readers find this message repeated in various ways throughout the gospels in stories such as that in which Jesus told a young man that it is easier for a camel to pass through the eye of a needle than for a rich man to enter the Kingdom of Heaven.

Matthew could not have made it clearer that the miracle stories were parables than in the passage introducing his eleventh chapter. Now when Jesus had finished instructing his disciples, he went on from there to teach and proclaim his message in their cities.

> When John heard in prison what the Messiah was doing,
> he sent word by his disciples and said to him, "Are you
> the one who is to come, or are we to wait for another?"
> Jesus answered them, "Go tell John what you hear and
> see: the blind receive their sight, the lame walk, the lepers
> are cleansed, the deaf hear, the dead are raised, and the
> poor have good news brought to them. And blessed is
> anyone who takes no offense at me."
>
> Matthew: 11.1-6

---

[96] P.1., The New Testament, *The New Oxford Bible.*

The last line of the above passage in other translations reads: "and happy is the man who does not find me a stumbling block." Continuing to establish Jesus' authority, Matthew's next passage aims to prove to deeply religious Jews that through Jesus an earlier prophecy has been fulfilled. For example, Isaiah had said:

> "All prophetic vision has become for you like a sealed book. Give such a book to one who can read and say, 'Come, read This;' and he will answer, 'I cannot', because it is sealed. Give it to one who cannot read and say, 'Come read this', and he will answer, 'I cannot read.'"
>
> Then the Lord said:
>
> "On that day deaf men shall hear when a book is read, and the eyes of the blind shall see out of the impenetrable darkness. The lowly shall once more rejoice in the Lord, and the poorest of men exult in the Holy One of Israel."
>
> Isaiah: 29.11-12, 18-20

Still building the authority of John and Jesus, Matthew next has Jesus "begin to speak to the people about John."

> "I tell you this: never has there appeared on earth a mother's son greater than John the Baptist, and yet the least in the kingdom of Heaven is greater than he.
>
> "Ever since the coming of John the Baptist the kingdom of Heaven has been subjected to violence and violent men are seizing it. For all the prophets and the Law foretold things to come until John appeared, and John is the destined Elijah, if you but accept it. If you have ears, then hear.
>
> "How can I describe this generation? They are like children sitting in the market-place and shouting to each other,

> "We piped for you and you would not dance
> 'We wept and wailed, and you would not mourn.'
>
> "For John came, neither eating or drinking, and they say,
> 'He is Possessed.' The Son of Man came eating and
> drinking, and they say, 'Look at him! A glutton and a
> drinker, a friend of tax-gatherers and sinners!' And yet
> God's wisdom is proved right by its results."
>
> Matthew: 11.11-19

It is not a return of Elijah that Jesus is predicting. It is the good things Elijah stood for and which John could now bring into being. However, as Jesus is pointing out, "only if you but accept it. If you have ears, then hear." Only with faith and by following the path God would have them follow, were the people of Israel to see prophecies become reality.

But, Jesus is saying in this passage by Matthew, you are not willing to accept any message from the messenger. - How like the men and women of the twenty-first century. Those who considered themselves the intellectually elite were resentful of anybody or anything that hinted at authority other than their own. - You scoffed at John, and refused to believe he had a message worth hearing. The reason you gave was that he fasted; so you labeled him "possessed." Yet when the Son of Man appeared who would eat and drink with tax-collectors and sinners, you branded him a glutton; and that was enough of an excuse to close your ears to his words as well. A messenger of God was damned if he did, and damned if he didn't. No matter who that messenger was, critics could always find a label to justify closing their ears.

Having spoken further about his own role in revealing the word of the Father, Jesus refers to the rigidity of the Law.

> "Come to me, all whose work is hard, whose load is
> heavy; and I will give you relief. Bend your necks to my
> yoke, and learn from me, for I am gentle and humble-
> hearted; and your souls will find relief. For my yoke is
> good to bear, my load is light."
>
> Matthew: 11.28-30

248

In reference to this passage, *The New Oxford Bible* notes: "The rabbis spoke of the *yoke* of the Law. Jesus regarded his claim as more demanding and more rewarding."[97] He is not saying "forget the Law." Instead he is emphasizing his earlier claim that he came not to abolish the Law, but to strengthen it. This then provides a lead-in for his next chapter, which he begins by repeating Mark's story of Jesus and the disciples who while walking through a cornfield on the Sabbath picked ears to eat. Matthew's conclusion, like Mark's is that the Sabbath was made for man, not man for the Sabbath. The Law was made for man, not man for the Law. Again, the point is that the way Jesus would have people live might, like the Law, be a *yoke;* but a much gentler and understanding *yoke.*

THE STRENGTHENING OPPOSITION

As in Mark, Matthew follows the story of the disciples picking and eating corn on the Sabbath with the story of Jesus healing a man in a synagogue on the Sabbath. Healing was considered work, and work was strictly prohibited on the Sabbath. Jesus was well aware that he was being watched by Pharisees who hoped to use this curing on the Sabbath as sufficient reason to bring charges against him. His response to those Pharisees is the same as the reader found in reading this story in Mark.

It is at this point, where Mark moved on to another story of Jesus' teaching, that Matthew inserts the following passage:

> Jesus was aware of it (the Pharisees plot to do away with him) and withdrew. Many followed, and he cured all who were ill; and he gave strict injunctions that that they were not to make him known. This was to fulfill Isaiah's prophecy:
>
> "Here is my servant, whom I have chosen, my beloved,
> on whom my favor rests
> I will put my Spirit upon him, and he will proclaim
> judgment among nations.
> He will not strive, he will not shout,

---

[97] *The New Oxford Bible*, fn. pp. 16-17.

> nor will his voice be heard in the streets.
> He will not snap off the broken reed,
> nor snuff out the smoldering wick, until he leads justice
> to victory.
> In him the nations shall place their hope."'
>
> Matthew: 12.15-21

It is important for readers to note that this passage refers to "nations", rather than to Israel. When this gospel was being written all nations except Israel were Gentile. Some translate this passage to say Gentiles instead of nations. The servant in Isaiah's prophecy is Israel (Isaiah: 42. 1-4). Her people had been chosen as the messengers to carry the word to all other nations. By inserting this prophecy from the revered prophet, Matthew has made Jesus the servant, the messenger carrying God's word.

Remember, Matthew is writing when the Gentile church has grown much faster than and is considerably larger than the Jerusalem church; and Matthew is working to prevent a split between Jews and Gentiles within the church. By referring to Isaiah's prophecy, Matthew has provided a reason for Jesus' message being carried to Gentiles. This missionary work is not undermining the religion of the Jews; it is but fulfilling Isaiah's prophecy.

As in Mark, another man is brought to Jesus for healing. When crowds began to voice their wonder, asking whether this healer was the Son of David, the promised Messiah, alarm resonated throughout the Pharisee community. They said: "It is only by Beelzebub prince of devils that this man drives devils out."

Knowing what they were thinking Jesus answered, as he did in Mark, that :

> "Every kingdom divided against itself goes to ruin; and no town, no household , that is divided against itself can stand. And if it is Satan who casts out Satan, Satan is divided against himself; how then can his kingdom stand? And if it is by Beelzebub that I cast out devils, by whom do your own people drive them out? If this is your argument, they themselves will refute you. But if it is by the Spirit of God that I drive out the devils, then be sure the kingdom of God has already come upon you...

250

> "...He who is not with me is against me, and he who
> does not gather with me scatters. "And so I tell you this:
> no sin, no slander, is beyond forgiveness for men except
> slander spoken against the Spirit, and that will not be
> forgiven. Any man who speaks a word against the Son of
> Man will be forgiven; but if anyone speaks against the
> Holy Spirit, for him there is no forgiveness, either in this
> age or in the age to come."
>
> Matthew: 12.25-28, 30-32

If "healing" (saving) by Jesus was called the work of Satan, where was the difference when "healing" was done by the disciples of the Pharisees? Matthew has Jesus saying it was no sin to slander the living Jesus who stood before the Pharisees. They were entitled to their opinion. However, it was absolutely unforgivable to attack God. If God was working through his messenger, the messenger could be slandered, but not the acts he was performing for God. That would be denying and slandering God.

Remember, Matthew is writing three generations after the death of Jesus. Some biblical scholars believe that in this passage Matthew may also be saying one could be forgiven for attacking Jesus while he lived, but not the Jesus who had been crucified and had risen. Pharisees and others who slandered Jesus while he was living, teaching, and healing (saving) could be forgiven, for they were not to realize Jesus was God's messenger. However, these scholars believe Matthew was also saying there was no such excuse for men and women living at the time of Matthew; for through Jesus' resurrection there now was proof of Jesus' role as God's messenger.

If Matthew is speaking of a living and a later resurrected Jesus, critics note that the words could not have been those of Jesus who had not been crucified or resurrected at that time the words were spoken. They could only be Matthew's addition. As Matthew continues his description of Jesus' censure of the Pharisees there are further indications that these are the words of Matthew, not Jesus.

> "Either make the tree good, and its fruit good; or make
> the tree bad, and its fruit bad; for the tree is known by its

> fruit. You brood of vipers! How can you speak of good
> things, when you are evil? For out of the abundance of
> the heart the mouth speaks. The good person brings
> good things out of a good treasure, and the evil person
> brings evil things out of an evil treasure. I tell you, on
> the day of judgment you will have to give an account for
> every careless word you utter; for by your words you will
> be justified, and by your words you will be condemned."
>
> Matthew: 12.33-37

The word "make" is used here in the same sense as a twenty-first century usage when someone asks, "What do you make of it?" Matthew's passage has Jesus saying, "Either *recognize* that a person is good, and his or her acts and words as good; or *recognize* that person as bad, and his or her acts and words as bad; for a person is known by what he does and says, by the way he or she lives."

> Then some of the scribes and Pharisees said to him,
> "Teacher, we wish to see a sign from you." But he
> answered them, "An evil and adulterous generation asks
> for a sign, but no sign will be given to it except for the
> sign of the prophet Jonah. For just as Jonah was three
> days and three nights in the belly of the sea monster, so
> for three days and three nights the Son of Man will be in
> the heart of the earth. The people of Nineveh will rise
> up at the judgment with this generation and condemn it,
> because they (the people of Nineveh) repented at the
> proclamation of Jonah, and see something greater than
> Jonah here. The Queen of the South (Queen of Sheba)
> will rise up at the judgment with this generation and
> condemn it, because she came from the ends of earth to
> listen to the wisdom of Solomon, and see, something
> greater than Solomon is here!"
>
> Matthew: 12.38-40

Matthew is continuing in his effort to make his Jewish audience accept Jesus in his role as God's messenger; a role that was supposed to have been the responsibility of Israel. The reference to an adulterous nation stems from Old Testament condemnations of Israel by prophets who berated her for forsaking her duty as God's messenger to the world. An "adulterous" nation was an unfaithful nation. The people of Israel were being labeled as unfaithful to God; of having abandoned the way God chose for them.

According to legend, Jonah, a prophet from Galilee had taught so successfully that non-Israelites accepted his message. However, he becomes angry when those non-Israelites (the people of Nineveh) are forgiven by God. In his petulance, Jonah deserts the mission assigned him by God. A violent storm at sea casts him overboard where "the Lord provided a large fish to swallow Jonah; and Jonah was in the belly of the fish three days and three nights." (Jonah 1:17). Note the symbolic three days and three nights.

The story of Jonah was meant to point out to Israel that God is merciful and will forgive those who return to their rightful role as God's chosen messengers. In inserting this reference to Jonah and the Ninevites, Matthew's Jesus is telling the doctors of law and the Pharisees that, while Gentiles are accepting Jesus' message, Israelites are in danger of condemnation for abandoning their role as God's messenger just because they are upset that the message is being accepted by others than Israelites. However, repentance and a return to God's way will save them as Jonah was saved.

Matthew then has Jesus implying that he is greater than Solomon. This is a passage that could never have been spoken by Jesus. Rather it is a further attempt by Matthew to convince his Jewish audience. Writing sixty years after Jesus' death, Matthew has Jesus predicting his own resurrection after three days in which he had been buried in the heart of the earth.[98] Furthermore, Jesus the modest teacher who preached humility, and would refuse a horse and chariot in order to enter Jerusalem on a small donkey, was not a braggart who would boast of being greater than Solomon.

Matthew has a Jesus speaking of his own power and wisdom as being a sign; a sign greater than any other sign from heaven that he was God's messenger doing God's work. This is Matthew's further rebuttal of Judaizers and others who wish to retain a church believing in resurrection, but which otherwise would reject the teachings of Jesus and would return to subservience to the Law. Jesus in this passage is

---

[98]   Tombs like that in which the gospels report that the body of Jesus was taken were man-made grottos hewn from hillsides.

supposed to be speaking to the Pharisees and the scribes (doctors of law), the very group striving to bring the church back under the Law sixty years after the crucifixion.

* * * * * * * * * * * *

Jesus adds a further comment reminiscent of his confrontation with the man in the synagogue in Capernaum (Mark: 1. 23-24) who had shouted: "What do you want with us, Jesus of Nazareth? Have you come to destroy us?" In Mark's story the demons within the man were "unclean". They tended to keep people tied to ritual and law, thereby placing a barrier between them and God. In Matthew's version, Jesus says to the scribes and Pharisees who had demanded a sign:

> "When an unclean spirit comes out of a man it wanders
> over the deserts seeking a resting-place, and finds none.
> Then it says, 'I will go back to the home I left.' So it
> returns and finds the house unoccupied, swept clean, and
> tidy. Off it goes and collects seven other spirits more
> wicked than itself, and they all come in and settle down;
> and in the end the man's plight is worse than before.
> That is how it will be with this wicked generation."
>
> Matthew: 12.43-45

It is not enough to empty ones' mind of evil or of wrong ideas of how one's life should be lived. That only leaves a void to be filled. Unless that new emptiness is filled with something good, leaving no room for anything else, the "evil" will always return.

THE TEACHER'S PARABLES

Turning once more to those parables Mark had recorded twenty years earlier, Matthew repeats the story of Jesus speaking to a crowd in parables. He begins with the parable of the man who went out to sow. As in Mark the disciples wish to know why he spoke in parables. In Matthew Jesus responds:

"The reason I speak to them in parables is that 'seeing
they do not perceive, and hearing they do not listen, nor
do they understand.' With them indeed is fulfilled the
prophecy of Isaiah that says:

'You will indeed listen, but never understand, and you
will indeed look, but never perceive. For this people's
heart has grown dull, and their ears are hard of hearing,
and they have shut their eyes; so that they might not look
with their eyes, and listen with their ears, and understand
with their heart and turn – and I would heal them.'

"But blessed are your eyes, for they see, and your ears,
for they hear. Truly I tell you, many prophets and
righteous people longed to see what you see, but did not
see it, and to hear what you hear, but did not hear it."

Matthew: 13.13-17

In Mark's gospel the disciples fail to understand the parable and
Jesus says to them: "You do not understand this parable?" How then
are you to understand any parable?" In Matthew the disciples
understand, but the people do not. Such small differences like this
should not be blown out of proportion as they all too frequently are.
The point both Mark and Matthew were making was that Jesus, and
they themselves, would teach only by parable. Matthew adds still a
further notice of the intent to teach only in parables, whether by Jesus,
or as the writer of the gospel.

Jesus told the crowds all these things in parables; without
a parable he told them nothing. This was to fulfill what
had been spoken through the prophet.

"I will open my mouth to speak
in parables
I will proclaim what has been hidden
from the foundation
of the world."

Matthew: 13.34-35

This passage raises questions for those who would see only literal meaning in the gospels; yet as a warning it has been unheeded by most readers for two millennia.

* * * * * * * * * * * *

Having sent all but the disciples away, Jesus spoke next of the kingdom of Heaven.

"The kingdom of Heaven is like a treasure lying buried in a field. The man who found it, buried it again; and for sheer joy went and sold everything he had, and bought that field.

"Here is another picture of the kingdom of Heaven. A merchant looking out for fine pearls found one of very special value; so he went and sold everything he had, and bought it.

"Again the kingdom of Heaven is like a net let down into the sea, where fish of every kind were caught in it. When it was full, it was dragged ashore. Then the men sat down and collected the good fish into pails and threw the worthless away. That is how it will be at the end of time. The angels will go forth, and they will separate the wicked from the good, and throw them into the blazing furnace, the place of wailing and grinding of teeth.

Matthew: 13.44-50

As with all parables this may be read literally or figuratively. Two points are being made in the above passages of this parable. Those who see this as a parable to be accepted as another figurative passage note Matthew's repeated emphasis on cost, the price to be paid.

The cost is much as it was with the young rich man seeking to enter the kingdom of God who was told by Jesus that a man with worldly possessions would find entering the kingdom to be as difficult as it would be for a camel to pass through the eye of a needle.

The cost, the giving up of attachment to material possessions and shedding worldly concerns, is great. However, for those who would enter the kingdom of Heaven, the cost is small compared to the value to be gained. Matthew's second point is made with his mention of the dragnet. Many will faithfully attend services. Many will give money. Many will pray. Many will be drawn to the kingdom of Heaven for what it promises. But, only those who actually live as God would have them live will find that peace that is the kingdom of Heaven.

Matthew's reference to the end of time (Day of Judgment) reflected the continuing belief among most Christians of the time that the much prophesized Armageddon and the end of the world was but a short time away. Having concluded these parables about the kingdom of Heaven, Jesus asks:

> "Have you understood all of this?" he asked; and they
> answered "Yes." He said to them, "When, therefore, a
> teacher of the law (Scribe or Pharisee) has become a
> learner in the kingdom of Heaven, he is like the house-
> holder who can produce from his store both the new and
> the old."
>
> Matthew: 13.51-52

Drawing once more from Mark's collection of traditions Matthew repeated the story of Jesus' return to his hometown where, when his message was ignored, Jesus had said: "Prophets are not without honor except in their own country and their own house." It is then, Matthew said, that Jesus learned of the beheading of John the Baptist. At this point Jesus "withdrew from there to a deserted place to be by himself."

Solitude was hard to find. Crowds followed by land, meeting him as he came ashore, and Mark's story of the feeding of the five thousand is repeated here. The purpose and meaning of this story are the same as were noted in our earlier reading of Mark. Again, Jesus walks on the water of the sea, but Matthew adds a passage not found anywhere else in the gospels. The disciples have just recognized that it is Jesus walking toward them on the water.

> Peter answered him, "Lord, if it is you, command me to come to you on the water." He said, "Come." So Peter got out of the boat, started walking on the water, and came to Jesus. But when he noticed the strong wind, he became frightened, and beginning to sink , he cried out, "Lord, save me!" Jesus immediately reached out his hand and caught him, saying to him, "You of little faith, why did you doubt?" When they got into the boat, the wind ceased. And those in the boat worshipped him, saying, "Truly you are the Son of God'."
>
> Matthew: 14.28-33

A literal reading sees Jesus walking on water and telling Peter to walk to him. Then, Peter being struck with doubt begins to sink but is saved when Jesus grasps his hand.

As a parable meant to be read figuratively a broader picture unfolds. Peter represents all people who have faith, but whose faith can be shaken when they feel threatened. Matthew is warning those faithful Christians who fear persecution, ostracism from society, material losses, or other reaction against them for their belief. Never weaken, never doubt, he says. Hold fast to your belief. Let nothing shake your faith in Jesus' message; only that can save you.

Matthew next repeated Mark's story of Jesus being criticized because his disciples did not wash their hands before they ate. In addition to what the reader has already read in Mark about Jesus' reaction, Matthew adds:

> Then he called the crowd to him and said to them, "Listen and understand: it is not what goes into the mouth that defiles a person, but it is what comes out of the mouth that defiles." Then the disciples approached and said to him, "Do you know that the Pharisees took offense when they heard what you said?" He answered, "Every plant that my heavenly Father has not planted will be uprooted. Let them alone; they are blind guides of the

> blind. And if one blind person guides another, both will
> fall into a pit." But Peter said to him, "Explain this
> parable to us." Then he said, "Are you also without
> understanding? Do you not see that whatever goes into
> the mouth enters the stomach, and goes out into the
> sewer? But what comes out of the mouth proceeds from
> the heart, and this is what defiles. For out of the heart
> come evil intentions, murder, adultery, fornication, theft
> false witness, slander. These are what defile a person, but
> to eat with unwashed hands does not defile."
>
> Matthew: 15.10-20

This parable is easily understood. But, the reader should also note its importance as one more deliberate challenge to Pharisees who insisted that one who did not abide strictly to the law was a sinner. Matthew's Jesus is not merely preaching to his followers. He is hurling challenges at the Pharisees, Sadducees, and Scribes. If he continues in this manner, a showdown cannot be avoided. His actions and words from this point on make clear that he had absolutely no intention of avoiding such a final confrontation from which he either would emerge leading the crowds, or would emerge the victor by way of the cross. As in Mark it is clear to Jesus where his acts and words are leading, and his acts and words are chosen accordingly.

In striving for continuity in Mark's message, we skipped a parable which is now repeated in Matthew. Because Matthew is so deeply concerned with the need to make his Jewish audience understand that it is God's will that Jesus minister unto and carry the word of God to others, not just to Israelites, the following parable fits well here.

> Jesus then left that place and withdrew to the region of
> Tyre and Sidon. And a Canaanite woman from those
> parts came crying out, "Sir! Have pity on me, Son of
> David; my daughter is tormented by a devil." But he said
> not a word in reply. His disciples came and urged him:
> "Send her away; see how she comes shouting after us."
> Jesus replied, "I was sent to the lost sheep of the house
> of Israel, and to them alone." But the woman came and
> fell at his feet and cried, "Help me, sir." To this Jesus

> replied, "It is not right to take the children's bread and throw it to the dogs." "True, sir," she answered; "and yet the dogs eat the scraps that fall from the master's table." Hearing this Jesus replied, "Woman, what faith you have! Be it as you wish! And from that moment her daughter was restored to health."
>
> Matthew: 15.21-28

This is a multi-point parable. To his Jewish readers Matthew, as did Mark, has Jesus moving out of Israelite territory into a Gentile land. He then is approached by a Canaanite woman, not only a Gentile, but a Gentile from the land, the people, and the religion that the people of Israel had historically held in contempt and had seen as the enemy from whom they had earlier seized the "promised land".

Jewish readers are once more reminded that Jesus had been sent to the "lost" people of Israel to help them once more find their way as God's messengers of the Word. Now comes the sharp contrast. The woman recognizes Jesus as the Messiah, the Son of David, who Jesus' own people, the Jews, failed to recognize. A Gentile has recognized Jesus as God's messenger, while those to whom he had been sent have failed to recognize him as such. He may have been sent to save Israel, but now is reaching out to everyone of faith. He is going beyond his original mission in order to minister unto anyone with faith, no matter where they might be or who they might be.

When Matthew began writing his gospel sixty years after the death of Jesus the young Christian church was under continual attack by Pharisees and other Judaizers. They insisted that the church sever all ties to Gentiles. Matthew is now telling them that they had not had the faith to follow when Jesus pointed the way, but Gentiles had that faith then and were still following the way of Jesus. So, how can you, who would try to make this new Christian church a sanctuary for Jews only, now deny participation by Gentiles in this church. Israel, it is your refusal to listen to Jesus and to follow him in your chosen role as the God's messenger to the rest of the world that has forced the new church to carry the message in your stead. Stop complaining, Matthew is saying, this is the result of your own actions.

As in Mark, Matthew has Jesus once more on the road, where he continues to heal those he finds in need of his ministrations. Telling his disciples that he felt sorry for these people, he directed that the

crowd of four thousand be fed. He has just healed (saved) those who
had come to him. Now he will feed the multitude. And as in Mark,
upon returning to their boat the disciples will complain of having
brought no bread:

> "Why do you talk of bringing no bread? Where is your
> faith? Do you remember the five loaves for the five
> thousand, and how many baskets you picked up? Or the
> seven loaves for the four thousand, and how many
> basketfuls you picked up? How can you fail to see I am
> not speaking about bread?"
>
> Matthew: 16.8-11

* * * * * * * * * * * *

Matthew moves on, placing Jesus in the territory of Caesarea
Philippi, where he asks his disciples:

> "'Who do people say that the Son of Man is?' And they
> said, 'Some say John the Baptist, but others, Elijah, and
> still others Jeremiah or one of the prophets.' He said to
> them, 'But who do you say that I am?' Simon Peter
> answered, 'You are the Messiah, the son of the living
> God.' And Jesus answered him, 'Blessed are you, Simon
> son of Jonah! For flesh and blood has not revealed this
> to you, but my Father in heaven. And I tell you, you are
> Peter, and on this rock I will build my church, and the
> gates of Hades will not prevail against it. I will give you
> the keys of the Kingdom of heaven, and whatever you
> bind on earth will be bound in heaven, and whatever you
> loose on earth will be loosed in heaven. Then he sternly
> ordered his disciples not to tell anyone that he was the
> Messiah."
>
> Matthew: 16.13-20

The use of the name Peter at this point is interesting. Jesus
spoke Aramaic. The word that meant rock in that language could also
be interpreted in Greek as the proper noun "Peter", and the gospels

were written in Greek. "You are the rock (Peter), and on this rock I will build my church." Simeon (Hebrew) or Simon (Greek) had been the original name by which "Peter" was known in the New Testament. At this point in the gospel, Matthew has Jesus referring to Simon as a rock because of his faith and loyalty.

Readers will have noted that the beginning of this passage was drawn from Mark. However, whether one reads this passage literally or figuratively one realizes the latter part of the passage could not have been spoken by Jesus, and is Matthew's addition. Jesus did not come to create a new church, but rather to reform and strengthen the religion into which he had been born and had lived to this point in his life. By word and action he has repeatedly made this clear. There was no church until Paul, Barnabas and Jewish reformers under Peter created such a church in the decades after the death of Jesus.

Peter's influence was considerable in the years immediately following Jesus' death. For roughly fifteen years he was the unquestioned leader of the small but growing Jewish religious community organized as a church to follow the teachings of Jesus. However, never having had the advantage of training in Mosaic Law, he was pressed by others more learned to take a stand against Gentile influences and practices of those churches started by Paul, Barnabas and other early missionaries. As we have seen, his influence was rejected by Paul and Barnabas as the church grew among Gentiles.

When, under considerable pressure from Paul and other leaders of the Gentile churches, Peter brought uncircumcised Gentiles into his Roman church his influence declined and his control over the Roman church was lost. He could no longer claim to be its leader when he died in 64AD, just three years before the death of Paul. Matthew is writing several generations after the death of Jesus; when the church is being threatened from within as well as without. He has Jesus anointing Simon with the title "Rock" (Peter). This was the Peter respected among Christian Jews who knew of his role in that original Jerusalem church that had adhered to most of the Law. Matthew has made this accepted and respected Peter the "rock" on which he has Jesus saying he built his church.

Over the three centuries following the crucifixion, control of the church was being consolidated among leaders in Rome; even at the expense of bishops assassinating bishops in their struggle for control. It was there that the decisions were made as to what to include in the New Testament, and how it should be edited. And it was during that time that the memory of Peter became a "rock" on which the eventual consolidated church would be built. And that which was built was far different from the reform, strengthening, and *simplifying* that Jesus had sought to bring to the religion to which he had belonged all of his life.

CHAPTER 17

THE KINGDOM OF HEAVEN

At this point in his gospel, like Mark before him, Matthew moves to establish Jesus as the truly beloved messenger sent by God. He is described as having taken Peter, James, and John (the brother of James) to the top of a high mountain.

> And he was transfigured before them, and his face shone like the sun, and his clothes became dazzling white. Suddenly there appeared to them Moses and Elijah, talking with him. Then Peter said to Jesus, "Lord it is good for us to be here; if you wish, I will make three dwellings here, one for you, one for Moses, and one for Elijah." While he was speaking, suddenly a bright cloud over-shadowed them, and from the cloud a voice said, "This is my Son, the Beloved; with him I am well pleased; listen to him!" When the disciples heard this they fell to the ground and were overcome with fear. But Jesus came and touched them, saying, "Get up and do not be afraid." And when they looked up, they saw no one except Jesus himself alone.
>
> As they were coming down the mountain, Jesus ordered them, "Tell no one about the vision until after

> the Son of Man has been raised from the dead." And the disciples asked him, "Why then, do the scribes say that Elijah must come first?" He replied, "Elijah is indeed coming and will restore all things; but I tell you that Elijah has already come, and they did not recognize him, but did whatever they pleased. So also the Son of Man is about to suffer at their hands." Then the disciples understood he was speaking to them about John the Baptist.
>
> Matthew: 17.2-13

Jesus' credibility as God's messenger is still being established. The religion of the Jews did not include resurrection. But, according to the scriptures Moses and Elijah had been swept up into heaven while still alive. Both were revered as founders of the religion of the Jews, and Elijah as the first and greatest of the prophets.

"And his (Jesus') face shone like the sun." - Moses "came down from Mount Sinai with the two stone tablets of the Tokens in his hands, and when he descended, he did not know that the skin of his face shone because he had been speaking with the Lord. When Aaron and the Israelites saw how the skin of Moses face shone, they were afraid to approach him." (Exodus: 34. 29-31).

In this passage, particularly important to Jews of the time, were Jesus' transfiguration (his shining face); the presence of Moses and Elijah, and their acceptance of Jesus; the voice of God claiming Jesus as his Son, the Beloved, to whom all were told to listen. Though not the Messiah Jews were taught to expect; not the Messiah who would lead armies and make Israel the ruler of the world, Jesus was to be listened to as the true Messiah sent by God.

Read literally, Moses and Elijah did appear; and Elijah had earlier appeared as John the Baptist to introduce Jesus to the world; and God spoke from a cloud before witnesses.

Read figuratively, the passage is seen as an attempt by the gospel writer to give stature to Jesus. The figurative reader does not see in this an attempt to lead people to worship Jesus, but rather as an attempt to open the ears of those not yet ready to accept the message Jesus was bringing to them.

Having now attempted to open the eyes and ears of his readers, Matthew moves on with his discourse on the Kingdom of Heaven. As with Mark and Luke, Matthew adopts Jesus' method of teaching by parables.

> At that time the disciples came to Jesus and asked, "Who is the greatest in the kingdom of Heaven?" He called a child, set him in front of them and said, "I tell you this: unless you turn around and become like children, you will never enter the kingdom of Heaven. Let a man humble himself till he is like a child, and he will be the greatest in the kingdom of Heaven. Whoever receives one such child in my name receives me. But if a man is a cause of stumbling to one of these little ones who have faith in me, it would be better for him to have a millstone hung round his neck and be drowned in the depths of the sea. Alas for the world that causes of stumbling arise! Come they must, but woe betide the man through whom they come!"
>
> Matthew: 18. 1-7

If the Kingdom of Heaven is within an individual like a small seed waiting to grow, there is within a child uncluttered room for it to grow. As increasing material desires and concerns begin to fill the life of an individual as he or she grows, they leave little room for the Kingdom to grow. Only by turning around and becoming like children can one enter the Kingdom of Heaven. Jesus is not saying an individual should behave like a child, but rather that he or she should look upon God as his or her father and live as a father would have his child live. Have faith in the Father, and drop your other concerns and desires. Jesus has himself frequently referred to his disciples as his children (little ones). This is a most important point in the parable. In referring to putting stumbling blocks in the path of one of God's children Jesus is not talking of the purity of a child. He is warning those who would attempt to undermine the faith of one of these early believers who have such faith in the father.

In a passage definitely not to be taken literally, Matthew stresses the gravity of the warning just delivered. He has Jesus saying that if one stumbles (falls from the path of righteousness) and it is the fault of his foot, or hand, or eye he should amputate or pluck out that offending member of his body.

Matthew moves on:

> "If a shepherd has a hundred sheep, and one of them goes astray, does he not leave the ninety-nine on the mountains   and go in search of the one that went astray? And if he finds it, truly I tell you, he rejoices over it more than over the ninety-nine that never went astray. So it is not the will of your Father in heaven that one of these little ones should be lost."
>
> Matthew: 18.12-14

This parable about the lost sheep is not part of a message from Jesus, but has been added by Matthew which becomes more apparent in the passage directly following the story of the lost sheep.

> "If another member of the church[99] sins against you, go and point out the fault when the two of you are alone. If the member listens to you, you have regained that one. But if you are not listened to, take one or two others along with you, so that every word may be confirmed by the evidence of two or three witnesses. If the member refuses to listen to them, tell it to the church (congregation); and if the offender refuses to listen even to the church, let such a one be to you as a Gentile and a tax collector. Truly I tell you, whatever you bind on earth sill be bound in heaven, and whatever you loose on earth will be loosed in heaven. Again truly I tell you, if two of you agree on earth about anything you ask, it will be done for you by my Father in heaven. For where two or three are gathered in my name, I am there among them."
>
> Matthew: 18.15-20

It is essential that readers of Matthew continue to keep in mind the audience for whom he is writing and the reason for his writing.

---

[99]   Other translations do not use the word church. Instead they refer to "your brother" and to the "congregation".

Paul had been plagued with congregations being split by dissension and with members of his churches who vied with each other in trying to grab control of their local churches. Matthew is writing sixty years after the death of Jesus and almost two generations had elapsed since Paul had written to his churches berating them and warning them concerning dissidents within the church.

But, there was no church; there were no Christian congregations until after Jesus had been crucified. Matthew's reference to the "little ones," the disciples and other followers of Jesus, being saved after being lost refers to Christians. However, Jesus had been trying to reform the religion in which he had been reared. Christianity, as a separate religion, was brought into being by such missionaries as Paul and Barnabas. Matthew's reference to dissidents in the "church" again highlights a major reason for his writing his gospel; namely to prevent a fragmenting of the church as it existed sixty years after Jesus' death.

Matthew, in his version of the parable of the healing of the leper, emphasizes the point that Jesus had not in any way tried to establish a new religion, but rather had been trying to reform the Jewish religion in which he had been raised. According to Mark, upon healing the man Jesus had directed him to speak to no one about it. Matthew added that Jesus said the man was to tell no one, *but* was to show himself to the priest and make the required offering laid down by Moses for cleansing. This completion of cleansing obviously could only be done within the ritual of the Jewish religion of that time.

In this eighteenth chapter Matthew has been telling his audience how members of the congregations should conduct their lives within the church. He concludes with a parable about the need for forgiveness.

> "The Kingdom of Heaven, therefore, should be thought of in this way: There was once a king who decided to settle accounts with the men who served him. At the outset there appeared before him a man whose debt ran into millions. Since he had no means of paying, his master ordered him to be sold to meet the debt, with his wife, his children, and everything he had. The man fell prostrate at his master's feet. 'Be patient with me,' he said, 'and I will pay in full'; and the master was so moved with pity that he let the man go and remitted the debt.

But no sooner had the man gone out than he met a fellow-servant who owed him a few pounds; and catching hold of him he gripped him by the throat and said,' Pay me what you owe.' The man fell at his fellow-servant's feet, and begged him, 'Be patient with me, and I will pay you'; but he refused, and had him jailed until he should pay the debt. The other servants were deeply distressed when they saw what happened, and they went to their master and told him the whole story. He accordingly sent for the man. 'You scoundrel!' he said to him; 'I remitted the whole of your debt when you appealed to me; were you not bound to show your fellow-servant the same pity as I showed you?' And so angry was the master that he condemned the man to torture until he should pay the debt in full. And that is how my heavenly Father will deal with you, unless you each forgive your brother from your hearts."

Matthew: 18.23-35

* * * * * * * * * * * *

In his next chapter, the 19th, Matthew drew directly from Mark. He uses Mark's parables about divorce, letting children come to Jesus, and the impossibility of a rich man entering the Kingdom of Heaven. He opens his 20th chapter with the parable comparing treatment in the Kingdom of Heaven with the treatment of laborers in a vineyard.

"For the Kingdom of Heaven is like a landowner who went out early in the morning to hire laborers for his vineyard. After agreeing with the laborers for the usual daily wage, he sent them into his vineyard. When he went out about nine o'clock, he saw others standing idle in the marketplace; and he said to them, 'You also go into the vineyard, and I will pay you whatever is right.' So they went. When he went out again about noon and about three o'clock, he did the same. And about five o'clock he went out and found others standing around; and he said to them, 'Why are you standing idle all day?' They said to him, 'Because no one has hired us.' He said

to them, 'You also go into the vineyard. When evening
came, the owner of the vineyard said to his manager,
'Call the laborers and give them their pay, beginning with
the last and going to the first.' When those hired at five
o'clock came, each of them received the usual daily wage.
Now when the first came, they thought they would
receive more; but each of them also received the usual
daily wage. And when they received it they grumbled
against the landlord saying, 'These last worked only one
hour, and you have given them equal to us who have
borne the burden of the day in the scorching heat.' But
he replied to one of them, 'Friend, I am doing you no
wrong; did you not agree with me for the usual daily
wage?' Take what belongs to you and go; I choose to
give this last the same as I give you. Am I not allowed to
do what I choose with what belongs to me? Or are you
envious because I am generous?' So the last will be first,
and the first will be last.

Matthew: 20.1-16

Although using different parables Mark, Matthew, and Luke
have delivered the same message: "the last will be first and the first will
be last." Matthew's parable making the further point that the master is
not bound by some formula or contract, but may choose as he will the
manner in which he will treat each individual.

In Mark, Jesus has just been speaking to his disciples about the
rich man who could not achieve the Kingdom of God, even though he
has faithfully followed the law and has given generously to the temple.
Jesus has just told them it is impossible for any man to enter the
Kingdom of God; at which point Peter says to him, "We here have left
everything to become your followers." How, he wants to know, is it
that we can not enter the Kingdom of God; and if we cannot be saved,
who can be? Jesus answered, "For men it is impossible, but not for
God." Peter then lists things the disciples had given up to join Jesus;
implying that they should have priority. Jesus replied: "But many who
are first will be last and the last first." The disciples had not yet learned
what Jesus meant by the Kingdom of Heaven.

Luke, as we shall see, used an entirely different parable to stress this same point that the first will be last and the last will be first. It matters not when one gains faith or how closely one has stuck to rules or laws. The master is not bound by any rule in passing judgment or making any other decision. Do not be jealous, if a late comer enjoys the same reward as you.

Drawing once more from Mark, Matthew repeats the story of the mother of James and John asking Jesus to let them sit next to him on the throne.[100] He concludes the story with Jesus saying, "Whoever wishes be great among you must be your servant, and whoever wishes to be first among you must be your slave; just as the Son of Man came not to be served but to serve, and to give his life as a ransom for many."

> As they were leaving Jericho he was followed by a great crowd of people. At the roadside sat two blind men. When they heard it said that Jesus was passing they shouted, "Have pity on us Son of David." The people told them sharply to be quiet. But they shouted all the more. "Sir, have pity on us, Son of David." Jesus stopped and called the men. "What do you want me to do for you?" he asked. "Sir," they answered, "we want our sight." Jesus was deeply moved, and touched their eyes. At once their sight came back, and they followed him."
>
> Matthew: 20.29-34

Mark and Luke recount this story with only one blind man calling to be cured (saved). A figurative reader, looking beyond a literal healing of a blind man, will note the point Matthew is making for his Jewish audience; namely that Jesus did not do what he did because people were accepting him as the Messiah (Son of David), but rather out of love and compassion for fellow humans. In this parable he opened eyes, not in response to adulation or because he was the

---

[100]   Matthew has the two brothers, rather than their mother, asking for these high positions in the material kingdom they believed Jesus would rule as the Messiah.

Messiah, but because he had the need to open the eyes of his people to the message of God so they might be saved (cured).

> They were now nearing Jerusalem; and when they reached Bethpage at the Mount of Olives, Jesus sent two disciples, with these instructions: "Go to the village opposite, where you will at once find a donkey tethered with her foal beside her; untie them, and bring them to me. If anyone speaks to you, say, 'Our Master needs them'; and he will let you take them at once." This was to fulfill the prophecy which says. "Tell the daughter of Zion, 'Here is your king, who comes to you in gentleness, riding on an ass, riding on the foal of the beast of burden.'"
>
> Matthew: 21.1-5

In this attempt to strengthen Jesus' credentials in the eyes of his Jewish audience Matthew has reminded his readers that the prophets had foretold a messiah arriving on a donkey rather than in a handsome chariot.

> "Rejoice, rejoice, daughter of Zion, shout aloud, daughter of Jerusalem; for see, your king is coming to you, his cause won, his victory gained, humble and mounted on an ass, on a foal, the young of a she-ass. He shall banish chariots from Jerusalem; the warrior's bow shall be banished, He shall speak peaceably to every nation, and his rule shall extend from sea to sea, from the River to the ends of the earth."
>
> Zechariah: 9.9-10

Biblical scholars believe Matthew misinterpreted the poetic passage in Zechariah as meaning two animals rather than one. To the literal reader there is the problem of the differing versions in Mark and Matthew. The figurative reader, who takes into account Matthew's need to prove Jesus fulfilled the prophecies of the Jewish scriptures, sees no problem in this.

And now Jesus has arrived in Jerusalem.

CHAPTER 18

JERUSALEM

Sacrifice and Resurrection

Mark tells us about Jesus cleansing the temple on his second day in Jerusalem. Matthew, on the other hand, opens his description of Jesus' last week with Jesus going directly to the temple upon entering Jerusalem. Whereas cynics highlight such discrepancies, this difference in time is not important. It does not alter the message. Drawing further from Mark, Matthew describes the cleansing of the temple; but then adds the following:

> "In the temple blind men and cripples came to him, and he healed them. The chief priests and doctors of the law saw the wonderful things he did, and heard the boys in the temple shouting, 'Hosanna to the Son of David!', and they asked him indignantly, 'Do you hear what they are saying?' Jesus answered, 'I do; have you never read the text, Thou has made children and babes at the breast sound aloud thy praise'? Then he left them and went out of the city to Bethany, where he spent the night."
>
> Matthew: 21.12-17

In this added passage Matthew provides a further reason for the Sadducees to fear Jesus. Within the temple, of all places, are found men blind to the way of God. They are not able to see the path God would have his servant (Israel) take. Even though the way has been laid out for them, they have remained blind to it. Furthermore, they are unable

274

to find their way to the Kingdom of Heaven. That their eyes could be opened, where the priests had failed (or where priests may even have had no wish to bring about a change in the attitudes and beliefs of the "blind"), seemed to have been of no concern to the priests until a mere peasant from Galilee arrived and opened those eyes. This was a challenge, a threat the Sadducees absolutely could not ignore.

After returning to Mark's outline by repeating the parable of the fig tree, Matthew then follows with the story of the chief priests and elders asking by what authority Jesus acted.

> "When he entered the temple, the chief priests and the elders of the people came to him as he was teaching, and said, 'By what authority are you doing these things, and who gave you this authority?' Jesus said to them, 'I will also ask you one question; if you tell me the answer, then I will also tell you by what authority I do these things. Did the baptism of John come from heaven, or was it of human origin?' And they argued with one another, 'If we say, 'From heaven,' he will say to us, 'Why then did you not believe him?' But if we say, 'Of human origin,' we are afraid of the crowd; for all regard John as a prophet.' So they answered Jesus, 'We do not know.' And he said to them, 'Neither will I tell you by what authority I am doing these things."
>
> Matthew: 21.23-27

Jesus, realizing that no matter what he says the chief priests and the elders will not believe him, refuses to answer them. Readers already have noted this in their reading of Mark. However, whereas Mark ends his eleventh chapter with this story, Matthew (apparently considering his audience) feels it necessary to add further to the story as a means of demonstrating that Jesus' authority exceeds that of the priests.

> "But what do you think? A man had two sons; he went to the first and said, 'Son go work in the vineyard today.' He answered, 'I will not'; but later changed his mind and went. The father went to the second and said the same; and he answered, 'I go sir'; but he did not go. Which of the two did the will of his father? They said, 'The first.'

> Jesus said to them, 'Truly I tell you, the tax collectors and the prostitutes are going into the kingdom of God ahead of you. For John came to you in the way of righteousness and you did not believe him, but the tax collectors and prostitutes believed him; and even after you saw it, you did not change your minds and believe him."
>
> Matthew: 21.28-32

In this added paragraph by Matthew, Jesus once more emphasizes that we mortals cannot know how God will judge. It is not one's position or title, but rather faith that will be the determiner. Did you priests and scribes believe God's messenger, or did you ignore the message while those you hold in contempt accepted the messenger and the message?

Though his followers called him rabbi, Jesus had never been so ordained. Yet now he is challenging the authority of the highest religious authorities; the very ones who would judge him. Matthew is, by this passage, discrediting any Jewish religious authorities who would deny the greater authority of Jesus; thereby telling Jewish Christians, and Jews who might be considering converting to Christianity, that even the chief priests and elders of the temple could not deny Jesus' authority any more than they could deny the authority of John the Baptist.

At this point Matthew returns to the parables he has selected from Mark. He repeats the parable of the landlord who sent messengers to his servants in his vineyard; all of whom were turned away or even beaten. Finally the landlord sent his son who was killed by the servants. Matthew then adds the parable about the stone the builders rejected; the stone which later became the cornerstone. And, as in Mark he adds: "When the chief priests and the Pharisees heard his parables, they realized he was speaking about them. They wanted to arrest him, but they feared the crowds, because they (the crowds) regarded him as a prophet." (Matthew: 21. 45-46)

> "Then, Jesus spoke to them again in parables: 'The kingdom of Heaven is like this. There was a king who gave a wedding banquet for his son. He sent his slaves to call to call those who had been invited to the wedding

> banquet, but they would not come. Again he sent other
> slaves, saying, 'Tell those who have been invited: 'Look, I
> have prepared my dinner, my oxen and my fat calves
> have been slaughtered, and everything is ready; come to
> the wedding banquet.' But they made light of it and
> went away, one to his farm, another to his business, while
> the rest seized his slaves and mistreated them, and killed
> them. 'The king was enraged. He sent his troops,
> destroyed those murderers, and burned their city. Then
> he said to his slaves, 'The wedding is ready. But those
> invited were not worthy. Go therefore into the main
> streets, and invite everyone you find to the wedding
> banquet.' Those slaves went out into the streets and
> gathered all whom they found, both good and bad; so the
> wedding hall was filled with guests.
>
> Matthew: 22.1-10

Read literally, this passage does not carry much of a message. If a reader chooses to read the passage figuratively, she or he must first keep in mind that Matthew is addressing fellow Jews; and secondly that the Kingdom of Heaven is not a place, but a blessed state of peace.

In this parable the people of Israel, the chosen people, have been invited to enter the Kingdom of Heaven. However, their material concerns occupy them so much that they have no room within themselves for the kingdom. Their eyes and ears are closed to the invitation. God's servants, John the Baptist and Jesus, were "seized, mistreated, and killed" when sent to repeat the invitation to the people of Israel. God, portrayed in this parable as the king, then rids himself of any further responsibility for the invited guests.

This passage is totally Matthew's parable. The killing of the murderers and the burning of their town may be seen as the destruction of Jerusalem in 70 A.D; something only Matthew could have known. Jesus died forty years before the destruction of Jerusalem. Paul died three years before the city was razed. Mark, the disciple of Peter and companion of Paul, completed his gospel before the fall of Jerusalem. Only by the time the later gospels were written (Matthew, Luke, John) could the writers know of the destruction of Jerusalem.

The king (God) then sends other servants (missionaries like Barnabas and Paul) out among those who had not been chosen to receive the invitation (the Gentiles). These servants were to bring all who were not among the first chosen to the feast (the Kingdom of Heaven).

Fearing the growing crowds of Jews who would now support Jesus, the Pharisees try to lead Jesus into a trap whereby Roman or other secular authorities would bear the onus for getting rid of Jesus. To this end they question him about payment of taxes to the emperor. Readers are familiar with this parable, having read it earlier in the "Gospel According to Mark". Matthew follows this with the questioning by Sadducees about the role, after resurrection, of a widow who was married to a succession of brothers. This is followed, as in Mark with further questioning by Pharisees. At this point Matthew adds a particularly sharp criticism aimed at those critics of the Christian church who would drag it back under the heel of the Pharisees and the Law.

> "Jesus then addressed the people and his disciples, 'The doctors of the law and the Pharisees sit in the chair of Moses; therefore do what they tell you; pay attention to their words. But do not follow their practice; for they say one thing and do another. They make up heavy packs and pile them on men's shoulders, but will not raise a finger to lift the load themselves. Whatever they do is done for show. They go about with broad phylacteries and with large tassels on their robes; they like to have places of honor at feasts and the chief seats in synagogues, to be greeted respectfully in the street, and to be addressed as 'rabbi'.
>
> "But you must not be called 'rabbi'; for you have one Rabbi, and you are all brothers. Do not call any man on earth 'father'; for you have one Father, and he is in heaven. Nor must you be called teacher'; you have one Teacher, the Messiah. The greatest among you must be your servant. For whoever exalts himself will be humbled; and whoever humbles himself will be exalted.
>
> "Alas, alas for you (woe unto you), lawyers and Pharisees, hypocrites that you are! You shut the door of the kingdom of Heaven in men's faces; you do not enter yourselves, and when others are entering you stop them.

"Alas for you (woe unto you), lawyers and Pharisees, hypocrites! You travel over sea and land to win one convert; and when you have won him you make him twice as fit for hell as you are yourselves.

"Alas for you, blind guides! You say, 'If a man swears by the sanctuary, that is nothing; but if he swears by the gold in the sanctuary, he is bound by his oath.' Blind fools! Which is more important, the gold, or the sanctuary which sanctifies the gold? Or you say, 'If a man swears by the altar, that is nothing; but if he swears by the offering that lies on the altar, he is bound by his oath.' What blindness! Which is the more important, the offering, or the altar which sanctifies it? To swear by the altar, then, is to swear both by the altar and by whatever lies on it; to swear by the sanctuary is to swear both by the sanctuary and by him who dwells there; and to swear by heaven is to swear both by the throne and by him who sits upon it.

"Alas for you, lawyers and Pharisees, hypocrites! You pay tithes of mint and dill and cummin; but you have overlooked the weightier demands of the Law, justice, mercy, and good faith. It is these you should have practiced, without neglecting the others. Blind guides! You strain off a gnat, yet gulp down a camel.!

"Alas for you, lawyers and Pharisees, hypocrites! You clean the outside of the cup and dish which you have filled inside by robbery and self-indulgence! Blind Pharisee! Clean the inside of the cup first; then the outside will be clean also.

"Alas for you, You are like tombs covered with whitewash; they look well from the outside, but inside they are full of dead men's bones and all kinds of filth. So it is with you: outside you look like honest men, but inside you are brimful of hypocrisy and crime.

"Alas for you, lawyers and Pharisees, hypocrites! You build up the tombs of the prophets and embellish the monuments of the saints, and you say, 'If we had been alive in our fathers' time, we should never have taken part with them in the murder of the prophets.' So you acknowledge that you are the sons of the men who killed the prophets. Go on then, finish off what your fathers began!

"You snakes, you viper's brood, how can you escape being condemned to hell? I send you therefore prophets, sages and teachers; some of them you will kill and crucify, others you will flog in your synagogues and hound from city to city. And so, on you will fall the guilt of all the innocent blood spilt on the ground, from innocent Abel to Zechariah son of Berachiah, whom you murdered between the sanctuary and the altar. Believe me, this generation will bear the guilt of it all.

"O Jerusalem, Jerusalem, the city that murders prophets and stones the messengers sent to her! How often have I longed to gather your children, as a hen gathers her brood under her wings; but you would not let me. Look, look! there is your temple, forsaken by God. And I tell you, you shall never see me until the time when you say, 'Blessings on him who comes in the name of the Lord.'"

Matthew: 23.1-39

Because the Pharisees from their authoritative position are quoting from the scriptures you should listen carefully to their teachings. Do what they say, Jesus says, but not what they do, for they are hypocrites who say one thing but do another. They burden you with all types of rules and tell you how you must bear the responsibility for living according to them, but they do nothing to help you bear that burden.

Nineteen verses of this chapter (23: 13-32) are often referred to as the seven woes. They are aimed at Pharisees; not all Pharisees; only those leading the new Pharasaism. This chapter is definitely Matthew; a Matthew using Jesus' confrontation in the temple as an opportunity to denounce the Pharisees. Remember that the temple was destroyed in 70 AD. The Pharisees had, since 100 BC, been trying to break the chokehold the priests of the Temple had on the religion of the Jews. That did not mean they intended to make it purely a congregational religion. However, they were actively trying to wrest control of the religion out of the hands of the Temple priests. An important instrument in this struggle was the synagogue, which the Pharisees developed and strengthened. Through the synagogue the Pharisees were telling people that they could worship other than at the temple. The Pharisees had long opposed the sensationalism of the bloody sacrifices carried out by the temple priests.

With the destruction of the temple the priests lost most of their hold over the people. The synagogue became increasingly important; and under control of Pharisees the religion of the Jews over the next two and a half centuries, not only in Israel, but throughout the Diaspora, was the high period of the new Pharasaism. By the time of Matthew and Luke, Pharasaism was the mode of the Jewish religion with which the Christian church was confronted.

When Jesus was challenging the religious authorities of his time, the Sadducees held the political power within the Jewish religious community. It was they who Jesus confronted, and they who carried the most weight in determining the fate of Jesus. Matthew is faced not only with dealing with that role of the Sadducees in the crucifixion of Jesus, but also with the later role of the Pharisees who were in Matthew's time the major force in trying to bring the Christian church back under the Law. The Sadducees had been Jesus' primary opponent; but now sixty years later it was the Pharisees who were threatening the Christian church. To understand why Matthew would take an entire chapter to attack the Pharisees, one needs to appreciate Matthew's dilemma. Earlier in his gospel he has tried to keep Jewish Christians in the church and to attract further converts. At this point he shifts to an attack on the leaders of the Pharisaic religion whom he sees as actively trying to bring down the new Christian church. Readers should note how carefully Matthew avoids attacking Jews or the religion of the Jews. His attack concentrates on the Pharisees.

PREPARING FOR THE END

At his point Matthew shifts from his denunciation of the Pharisees and begins a series of predictions of disasters ahead and of what would happen when the Messiah was gone.

> "As Jesus came out of the temple and was going away, his disciples came to point out to him the buildings of the temple. Then he asked them, 'You see all these, do

> you not? Truly, I tell you, not one stone will be left here upon another; all will be thrown down.'
>
> "When he was sitting on the Mount of Olives, the disciples came to him privately, saying, 'Tell us, when will this be, and what will be the sign of your coming and of the end of the age?' Jesus answered them, 'Beware that no one leads you astray. For many will come in my name, saying, 'I am the Messiah! And they will lead many astray. And you will hear of wars and rumors of wars; see that you are not alarmed; for this must take place, but the end is not yet. For nation will rise against nation, and kingdom against kingdom, and there will be famines and earthquakes in various places: all this is but the beginning of the birth pangs."
>
> Matthew: 24.1-8

A new reader of the New Testament will note that this passage is almost word for word the same as that found in Mark. Actually this entire 24th chapter of Matthew is a repetition of what readers have already found in Mark (13. 3-37).

In discussing Mark we saw various interpretations of the reference to the destruction of the temple. Mark wrote before the temple was destroyed. Whereas Mark could be using the temple as symbol of the fall of Jerusalem and defeat of the Jews, Matthew is writing twenty years after the Romans destroyed the temple while putting down a revolt by the Jews.

The New Oxford Bible notes that: "These verses, together with the discourse that follows, seem to merge teachings about an immediate destruction of Jerusalem with details associated in Scripture with the end of human history. These teachings were set down by the Evangelist in the light of events between A.D. 30 and 70. It is difficult to be certain what the original form of Jesus' words was."[101]

Matthew knew what had happened in those years between Jesus' death and Mark's writing; but he also knew what had happened in the twenty or more years that had passed since Mark wrote. The temple in Jerusalem had been destroyed, the power of the priests had been greatly diminished with the destruction of the temple, and once

---

[101]   Footnote, p. 36 "New Testament", *The New Oxford Bible*.

more thousands of Israelites left Israel for cities throughout the Mediterranean region.

Matthew, as did Mark, now has Jesus move to the Mount of Olives. This was an important reference for Jews of that time. The Mount of Olives is frequently mentioned in the gospels; and devout Jews would recall Zechariah's prophecy concerning the coming of the end: "Then the Lord will go forth and fight against those nations as when he fights on a day of battle. On that day his feet shall stand on the Mount of Olives, which lies before Jerusalem on the east..." (Zechariah: 14. 3-4). It is important that Jesus, especially as the Jewish Messiah described by Matthew, make his pronouncement and prophecy of the future and of an impending "end of the age" from this spot.

It is here, on the Mount of Olives, that the disciples gather round to ask Jesus, "and what will be the sign of your coming and of the end of the age?" As in Mark, the remainder of this chapter is devoted to warning the disciples of the pitfalls and persecution that lay ahead. It ends with the warning about the coming of final judgment.

> "Who then is the faithful and wise slave, whom his master has put in charge of his household, to give the other slaves their allowance of food at the proper time? Blessed is that slave whom his master will find at work when he arrives. Truly I tell you, he will put that one in charge of all his possessions. But if that wicked slave says to himself, 'My master is delayed,' and he begins to beat his fellow slaves, and eats and drinks with drunkards, the master will come home on a day when he does not expect him and at an hour he does not know. He will cut him in pieces (cut him off) and put him with the hypocrites, where there will be weeping and gnashing of teeth."
>
> Matthew: 24.45-51

In his next chapter, Matthew continues to emphasize that one will never know when or for what he or she will be judged. Live a life in which you are always ready, Jesus tells his disciples.

> "When the day comes the kingdom of Heaven will be like this. Ten bridesmaids who took their lamps and

went to meet the bridegroom. Five of them were foolish, and five were wise. When the foolish took their lamps, they took no oil with them; but the wise took flasks of oil with their lamps. As the bride-groom was delayed, all of them became drowsy and slept. But at midnight there was a shout, 'Look! Here is the bride-groom! Come out and meet him.' Then all the bridesmaids got up and trimmed their lamps. The foolish said to the wise, 'Give us some of your oil, for our lamps are going out.' But the wise replied, 'No! there will not be enough for you and for us; you had better go to the dealers and buy some for yourselves. And while they went to buy it, the bridegroom came, and those who were ready went with him to the wedding banquet; and the other bridesmaids came also, saying, 'Lord, lord, open to us.' But he replied, 'Truly I tell you, I do not know you.' Keep awake therefore, for you know neither the day nor the hour."

Matthew: 25. 1-13

This parable may remind the reader of Jesus' earlier parable about the bridegroom eating while Pharisees fasted. It was not uncommon for Jesus to be referred to as the bridegroom. This is followed by a parable in a similar vein.

"It is like a man going abroad, who called his servants and put his capital in their hands; to one he gave five bags of gold, to another two, to another one, each according to his capacity. Then he left the country. The man who had the five bags went at once and employed them in business, and made a profit of five bags, and the man who had two bags made two. But the man who had been given one bag of gold went off and dug a hole in the ground, and hid his master's money. A long time afterwards their master returned, and proceeded to settle accounts with them. The man who had been given the five bags of gold came and produced the five he had made: 'Master, he said, you left five bags with me; look I

> have made five more.' 'Well done, my good and trusty
> servant!' said the master. 'You have proved trustworthy
> in a small way; I will now put you in charge of something
> big. Come and share your master's delight.' The man
> with the two bags came and said, 'Master, you left two
> bags with me; look, I have made two more.' 'Well done,
> my good and trusty servant! said the master. 'You have
> proved trustworthy in a small way; I will now put you in
> charge of something big. Come share your master's
> delight.' Then came the man who had been given one
> bag came and said, 'Master, I knew you to be a hard man:
> you reap where you have not sown, you gather where you
> have not scattered; so I was afraid, and I went and hid
> your gold in the ground. Here it is – you have what
> belongs to you.' 'You lazy rascal!' said the master. You
> knew that I reap where I have not sown, and gather
> where I have not scattered? Then you ought to have put
> my money on deposit, and on my return I should have
> got it back with interest. Take the bag of gold from him,
> and give it to the one with ten bags. For the man who
> has will always be given more, till he has enough and to
> spare; and the man who has not will forfeit even what he
> has. Fling the useless servant out into the dark, the place
> of wailing and grinding of teeth!'"
>
> Matthew: 25.14-30

This is an interesting story when read literally; but when read literally it is difficult to find a religious message. It seems to deal entirely with the very material world Jesus has repeatedly said stood between humans and the kingdom of God.

As a parable it was meant to be read figuratively. Here the reader finds a further description of what could happen at the time of the final judgment. The bags of gold were all those things God had given humans; life, the capacity to make choices, and an awareness of God's will. Like the bridesmaids, the three men were free to choose the path to follow. Five bridesmaids were too busy thinking of other things to bother to take extra oil with them and were not ready for the bridegroom's arrival. Two of the men used what God had given all humans and used their lives to carry out the will of God. The third

man had done nothing positive. He had existed; and though receiving
God's gifts he failed to use them as a good and trustworthy servant of
God. It is not enough to exist. One should try to leave the world a
better place than when he or she entered it. What have these men done
with their lives and God's gifts to help bring the kingdom closer to
others?

Matthew explains further this role of the man or woman who
will eventually face the Day of Judgment. It did not matter that the
three men received unequal gifts. They had the ability to do the best
with what they had. This theme is expanded in the following familiar
passage concerning the separation of those who would inherit the
kingdom from those who would be rejected.

> "When the Son of Man comes in his glory, and the angels
> with him, then he will sit on the throne of his glory. All
> the nations will be gathered before him, and he will
> separate people, one from another as a shepherd
> separates the sheep from the goats, and he will put the
> sheep at his right hand and the goats at the left. Then the
> king will say to those on his right hand, 'Come, you that
> are blessed by my Father, inherit the kingdom prepared
> for you from the foundation of the world; for I was
> hungry and you gave me food, I was thirsty and you gave
> me something to drink, I was a stranger and you
> welcomed me, I was naked and you gave me clothing, I
> was sick and you took care of me, I was in prison and
> you visited me.' Then the righteous will answer him,
> 'Lord when was it that we saw you hungry and gave you
> food, or thirsty and gave you something to drink? And
> when was it that we saw you naked and gave you
> clothing? And when was it that we saw you sick or in
> prison and visited you?' And the king will answer them,
> 'Truly I tell you, just as you did it to one of the least of
> those who are members of my family, you did it to me.'"
>
> Matthew: 25.31-40

This parable goes still further in describing the rejection of
those who failed to do what had been done by those chosen to inherit
the kingdom. Being a high priest, a scribe, a Sadducee, or a Pharisee

guarantees nothing. Being a wealthy merchant, wearing fine robes while giving large sums to charities, is not enough. It is not gifts of money, nor achievement of high position within the religious establishment that guarantees salvation. The poorest person who gives time from his or her life to help others is considered far more worthy than those who are too busy, or have no inclination, to give of themselves. This is reminiscent of Paul's exhortation forty years earlier that all humans will be judged by the way they lived (Romans: 2. 1-16).

The three parables of this chapter were meant to be read together. The second builds on the first, and the third expands still further on the theme of how people will be judged by what they have done or failed to do. Remember the positive aspect of the Golden Rule. "*DO* unto others as you would have them do unto you." Don't, Matthew is saying, assume you are good because you are neutral and are doing nothing to harm another. You *must* act; you *must* do; and by what you do you will be judged.

Mark had warned that the "master" could come at any time. Be ready, he admonished his readers; be ready at all times. In those earliest years of the new church, converts believed the world would come to an end at any moment. Twenty years later, Matthew includes the three parables we have just quoted; parables apparently not available to Mark or Paul. Why?

When one finds material in Matthew or Luke that was never mentioned by Paul or Mark, the question arises as to why twenty years later this material was added. Again, readers need to put themselves in Matthew's sandals in Matthew's time. The church is being threatened through the growing competition of mystery religions offering both physical resurrection and miracles performed by founders born of virgins. Part of the struggle to hold this young church together calls for it to match or surpass claims that are drawing its members into those other religions. Survival of the church is the only way the message of Jesus can be carried to the people. The church is the vehicle. The stories of Jesus' birth and of his physical resurrection were not part of Jesus' message. They were, on the other hand, important additions in this struggle for survival of the vehicle that carries the message.

The world of Matthew's time has not come to an end. Believers who have flocked to the church are now asking whether the prediction of an imminent day of judgment has been nothing but a gimmick. Why then, these early converts wonder, should we bother about living according to what Jesus said was God's way. The three parables

Matthew inserts at this juncture hammer home the point that no one can know just what year, or day, or hour the Lord will appear and judgment will be passed Judgment will not be based on one's future intentions or one's behavior years before, but on how one is living when the Lord suddenly, and without fanfare or prior announcement, appears. This is no time to vacillate about your faith in your religion, says Matthew in response to these doubts. This is no time to take a vacation, no matter how brief, from faith and the way of life taught by Jesus. Always be ready, warns Matthew in these parables.

* * * * * * * * * * * *

Two days before Passover was to be observed:

> "Then the chief priests and the elders of the nation met in the palace of the High Priest, Caiaphas; and there they conferred together on a scheme to have Jesus arrested by some trick and put to death. 'It must not be during the festival,' they said, 'or there may be rioting by the people.'"
>
> Matthew: 26.3-5

Note the deep fear expressed by the chief priests and elders; fear that the people would rise against them in support of Jesus. This could even grow to be an all out rebellion against the authority of the priests and Sadducees. This is so different than the theme of centuries of preaching, and of twenty-first century novels and motion pictures, in which the masses of Jews were about to call for Jesus' death. In this passage the conspirators are scheming to bring about Jesus' death in such a way that the "people" would be unaware until it was too late for them to prevent the crucifixion.

Matthew now repeats Mark's stories of the Last Supper, Jesus' prayer at Gethsemane, betrayal by Judas, the denials by the disciples, the trial by the Governor, the crucifixion, and the placing of Jesus in a tomb. He then adds a last chapter which goes beyond what Mark had written.

"The Sabbath was over, and it was about daybreak on Sunday, when Mary of Magdala and the other Mary came to look at the grave. Suddenly there was a violent earthquake; an angel of the Lord descended from heaven; he came to the stone and rolled it away, and sat himself down on it. His face shone like lightening; his garments were white as snow. At the sight of him the guards shook with fear and lay like dead.

"The angel then addressed the women: 'You,' he said, 'have nothing to fear. I know you are looking for Jesus who was crucified. He is not here; he has been raised again, as he said he would be. Come and see the place where he was laid, and then go quickly and tell his disciples: 'He has been raised from the dead, and is going on before you into Galilee; there you will see him.' That is what I had to tell you.

"They hurried away from the tomb in awe and great joy, and ran to tell the disciples. Suddenly Jesus was there in their path. He gave them his greeting, and they came up and clasped his feet, falling prostrate before him. Then Jesus said to them, 'Do not be afraid. Go and take word to my brothers that they are to leave for Galilee. They will see me there.' "The women had started on their way when some of the guard went into the city and reported to the chief priests everything that had happened. After the meeting with the elders and conferring together, the chief priests offered the soldiers a substantial bribe and told them to say, 'His disciples came by night and stole the body while we were asleep.' They added, 'If this should reach the Governor's ears, we will put matters right with him and see that you do not suffer.' So they took the money and did as they were told. This story became widely known, and is current in Jewish circles to this day.

"The eleven disciples made their way to Galilee, to the mountain where Jesus had told them to meet him. When they saw him they fell prostrate before him, though some

> were doubtful. Jesus then came up and spoke to them. He said, 'Full authority in heaven and on earth has been committed to me. Go forth therefore, and make all nations my disciples; baptize men everywhere in the name of the Father and the Son and the Holy Spirit, and teach them to observe all that I have commanded you. And be assured, I am with you always, to the end of time.'"
>
> Matthew: 28.5-20

Matthew is aware that Paul, other early founders of the church, and Mark who was recording the gospel being preached in those first years of the church, believed in spiritual, not physical resurrection. But, he has to deal with the growing attraction of physical resurrection as preached by the various religions throughout the region. He elaborates, therefore, on the resurrection by describing a physical reappearance of Jesus. Still, he retains the important message carried in Mark. "Go forth therefore, and make *all* nations my disciples; baptize men everywhere in the name of the Father and the Son and the Holy Spirit, and teach them to observe all that I have commanded you."

Matthew has spent his gospel up to this point explaining to fellow Jews why they should accept the word of Jesus. He has lauded Jesus as the long expected Messiah. He has witnessed demands from Judaizers that all Christians should live according to rules governing everything from diet to circumcision. He has used his gospel to fight for survival of a church free from the law and the rule of Pharisees and priests. And now, in his last words he aggressively justifies the spread of the church among Gentiles: "Go forth therefore, and make *all* nations my disciples."

Matthew ties this message to the crucifixion; to the ultimate sacrifice of the teacher. To those Jews who have accepted enough of Jesus' teaching to join the Christian church, Matthew throws out this final challenge. He calls for throwing off the shackles that would prevent the church from becoming a universal church, rather than just a limited reform sect of the Jewish religion of that time. The missionary movement among the Gentiles and the rapid spreading of the gospel among Gentiles is not a matter of personal ambition of those who are carrying the message by organizing new churches. Instead, through the spiritually resurrected Jesus comes the pledge that in carrying this message to the Gentiles: "Be assured, I am with you always, to the end of time."

CHAPTER 19

LUKE

Just as we cannot with certainty identify the authors of the gospels of Mark and Matthew, so we cannot with certainty identify the author of *The Gospel According To Luke*; though there is considerable support for the theory that he was a physician who as a young man had accompanied Paul on some of his travels. We do know the author was well educated; his literary style leading some to praise his gospel as one of the most beautiful literary works of all time.

Unlike Paul, Mark, and Matthew; it is most likely Luke was a Gentile. His gospel is definitely aimed at a Gentile audience. Not only had he little need to make reference to the prophets and the scriptures; he actually avoided doing so wherever possible, and also carefully avoided reference to Jesus as the *Jewish* Messiah. As we earlier noted, at least half of Matthew's gospel was taken directly from *The Gospel According To Mark,* to which he then added passages to show how Jesus fulfilled the prophecies of the Jewish scriptures. Luke also drew at least half his gospel directly from Mark's gospel but, in contrast to Matthew, the passages Luke added emphasize the kindness, thoughtfulness, and humanity of Jesus. This is most noticeable in such parables as those concerning the Lost Coin, the Good Samaritan, and the Prodigal Son.

While avoiding scriptural references which would mean nothing to, or would raise questions for, his Gentile audience, Luke also avoided terms that would tend to label Jesus as a Jewish prophet or teacher. Luke never has disciples addressing Jesus as "rabbi", though Luke also saw him as a teacher. Instead, they call him "Master," a term which in Greek would connote a teacher.

Like Matthew, Luke wrote his gospel some fifty-five or sixty years after the death of Jesus. He makes it quite clear that he had no personal acquaintance with the events about which he was writing. Rather, he is presenting an interpretation of events as he believed they should be viewed in the context of Jesus' teaching.

> "Since many have undertaken to set down an orderly account of the events that have been fulfilled among us, just as they were handed on to us by those who from the beginning were eyewitnesses and servants of the word, I too decided, after investigating everything carefully from the first, to write an orderly account for you, most excellent Theophilus, so that you may know the truth concerning the things about which you have been instructed."
>
> Luke: 1.1-4

Not only has Luke pointed out that he had in no way personally witnessed the events about which he was writing, but that there had been numerous written accounts available to him. Of these earlier writings, other than the letters of Paul, a few of the earliest epistles, and the gospel of Mark, we have no record for they were not among the gospels or epistles chosen and saved by the men who, a century after Luke, would be charged with compiling the beginnings of our present bible.

The Gospel According To Luke, then, became the interpretation of Christianity Luke wished to pass on to Gentiles.

LUKE'S INTRODUCTION OF JESUS

Like Matthew, Luke begins by building credentials for Jesus; opening with an account of the miraculous birth of a son to Elizabeth and Zechariah. According to Luke, Elizabeth had been barren throughout their married life until the angel Gabriel appeared before Zechariah and informed him that Elizabeth would bear a son.

> "Do not be afraid, Zechariah; your prayer has been heard; your wife Elizabeth will bear you a son, and you shall name him John. Your heart will thrill with joy and many will be glad that he was born; for he will be great in the eyes of the Lord. He shall never touch wine or strong drink. From his birth he will be filled with the Holy Spirit; and he will bring back many Israelites to the Lord their God."
>
> Luke: 1.13-16

In this manner Luke introduces John the Baptist, giving John a somewhat divine stature;[102] a stature that becomes important when later John will tell the crowds awaiting baptism that "there is one to come who is mightier than I." Luke follows this introduction with a description of Gabriel's visit to Mary six months later; at which time he tells her:

> "Do not be afraid, Mary, for God has been gracious to you; you will conceive and bear a son, and you shall name him Jesus. He will be great; he will bear the title 'Son of the Most High'; the Lord God will give him the throne of his ancestor David, and he will be king over Israel for ever; his reign shall never end. 'How can this be?' said Mary; 'I am still a virgin.' The angel answered, 'The Holy Spirit will come upon you; and for that reason the holy child to be born will be called 'Son of God'."
>
> Luke: 1.30-35

Once more, a literal reading and a figurative reading diverge. Critics challenge the literalist by asking how we can today know exact conversations occurring almost two thousand years before the invention of tape recorders and when no witnesses were present to record the conversations in any other manner. Furthermore, they point

---

[102]   Matthew knew his fellow Jews would need no introduction to John the Baptist. However, Gentiles for whom Luke was writing were far less likely to have heard of John; therefore this building of background, which included the announcement by the angel Gabriel, was important in giving John the status from which he would in turn would introduce Jesus.

out, Paul, Mark, and Matthew failed to note the angel Gabriel's conversation with Zechariah, yet roughly ninety-five years after the event Luke came up with the exact conversation.

It was after the birth of Elizabeth's child, John, that Luke has Joseph and Mary travel from Nazareth to Bethlehem to register.

> This was the first registration of its kind; it took place when Quirinius was governor of Syria. For this purpose everyone made his way to his own town; and so Joseph went up to Judea from the town of Nazareth in Galilee, to register in the city of David, called Bethlehem, because he was of the house of David by descent; and with him went Mary who was betrothed to him.
>
> Luke: 2.1-5

Luke was a fine writer, but his knowledge of the history and geography of the Middle East did not match his literary expertise. In the above passage, as earlier noted when reading Matthew, Luke inaccurately uses a trip to register in Bethlehem as a reason for Joseph and Mary to be in the city of David at the time of Jesus' birth. That registration was not ordered by Quirinius until Jesus was twelve or thirteen years old.[103]

As with Matthew, Luke wrote when Christian churches were tying to survive or grow while surrounded by religions claiming founders born of virgins; a claim also made repeatedly on behalf of emperors, Pharaohs, and legendary heroes for more than two thousand years before Jesus was born. Amid such competition, trying to draw converts to a new religion built around the teachings of one who was not a miracle worker "born of a virgin" might seem a near hopeless task to early Christian missionaries.

Matthew, writing for a Jewish audience refers repeatedly to Jesus' birth fulfilling prophecies found in the scriptural accounts of the prophets. Luke refers to Jewish scriptures, but he does not cite them as prophecies.[104] In Matthew's version of Jesus' birth, Mary and Joseph were living in a house in Bethlehem, and only after Jesus birth did the flee to Egypt and eventually to Nazareth. This fitted well into Jewish

---

[103] Twelve or thirteen depending on what month Jesus was born.
[104] "Light in the Darkness", Marcus J. Borg, Distinguished professor of Religion at Oregon State University, *Christian Century*, December 16, 1998.

prophecies. Luke, on the other hand, describes a family living in Nazareth and making a trip to Bethlehem.

Christians who do not accept the above passage literally are not troubled by this. They see no need to become bogged down with concern over Luke's and Matthew's differing efforts to establish Jesus' credibility and authority in their introductions. Twenty-first century Christians do not face competitive religions claiming messengers born of virgins. They need, however, to find and heed the message.[105]

Luke adds another story not found anywhere else in the Bible.

> Now every year his parents went to Jerusalem for the festival of the Passover. And when he was twelve years old, they went up as usual for the festival. When the festival was ended and they started to return, the boy Jesus stayed behind in Jerusalem, but his parents did not know it. Assuming he was in the group of travelers, they went a day's journey. Then they started to look for him among their relatives and friends. When they did not find him, they returned to Jerusalem to search for him. After three days they found him in the temple, sitting among the teachers, listening to them and asking them questions. And all who heard him were amazed at the understanding of the answers. When his parents saw him they were astonished; and his mother said to him, "Child, why have you treated us like this? Look, your father and I have been searching for you in great anxiety." He said to them, "Why were you searching for me? Did you not know that I must be in my Father's house?"   Luke: 2.41-49

[105] Peter died 34 years after Jesus was crucified, and Paul 37 years after Jesus' death. Mark 's gospel was written about 38 or 39 years after Jesus' death. Nothing is mentioned by them about Jesus' birth. Considering the prevalence of virgin births claimed for political and religious leaders throughout the region, it is difficult to imagine that no local Christian churches would have adopted virgin birth stories during the twenty years between the time of the deaths of early church leaders (such as Peter and Paul) and the writing of the gospels of Matthew and Luke. If such stories later began to sweep through the as yet relatively unorganized Christian community which at that time had no bible or central authority, it is understandable that Matthew and Luke would feel it necessary to include and explain a virgin birth. Each handled it in the manner appropriate for his particular audiences.

Again critics find fuel for their fires. Why, they ask, did Paul, Mark, and Matthew know nothing of Jesus' childhood, while Luke is able to find this story, with the exact conversation, more than eighty years after Jesus is supposed to have sat with the scholars? Furthermore, Luke says that every year Jesus' parents traveled the long road to Jerusalem to celebrate Passover. Joseph might have made this trip, but Mary and the children were under no such obligation. If every family throughout Israel and Judah were to make this trip annually, who tended the sheep, watered and fed the cattle, kept the local shops, and otherwise kept the country running? Where would these thousands of people have stayed and how would they have been fed?

Such questions can cast doubt on the veracity of Luke's gospel; but only if it is read literally. Luke's lack of first hand knowledge of distances, customs, and other conditions in Israel and Judah are evident in this passage. Readers should remember that Luke said he had no first hand knowledge of events in that region or that time period. He is thought to have been living in Antioch when preparing this gospel.

For those who read this gospel figuratively, this is in no way disillusioning nor does it otherwise diminish the value of Luke's gospel. They see this passage as a continuation of Luke's attempt to build the reputation and the authority of the messenger before introducing the message. Early organizers of Christianity appear not to differ greatly from the founders of the mystery religions surrounding them in their concern that their message could be lost, if they did not emphasize the stature of the messenger. Methods used two thousand years ago by gospel writers to keep the message alive should not become obstacles for twenty-first century Christians pursuing that message.

Luke moves on with a description of the work of John the Baptist and the eventual arrival of Jesus to be baptized by John. It is at this point that he inserts the genealogy of Jesus. We noted the differences between the genealogy according to Matthew and that according to Luke when we earlier discussed *The Gospel According To Matthew*. Whereas Matthew emphasized Jesus as a descendant of the royal line of the House of David, Luke avoids the Jewish royal line, but moves the genealogy back to Adam; thereby making Jesus a descendant of the first man created by God; something Jesus would hold in common with all humankind.

Borrowing from Mark's gospel, Luke next briefly mentions the forty days spent facing temptations in the wilderness. From there Luke has Jesus returning directly to Galilee. Unlike Matthew he does not discuss the work of Jesus upon his return, except to say in two sentences that Jesus began to teach in synagogues in the area, before describing Jesus' preaching in the synagogue in his home town of Nazareth.

According to Matthew, Jesus had been preaching in various localities before returning to Nazareth. He had spent forty days in the wilderness and then had returned to Galilee, making his home in Capernaum. He preached throughout Galilee where he healed many while crowds followed him. He had given his Sermon on the Mount, and had continued his work for some time. It is then that Matthew has Jesus returning to Nazareth where in the synagogue he taught and was reproached by the people who had taken offense from his teaching. It was then that Jesus told them: "Prophets are not without honor except in their own country and their own house."

Luke at this point goes into more detail about the teaching in the Nazareth synagogue. He tells of Jesus reading from a scroll of Isaiah, after which he began to preach.

> "The Spirit of the Lord is upon me, because he has anointed me to bring good news to the poor. He has sent me to proclaim release to the captives and recovery of sight to the blind, to let the oppressed go free. To proclaim the year of the Lord's favor." He rolled up the scroll, gave it back to the attendant, and sat down; and all eyes in the synagogue were fixed on him.
>
> He began to speak: "Today", he said, "in your hearing this text has come true." There was a general stir of admiration; they were surprised that words of such grace should fall from his lips. "Is this not Joseph's son, they asked." Then Jesus said, "No doubt you will quote the proverb to me, 'Physician, heal yourself', and say, 'We have heard of all your doings at Capernaum; do the same here in your own home town.' "I tell you this, he went on: "no prophet is recognized in his own country. There were many widows in Israel, you may be sure, in Elijah's time, when for three years and six months the skies never opened, and famine lay hard over the whole country; yet it was to none of those Elijah was sent, but to a widow at Serepta in the territory of Sidon. Again in the time of the

298

> prophet Elisha there were many lepers in Israel, and not
> one of them was healed, but only Naaman , the Syrian."
> At these words the whole congregation were infuriated.
> They leapt up, threw him out of the town, and took him
> to the brow of the hill on which it was built. But he
> walked straight through them all and went away.
>
> Luke: 4.18-30

Some translations have Jesus being taken to the edge of a cliff from which he was to be thrown. With this story, Luke has given his readers a picture of a Jesus who was being cast out by his own people and whose message has been rejected. Jesus had told the congregation they were not to believe that just because they were Israelites they would receive God's blessings or be reconciled. For emphasis he used an "Old Testament" story in which a non-Israelite was saved (healed) when all Israelites around him were not. He was telling the congregation that though he, the prophet, was without honor in his own country his message would be received by "foreigners".

Neither Mark nor Matthew related that story. Matthew has only pointed out that Jesus was the prophet rejected in his home town. Luke's version prepares his Gentile readers to accept Jesus as the prophet rejected by Israel and destined by God to bring the word to the rest of the world. He has thus separated Jesus and his teachings from a national label.

Luke then repeats, in Mark's words, the story of Jesus being challenged in the synagogue in Capernaum by the man who shrieked: "What do you want with us, Jesus of Nazareth? Have you come to destroy us?" This is followed by accounts of Jesus healing those who were brought to him.

Mark and Matthew tell of Jesus walking beside the sea where seeing Simon (Peter) and Andrew he called for them to join him and become fishers of people. Luke, at this point, tells of Jesus stepping into Simon's boat and telling Simon to move his boat to deep water and then put down his nets. The catch is so great that it almost causes the boat to capsize. Simon Peter then falls to his knees in awe and says; "Go away from me, Lord, for I am a sinful man!" (Luke: 5. 8)

Luke is portraying Peter as a strong man with human frailties. But, here Peter is also seen as one who recognizes what the *New Oxford Bible* calls "a more-than-human-power (to which) he responds by personal self-judgment."[106]   Jesus replies by telling Peter, and his companions Andrew, James, and John not to be afraid, but to join him and become fishers of men.

In this passage, Luke has made Peter a man who in his wisdom has come to a conclusion about the goodness and power of Jesus. Whereas Mark and Matthew give no reason for the four to drop their work and follow a stranger, Luke has shown them making their choice after concluding that Jesus was someone "with more than human power". Luke has done more than just highlight Jesus' "power"; he has shown the disciples to be thinking men, not merely men who without thought dropped what they were doing and followed a stranger like innocents following the Pied Piper. Luke had noted earlier that after leaving the wilderness:

> …Jesus, armed with the power of the Spirit, returned to Galilee; and reports about him spread through the whole country-side. He taught in their synagogues and all men sang his praises.
>
> So he came to Nazareth, where he had been brought up, and went to synagogue on Sabbath day as he regularly did.
>
> Luke: 4.14-16

Luke concludes this passage by quoting the sermon that resulted in Jesus being ejected from the synagogue by the congregation. With this he has made it clear that Jesus' reputation had spread throughout the region before he asked the four fishermen to join him. Therefore, the four who would join Jesus were not ignorant of his teachings and his reputation.

The remainder of Luke's fifth chapter is given to those parables about healing, eating with tax gatherers, patching an old cloak with new cloth, or pouring new wine in an old wineskin, which he drew from Mark. He begins the sixth chapter with the passage about the disciples picking ears of corn and eating them on the Sabbath. This is followed

---

[106]   *The New Oxford Bible*, footnote, p.85 NT.

300

by the story of healing on the Sabbath despite the critical Pharisees and lawyers who were present and objected.

It is at this point that Luke's Jesus "came down the hill...and took his stand on level ground," and began to speak.[107] Both those who are reading literally and those who seek a message from a figurative reading should note the similarities and differences between Matthew's Sermon on the Mount and Luke's Sermon on the Plain.

> "How blest are you who are in need; the kingdom of God is yours.
>
> "How blest are you who now go hungry; your hunger shall be satisfied.
>
> "How blest are you who weep now; you shall laugh.
>
> "How blest you are when men hate you, when they outlaw you and insult you, and ban your very name as infamous, because of the Son of Man. On that day be glad and dance for joy; for assuredly you have a rich reward in heaven; in just the same way did their fathers treat the prophets.
>
> "But alas for you who are rich; you have had you time of happiness.
>
> "Alas for you who are well-fed now; you shall go hungry.
>
> "Alas for you who laugh now; you shall mourn and weep.
>
> "Alas for you when all speak well of you; just as did their fathers treat the false prophets.
>
> "But to you who hear me I say:

[107] As noted in the *The New English Bible,* footnote, p. 76 NT, Matthew chose the mount for the spot from which to preach, but Luke "thinks of mountains for settings requiring privacy; public teaching tends to take place on level ground."

"Love your enemies; do good to those who hate you; bless those who curse you; pray for those who treat you spitefully. When a man hits you on the cheek, offer him the other cheek too; when a man takes your coat, let him have your shirt as well. Give to everyone who asks you; when a man takes what is yours, do not demand it back. Treat others as you would like them to treat you.

"If you love only those who love you, what credit is that to you? Even sinners love those who love them. Again, if you do good only to those who do good to you, what credit is that to you? Even sinners do as much. And if you lend only where you expect to be repaid, what credit is that to you? Even sinners lend to each other to be repaid in full. But you must love your enemies and do good; and lend without expecting return; and you will have a rich reward; you will be sons of the Most High, because he himself is kind to the ungrateful and wicked. Be compassionate as your father is compassionate.

"Pass no judgment, and you will not be judged; do not condemn, and you will not be condemned; acquit and you will be acquitted; give, and gifts will be given you. Good measure, pressed down, shaken together, and running over, will be poured in your lap; for whatever measure you deal out to others will be dealt to you in return."

Luke: 6.20-38

Like Matthew, Luke has gathered many of Jesus' teachings into a single sermon. This is far more effective than trying to present individual small fragments in a variety of settings, for it provides a strong base on which the new Christian theology can grow and the church can build.

As in Matthew "How blest are you" is past tense. Those positive things listed by Luke are done by individuals who have been blest with the ability to do those things, However, unlike Matthew, Luke adds the passages in which Jesus warns (Alas or Woe to) the wrongdoer. Like Matthew he includes the Golden Rule and the warning against passing judgment.

Then comes the controversial passage speaking of turning the other cheek and of being confronted with a robber who steals one's coat. This highlights Jesus' call for those who are harmed by others to refrain from violent resistance or retaliation. The robber has stolen your coat; do not try to stop him from stealing your shirt as well. This is a part of Jesus' sermon in which he calls for people to love their enemies, which Jesus would practice even on the cross.

This is a very difficult passage for those who choose to read the bible literally. Here is a commandment, an order, by Jesus telling people they must not resist criminals or use force to resist wrongdoers. The literal reader will realize that he or she does not know anyone, including themselves who could or would obey that directive to the point of accepting harm to their loved ones. Yet, the command is clear. Does one who reads this passage literally now find it necessary to make choices as to what to obey and what to ignore; and if so does that apply only to this single command? Where does one begin and end such choices?

Luke knew humans could never completely adhere to this course of action. Fathers and mothers would act to protect their children; people would protect property essential for the feeding, clothing, and housing of their families. He knew nations would resist invaders who would loot, rape, and kill their people. This call for non-resistance to those who would bring harm to one or one's family is presented as an ideal which humans should strive to approach. It is the ideal, the ultimate goal. Though it cannot be reached by humans, they should attempt to come as near as possible to reaching it.[108] The important message is "Love your enemies."

Though the Beatitudes and the admonitions and parables that follow are presented by Luke as the Sermon On the Plain, the reader should remember that when Jesus teaches as he does in this "sermon" he is teaching his disciples and other followers who have by now grown in number to the point of being referred to as a crowd. He next moves

---

[108] Mark, Matthew, and Luke relate the story of the young rich man who asked how he could enter the kingdom of heaven. When his disciples asked how anyone give up everything , even concerns for loved ones, Jesus told them , "For men this is impossible; but everything is possible for God." That is another example of setting a goal unattainable for humans, but nevertheless a goal toward which all those with faith should never cease to travel.

on to the parable in which Jesus asks whether the blind can lead the blind. Nothing is to be learned from one whose eyes are closed to the word. However, Jesus adds, one who follows a teacher whose eyes are open can eventually learn to live like the teacher. He further warns of hypocrisy when one criticizes a fellow human for biases (the speck in his eye) while blind to his own greater biases (the log in his own eye).

Luke brings Jesus' sermon to a close with further parables which we earlier discussed when reading Matthew. Then, having completed his sermon, Jesus left for Capernaum.

CHAPTER 20

HEALING AND TEACHING

Some readers are disturbed by the differences in wording between Matthew and Luke, even in the Sermon on the Mount or the Plain; but there need be no concern about these differences, if one keeps in mind the priorities of each of the writers of the gospels. Mark wrote to record the oral traditions that had become the basis of the teachings of Paul, Peter, Barnabas and other founders and organizers of the first Christian churches.

Matthew and Luke faced new challenges. This new religion had been changing and developing throughout the twenty years since Mark had written his gospel. It was still being formed as a religion. There was of course no bible; after all, the gospels of Matthew, Luke, and John, and the Acts and later epistles did not yet exist. Those early church services would hardly be recognizable by twenty-first century Christians.

Matthew and Luke had to be concerned not only with the present but also with the future of that young church which still had no central organization or means of communication that could reach all the local churches. Those problems which had so frustrated Paul had not only not been eliminated, but had grown. To meet these problems, Matthew and Luke prepared their gospels; each using Mark's collection of oral traditions as a core around which each added material that in effect was a response to the challengers of the young church. Each, was in his own way working to prevent the church from splintering or collapsing; while at the same time framing Jesus' message in a manner that would best assure the future of the new religion that would be the vehicle to carry that message.

If there had been no threat to the existence of the church, it is likely that neither would have seen the need to write his gospel; or at least not in the form that they did. In the twenty-first century with established church doctrines, multiple denominations, and churches and cathedrals it is difficult to imagine how close the young religion was to fading away as did many mystery religions around them. On every side there were elements pulling and pushing for control, for merging the religion with another, or for actual dissolution of the new faith. Without stepping into the sandals of those apostles it is almost impossible to appreciate their struggle to save the church and to secure the future of this new religion while they were still building its theology.

Whereas Matthew's additions to Mark's collection were aimed at holding Jewish members within the church while also building for the future, Luke's additions sought to hold the church's Gentile members within the fold while at the same time continuing to expand the church amidst a sea of competing mystery religions and conflicting philosophies.

As we keep in mind these various audiences to whom gospel writers were directing their messages and the critical period in the young church's development when survival was at stake, we may better understand and not be disturbed by the differing approaches of the four gospels. The church was all important to those apostles for it was the church that was to carry the message throughout the ages.

Serious readers of the gospels and the epistles should watch for the changes and the ongoing development as this new young religion grew. As we have already noted, Jews who accepted some of Jesus teaching and wove them into their own religion as additions and reforms were the earliest congregations. But, as Paul had predicted, after missionaries brought Jesus' teachings to the Gentiles, Gentile churches and Gentile congregations soon far outnumbered Jewish congregations. As this new religion was adopted by Gentiles, it grew and changed to become Gentile in its form and content; the religion that came to the Gentiles became itself Gentile.

These changes had begun well before the arrival of Paul,[109] and would be important in shaping Paul's ever maturing theology. Luke, some forty years after Paul's letter to the Romans, further reflects this maturing of Christianity. Like Gnostics and Stoics he does not present an Old Testament God of Vengeance. His Jesus is a compassionate agent of God, bringing a message of love, even love for one's enemies. His Jesus is not a Messiah of a chosen nation, but is God's messenger to all people of the world. Only among the Gentiles could this version of Christianity have been formed.

THE COMPASSIONATE JESUS

Upon Jesus arrival in Capernaum a group of respected leaders of the Jewish community came to speak to him on behalf of a Roman centurion who they said was "a friend of our nation and it is he who built our synagogue." A servant for whom the centurion had great respect was near death, and these elders had come to ask Jesus to save the servant's life.[110] However, as he neared the centurion's house, Jesus was met by other friends of the centurion who carried a message from the centurion:

> "Do not trouble further, sir; it is not for me to have you under my roof, and that is why I did not presume to approach you in person. But say the word and my servant will be cured. I know from my position I am myself under orders, with soldiers under me. I say to one, 'Go', and he goes; to another, 'Come here', and he comes; and to my servant, 'Do this', and he does it.

---

[109]   Jewish "Christian" congregations though adopting some of Jesus' teachings still retained the basic structure of their religion and their adherence to the Law. Gentiles had already adopted and put into practice numerous basic tenets of Stoicism and Gnosticism, as well as those of mystery religions in the region. It would be these Gentiles who would mould Christianity until it became the basis of modern Christianity.

[110]   Among the servants or "slaves" of Roman officials there were often Greeks or other well educated non-Romans. They might be philosophers, astronomers, physicians, or learned men of other fields. They sometimes became mentors and friends of their "masters", as contrasted to house or field slaves.

> When Jesus heard this, he admired the man, and turning
> to the crowd that was following him. he said, 'I tell you,
> nowhere, even in Israel, have I found faith like this.' And
> the messengers returned to the house and found the
> servant in good health."
>
> Luke: 7.6-10

As in Matthew's version, emphasis is on the faith of the Gentile centurion and especially on the point that the healing was "earned" through this faith. Using the people of Israel as an example of those who all too often had little or no faith in Jesus' message, this emphasis notes that it was not the nation, or location, or organization to which a person belonged, but rather the individual's faith, that brought salvation.

Luke moves on to the story of Jesus raising the dead son of a grieving widow. Not only do these stories serve to emphasize the role of faith, they also highlight Jesus' deep compassion. At this point John the Baptist has sent two of his disciples to ask Jesus whether he was the "one to come." As he did in Matthew, Jesus answered by directing them to tell John that they had seen and heard:

> "How the blind recovered their sight, the lame walk, the
> deaf hear, the dead are raised to life, the poor are hearing
> the good news – and happy is the man who does not find
> me a stumbling block."
>
> Luke: 7.21-23

With this message for John, Luke makes clear that in this series of parables healings are not of physical disabilities; but that the diseases to be cured symbolize the eyes and ears that had been unable to receive the word of God, those whose lives were crippled by their sins, and those apparently completely lost (dead) who were raised (reconciled). You have seen what I have been doing and how the message of faith is being passed on to those in need of reconciliation, Jesus is telling John's messengers. Go back and tell John what you have witnessed.

Having extolled the works of both Jesus and John in these verses, Luke then takes Jesus to the home of a Pharisee.

One of the Pharisees asked Jesus to eat with him, and he went into the Pharisee's house and took his place at the table. And a woman in the city, who was a sinner, who learned that he was eating in the Pharisee's house, brought an alabaster jar of ointment. She stood behind him at his feet, weeping, and began to bathe his feet with her tears and to dry them with her hair. Then she continued kissing his feet and anointing them with the ointment. Now when the Pharisee who had invited him saw it, he said to himself, "If this man were a prophet, he would have known who and what kind of woman this is who is touching him – that she is a sinner." Jesus spoke up and said to him, "Simon, I have something to say to you." "Teacher," he replied, "Speak."

"A certain creditor had two debtors; one owed five hundred dinarii, and the other fifty. When they could not pay, he cancelled the debts for both of them. Now which of them will love him more?" Simon answered, " I suppose the one for whom he cancelled the greater debt." And Jesus said to him, "You have judged rightly." Then turning toward the woman, he said to Simon , "Do you see this woman? I entered your house; you gave me water for my feet, but she has bathed my feet with her tears and dried them with her hair. You gave me no kiss, but from the time I came in she has not stopped kissing my feet. You did not anoint my head with oil, but she has anointed my feet with ointment. Therefore, I tell you, her sins, which were many, have been forgiven; hence she has shown great love. But the one to whom little is forgiven, loves little." Then he said to her, "Your sins are forgiven." But those at the table with him began to say among themselves, "Who is this who even forgives sins?" And he said to the woman, "Your faith has saved you, go in peace."

Luke: 7.36-50

Mark and Matthew included the parable of a woman who anointed Jesus' head with oil. In their versions Jesus was visiting the home of Simon, a leper. Around the table the others present criticized the woman sharply for wasting expensive oil when the money it would have brought, if sold, could have been given to the poor. Mark and Matthew conclude the story by having Jesus say:

> "Let her alone; why do you trouble her? She has performed a good service for me. For you will always have the poor with you, and you can show kindness to them whenever you wish; but you will not always have me. She has done what she could; she has anointed my body beforehand for burial. Truly I tell you, wherever the good news is proclaimed in the whole world, what she has done will be told in remembrance of her."
>
> Mark: 14.6-9

Matthew's version is almost a direct copy of Mark's. However, Luke uses the story for a different purpose. His conclusion uses this parable to show the compassion involved in forgiveness of one who has sinned many times.

Once more the literal reader is faced with a choice of which version to accept. Obviously these were parables created by the writers of the gospels. Matthew and Luke each report an "exact" conversation as though it had actually been recorded more than a half century earlier. Yet they differ in what was said and in the lesson to be learned from the story. One who reads these parables figuratively rather than as actual historical accounts, sees them as the means chosen by each writer to get across what he considered the more important part of Jesus message that could be illustrated by the story.

* * * * * * * * * * * *

It is here, as Luke opens his eighth chapter that he relates the parable of the sower in which Jesus tells his disciples that all his teaching would be in the form of parables; the remainder of the chapter consisting of parables the reader has already met in Mark and Matthew. The ninth chapter continues with further parables, the transfiguration, the feeding of five thousand, and other passages from which readers have sought meaning when reading Mark and Matthew. However, it is in the tenth chapter that Luke adds the parable of the Good Samaritan, not told by either Mark or Matthew.

> Just then a lawyer stood up to test Jesus. "Teacher," he said, "what must I do to inherit eternal life?" He said to him, "What is written in the law? What do you read there?" He answered, "You shall love the Lord your God with all your heart, and all your soul, and with all your strength, and with all your mind; and your neighbor as yourself." And he said to him, "You have given the right answer, and you will live"
>
> But wanting to justify himself, he asked Jesus, "And who is my neighbor?" Jesus replied, "A man was going down from Jerusalem to Jericho, and fell into the hands of robbers, who stripped him, beat him, and went away, leaving him half dead. Now by chance a priest was going down that road; and when he saw him, he passed on the other side. So likewise a Levite, when he came to the place and saw him, passed by on the other side. But a Samaritan while traveling came near him; and when he saw him, he was moved with pity. He went to him and bandaged his wounds, having poured oil and wine on them. Then he put him on his own animal, brought him to an inn, and took care of him. The next day he took out two denarii, gave them to the innkeeper, and said, 'Take care of him; and when I come back, I will repay you whatever more you spend.' Which of these three do you think was a neighbor to the man who fell into the hands of the robbers?" He said, "The one who showed him mercy." Jesus said to him, "Go and do likewise."
>
> Luke: 10.25-37

Luke drives home two points. His first, by noting that the two men who passed by the injured man were a priest and a Levite. The priest represents the highest authority of religious law. Lay assistants to Temple priests were chosen from men of the tribe of Levi. Thus both were deeply religious men; not bad or callous men. Their positions of responsibility required strict obedience to the Law. Without approaching the unconscious man they could not know whether he was alive or dead; and according to the rules of their religion, if they approached a dead body they would no longer be found fit to serve in the Temple. In this parable it is left to the lawyer to determine whether strict adherence to man-made religious rules is more important than saving a fellow human.

Luke makes the second important point of this parable when he identifies this fellow human, who finds compassion more important than man-made religious rules, as a Samaritan. Samaria, an area of about 40 miles by 35 miles lay along the Mediterranean just south of Galilee. Mainly because of its location its people had not been deported at the time of the Babylonian Exile. Those Jews who chose to return to Judah,[111] after Cyrus the Great had conquered Babylon in 538 BC and granted them permission to leave, so deeply resented those who had not been included in the Exile that they refused to let the Jews of Samaria take part in building the Second Temple. When denied the privilege of sharing in the rebuilding of the Jerusalem Temple, the Samaritans built their own Temple on a site roughly 25 miles north of Jerusalem. This deep contempt for Samaritans grew and spread throughout the rest of Israel and Judah over the next five centuries, being very much alive at the time of Jesus.

"And who is my neighbor?"

---

[111]   Babylon at the time of the Exile was a city surrounded by other cities and towns. This complex was connected by roads, canals, and fortifications. It had spread to both sides of the Euphrates river which was spanned by a stone bridge 3,032 feet long. One of the cities walls was 300 feet high, with towers 420 feet tall. There were massive buildings including elaborate temples. Beautiful hanging gardens added to the spectacle. Circling the metropolitan area required a ride of between 40 and 50 miles. As a trade center, Babylon was crowded with caravans from India and Africa. To Israelites from a small and somewhat isolated nation this was a most awesome experience. They eventually fell into three general categories. There were those who abandoned their religion and adopted the way of life of Babylonians. There were those who remained faithful to their religion but had become involved in commerce, who, when Cyrus declared an end to the Exile, moved to other commercial centers throughout the Middle East where they eventually established Jewish communities and synagogues. Then there were those, including many of the less affluent, who returned to Judah and Israel. It was this group, which had remained steadfastly faithful to its religion and to its sense of nationhood, that deeply resented those who had not experienced the deportation to Babylonia.

For a thousand years only those among the "chosen people" had been considered neighbors'; everyone else was a "foreigner". In this parable Jesus leaves no doubt that to him this was unacceptable. At that time, when even Samaritans were being treated as foreigners by other Jews, the last person one would expect to see coming to the aid of a Jew was a "foreigner".

The contrast could not be clearer in this parable. Good men, leaders of Temple worship, were compelled by man-made religious rules to avoid the body of a man who might be dead; yet a "contemptible" Samaritan from whom other Jews were led to expect nothing good was the one whose compassion overrode all other rules. Having just previously completed a series of parables dealing with Jesus' teaching in Israel and Judah, Luke has now inserted this strong parable in which all humans are neighbors. Although those previous chapters had described Jesus work in Israel and Judah, the story of the Good Samaritan tells Gentiles this is a religion, and a Jesus, for all.

* * * * * * * * * * * *

Luke follows the parable of the Good Samaritan with chapters devoted to parables and stories readers earlier found in Mark and Matthew. He then opens his fifteenth chapter with the story of the shepherd's concern for a lost sheep; a story readers found earlier in Matthew.

So, he told them this parable: "Which one of you, having a hundred sheep and losing one of them, does not leave the ninety-nine in the wilderness and go after the one that is lost until he finds it? When he has found it, he lays it on his shoulders and rejoices. And when he comes home, he calls together his friends and neighbors, saying to them, 'Rejoice with me, for I have found my sheep that was lost.' Just so, I tell you, there will be more joy in heaven over one sinner who repents than over ninety-nine righteous persons who need no repentance."

Luke: 15.3-7

The shepherd does not carelessly or recklessly leave the ninety-nine sheep to graze peacefully in a quiet meadow. His confidence in them is sufficient for him to leave them in the wilderness while he searches for the one that is lost. He knows they will not stray. They are those whose faith holds them to the righteous path even amidst the problems and temptations of the world in which they live. God, as seen in this parable, will in his compassion find ways to find those who have not been able to find him. Jesus, may be seen as the agent God has chosen for that task.

Matthew moved directly from this parable to a passage in which Jesus speaks of discipline within the "church" (brother treating brother), although there was not yet a church until after Jesus' death. In contrast, Luke feels the need to emphasize further the compassionate Jesus. He moves directly to a second parable emphasizing the compassion of God who will always seek those who are lost. His conclusion to the parable of the shepherd provides a perfect lead-in to his parable of the Lost Coin.

> "Just so, I tell you, there will be more joy in heaven over one sinner who repents than over ninety-nine righteous persons who need no repentance.
>
> "Or what woman having ten silver coins, if she loses one of them, does not light a lamp, sweep the house, and search carefully until she finds it? When she does find it, she calls together her friends and neighbors, saying, 'Rejoice with me, for I have found the coin that I had lost.' Just so, I tell you, there is joy in the presence of the angels of God over one sinner who repents."
>
> Luke: 15.7-10

Again the emphasis is on that which is lost. And again when the lost is found there is great rejoicing. A literal reading notes the effort to find the one who is lost and the joy upon finding the one who was lost. A figurative reading also notes that Luke's parable "illustrates God's concern for those who lack the ability to find him; he seeks them."[112] This is a positive instruction for the Christians of the young church.

---

[112]   Fn. p.106 NT, *The New Oxford Bible*.

Luke is exhorting them: do not be smugly satisfied because you are among fellow believers who have found God. Go forth and seek those who have not been able to find him.

Readers should remember at this point that this is Luke's parable. It is not found elsewhere. It is Luke's exhortation at a time when the young church is at a critical point; the very existence of this new Christianity among Gentiles is at stake. Complacency could not be tolerated. This had to be a church with a mission; and part of that mission had to be the spreading of the gospel.

Although the parable has shown the concern of God for the lost one, it has had Jesus speaking, thereby emphasizing the compassion of Jesus. Still Luke is not satisfied that his message is going to get across to his readers. He now adds a third parable which places even more emphasis on the ability of the one who was lost to return to his faith.

"Then Jesus said, 'There was a man who had two sons. The younger of them said to his father. 'Father give me the share of the property that will belong to me.' So he divided his property between them. A few days later the younger son gathered all he had and traveled to a distant country, and there he squandered his property in dissolute living. When he had spent everything, a severe famine took place throughout that country, and he began to be in need. So he went and hired himself out to one of the citizens of that country, who sent him to his fields to feed the pigs. He would gladly have filled himself with the pods that the pigs were eating, and no one gave him anything. But when he came to himself he said, 'How many of my father's hired hands have bread enough and to spare, but here I am dying of hunger! I will get up and go to my father, and I will say to him, 'Father, I have sinned against heaven and before you; I am no longer worthy to be called your son; treat me like one of your hired hands.' So he set off and went to his father. But while he was still far off, his father saw him and was filled with compassion; he ran and put his arms around him and kissed him. Then the son said to him, 'Father, I have sinned against heaven and before you; I am no longer worthy to be called your son.' But the father said to his slaves, 'Quickly, bring out a robe – the best one – and put it on him; put a ring on his finger and sandals on his feet. And get the fatted calf and kill it, and let us eat and celebrate; for this son of mine was dead and is alive again; he was lost and is found!' And they began to celebrate.

"Now his elder son was in the field and when he came and approached the house; he heard music and dancing. He called one of the slaves and asked what was going on. He replied, 'Your brother has come, and your father has killed the fatted calf, because he has got his son back safe and sound.' Then he became angry and refused to go in. His father came out and began to plead with him. But he answered his father, 'Listen! For all these years I have been working like a slave for you, and I have never disobeyed your command; yet you have never given me even a young goat so that I might celebrate with my friends. But when this son of yours came back, who had devoured your property with prostitutes, you killed the fatted calf for him!' Then the father said to him, 'Son, you are always with me, and all that is mine is yours. But we had to celebrate and rejoice, because this brother of your was dead and has come to life; he was lost and has been found.'"

Luke: 15.11-32

In this parable Luke has made his concept of a compassionate Jesus even clearer. Readers, at the time of his writing, were well aware of the large numbers of young Jews who had left their homes in what they would have considered "small town" Israel or Judah to find their fortune in the thriving Gentile cities throughout the Middle East and the countries bordering the Mediterranean. Although the audience Luke was addressing would understand the attractions causing this young man to leave his father's farm, prosperous though it was, most would never have predicted the father's compassionate reaction.

Once more it is important for the reader to step into the sandals of the gospel writer. The young man of whom Luke writes is the typical youthful rebel throughout all time. All that his parents believe, and the society in which he lives, and anything representing authority such as accepted standards of moral behavior are "old fashioned" and only for those who cannot see the real world that he in his youthful wisdom believes he understands far better than his father. In his contempt for all that "old fashioned" stuff that he has abandoned, he has also abandoned the faith of his people.

When his life begins to fall apart he is forced to work in the fields with pigs. Association with pigs was for Jews in those times a most humiliating experience; an indication that the young man had sunk about as far as anyone could sink. Maybe his father was brighter than the young man had previously thought, and all he left behind had not been a society of stupid people who could not see things as he had seen them. And finally he even begins to see the value of all he left behind. He sees his errors, his sins, and wants only to return to his father. He cannot expect forgiveness. He does not expect to be received as a son. All he wants is a chance to come home.

The father upon seeing his son in the distance runs to meet him. In those days it was undignified for an elder to run, but nothing was more important to the father than welcoming his son back into the fold. The robe was reserved for festive occasions, and the father ordered not only the robe, but the best robe. Furthermore, the father ordered an elaborate feast and joyous celebration.

When the elder son expressed his anger the father had said: "But we had to celebrate and rejoice, because this brother of yours was dead and has come to life; he was lost and has been found."

Luke has used the expression "was dead and has come to life", in the same manner in which it was used in earlier parables in which Jesus brought the dead back to life. The young man had been lost. He symbolizes those who have completely abandoned their God, and have broken all the rules of Christian living. Yet, when at the lowest depths of depravity, the young man found the faith he had held in contempt now held promise of a better life.

He returns to the arms of his father who does not reject him because of his past, but welcomes him with joy. The older son had, like the sheep left in the wilderness, been expected to retain his faith. The climb back from the depths to which the young man had sunk was to the father a show of strength. This was a grasping for faith by one seeking his father; more difficult in his father's eyes than having never been faced with the challenge of the lost seeking the father.

Luke leaves it to the reader to answer the questions: Who is the father? Where is the home? Who does the young man symbolize? As a Christian, how should one look upon those who do not have faith or have done what Christians believe is evil? Should the Christian as in the parable of the lost sheep or the parable of the lost coin refuse to accept the loss? Will the Christian welcome warmly others who seek God, even when those fellow Christians may not share all the same values, goals, and prejudices?

In showing Christians a Jesus of compassion; Luke completely rejects the concept of a God of vengeance. This God does not wield a flaming sword with which to slay the wrongdoer. This God is a God of love who, rather than punishing those who are lost, reaches out to them. Luke speaks of a Jesus and a God who understand the non-believers and the "sinners", and who seek to save them rather than punish them.

There is much to be found in the parable of the Good Samaritan and in the three parables about the lost who were found. The need to add three of these four parables that are not found in other gospels sets Luke apart in his need to emphasize the compassion of Jesus.

* * * * * * * * * * * *

Probably no parable in the New Testament is as puzzling or difficult to interpret as that with which Luke opens his 16th chapter. Difficult in that various interpretations have been offered, but determining which Luke wished to have his readers discover is still a mystery.

> "Then Jesus said to the disciples, 'There was a rich man who had a manager, and charges were brought to him that this man was squandering his property. So he summoned him and said to him, 'What is this I hear about you? Give me an accounting of your management, because you cannot be my manager any longer.' Then the manager said to himself, 'What will I do, now that my master is taking the position away from me? I am not strong enough to dig, and I am ashamed to beg. I have decided what to do so that, when I am dismissed as

> manager, people will welcome me to their homes. So
> summoning his master's debtors one by one, he asked
> the first, 'How much do you owe my master?' He
> answered, 'A hundred jugs of olive oil.' He said to him,
> 'Take your bill, sit down quickly, and make it fifty.' Then
> he asked another, 'And how much do you owe?' He
> replied, 'A hundred containers of wheat.' He said to him,
> 'Take your bill and make it eighty.' And his master
> commended the dishonest manager because he had acted
> shrewdly; for the children of his age are more shrewd in
> dealing with their own generation than are the children of
> the light. And I tell you, make friends for yourself by
> means of dishonest wealth so that when it is gone, they
> may welcome you into the eternal homes.'
>
> Luke: 16.1-9

Left at this point a literal reader has to wonder at Luke apparently commending a dishonest manager for skillfully evading punishment for his crime. Is dishonesty and hypocrisy being lauded?

In the first written material to be included in the *New Testament* (Paul's letter to the Thessalonians) Paul has referred to the "children of light." In the arid barren hills of ancient Judah's wilderness hundreds of religious and legal manuscripts were hidden in caves by Jewish fugitives. In1947, a shepherd came upon the first of these "Dead Sea Scrolls." Among some four hundred manuscripts since uncovered were teachings of the Essenes, one of which was "The War of the Sons of Light Against the Sons of Darkness." *The Gospel According to John,* written about ten yeans years after that of Luke, includes further reference to the light and the dark in a passage in which John describes Jesus' response to a crowd's concern that, according to the Law, the Messiah cannot be "lifted up", but must remain forever.

> "Jesus said to them, 'The light is with you for a little
> longer. Walk while you have the light, so that the
> darkness may not overtake you. If you walk in the
> darkness, you may not know where you are going.
> While you have the light, believe in the light, so that you
> may become the children of the light.'"
>
> John: 12.35-36

Paul's references to the children of light, and later references by Luke and John, were used to differentiate those who were following the teachings of Jesus (the Christians) from those still in the "dark." In Luke's parable such cleverness as displayed by the dishonest manager could be found in the way the worldly. Those still in the dark could use their worldly "skills" to take advantage of their fellow beings; something those who are "spiritually enlightened", the unworldly, would not be able to do. An explanatory note in *The New Oxford Bible* points out that though dishonest, "the manager was prudent in using the things of this life to ensure the future; believers should do the same."[113] This does not mean believers should also be dishonest, but rather that they do things in this life that will ensure their future as "children of the light."

The New English Bible offers a somewhat different explanation when it notes that the last sentence (verse 9) of Luke's passage quoted above could be construed as perhaps commending the dispensing of wealth "in acts of charity."[114] Is Jesus saying that non-Christians, those who have not seen the light, could still through their acts of charity "be welcomed into the eternal home;" that those who have not seen the light, but who do good even when unaware of the way of Jesus, could be saved through their good acts?

This latter interpretation makes those first nine verses of Luke's sixteenth chapter a more logical introduction to the rest of that chapter which speaks of the manner in which wealth is employed, and the character of the worldly. This is especially important, if Luke intended interpreters of the parable to see Jesus as the Master, and the manager as representing all of the worldly (non-enlightened). It would mean that non-Christians who lived a good life, performing good acts, would not be denied salvation. In this vein Luke continued:

> "The man who can be trusted in little things can be
> trusted also in great: and the man who is dishonest in
> little things is dishonest also in great things. If then, you
> have not proved trustworthy with the wealth of this

---

[113] Footnote, p.107 NT, *The New Oxford Bible*.

[114] Footnote, p. 94 NT, *The New English Bible*.

320

> world, who will trust you with the wealth that is real?
> And if you have proved untrustworthy with what belongs
> to another, who will give you what is your own?
>
> "No servant can be the slave of two masters; for either
> he will hate the first and love the second, or he will be
> devoted to the first and think nothing of the second.
> You cannot serve God and Money
>
> "The Pharisees, who loved money, heard all this and
> scoffed at him. He said to them, "You are the people
> who impress your fellow-men with your righteousness;
> but God sees through you; for what sets itself up to be
> admired by men is detestable in the sight of God.
>
> "Until John (the Baptist), it was the Law and the
> prophets; since then, there is the good news of the
> kingdom of God, and everyone forces his way in.
>
> "It is easier for heaven and earth to come to an end than
> for one dot or stroke of the Law to lose its force."
>
> Luke: 16.9-17

Luke continues to pursue the theme of the rich versus the poor; a theme not only found elsewhere throughout the old and new testaments, but in philosophies and religions elsewhere in the Mediterranean world. The rich are used to represent those so occupied with their material world that the seed of the Kingdom of God has no room to grow within them and they cannot, therefore, be other than unrighteous. The poor, with little or no material wealth to be protected or enlarged, symbolize those who have time for the word and room for the seed so can be righteous, as in the parable of Lazarus and the rich man with which Luke immediately followed the passage above.

However, there is an inconsistency here in all the gospels; an inconsistency necessary for their writers to get their points across. For example, there are parables such as that of the young rich man who was told that it was more difficult for a rich man to enter the kingdom of heaven than for a camel to pass through the eye of a needle, and Luke's parable in which a rich man ended up in Hades while the poor Lazarus was carried by angels to be with Abraham. Then in sharp contrast, Luke has the wealthy father, representing God, showing compassion for his prodigal son, and earlier parables in the gospels tell of the good rich man sending servants, and later his son to the men in his vineyards, only to have those workers kill the son. In these latter parables God is represented as the father or the master. A reader should be aware of the manner in which the rich man and the poor man are used as symbols, and should look for the messages rather than looking no further than the labels. What are these men or women supposed to represent? Parables are meant to carry a deeper message than a mere condemning or praising of various characters.

CHAPTER 21

ACCEPTING THE CONFRONTATION

Because they shared a common core of parables and passages relating to Jesus' work, the gospels of Mark, Matthew, and Luke came to be known as the synoptic gospels. Matthew's and Luke's additions of parables and passages not included in Mark's earlier collection of oral traditions have been attributed to their drawing from an unknown source which biblical historians of the past have referred to as "Q". As both literal and figurative readers of these two gospels shall have observed, even these additions differ. So, "Q", unlike Mark is not a single common source for both Matthew and Luke. Their sources differ just as their interpretations differ. Why?

This should be surprising only to a reader who assumes "Q" is a written source or the creation of one person. However, as we have noted, the years between the time when Mark wrote his gospel and the time when Matthew and Luke wrote their gospels were a period of rapid growth for the young church. People moving from a town where they had been a member of a Christian church would often be among the movers and doers opening a church in the town or city to which they had moved. They could also carry local practices and beliefs from one church to another.

It is unlikely that more than one or two of the original disciples who had traveled with Jesus, observing his acts and listening to his teachings, were able to read or write. No two individual's observations ever being exactly alike, it would have been most unlikely that any two of the Christian communities they created had exactly the same descriptions and interpretations upon which to build. As those who became the apostles went forth to carry Jesus' message, their oral presentations would become a part of the growing body of oral traditions from which later writers would draw. It is wise to recall that Luke began his Gospel by noting these many written accounts, other than Mark, which the framers of the New Testament would later discard.

> "Since many have undertaken to set down an orderly account of the events that have been fulfilled among us, just as they were handed down to us by those who from the beginning were eyewitnesses and servants of the word, I have decided, after investigating everything carefully from the very first, to write an orderly account for you Theophilus, so that you may know the truth concerning the things about which you have been instructed."
>
> Luke: 1.1-4

There was no New Testament. With the lack of overall organization and communication it was inevitable that early Christianity would sprout many local interpretations of what had gone on before. Some of these local versions would spread to other churches, and a few would become widely accepted. A story preached repeatedly could, after two or more decades, be accepted as "history". Parables such as that of the lost sheep would become as well known as the parables in Mark's gospel. Other parables and stories would vary as they were carried orally from church to church throughout the Roman Empire.

Congregations would thus come to share a common belief in the story of Jesus being born of a virgin, yet with versions differing from region to region, like the differing versions of Matthew and Luke. Congregations could have a common belief in the resurrection but with differing versions such as appear in Matthew's and Luke's stories of the resurrection. They have certain parables in common, such as that of the lost sheep; but other parables like the Good Samaritan and the Prodigal Son reflect the writer's belief that, in addressing his particular audience, these additional parables were essential for making clear a particular teaching of Jesus.

LESSONS FOR THE DISCIPLES

Matthew warned against one person causing another to sin, to stumble. This he followed with the story of the lost sheep. Luke, like Matthew, tells of Jesus warning his disciples against causing another to stumble, but this warning comes after the parable of the lost sheep and feeds into this further instruction:

> "If your brother wrongs you, reprove him; and if he repents, forgive him. Even if he wrongs you seven times in a day and comes back to you seven times saying, 'I am sorry,' you are to forgive him."
>
> Luke: 17.3-4

Like Matthew, Luke is concerned about the increasing divisiveness among members of the church (brothers). He does not go into the detail that Matthew did as to how this should be handled within a congregation, but he does make a strong point about forgiveness. The one who is wronged must forgive. If he or she does not forgive, the split only widens. Therefore, if the one who is wronged has the welfare of the church at heart, he or she must assume the responsibility for healing those wounds created by the one who has wronged him or her.

Even in that very young church of the days of Luke and Matthew there were those who would refuse to consider any interpretation of the scriptures, or of Jesus' word, other than their own. Throughout the two thousand years that followed, and up to the present, such schisms have continued as individuals and groups declare that they are unable to work as "brothers" because their interpretations of the word differ from that of their "brothers and sisters." Unfortunately, the division between "brethren" who read the parables literally and those who read them figuratively is so great that they all too often find it impossible to worship in the same sanctuaries.

To Luke there is a great difference between real faith and that which individuals or groups profess to be their faith. He tells his readers that in responding to the disciples plea that he "increase their faith," Jesus said, "If you had faith no bigger than a mustard-seed, you could say to this mulberry-tree, 'Be rooted up and replanted in the sea,' and it would obey at once" (Luke: 17. 5-6). This exaggeration, used also by Mark and later by Matthew, refers not to a power possessed by disciples or by any other human who has faith. This parable deliberately exaggerates in order to make the point that it is not the individual's faith that can handle such an exaggerated problem, but rather that it is God, in whom one has faith, who can meet all such challenges. Luke makes this point repeatedly and adds emphasis with this continuation of the parable in which Jesus adds:

> "Who among you would say to your slave who has just come in from plowing or tending sheep in the field, 'Come here at once and take your place at the table?' Would you not rather say to him, 'Prepare supper for me, put on your apron and serve me while I eat and drink; later you may eat and drink?' Do you thank the slave for doing what was commanded?' So it is also, when you have done all that you were ordered to do, say, 'We are worthless slaves; we have done only what we ought to have done!'"
>
> Luke: 17.7-10

As noted in *The New Oxford Bible*, "One's relation to God makes obedience to God a duty to be fulfilled and not an occasion for reward."[115] Jesus is in a sense rebuking his disciples. Faith, he explains, is not some sort of magic that will enable you to do all things. No increase in your faith can give you such powers. You are God's servants. It is your duty to do God's will. Your faith should be faith in God who can do all things.

Luke continues with still a further parable emphasizing that it is not faith that can do all things; it is God in whom one has faith who has such power.

> "On the way to Jerusalem Jesus was going through the region between Samaria and Galilee. As he entered a village, ten lepers approached him. Keeping their

---

[115]   *The New Oxford Bible*, fn., p. 108 NT .

> distance, they called out, saying, 'Jesus, Master, have
> mercy on us!' When he saw them, he said to them, 'Go
> and show yourselves to the priests.' And as they went,
> they were made clean. Then one of them, when he saw
> that he was healed, turned back, praising God with a loud
> voice. He prostrated himself at Jesus' feet and thanked
> him. And he was a Samaritan. Then Jesus asked, 'Were
> not ten made clean? But the other nine, where are they?
> Was none of them to return and give praise to God
> except this foreigner?' Then he said to him, 'Get up and
> go your way; your faith has made you well.'"
>
> Luke: 17.11-19

Once more Luke has made the point that this new religion is a
religion for all. Faith knows no barriers. The Samaritan in this case is
considered a foreigner, yet has recognized that it was God, in whom he
had faith, who had been the healer. The nine Jews apparently took it
for granted that their faith brought about their healing and failed to see
God as the healer; faith was enough; there was no need for thanks.

Like Mark and Matthew, Luke tries to make his audience
understand that the Messiah is not to be a worldly leader sent by God
to establish a national kingdom over which the Messiah would rule in
the name of God. To once more make this point Luke presents a
parable here in which Pharisees ask Jesus when the Kingdom of God is
coming. Once more Jesus explains that it will not be at some
identifiable future date, nor will there be a sign or a warning that it is
about to come.

> "The kingdom of God is not coming with things that can
> be observed; nor will they say 'Look, here it is!' or 'There
> it is!' For, in fact, the kingdom of God is among you.'"
>
> Luke: 17.20-21

The kingdom is here, Jesus says; you do not need to look for it;
you only need to make room for it within you and among you. It is
neither something still to come, nor a *place* to which you will go in the
future; *it is already here.*

Luke's next three chapters, 18-21, repeat parables the reader has already found and discussed in Mark and Matthew.[116] At the same time he has brought Jesus to Jerusalem where Jesus has told his disciples he would end his days. Luke does not go into details about the cleansing of the temple. His version leads one to assume Jesus, who was then teaching in the temple daily, had "taken control of the temple."[117] Here Luke makes the important point that Jesus is popular with the people; that it is the Chief Priests, Doctors of Law (scribes), and other leaders who seek to have Jesus killed.

> "Every day he was teaching in the temple. The chief priests, the scribes, and the leaders of the people kept looking for a way to kill him; but they did not find anything they could do, for all the people were spellbound by what they heard."
>
> Luke: 19.47-48

When Luke introduces Judas Iscariot as the traitor, he says: "Then Satan entered into Judas called Iscariot, who was one of the twelve." (Luke: 22. 3.) When Luke also says Judas accepted money for his betrayal of Jesus, the phrase that Satan entered into him becomes important. As we have noted, Satan was not meant to be a person, but rather was a personification of the temptations of the material world. If Judas *Iscariot* was a member of the Sicarii (those terrorists who would use any means to drive out the Romans and who were known for their assassinations of those who stood in the way of such action), Satan represents a more powerful temptation than money could ever be.

To Judas, Jesus was no longer a potential force for the overthrow of the Romans. Jesus may have gained a large following, but

---

[116]   Praying by the Pharisee and the tax collector; Jesus and the children; Comparison of passing through the eye of a needle and a rich man entering the Kingdom of God; Healing the blind man; the parable of the pounds left with the servants for investing; Jesus response to the Chief Priests about his authority; the man who turned his vineyard over to his tenants and later sent servants and eventually his son to collect what they owed; Give to Caesar that which is Caesar's and to God things that are Gods; whose wife will a widow be when resurrected?; The poor widow giving her last penny at the temple treasury; and others.

[117]   *The New English Bible*, fn. p. 99 NT.

by teaching peace and the unimportance of a material kingdom Jesus would, in the eyes of Judas, be betraying the cause for which Sicarii were willing to die. If - at the very time when Jesus was at his peak and was being hailed by the crowds as a "prophet" promising a new way of life - he were to be executed by the "Jewish" collaborators (Priests and other Sadducees) and the Romans, it might be possible to ally those crowds to the cause of the Sicarii. This is a point about which historians and theologians may well differ. Either way, Judas is the one who betrays Jesus. This difference of interpretation of Judas' motive is fueled by the fact that Matthew, and later John, will attribute Judas betrayal of Jesus solely to his greed for money, whereas Luke speaks of Satan entering into Judas. Luke has Judas accepting money offered by the Chief Priests, but Matthew has Judas asking the Chief Priests, "What will you give me if I betray him to you."

THE LAST DAYS

> "Every day he was teaching in the temple, and at night he would go out and spend the night on the Mount of Olives, as it was called. And all the people would get up early in the morning to listen to him in the temple."
>
> Luke: 21.37-38

The Mount of Olives was close to the temple; the distance being little more than the distance from one end of the temple enclosure to the other. So, with the coming of Passover, Jesus instructed his disciples to arrange for a nearby room in the city and to prepare it for the Passover meal. "When the hour came, he took his place at the table, and the apostles with him." Jesus began by speaking of the short time he would have with them.

> "Then he took a loaf of bread, and when he had given thanks, he broke it and gave it to them, saying, 'This is my body, which is given for you. Do this in remembrance of me.'"
>
> Luke: 22.19

According to Mark, when Jesus divided the bread he said: "Take, this is my body." According to Matthew, Jesus said: "Take, eat, this is my body. But Luke, in expanding the statement, has Jesus saying: "This is my body, which is given for you. Do this in remembrance of me." Apparently Luke realized the need to add words which would make the meaning of Jesus' act clearer for the early Christians. In Luke's version Jesus clearly predicts his death within days or hours. It is a death he could avoid by leaving Jerusalem to teach once again in Galilee or in the wilderness. However, he is choosing to face the inevitable; to sacrifice his life that his message might be kept alive. "This is my body, *which is given - for you.*" Given for you that you may never forget. In remembering me, remember the message I have brought, and keep it alive.

> "And he did the same with the cup after supper, saying, 'This cup that is poured out for you is the new covenant in my blood.'"
>
> Luke: 22.20

The original covenant with God, made through Moses, had been sealed in blood as were all major covenants of the time. Like Mark and Matthew, Luke describes Jesus use of wine as a substitute for blood; the apostles around the table being told that the blood Jesus would shed through his death on the cross would seal a new covenant between believers and God.

Having returned to the Mount of Olives, Jesus told his disciples to pray and then moved on a "stone's throw" further where he could pray in private. One who reads the next passage literally does not ask how it was possible for Luke or other Gospel writers to know what Jesus said in a private prayer. To one reading figuratively the importance of this passage is its use to show that Jesus knowingly accepted the fate that lay before him. Later, most likely some two hundred years later when the New Testament was being compiled in Rome, two verses were added.

> "Then an angel from heaven appeared to him and gave him strength. In his anguish he prayed more earnestly, and his sweat became like great drops of blood falling to the ground."
>
> Luke: 22.43-44

Once more the skeptic asks how anyone could be aware of the coming of an angel or the condition of Jesus, if he were praying in private out of sight of even his disciples. However, realizing these two verses were added sometime in the second century after Jesus death a reader finds the skeptic's comments irrelevant. Those verses reflect the type of material being added to the earlier oral traditions as Christianity continued to develop throughout the century after Jesus' death. That these additions were made during the second century after Jesus' death, but were not included in the original Gospels of Mark, Matthew, or Luke, or in the writings of Paul, is but one example of how the traditions about Jesus continued to grow for centuries after his death. In no way should such mythical comments about the messenger affect the validity of the message.

Luke continues as did Mark and Matthew with the account of the arrest and trial of Jesus. Luke's version of the comments by Pilate make even more clear to his readers the role of the Jewish religious leaders and their assistants, and lack of participation by the rest of the Jewish population. According to Luke, Pilate had said that he found "no basis for an accusation against this man." (Luke: 23. 4)

When those who had brought Jesus before Pilate heard this they strenuously objected:

> "But they were insistent and said, 'He stirs up the people by teaching throughout all Judea, from Galilee where he began even to this place.'"
>
> When Pilate heard this, he asked whether the man was a Galilean. And when he learned that he was under Herod's jurisdiction, he sent him off to Herod, who was himself in Jerusalem at that time. When Herod saw Jesus he was very glad, for he had been wanting to see him for a long time, because he had heard about him and was hoping to see him perform some sign. He questioned him at some length, but Jesus gave him no answer. The chief priests and the scribes stood by, vehemently accusing him. Even Herod with his soldiers treated him with contempt and mocked him; then he put an elegant robe on him, and sent him back to Pilate. That same day

> Herod and Pilate became friends with each other; before this they had been enemies.
>
> "Pilate then called together the chief priests, the leaders, and the people, and said to them, 'You brought me this man as one who was perverting the people; and here I have examined in your presence and have not found him guilty of any of your charges against him. Neither has Herod, for he sent him back to us. Indeed he has done nothing to deserve death. I will therefore have him flogged and release him.'"
>
> Luke: 23.5-16

Pilate would again be shouted down by the priests and their entourage demanding Jesus' death, but Pilate would address them a third time, asking: "Why, what evil has he done?" But, the accusers continued their demands until Pilate finally gave way.

Luke describes the crucifixion in much the same manner as did Mark and Matthew. When the women who had prepared spices returned to the tomb to which Jesus' body had been borne three days before, they were amazed and even frightened. In front of such tombs a trough or gutter was cut from the earth or stone paving. From a huge stone a circular slab was carved. This large disk stood upright and could be rolled in the shallow trough to close or open the entrance to the tomb. Now the stone had been rolled aside. The women, Mary Magdalene, Mary mother of Jesus, Joanna, Mary mother of James, and the other women who had followed Jesus from Galilee reported their discovery to the disciples.

When read literally the remaining verses of Luke's gospel paint a picture of Jesus returning in physical form, and speaking to the women and later to the disciples. He is, through his words to them, entrusting them to carry forth the message he had been bringing to them during their three years together.

To be able to write so that a literal reading carried the same message that was buried and awaiting discovery by one who read figuratively was not an every day talent. Readers who dig for a deeper meaning in this description by Luke note that the women and men did not recognize a physical Jesus. Their eyes were closed to all but their grief until they were opened with the realization that they were expected to carry on the work Jesus had begun.

> "As they (the women) came near the village to which
> they were going, he walked ahead as if he were going on.
> But they urged him strongly, saying, 'Stay with us,
> because it is almost evening and the day is nearly over.'
> So he went in to stay with them. When he was at the
> table with them, he took the bread, blessed and broke it,
> and gave it to them. Then their eyes were opened, and
> they recognized him; and he vanished from their sight."
>
> Luke: 24.28-31

A literal reading portrays a Jesus returning in flesh and talking with, and eating with, the women who failed to recognize him even though they had been close to him for years. When they do recognize him, he vanishes.

Reading this passage as a figurative presentation by Luke, a reader does not find Jesus being portrayed as returning in flesh after a physical resurrection. Instead, the women are seen as discussing the Jesus they lost; their eyes being closed to the reality of the moment. They are speaking of the physical Jesus and what he had meant to them; until the moment when they realize that what Jesus had taught was not lost, that his spirit has been resurrected, at which moment the physical Jesus is replaced by the Word he has passed on to them.[118] So too, according to Luke, the disciples recognize that they are to carry on. He makes it clear that this was not a physical Jesus who had returned when he has Jesus speak to the disciples saying: "These are my words that I spoke to you when *I was still with you*." (Luke: 24. 44)

> "Then he *opened their minds* to understand the scriptures,
> and he said to them 'Thus it is written, that the Messiah
> is to suffer and rise from the dead on the third day, and
> that repentance and forgiveness of sins is to be

---

[118] *The New Oxford Bible* in a footnote concerning the meeting of the women and Jesus on the road, and which is applicable to the time with Jesus as he broke bread with them, concisely comments that "The distinction is between perception and recognition." p. 121 NT.

> proclaimed in his name to all nations, beginning from Jerusalem. You are witnesses of these things. And see, I am sending upon you what my Father promised, so stay here in the city until you have been clothed with the power from on high."
>
> Luke: 24.44-49

Luke's final emphasis aims to make Jews, and the Gentiles to whom he was primarily directing his gospel, recognize that this was a religion for all people, not just for a chosen few. "Repentance and forgiveness of sins is to be proclaimed in his name *to all nations*."

CHAPTER 22

THE GOSPEL ACCORDING TO JOHN

Not only is the author of this gospel unknown, but according to most biblical scholars more than one author had a hand in preparing the gospel. These may have been disciples of the apostle John who were bringing his teachings together in the form of a gospel. Furthermore, it is generally accepted among biblical scholars and historians that the last chapter was added well after the original author or authors had completed their writing of the gospel. However, for ease of reference we shall use the name John whenever referring to the authors of this gospel.

John's gospel is quite unlike the three synoptic gospels we have discussed; his concept of God being more like that of Paul than that of Matthew, or Luke. His emphasis is on the relationship of individuals to God; not on a Messiah relating to a nation, or a congregation, or to Christians as a whole. For John, Jesus is bringing the Word to each individual as a means of salvation for that individual. Jesus becomes the messenger bringing *personal* salvation.

The young church is growing rapidly; not only in membership, but in the depth of its theology at the time John is writing in Ephesus. This was at least seventy years after the death of Jesus; roughly a half century after Paul wrote his letter to the Romans at the peak of his career, a generation and a half after Mark penned his gospel, and ten or fifteen years after the gospels of Matthew and Luke. This is a different kind of gospel, with a different purpose. It does not show the depth of concern of earlier gospels over problems threatening to split the church. In contrast, its emphasis on a theological interpretation of events has led Christians throughout the years to refer to it as the "spiritual Gospel." Even the different order in which this gospel has arranged events as contrasted to the synoptic gospels has a purpose. In John these events are presented in such a manner that each becomes a base upon which a particular theological interpretation can be built.

John has frequently been referred to as a mystic, but he is more than that. We have seen how Stoicism and the mystery religions played a role in Paul's thinking. John differs in that his writings reflect more the influence of Gnosticism. However, readers should not assume that because of this influence John had become one of the early church's Christian Gnostics. Far from it. John did not accept the pessimistic view of Christian Gnostics that all that existed in the world was evil.

Mystery religions had become increasingly popular in the Mediterranean world during the four centuries from the days of Plato until the birth of Jesus; and their popularity would continue to grow as they spread further into North Africa and Anatolia during the three hundred years after the death of Jesus. It was typical of mystery religions that the founder of such a religion would eventually be considered divine by his followers. After his death he would be worshipped to the point where often the sole reason for continued existence of the religion was worship of the founder. These founders were considered by their followers to be revealers of the truth, leading modern historians to speak of their religions as "revealed religions."

Mystery religions preached salvation through uniting with God. As these religions grew and spread throughout Greece, the Middle East, and Egypt, religious rituals became the major part of religious services, and were considered the means by which an individual was united with God. Gnostics, on the other hand believed humans had long before fallen from their close relationship with God. They had fallen from a higher level into the evil world. Their unconscious selves needed to become once more aware of their origin; of their individual spirit's relationship to God. Therefore, salvation came through the individual finally becoming aware of that spirit which existed within him or her. This particular knowledge, which had been lying dormant within the individual, would only be reawakened by divine revelation. This was the Gnostics' path to salvation.

During the roughly seventy years between the time of Jesus' death and the writing of the "Gospel According To John", early Christian thought was continually being influenced by the mysteries and Gnosticism. Although Paul and John were influenced by Stoicism, Gnosticism, and the mysteries, they never became adherents or disciples of these philosophies/religions.

In his gospel, John does not cover many of those acts and travels of Jesus that were so important to Mark, Matthew, and Luke. He, instead, places his emphasis on theology; often by offering expanded discourses by Jesus. His intent becomes apparent as he introduces his gospel.

INTRODUCING THE WORD

> When all things began, the Word already was. The Word dwelt with God, and what God was, the Word was. The Word, then, was with God at the beginning, and through him All things came to be; no single thing was created without him. All that came to be was alive with his life, and that life was the light of men. The light shines on in the dark, and the darkness has never mastered it."
>
> John: 1.1-5

Eternally, even before any imaginable beginning, there existed the Word (Logos). The Word had always been with God; it was timeless; there was no beginning, for the Word had been there before a beginning. "The Word, then, was with God *at the beginning.*" The Word, then, was the creative intelligence that brought the universe into being.[119]

---

[119] For ancient Greeks Logos meant not only "word", but plan or reason. More than 500 years before the birth of Jesus the Greek philosopher Heraclitus had developed the idea that the logos had reasoning power and created the universe, and that humans failed to understand that there was reason for and in their very existence. Therefore, they lived in a world naively defined in their own terms. He was followed by Zeno (the founder of Stoicism)who described the logos as the completely rational and spiritual basis for all that had been created and now existed. (continued)

For the reader, John offers the most complex message of all the gospels. He has presented the Word as though it were a separate entity, "When all things began, the Word already was." Yet, this is followed by, "The Word was with God, and what God was, the Word was." Stoics and other Greek philosophers had earlier spoken of the Logos. In the Jewish communities that had spread throughout the Mediterranean world these Greek influences gave birth to Hellenistic Judaism. It was during Jesus' lifetime that its outstanding proponent, the Jewish philosopher Philo,[120] described the Logos as being separate from God, and also as actually being God, and as a characteristic of God.

One who reads John's introductory passage literally will probably not be concerned with these influences. However, one who reads John figuratively will note how most of the difference between John's gospel and those of Mark, Matthew, and Luke reflects these influences. "When all things began the Word already was." Then the following, "The Word was with God, and what God was, the Word was." John's emphasis on Jesus being the logos, which temporarily assumed human form, not only reflected the manner in which Greek philosophy influenced John, but was certain to attract Greek interest in John's theology.

We must, at this point, also note John's use of the word "life." *The New English Bible* notes: "Life in John always means eternal (not merely natural) life (see John 3: 15). This life becomes the *light of men* in that it reveals the Father to them."[121]

Gnosticism's influence is apparent in verses following the definition of the Word. "All that came to be was alive with his life, and that life was the light of men. The light shines in the dark, and darkness has never mastered it." Later, in the fourteenth verse John will identify Jesus as the Word: "And the Word became flesh and lived among us, and we have seen his glory, the glory as of a father's only son, full of grace and truth."

The New Oxford Bible notes: "The Word (Greek 'logos') of God is more than speech; it is God in action, creating (Genesis 1.3; Ps 33.6), revealing (Amos 3.7-8), redeeming (Ps. 107.19-20)."

[120]   Philo lived in Alexandria, Egypt. He was born sometime between 15 and 10 BC, and died between 45 and 50 AD.
[121]   *The New English Bible*, fn., p. 108 NT.

John, like the Gnostics, speaks of the need for divine revelation as the path to salvation. He makes Jesus the "light", the Word, arriving in human form to bring that light to each individual, thereby bringing salvation through revealing to each individual his or her individual relationship to God. As had the ancient religions and philosophies of China, India, Babylonia, Greece, and Egypt for millennia before him, John employs light and darkness to represent good and evil. In John this contrasts the light that is the way of God with the darkness of total evil which forever seeks, but fails, to master God's will.

This Jesus, who in John's fourteenth verse is identified as the Word that became flesh to bring the "light" into the world of humans, is eternal, for the Word existed before the "beginning". *The New Oxford Bible* notes: "Apart from him both physical (Col 1: 17) and spiritual life would recede into nothingness (John 5. 39-40; 8: 12). Darkness is total evil in conflict with God; it cannot overcome."[122]

The Gnostics' belief that salvation was the result of revelation, when the individual's relationship to God was revealed to the unconscious self, was not an idea foreign to the Greek Platonists. Socrates, living four hundred years before Jesus and two centuries before the advent of Gnosticism, would be remembered for his saying, "Know thyself." For John, salvation was the result of coming to know God's will. Jesus was the light that drove out that darkness that represented the lack of knowledge of God. Humans had to know themselves, to understand their true relationship with God. If they had this knowledge, and actually believed what had been revealed to them, they would make the right moral choices in their relationships with one another.

For both literal and figurative readers it is important to understand John's introduction to his gospel, because this is the theme of his entire gospel. He has written this gospel to show his readers that Jesus is the light; the only light that could dispel darkness and thereby reveal God to the individual. To John it is all important that one sees Jesus as the Word in human form. For John, only those can be called Christians who thus see Jesus as the Word that temporarily became flesh.

For the literal reader there may be a problem. According to John the Word existed before the beginning, and Jesus is the Word,

---

[122] *The New Oxford Bible*, fn. p. 125 NT.

therefore he has existed since before the beginning; was a part of the beginning. John opened his gospel saying: "In the beginning was the Word, and the Word was with God, and the Word was God." Then, from a literal reading a reader must assume that Jesus and God are one, and that God in the form of Jesus left all else to spend thirty six years walking among humans. And, if Jesus is God, critics will ask, "How then can God be the Father and Jesus his son?"

Critics further ask, if Jesus is the Logos, and therefore the creator, why did he not arrive in the world as an adult ready to preach? Why, they ask was it necessary for him to be born of a woman and then spend thirty-three years growing to the point where he could act as the Logos? John touches on none of these points, for his concern is that people recognize that Jesus represents the Word, the purpose and plan for the world and its humans, and that he be listened to accordingly. Having *faith* in the plan and purpose for all humanity is the aim John has for all individuals.

John continues his introduction by next describing the role of John the Baptist as one sent by God to introduce Jesus.

There was a man sent from God, whose name was John. He came as a witness to testify to the light, so that all might believe through him. He himself was not the light, but he came to testify to the light. The true light, which enlightens everyone, was coming into the world.

He (Jesus) was in the world, and the world came into being through him; yet the world did not know him. He came to what was his own, and his own people (the people of Israel) did not accept him. But to all who received him, who believed in his name, he gave power to become children of God, who were born, not of blood or of the will of the flesh, or the will of man, but of God.

And the Word became flesh (human) and lived among us, and we have seen his glory, the glory as of a father's only son, full of grace and truth. John (the Baptist) testified to him and cried out, "This was he of whom I said, 'He who comes after me ranks ahead of me because he was before me.' From his fullness we have all received, grace upon grace. The law indeed was given

> through Moses; grace and truth came through Jesus
> Christ. No one has ever seen God. It is God the only
> Son, who is close to the Father's heart, who has made
> himself known."
>
> John: 1.6-18

Chronology is not one of John's strong points. In John's gospel Jesus is with John the Baptist when he selected his first disciples, in contrast to the synoptic gospels which had him walking along the shores of the Sea of Galilee.

> "The next day John again was standing with two of his
> disciples, and as he watched Jesus walk by, he exclaimed,
> 'Look, here is the Lamb of God!' The two disciples
> heard him say this, and they followed Jesus. When Jesus
> turned and saw them following, he said to them, 'What
> are you looking for?' They said to him, 'Rabbi' (which
> translated means Teacher), where are you staying?' He
> said to them, "Come and see." They came and saw
> where he was staying, and they remained with him that
> day. It was about four o'clock in the afternoon. One of
> the two who heard John speak and followed him was
> Andrew, Simon Peter's brother. He first found Simon
> and said to him, "We have found the Messiah" (which is
> translated Anointed). He brought Simon to Jesus, who
> looked at him and said, "You are Simon son of John.
> You are to be called Cephus (which is translated Peter,
> the Rock)." The next day Jesus decided to go to Galilee.
>
> John: 1.35-43

Where did Jesus find Peter and invite him to be a disciple; on the northwest shore of the Sea of Galilee or at the edge of the wilderness where John the Baptist was teaching? These discrepancies may raise questions among literal readers, and certainly provide fodder for critics. However, for those who read the gospels figuratively this is of no consequence. We have quoted the above passage here only as an example of how various passages in John are out of sequence with the other three gospels. Those who read figuratively note that such passages are only important insofar as they succeed in delivering John's message; a point he makes in his twentieth chapter

> There are indeed many other signs that Jesus performed in the presence of his disciples, which are not recorded in this book. *Those here written have been recorded in order that you may hold the faith that Jesus is the Christ, the Son of God,* and that through this faith you may possess life in his name.
>
> John: 20.30-31

John has made it clear that he was not concerned with presenting an accurate history; hoping instead to show individuals the path to salvation through faith in Jesus. Mark, Matthew, and Luke had established credentials for the teacher Jesus, and had used parables to carry Jesus' message to their readers   John believed it essential to go beyond the aims of those gospels in his parables. He aims to bring to individuals of this new religion a deeper and more important theological message; a message in which each individual's salvation is based on his or her personal knowledge of his or her relationship with God.

CAN ANYTHING GOOD COME OUT OF NAZARETH

> The next day Jesus decided to go to Galilee. He found Philip and said to him, "Follow me." Now Philip was from Bethsaida, a city of Andrew and Peter. Philip found Nathanael and said to him, "We have found him about whom Moses in the law and also the prophets wrote, Jesus son of Joseph from Nazareth." Nathanael said to him, "Can anything good come out of Nazareth?" Philip said to him, "Come and see." When Jesus saw Nathanael coming toward him, he said of him, "Here is truly an Israelite in whom there is no deceit1!" Nathanael asked him, "Where did you get to know me?" Jesus answered, "I saw you under the fig tree before Philip called you." Nathanael replied, "Rabbi, you are the Son of God! You are the King of Israel!" Jesus answered, "Do you believe because I told you that I saw

342

> you under the fig tree? You will see greater things than
> these." And he said to him, "Very truly, I tell you, you
> will see heaven opened and the angels of God ascending
> and descending upon the Son of Man."
>
> John: 1.43-51

As John has Jesus returning to Galilee, he adds that Philip, Andrew, and Peter were all from Bethsaida, which was on the northern shore of the Sea of Galilee. This, as in the synoptic gospels will place the three disciples along the shore of the Sea of Galilee, though after they had been recruited at the edge of the wilderness.

John will now recount seven of the miracles attributed to Jesus in the earlier gospels. However, he refers to these as *signs* that Jesus is indeed the true messenger who can and will bring the light of revelation in his teaching; not as miracles to impress listeners and readers.

> On the third day there was a wedding in Cana-in-
> Galilee. The mother of Jesus was there, and Jesus and
> his disciples were guests also. The wine gave out, so the
> mother of Jesus said to him, "They gave no wine left."
> He answered, "Your concern, mother, is not mine. My
> hour has not yet come." His mother said to the servants,
> "Do whatever he tells you." There were six stone water-
> jars standing near, of the kind used for Jewish rites of
> purification; each held from twenty to thirty gallons.
> Jesus said to the servants, "Fill the jars with water," and
> they filled them to the brim. "Now draw some off," he
> ordered, "and take it to the steward of the feast;" and
> they did so. The steward tasted the water now turned to
> into wine, not knowing the source; although the servants
> who had drawn the wine knew. He hailed the
> bridegroom and said, "Everyone serves the best wine
> first, and waits until the guests have drunk freely before
> serving the poorer sort; but you have kept the best wine
> till now."
>
> This deed at Cana-in-Galilee is the first of the signs by
> which Jesus revealed his glory and led his disciples to
> believe in him.
>
> John: 2.1-11

John has brought Jesus' mother into the picture in a way none of the earlier gospel writers had. He has her accompanying Jesus in his travels and has her present when the first of the signs of his "glory" are revealed. John thus uses her to represent worldly concerns in contrast to what Jesus foresees as his future role. "Your concern, mother, is not mine. My hour has not yet come."

When would Jesus' hour come? According to John, that would be when God decided the time was right for Jesus to make known his role; not when Mary or anyone else thought it the appropriate time. This raises a question. John has begun his gospel by explaining that the Word existed before all else and that the Word was with God. Later in his gospel he says Jesus is the Word become flesh. If God is to determine when Jesus is to be revealed for what he was, this implies that Jesus is being directed by God. But, critics ask, if Jesus is the Word incarnate, and the Word is also God, how can the Word give instructions to itself? Or, does this imply that the decision is Jesus' to make, and will not be the result of any worldly pressures or temptations?

This question arises because of John's conviction that all Christians must see the "glory" of Jesus being revealed to the world. He has followed this passage with Jesus turning water into wine, thereby having Jesus finally deciding to give the first sign of who and what he was. Reading literally, one sees the conflicting ideas of the role of Jesus as the Word became flesh and God who is also the Word. In a figurative reading, the reader sees John doing what the other gospel writers had done before him. He is trying to make certain that Jesus' message will be accepted, by using signs (miracles) to reveal Jesus as the true light that will reveal for each individual his or her true relationship with God.

John moves Jesus and his mother and four brothers directly from Cana to Jerusalem, where Jesus goes immediately to the Temple. The story of the cleansing of the Temple is repeated at this point, but with John's emphasis on the challenge by the authorities. After driving out the money changers and the dealers in sacrificial animals and birds, Jesus is confronted by the Temple authorities.

> Then he turned to the dealers in pigeons: "Take them out." he said, "You must not turn my Father's house into

344

> a market." His disciples recalled the words of the
> Scripture, "Zeal for thy house will destroy me." The
> Jews challenged Jesus: [123] 'What sign," they asked, "can
> you show as authority for your action?" "Destroy this
> temple," Jesus replied, "and in three days I will raise it
> again." They said, "It has taken forty-six years to build
> this temple. Are you going to raise it again in three
> days?" But the temple he was speaking of was his body.
> After his resurrection his disciples recalled what he had
> said, and they believed the Scripture and the words Jesus
> had spoken.
>
> John: 2.18-22

The reference to raising himself from the dead in three days is, as in references in other gospels, a product of Christology. Jesus act of cleansing the temple was an act of such importance that it would have been well remembered. The words about turning his Father's house into a den of robbers, or as in John's gospel a marketplace, reflect Scriptural passages. Important here is John having Jesus refer to the Temple as his Father's house. The three synoptic gospels have Jesus asking "Does not the Scripture say My house shall be called a house of prayer for all nations." John does not have Jesus refer to the Scripture, but rather has him directly refer to the Temple as "My Father's house." Here, John has Jesus declaring his relationship to God, or as the *New Oxford Bible* notes, "My Father's house is a claim of lordship." [124]

John continues to speak of signs:

> When he was in Jerusalem during the Passover festival,
> many believed in his name because they saw the signs of
> what he was doing. But Jesus on his part would not
> entrust himself to them, because he knew all people and
> needed no one to testify about anyone for he himself
> knew what was in everyone.
>
> John: 2.23-25

---

[123] The term "Jews" referred to the Temple authorities, not to the Jewish population as a whole, for Jesus and his disciples and all the crowds to whom he preached were also Jews.
[124] *The New Oxford Bible*, fn. p. 127 NT.

John has presented an interesting passage at this point. He has been using signs to reveal and prove that Jesus is the Word in flesh; yet here he is saying that anyone who believes in Jesus because they are awed by these signs, rather than by the message he brings, has ears that do not hear. *The New Oxford Bible* notes: "Faith which rests merely on *signs* and not on him to who they point is shallow and unstable." This is still as much a message for the twenty-first century Christian as it was for the Christians of John's lifetime. Do people consider themselves to be Christians because of the miracles they associate with Jesus' birth, death, and acts, or because they have heard and have faith in the message he brought?

THE FIRST DISCOURSE

> There was one of the Pharisees named Nicodemus, a member of the Jewish Council (Sanhedrin), who came to Jesus by night. "Rabbi," he said, "we know that you are a teacher sent by God; no one could perform these signs of yours unless God was with him." Jesus answered, "In truth, in very truth I tell you, unless a man has been born over again he cannot see the kingdom of God." "But how is it possible." said Nicodemus, "for a man to be born when he is old? Can he enter his mother's womb a second time and be born?" Jesus answered, "In truth I tell you, no one can enter the kingdom of God without being born from water and spirit. Flesh can give birth only to flesh; it is spirit that gives birth to spirit. You ought not to be astonished, then, when I tell you that you must be born over again. The wind blows where it wills; you hear the sound of it, but you do not know where it comes from, or where it is going. So with everyone who is born from spirit."
>
> Nicodemus replied, "How is this possible?" "What!" said Jesus. "Is this famous teacher of Israel ignorant of such things? In very truth I tell you, we speak of what we know, and testify to what we have seen, and yet you reject our testimony. If you disbelieve me when I tell you

> about things on earth, how are you to believe if I should
> talk about things in heaven?"
>
> John: 3.1-12

Greek concepts of the Logos, and the divine revelation theory of the Gnostics, are reflected in the third verse above. "Very truly, I tell you, no one can see the Kingdom of God without being born again (or as in other translations, born from above)." In John's passage, Jesus tells Nicodemus that only God can reveal the Kingdom of God to an individual; a revelation made possible only by the light being sent in the person of Jesus.

Nicodemus taking Jesus' words literally cannot imagine being born again. In the synoptic gospels Jesus explains to his disciples: "To you the secret of the kingdom of God has been given; but to those who are outside everything comes by way of parables, so that (as the Scripture says) they may look and look, but see nothing; they may hear and hear, but understand nothing; otherwise they might turn to God and be forgiven."[125] John achieves two things with his parable. As in the other gospels he makes certain that his readers know he is using parables, and that the reader needed to dig for their message.

Nicodemus is seen as a famous scholar, a man of considerable intelligence and supposedly of wisdom; yet Jesus finds it necessary to explain that it is through baptism (water) and revelation of the spirit that one is born again. All humans are born of and are flesh. They live in the material world. They were born with physical bodies. To see the kingdom of God the unconscious spirit within them must be awakened (reborn). It is the light of the Logos in the form of Jesus that has been sent to bring about this rebirth.

Greek philosophers had been noting this distinction between "flesh" and the "spirit" for centuries before the birth of Jesus. There would be no difficulty in accepting John's use of this contrast between the flesh and the spirit throughout the Hellenistic world. Later John will say God is spirit, and those who worship him must worship in Spirit and truth."[126] Like the Gnostics, when John says God is spirit he

---

[125]   Mark: 4. 11-12

[126]   John: 4. 24

is saying a bit of God rests within each individual, and waits to be revealed to that individual as the individual is "reborn".

John continues his theological explanation by means of his story of Jesus speaking to Nicodemus.

> "No one has ascended into heaven except the one who descended from heaven, the Son of Man. And just as Moses lifted up the serpent in the wilderness, so must the Son of Man be lifted up, that whoever believes in him may have eternal life.
>
> "For God so loved the world that he gave his only Son, so that everyone who believes in him may not perish but may have eternal life."
>
> John: 3.13-16

The literal reader may see these passages as an account of Jesus actually speaking to Nicodemus. At this point there is a problem with that literal reading. None of the earlier gospels carry this lengthy conversation with Nicodemus. It was apparently unknown to Mark and even later to Matthew and Luke. Now, roughly seventy years after Jesus' death John is offering a verbatim account of Jesus' words to Nicodemus. To one reading this as a figurative account within a parable, these words can only be seen as John's interpretation of Jesus' role being presented in the form of a discourse by Jesus. John will do this frequently in his gospel. He will offer a theological explanation in a manner he believes will be most likely to get his point across; that manner being dialogues in which Jesus explains what is essentially John's theology.

Just what did John mean when he has Jesus saying: "And just as Moses lifted up the serpent in the wilderness, so must the Son of Man be lifted up." According to the Scriptures, the people following Moses from Egypt found themselves with little food or water, and suffering from their long trek through the desert. So embittered had they become that they began to castigate Moses and eventually berated God. At that point poisonous serpents appeared and bit many who then died. God, in response to Moses' plea, instructed him to make a serpent and lift it up where all could see it. The serpent that Moses fashioned in bronze was then fastened to a pole. Thereafter, whenever one of the

Israelites was bitten by a serpent he or she had only to look upon the bronze serpent to be cured. It was not the serpent, but their faith in God who had directed that the serpent be made that cured them.

John's reference to Jesus being lifted up is often read to mean that he would be lifted upon the cross, and for those who saw him there, not as just another crucified being, but as the Son of Man who had been sent by God, would by their faith have gained eternal life. Like the serpent raised by Moses in the wilderness, Jesus on the cross would become a shining symbol of what God promised those with faith. In this passage we see John's words. Seventy years after the crucifixion he has Jesus' telling Nicodemus what could only take place after Jesus' death. John is making Jesus on the cross the reason for faith by all Christians; a faith in God and in the truth of the message he sent by way of Jesus, his messenger.

The sixteenth verse just does not fit with claims made Jesus in the three earlier gospels. Here Jesus is saying he is the Son of God, which makes God far less than the Logos that is a vast intelligence that created the earth. And, it does not fit the humble and modest Jesus of the other gospels. Even at this point in his gospel it is unlike John to have put such words in Jesus' mouth. There are biblical scholars, who in interpreting John's writing, are convinced that this verse was added later by another writer.

This becomes an important point for the earlier gospels written during the seventy some years between the death of Jesus and John's writing do not speak of Jesus as God's only son who, because God so loved the world, would be sacrificed that all others might have eternal life. This appears to be another of the insertions made in later years as the crucifixion and the image of Jesus on the cross grew in importance in Christian doctrine. Over the two centuries following Jesus' death church leaders found glorification of Jesus to be vital for the church's survival at a time when most mystery religions were falling by history's wayside. Without survival of the church there would have been no other vehicle to carry Jesus' message throughout the ages.

John now completes Jesus' conversation with Nicodemus with a passage that clearly reflects the influence of Gnosticism. The light that will reveal God and God's will is the Logos, and Jesus is the Logos in bodily form. John has Jesus continuing his talk with Nicodemus with Jesus saying:

> "Indeed, God did not send the Son into the world to condemn the world, but in order that the world might be saved through him. Those who believe in him are not condemned; but those who do not believe are condemned already, because they have not believed in the name of the only Son of God. And this is the judgment, that the light has come into the world, and people loved darkness rather than light because their deeds were evil. For all who do evil hate the light, so that their deeds may not be exposed. But those who do what is true come to the light, so that it may clearly seen that their deeds have been done in God."
>
> John: 3.17-21

According to John, Nicodemus came to Jesus in the night[127] and Jesus answered Nicodemus' questions with the explanations we have noted in the above passages. This was a private conversation with no modern recording devices, no one other than Jesus and Nicodemus being present, and yet John offers this as though it were the actual discussion between the two. Does that make it unimportant? Does that discredit everything John writes in his gospel?

Mark gave early Christians a gospel that presented what was being taught and preached in the early Christian churches of Paul, Barnabas, and Peter. Matthew and Luke felt a need to portray a Jesus whose stature would withstand competing claims of virgin births of the founders of mystery religions that were competing for adherents. To do this they added their stories of a virgin birth, not found in Mark, but similar to those found in the mystery religions. Mark wrote to provide a common basis for continuing the teachings of Paul and Peter and others at a time when new churches were being established by local leaders. Matthew wrote for a Jewish audience at a time that Judaizers threatened to divide the church. Luke wrote for gentiles, both within and without the church, who were being tempted by the promises of the mystery religions and of intriguers within the church.

---

[127]   This has been interpreted by some biblical scholars as meaning Nicodemus was in that darkness in which lived those who had not placed their faith in Jesus. Only those with such faith lived in the light.

By the time John was writing, even the religion of the Jews reflected more than a century of Hellenistic influence. John had grown up in that Hellenistic world. He does not repeat the stories of a virgin birth which would have been rejected by many Greeks and others in this Hellenistic culture. He too builds credentials for "God's messenger"; but by identifying Jesus as the Logos in flesh. The discourse in response to Nicodemus' query is a part of this lengthy introduction of Jesus and the establishing of his credentials as the Logos in human form. When this is recognized as the reason for John's creating a discourse by Jesus when he meets Nicodemus, one who reads figuratively does not reject John's entire gospel because of this fictional dialogue. It is John's theological concepts that the figurative reader seeks.

John moves from his story of the meeting of Nicodemus and Jesus to an account of John the Baptists' testimony as to the true identity of Jesus.

> Now a discussion about purification arose between John's disciples and a Jew. They came to John and said to him, "Rabbi, the one who was with you across the Jordan, to whom you testified, here he is baptizing, and all are going to him." John answered, "No one can receive anything except what has been given from heaven. You yourselves are my witnesses that I said, 'I am not the Messiah, but I have been sent ahead of him.' He who has the bride is the bridegroom. The friend of the bridegroom, who stands and hears him, rejoices greatly at the bridegrooms voice. For this reason my joy has been fulfilled. He must increase, but I must decrease."
>
> John: 3.25-30

The use of the word Jew should not be overlooked. John the Baptist and all his disciples are Jews as are all those to whom they administer. Why then should the man who was discussing purification be identified as a Jew? As this passage unfolds the figurative reader will find it is aimed at leading Israel to, and showing her, the Logos in the form of Jesus.

The use of the "bridegroom" as a metaphor appears in both Jewish Scripture and in Mark and Matthew. In Hosea it refers to the marriage of God and Israel. The gospel of John has John the Baptist using the same imagery. Here, John the Baptist speaks of himself as being the best man, the "friend of the bridegroom", whose role is to bring the bride to Jesus; the bride being Israel.

According to the earlier gospels, Jesus did not begin his teaching until after the arrest of John the Baptist. However, to use John the Baptist as the one to introduce the idea of Israel being led to believe in Jesus, the gospel of John needed to place the arrest after the above discussion between John the Baptist and his disciples. Again, this use of literary license should not distract from the intent of the gospel writer. It is still part of the introduction of Jesus and his role as the Logos incarnate.

CHAPTER 23

BRINGING THE LIGHT

In John's gospel, Jesus is passing through Samaria on his way back to Galilee when, weary from the long walk, he has stopped to rest at Jacob's well while his disciples go in search of food for a noon time meal. As a Samaritan woman comes to draw water from the well Jesus asks her to give him a drink, to which request she responds:

> "How is it that you, a Jew, ask a drink of me, a woman of Samaria?" (Jews do not use vessels in common with Samaritans.) Jesus answered her, "If you knew the gift of God, and who it is that is saying to you, Give me a drink, you would have asked him and he would have given you the living water." The woman said to him, "Sir, you have no bucket, and the well is deep. Where do you get that living water? Are you greater than our Ancestor Jacob, who gave us the well, and with his sons, and his flocks drank from it?" Jesus said to her "Everyone who drinks this water will be thirsty again, but those who drink of the water that I will give them will never be thirsty. The water that I shall give him will be an inner spring always welling up for eternal life." The woman said to him, "Sir, give me that water, so that I may never be thirsty, nor have to keep coming here to draw water."
>
> John: 4.7-15

It is interesting that John says: "Jesus, tired out by his journey was sitting by the well." Critics ask if Jesus was the Logos how could he be tired? Only a human would be "tired out". This is an important point, for it is the humanness of Jesus that makes his compassion for all fellow humans so meaningful.

Early church leaders taught that Christians were expected to live their lives free from sin, even as Jesus lived his life. But, others said that a sin free life was possible for Jesus only because he was divine, the Logos incarnate. No human could achieve such perfection because such perfection could only be achieved by a divine being, so no human should be expected to be free from sin. When John and others refer to Jesus' humanity, they make his compassion, his kindness and love for all others, and his entire way of life an example for all other humans, a goal which each human could at least strive to attain.

This can be confusing, because John quite definitely is writing to prove for his readers that there can be a divine relationship between true Christian worshipers and the Christ; a coming together; a uniting of God and the individual. This could only be accomplished if Jesus himself were divine. Proving this divinity is the motive for the writing of this entire gospel as John later explains in his twentieth chapter:

> There are indeed many other signs that Jesus performed in the presence of his disciples, which are not recorded in this book. Those here written have been recorded in order that you may hold the faith that Jesus is the Christ, the Son of God, and that through this faith you may possess life by his name.
> John: 20.30-31

The Samaritan woman is amazed that Jesus should ask her for a drink of water. She has recognized Jesus as a rabbi (teacher), and rabbis did not speak to women in public places. The reader will recall that although Samaritans were Jews, other Jews looked down on them because the Jews of Samaria had not shared the exile in Babylonia. Though the Babylonian exile had occurred more than five and a half centuries earlier, prejudice against Samaritans had not lessened.

This passage and the rest of the chapter describe further contacts with Samaritans and Gentiles. For those living in the Hellenistic world in which John has been raised, John is describing a Jesus whose divinity crosses all ethnic and national barriers.

For people of that time, "living water" referred to water flowing from a spring, rather than still water in a quiet pool. How, the Samaritan woman is asking, can you give me living water when you do not even have a bucket to lower into this deep spring-fed well? It is here that John introduces Jesus as the one who will bring eternal life; "living water" having centuries before been described in the Scriptures as being "the Lord."[128]

It is obvious that the woman still did not understand what Jesus meant when he spoke of living water when she added, "Give me the water, and then I shall not be thirsty, nor have to come all this way to draw water." However, moments later the woman begins to see Jesus as more than an ordinary traveler.

> "Sir," she replied, "I can see that you are a prophet. Our fathers worshipped on this mountain, but you Jews say that the temple where God should be worshipped is in Jerusalem." "Believe me," said Jesus, "the time is coming when you will worship the Father neither on this mountain, nor in Jerusalem. You Samaritans worship without knowing what you worship, while we worship what we know. It is from the Jews that salvation comes. But the time approaches, indeed it is already here, when those who are real worshippers will worship the Father in spirit and in truth. Such are the worshippers whom the Father wants. God is spirit, and those who worship him must worship in spirit and truth." The woman answered, "I know that the Messiah (who is called Christ) is coming. When he comes, he will tell us everything."

---

[128] *The New Oxford bible,* fn. p.129 NT. Reference is made to Jeremiah: 2. 13. "...my people have committed two evils: they have forsaken me, the fountain of living water, and dug out cisterns for themselves, cracked cisterns that can hold no water. Reference is also made to Jeremiah: 17. 13. "O hope of Israel! O Lord! All who forsake you shall be put to shame; those who turn away from you shall be recorded in the underworld, for they have forsaken the fountain of living water, the Lord."

> Jesus said, "I am he, I am speaking to you now."
>
> John: 4.19-26

Through words he attributes to Jesus, John makes the point that the place where one worships is of no importance. It is not a particular mountain, or totemistic rock, or sacred shrine, or even the temple that makes worship meaningful. It is important to keep in mind that John wrote this several generations after the first Christian churches were established, and therefore would have included Christian church sanctuaries in such a list. Worship of God should not be tied to ritual or location, and thus face limits of time and space. God should be worshipped at all times "in spirit and in truth".

By speaking of God as spirit, John does not mean something abstract and apart from humans. To John, as was true of the Gnostics, a part of that spirit was present in each individual, and true worship recognized that God as spirit has given a bit of "himself" to each individual.[129]

John has the woman saying: "I know that the Messiah (who is called Christ) is coming. When he comes he will tell us everything." In response John has Jesus telling her, "I am he, I who am speaking to you now." Taken literally, Jesus is saying he is the Messiah. Yet John has already made and will continue to make clear that Jesus is the Logos for all people. He is not a Messiah for the Jews, nor can he be the physical Messiah, if he is the Logos but temporarily in human form. Why then has John added this statement?

The woman expects that with the coming of the Messiah all her questions will be answered. Is Jesus saying, "I am the Messiah?" Is Jesus responding to her belief that only the Jewish Messiah will have the answers she seeks, and that he is that Messiah, or is he just saying, "I am he who will tell you everything?" Or, has John inserted this reference to the Messiah, and Jesus' response, as another strengthening of Jesus' authority for those who had not yet recognized him as the

---

[129]   *The New English Bible* p.113 NT, notes "That *God is spirit* does not mean for John that God is remote from history; rather it affirms his involvement in history. *The New Oxford Bible* translation: "But the hour is coming, and is now here, when the true worshippers will worship the Father in spirit and truth, for the Father seeks such as these to worship him." A note on p.130 NT referring to that passage comments, "Worship *in spirit* is our response to God's gift of himself (*the Father seeks*).

spirit in flesh? To find an answer to these questions the reader needs to step back 2,000 years, put himself or herself in John's sandals, and then ask what am I (John) trying to do.

No matter which answer the reader may decide upon, the important point is that Jesus has told the woman to believe what he has just told her of the need to worship in spirit and in truth, *because* he has the authority to make that statement. John's Jesus is that spirit incarnate; therefore the will of the spirit is obviously Jesus' will.

The disciples have returned from their quest for food. They are now urging Jesus to share their noon meal.

> "Rabbi, eat something." But he said to them, "I have food to eat that you do not know about." So the disciples said to one another, "Surely no one has brought him something to eat?" Jesus said to them, "My food is to do the will of him who sent me and to complete his work. Do you not say , 'Four months more , then comes the harvest?' But I tell you, look around you, and see how the fields are ripe for harvesting. The reaper is already receiving wages and is gathering fruit for eternal life, so that the sower and reaper may rejoice together. For here the saying holds true, 'One sows and another reaps.' I sent you to reap that for which you did not labor. Others have labored, and you have entered into their labor."
>
> John: 4.31-38

In John's parable Jesus portrays himself as the laborer who sowed the fields. He (Jesus), not the disciples, has introduced the light to the people. John, writing almost three quarters of a century after the death of Jesus, has seen how Christianity has grown since then. In this passage he sees Jesus' teachings and compassion, his willingness to die to bring and keep alive the light, and the resurrection of his spirit, as being the labor through which were sown the seeds of faith for Christians. John has Jesus telling the disciples it is now their task to harvest the results. The seed had been sown; the faith in the spirit had grown; the disciples are to reap and share that harvest by spreading that faith.

Read literally, this passage could be confusing. Jesus would be speaking as though his death and resurrection had already occurred, for they were part of the seed that had been sown. A figurative reading, on the other hand, recognizes that the words attributed to Jesus at this point are actually John's; and John is using them to point out that the duty of Christians and the church is to live by and to spread the light of the Logos throughout the world.

One should never be cynical when a gospel writer attributes his own words to Jesus in a parable. The writers of the gospels are putting into words what they consider to be the intent of and the crux of Jesus' teachings. The Sermon on the Mount is an excellent example of how gospel writers brought together in one sermon important lessons taught by Jesus on various occasions during his three years with his disciples.

The writers of John interpreted what they considered the deeper meaning of Jesus' teachings, and presented it in the form of words spoken by Jesus. There is nothing hypocritical in this. This was a sincere effort to present that interpretation to their Hellenistic world several generations after Jesus' death on the cross. It was a world in which the young Christian church was surrounded by competing and rivaling Gnosticism, Neo-Platonism, Judaism, Mystery Religions, Stoicism, Epicureanism, Emperor Worship, the teachings of Philo, and even the less complex Pauline theology.

Once again he visited Cana-in-Galilee, where he had turned the water into wine. An officer in the royal service was there, whose son was lying ill at Capernaum. When he heard that Jesus had come from Judaea into Galilee, he came to him and begged him to go down and cure his son, who was at the point of death. Jesus said to him, "Will none of you believe without some signs or portents?" The officer pleaded with him, "Sir, come down before my boy dies." Then Jesus said, "Return home; your son will live." The man believed what Jesus had said and started for home. When he was on his way down his servants met him with the news, "Your boy is going to live." So he asked them what time it was when he began to recover. They said, "Yesterday at one in the afternoon the fever left him." The father noted that this was the exact time when Jesus had said to him, "Your

> son will live", and he and all his household became believers.
>
> This was now the second sign which Jesus performed after coming down from Judaea into Galilee.
>
> John: 4.46-54

Though this passage may be brief, it makes several points. The woman at the well had been a Samaritan. An officer in the royal service would be a Roman. John could have used Jews in Galilee or Judaea in these parables. By choosing a Samaritan and a Gentile Roman he again makes the point that Jesus, the Logos incarnate, and his works were not limited by national or ethnic barriers. Furthermore Jews held Samaritans in contempt and Romans were considered an enemy occupying force which worshipped more than one God.

The earlier gospels used parables in which miracles carried messages. The blind could be made to see the will of God and the deaf made to hear the message of faith. John does not use this parable for that purpose. Instead, he uses the healing of the Roman officer's son as a sign that Jesus was the Logos sent in human form.

The most important point John is making here is found in Jesus' words: "Will none of you ever believe without seeing signs and portents?" It is disheartening to John that signs and prophetic comments are necessary to open eyes and ears to the message. By the time he is writing, far too many Christians had found these miracles and portents drowning out the message. In a very real sense their eyes were once more being blinded and their ears deafened to the Word. Why, John has Jesus asking, are all of you unable to accept the messenger and his message without these signs and portents? Have none of you faith except when it is accompanied by some miracle, or sign, or prophetic pronouncement? Where is your faith?

How prophetic John's concern. He foresaw Jesus' message being lost amid a growing reverence for and worship of a messenger who could perform miracles; the signs becoming the *raison d'etre* for so much of the continuing growth of the church throughout the next two thousand years.

JESUS, GOD'S AGENT

In John's gospel, Jesus moves around Palestine more often than in the synoptic gospels. This should not create a problem for the reader, for John is picking what he considers the most appropriate setting for each of Jesus' sermons and works; and it is not the setting, but the teaching that is important.

While still introducing Jesus as the bearer of the light, John has added a further sign with the opening of his fifth chapter. He begins with a story of Jesus who, on the Sabbath, healed a man who had been paralyzed for thirty-eight years. Of course this would be condemned by the authorities, which is the real aim of the story as it provides John with an opportunity to have Jesus defend himself against these attacks.

> It was works of this kind done on the Sabbath that stirred the Jews[130] to persecute Jesus. He defended himself by saying, "My Father has never yet ceased his work, and I am working too." This made the Jews still more determined to kill him, because he was not only breaking the Sabbath, but, by calling God his own Father, he claimed equality with God.
>
> To this charge Jesus replied, "In truth, in very truth I tell you, the Son can do nothing by himself; he does only what he sees the Father doing; what the Father does, the Son does. For the Father loves the Son and shows him all his works, and will show greater yet, to fill you with wonder. As the Father raises the dead and gives them life, so the Son gives life to men, as he determines. And again, the Father does not judge anyone, but has given full jurisdiction to the Son; it is his will that all should pay the same honor to the Son as to the Father. To deny honor to the Son is to deny it to the Father who sent him."
>
> John: 5.16-23

[130] John continues to refer to the religious/political establishment as the *Jews*. He does not mean the Jewish community, only the authorities. Not only were Jesus and his disciples Jews, but so were those he was healing on the Sabbath and the hundreds who gathered to hear him preach the Word.

The remainder of the chapter is a continuation of Jesus' testifying that he is truly the Son of God with all God's powers having been delegated to him. The Jesus of the synoptic gospels was modest, even humble at times. He did not want his disciples to refer to him as the Messiah. That Jesus would never have devoted an entire page-long speech to discussing his own importance.

Peter, always close to Jesus, helped establish the Jerusalem church shortly after Jesus' death on the cross. Paul, organized Christian churches among the Gentiles as early as eighteen years after Jesus' death. Mark recorded the teachings of those churches in his gospel about thirty-nine years after Jesus died. Matthew and Luke prepared their gospels about twenty years after Mark's gospel appeared. They added two different versions of the birth of Jesus and of his physical resurrection, but like Mark, Paul, and Peter they do not show that they had ever heard Jesus spend so much time telling others how important he was or that he was divine. Yet, John, some seventy years after the death of Jesus presents this passage as though it were a verbatim account of Jesus' words in defense of himself.

It is obvious that this is John's effort to make people understand that Jesus, whose teachings were so important, was speaking as God's agent among humans. In this, John left himself open to critics who would later challenge Jesus' divinity. They could point out that John had opened his gospel proclaiming Jesus as the Logos. If the Logos existed before time, and was the creator of all that existed, why did he spend so much time trying to convince his listeners that he, the Logos incarnate, had been sent by God. How could the all powerful Logos be a Son acting under orders from the Father? How could the all powerful creator, the Logos, drop to becoming the agent of another.

In their parables, Mark, Matthew, and Luke had given authority to Jesus by demonstrating his divinity through the performing of miracles. John, however, has made clear his concern that such use of miracles as indications of divine authority would backfire; emphasizing instead his use of signs, not miracles, to identify Jesus as the bearer of the light. So, at this point, he has had Jesus explain just who he is and what authority he wields.

Even as John used this approach in trying to make his readers believe in Jesus and his message, he could not help but realize it was possible that it would cause his readers to devote so much of their worship to praise and glorification of the messenger that they would find little, if any time, to receive the message. It was a difficult, but to John, a necessary balance. Today's reader should keep in mind the world in which John was writing two thousand years ago; a world with rivaling influences of the teachings of earlier Greek philosophers, of Stoics, of miracle religions, and of Gnostics; a world in which John has to make the Hellenistic world see Jesus as the one and only carrier of the light. *It was a world in which Christians were still a tiny minority.*

* * * * * * * * * * *

John opens his sixth chapter with the only parable to appear in all four gospels, the feeding of the five thousand. Mark, Matthew, and Luke have the disciples asking Jesus to send the crowds away to find food, and later will have Jesus explain to the disciples what he meant by the bread he gave them.

> Jesus went up the mountain and sat down there with his
> disciples. Now the Passover, the festival of the Jews, was
> near. When he looked up and saw the large crowd
> coming toward him, Jesus said to Phillip, "Where are we
> to buy bread for these people to eat?" He said this to
> test him, for he himself knew what he was going to do.
> Phillip answered him, "Six months' wages would not buy
> enough bread for each of them to get a little."
>
> John: 6. 3-7

With the words, "He said this to test him," John is making it clear from the beginning that Jesus is not speaking of physical food. Furthermore he has Jesus ask Phillip where the food was to come from, whereas Mark, Matthew, and Luke have the disciples ask Jesus how the crowd was to be fed. Perhaps a small point, but it does have Jesus instructing the disciples rather than criticizing them for their lack of understanding. He follows this with a further explanation of what Jesus meant, by having Jesus explain to the crowd that had followed him.

> When they found him on the other side of the sea, they
> said to him, "Rabbi when did you come here?" Jesus

362

> answered them, "Very truly, I tell you, you are looking
> for me, not because you saw signs, but because you ate
> your full of the loaves. Do not work for the food that
> perishes, but for the food that endures for eternal life,
> which the Son of Man will give you. For it is on him that
> God the Father has set his seal." Then they said to him,
> "What must we do to perform the works of God?" Jesus
> answered them, "This is the work of God, that you
> believe in him whom he has sent." So they said to him,
> "What sign are you going to give us then, so that we may
> see it and believe you? What work are you performing?
> Our ancestors ate the manna in the wilderness; as it is
> written, 'He gave them bread from heaven to eat.'" Then
> Jesus said to them, "Very truly, I tell you it was not
> Moses who gave you bread from heaven. For the bread
> of God is what comes down from heaven and gives life
> to the world." They said to him, "Sir, give us this bread
> always."
>
> John: 6.25-35

John is further stressing the point that feeding the five thousand was no physical miracle when he has Jesus point out to the crowd that they were not looking for him because they saw miracles, but because they had been filled with the "true bread" that endures for "eternal life". Once more John emphasizes the point that God's messenger is not to be believed because of miracles he is supposed to achieve. His Jesus tells the crowd that it was not Moses, nor is it now he (Jesus), who is bringing the people "the true bread from heaven." Only God gives the bread that "gives life to the whole world."

When read literally this can be confusing. Jesus is supposed to be the Logos, the creative power that brought the universe into being, but here presents himself again as the messenger sent by God who is superior to him. John, recognizing the need for further clarification, continues:

> Jesus said to them, "I am the bread of life. Whoever
> comes to me will never be hungry, and whoever believes
> in me will never be thirsty. But I have said to you that
> you have seen me and yet you do not believe. Everything

> that the Father gives me will come to me, and anyone
> who comes to me, I will never drive away; for I have
> come down from heaven, not to do my own will, but the
> will of him who sent me, that I should lose nothing of all
> that he has given me, but raise it upon the last day. This
> is indeed the will of my Father, that all who see the Son
> and believe in him may have eternal life; and I will raise
> them up on the last day."
>
> John: 6.35-40

With this passage, John has described Jesus as being sent into the world of humans as a physical representation of God's promise to those who believe.[131] Everything God sends by way of Jesus will be passed on to those who have faith. Jesus is the physical symbol of faith; the conduit for God's gift of eternal life. He has been given to humans so they might hear the message he bears, and when they have seen and heard, *and believe in him,* they shall have received God's gift of faith. Faith is being given them by God, it is not something humans create; but it is up to them to accept this gift.

THE GROWING RELIGION

This may well be a good moment for readers to pause and consider the growth and development of Christianity in those early years as reflected in the differing presentations and interpretations of Christianity by Paul and the various gospel writers.

In Jerusalem hundreds, even several thousand, eventually flocked to those synagogues where they could find rabbis teaching of Jesus' promise of resurrection. Jesus had been a strong believer and faithful adherent of Judaism. Remember, he had come not to destroy or replace his religion, but to reform and strengthen it. What is often in the twenty-first century referred to as the early "Christian" church was in fact only a reform movement within Judaism.

---

[131] John has Jesus' saying, "I have come down from heaven." As popular belief at that time held that heaven was just above ceiling in which the stars were embedded, it would seem logical to John's readers at that time to assume Jesus would have descended to arrive on earth.

Paul, trained as a Pharisee and believing strongly in the moral life under the Law, wished as did all sincere Pharisees that Judaism would become the universal religion binding all the world to its high standards of morality. However, Paul had grown up outside Israel, in a land where Jews were a small minority and Gentiles the great majority. It had only been eight years since Jesus' death and even a shorter time since the "Christian" reform movement had become organized within Judaism, when Paul became a convert to "Christianity."

The appeal of the strong morality of Judaism with its essential Law was still with Paul, but he knew that with its nationalistic emphasis it could never become a universal religion. He could, however, envision the benefits of the highly moral life of Judaism being carried to all peoples within a religion that was truly universal. He could visualize all the benefits of the Jewish religion to which Jesus and his disciples had belonged, but without those nationalistic requirements of the Law, and without the Scriptural limitations in which Moses, the prophets, and the wisdom writers spoke of Jews as the only "chosen people."

Upon coming to the conclusion that Judaism could never, despite its strong message of morality, become a universal religion, Paul had retired to Arabia where he remained for three years. For another year he lived in Damascus. During those years he had come to the conclusion that a religion built around the teachings of Jesus could truly become the universal religion which could carry the high morality of Judaism beyond national or ethnic borders. The people of the world could be united in one faith.

Paul spent another two years in Jerusalem with Peter, James and other founders of the "Jerusalem Church". His conviction that only the teachings of Jesus could unite all peoples finally caused him to leave the Jerusalem Church to join Barnabas in Antioch, where for the first time the followers of Jesus were given the name "Christians." It was with this envisioned potential that Paul and fellow missionaries carried this young religion into the Gentile world. His work and letters are important in revealing how his theological concepts would continue to mature throughout the remainder of his life.

By the time Mark wrote the first gospel one can see how far that early Christianity, so largely dependent on the developing theology of Paul, had developed beyond the limitations of the original "church" in Jerusalem. And just twenty years had elapsed since Paul had begun his missionary work with Barnabas.

By the end of the next two decades Matthew would present a Jesus and his teachings in a manner aimed to respond to the disbelief of his fellow Jews, and to convince them of the need for all to accept this new religion based on faith in the teachings of Jesus. The struggle to expand and keep the young church united had been a key point in Paul's writings. That continuing struggle is evident by the manner in which Matthew presented Mark's teaching in a way acceptable to Jews.

It is important to note that these founders and defenders of this new religion were deeply religious Jews who, like Paul, believed Judaism could never become a universal religion. According to the Scriptures, Israel was the servant of God "chosen" to carry God's message to all humans. However, the nationalistic limitations of the people "chosen" by God for this task had made it impossible for them to carry his message to the rest of the world. So it was that Jews like Paul, Mark, and then Matthew devoted their lives to building this new religion around the teachings of Jesus.

Luke, on the other hand, wrote primarily for Gentiles, presenting a compassionate Jesus, while emphasizing the role of love for and the understanding of fellow humans. At the same time, like Matthew he found it necessary to add stories of the virgin birth and an expanded role of the resurrection, to meet the challenges of competing religions.

Each generation of apostles expanded on the teachings of Jesus. Christianity was steadily growing with newly added parabolical illustrations and interpretations, and with further theological input by new leaders within the church.

Seventy years after Jesus death, John's gospel would present a theology quite different than that of the early Jerusalem church. None of the gospel writers had ever met Jesus' parents. None had ever personally seen or heard Jesus. They wrote well after Jesus' death. Only Mark knew Peter and had listened to his sermons. He was, therefore, the only one of the writers able to question Peter and Paul about what they had either personally or through witnesses learned of Jesus' life and work.

Matthew and Luke, as we have seen, used Mark's "historical" core around which to add new developments; Christianity was growing. It was still only sixty years since Jesus' death when they penned their gospels. Yet, today's reader can see how rapidly Christianity had already changed. It was not a religion at the time of Jesus' death. It was still a reform movement within Judaism at the time of Paul's conversion. It was in its infancy as a new religion at the time of Paul and Barnabas, and even when the "Gospel According to Mark" was penned. *But* it was always growing.

It would grow as men's and women's ideas grew, for all religions are 'man-made'. Usually they are created by disciples or other followers of a spiritual leader; but always developed and expanded by later followers. Jesus, as we have noted did not create Christianity. It was created by those who sought to perpetuate his teachings among Gentiles.

It is important for literal and figurative readers alike to keep this early growth in mind as they read the "Gospel According to John." Unlike the earlier gospels, it does not attempt an historical presentation. It is devoted to the exposition of John's theology; a theology in which the reader will see the strong Greek influence in that continuing growth of Christianity.

As we are reading we are watching men create and build a religion that would be called Christianity.

JESUS, THE GROWING THREAT

The crowd that had followed Jesus had just been told by him that, "In very truth I know you have not come here looking for me because you saw signs, but because you ate the bread and your hunger was satisfied." When they had demanded a sign so they might believe in him he had told them, "I am the bread of life."

> Then the Jews[132] began to complain about him because he said, "I am the bread that came down from heaven." They were saying, "Is this not the son of Joseph, whose father and mother we know? How can he now say, 'I have come down from heaven?'" Jesus answered them, "Do not complain among yourselves. No one can come to me unless drawn by the Father who sent me; and I will raise that person on the last day. It is written in the prophets, 'And they shall be taught by God.' Everyone

---

[132] Religious/political leaders and others who oppose Jesus; not meant to mean all Jews.

> who has heard and learned from the Father comes to me. Not that anyone has seen the Father except the one who is from God, he has seen the Father. Very truly, I tell you, whoever believes has eternal life. I am the bread of life. Your ancestors ate the manna in the wilderness, and they died. This is the bread that comes down from heaven, so that one may eat of it and not die. I am the living bread that came down from heaven. Whoever eats of this bread will live forever; and the bread that I will give for the life of the world is my flesh."
>
> John: 6.41-51

The above translation is taken from the *New Oxford Bible*. The translation of the last sentence as found in *The New English Bible* is perhaps clearer. "Moreover, the bread which I will give is my own flesh; I give it for the life of the world." In the earlier gospels Jesus has explained to his disciples that his frequent reference to bread is not to a leavened loaf but to the word he was bringing to the people. John's reference to this distinction is in Jesus' words, "the bread I will give is my own flesh." As the Logos incarnate, Jesus' flesh is the gift of faith sent by God.

As we have previously noted, the Jesus of Paul, Mark, Matthew, and Luke would never have talked so much about himself. He would never have paraded his power and authority. John is describing for his readers the Jesus he wants them to see and hear with open eyes and ears. When Matthew brought Jesus' teachings into a compact lesson he had the words appear to be spoken by Jesus in a single sermon on the mount. John is continuing to have his understanding of the role of Jesus, and of the religion that is being spread in Jesus' name, appear as words spoken by Jesus.

John's Jesus has brought God's gift of faith to humans on the physical earth. That faith is the bread of which Jesus is the living symbol. John does not include a detailed description of the Last Supper as did the other gospel writers. Instead it is here that he has Jesus say that whoever has accepted the faith he has brought to them will have eternal life and that he, as the living bread, will give his life to ensure eternal life for all those who believe in him.

Those who were "drawn by the Father" who sent Jesus, is a reference to the Scriptures which Pharisees and other Jewish scholars of those times would recognize: "It is (so) written in the Prophets"

Again there is a point of conflict in John's descriptions of Jesus. The Jesus he has introduced in his first chapters is the Logos incarnate. He is not human, but has assumed human form to be God's messenger. But, here John has Jesus saying he will give his life for the life of the world. At this point John has made Jesus a human who can be made to suffer and die on the cross. This is where it becomes increasingly difficult for the literal reader, for John's parables are deeply influenced by Greek philosophy and are aimed primarily at a Hellenistic audience familiar with Greek philosophy.

As we have noted, John does not include the giving of bread and wine during the Last Supper in his gospel. However, at this point he uses Jesus' reply to the skepticism of the "Jews" to offer a more complete explanation of the "flesh and blood" than do the descriptions of the Last Supper in earlier gospels.

> This led to a fierce dispute among the Jews. "How can this man give us his flesh to eat?" they said. Jesus replied, "In truth, in very truth I tell you unless you eat the flesh of the Son of Man and drink his blood you can have no life in you. Whoever eats my flesh and drinks my blood possesses eternal life, and I will raise him up on the last day. My flesh is real food; my blood is real drink. Whoever eats my flesh and drinks my blood dwells continually in me and I dwell in him. As the living Father sent me, and I live because of the Father, so he who eats me shall live because of me. This is the bread which came down from heaven; and it is not like the bread which our fathers ate: they are dead, but whoever eats this bread shall live for ever."
>
> John: 6.52-58

John stresses the difference between a literal and a figurative interpretation of Jesus' role and message in his next passage. Those who had been following Jesus only because of the miracles they had observed and the literal acceptance of his parables are revealed as ones who had not really understood nor really accepted God's gift of faith.

John is predicting the split between those who would understand the depth of Jesus' message and those who failed to see beyond the shallowness of mere signs and political potential.

"This was spoken in synagogue when Jesus was teaching in Capernaum. Many of his disciples on hearing it exclaimed. 'This is more than we can stomach! Why listen to such talk?' Jesus was aware that his disciples were murmuring about it and asked them, 'Does this shock you? What if you see the Son of Man ascending to the place where he was before? The spirit alone gives life; the flesh is of no avail; the words which I have spoken to you are both spirit and life. And yet there are some of you who have no faith.' For Jesus knew all along who were without faith and who was to betray him. So he said, 'This is why I told you that no one can come to me unless it has been granted to him by the Father.

"From that time on, many of his disciples withdrew and no longer went about with him. So Jesus asked the Twelve, 'Do you also want to leave me?' Simon Peter answered him, 'Lord to whom shall we go? Your words are words of eternal life. We have faith, and we know that you are the Holy One of God.' Jesus answered, 'And have I not chosen you, all twelve? Yet one of you is a devil.' He meant Judas, son of Simon Iscariot. He it was who would betray him and he was one of the Twelve."

John: 6.59-71

The three earlier gospels had vast crowds following Jesus, with only the High Priests, Sadducees, and Pharisees appearing to question him. John is having an early dropping off of followers who could not believe in him, who had little or no faith.

John then has Jesus traveling around Galilee because, "He did not wish to go about in Judea because Jews were looking for an opportunity to kill him." (John: 7. 1) According to John, it was at this juncture that Jesus' brothers were urging him to go with them to Judea where he could be seen and heard. They said to him:

370

> "Leave here and go into Judea, so that your disciples also
> may see the works you are doing; for no one who wants
> to be widely known acts in secret. If you do these things,
> show yourself, show yourself to the world." (For not
> even his brothers believed in him.) Jesus said to them,
> "My time has not yet come, but your time is always here.
> The world cannot hate you, but it hates me because I
> testify against it that its works are evil. Go to the festival
> yourselves. I am not going to this festival, for my time
> has not yet fully come." After saying this he remained in
> Galilee.
>
> John: 7.3-9

John has stressed the physical threat Jesus faces if he continues his teaching. In this account Jesus is completely aware of the fate that awaits him. This is not the right time for Jesus to go public; the right time being when his works are ready to be proven by his death on the cross. However, Jesus is not averse to going to Jerusalem for the festival of Booths (Tabernacles). He would go, but secretly, not openly where he would be immediately arrested.

> But after his brothers had gone to the festival, then he
> also went, not publicly but as it were in secret. The Jews
> were looking for him at the festival and saying, "Where is
> he?" And there was considerable complaining about him
> among the crowds. While some were saying, "He is a
> good man," others were saying, "No he is deceiving the
> crowd." Yet no one would speak openly about him for
> fear of the Jews.
>
> About the middle of the festival Jesus went up into
> the temple and began to teach. The Jews were astonished
> at it, saying, "How does this man have such learning,
> when he has never been taught?" Then Jesus answered
> them, "My teaching is not mine but his who sent me.
> Anyone who resolves to do the will of God will know
> whether the teaching is from God or whether I am
> speaking on my own. Those who speak on their own
> seek only their own glory; but the one who seeks the
> glory of him who sent him is true, and there is nothing
> false in him.

"Did not Moses give you the law? Yet none of you keeps the law. Why are you looking for the opportunity to kill me?" The crowd answered, "You have a demon!" "Who is trying to kill you?" Jesus answered them, "I have performed one work, and all of you are astonished. Moses gave you circumcision (it is of course not from Moses but from the patriarchs), and you circumcise a man on the Sabbath. If a man receives circumcision on the Sabbath in order that the law of Moses may not be broken, are you angry with me because I healed a man's whole body on the Sabbath? Do not judge by appearances, but judge with right judgment."

John: 7.10-24

Again readers must be aware that John uses the word "Jews" as a label identifying the leaders of the political/religious community. The crowds that had gathered to listen to him and to support him were Jews. All his followers during his lifetime were Jews. He is constantly working to reform the religion of the Jews in which he has great faith. The writer (or writers) of John's gospel appears, from his knowledge of Jewish religion and practices, to be a Hellenistic Jew. The use of the term "Jew" also made a point with Gentiles. By having Jesus doubted and persecuted by Jews he will not be seen as merely the representative of a "chosen people". His teachings are thereby freed of a nationalistic label (of being a religion of "Jews") and become the basis for a religion for all.

This particular visit to Jerusalem is not mentioned by Mark, Matthew, or Luke. John uses his story of the visit to the festival of Booths to show his readers a Jesus who knows he will eventually be executed, if he continues his work. He also is presenting a Jesus who is explaining that he is not violating his religion, but rather is carrying out its real intent. Those who would kill him represent those who would restrict that religion to the letter of the law, to ritual, and to man-made rules enforced by its leaders. John's theology reaches far beyond a religion within man-made boundaries.

Jesus is insisting that a man-made religion can put no restrictions on the will of God which goes far beyond the confines of the Temple, or the law, or the rulings of the Sadducees and Pharisees.

Considering the time when John is writing, we must assume he was also referring to attempts by those who would establish rigorous rules and rituals in the still young Christian church.

By describing differing opinions in the crowd of listeners around Jesus, John shows us a Jesus who does not bring about instant agreement and conversion whenever he speaks. Jesus' work is not easy as the story of the Sermon on the Mount and the feeding of the five thousand may have made it appear. It will only reach its culmination with his sacrifice on the cross. For John this makes Jesus' execution essential, if Jesus' teachings are to be understood, preserved, and carried throughout time.

John continues by describing the people of Jerusalem wondering why anyone would want to kill Jesus. Some said they knew his parents, and now ask how this peasant from Galilee could possibly be considered the Messiah. Once more Jesus explains that he has been sent by God; and many who believed him were saying, "When the Messiah comes, will he do more signs than this man has done?" (7. 31)

It was at this point that the Pharisees and the chief priests sent the temple police to arrest Jesus. When they returned empty handed, angry Pharisees demanded an explanation. The police responded, "Never has anyone spoken like this!" They had heard Jesus say:

> "If anyone is thirsty let him come to me; whoever believes in me, let him drink. As the Scripture says, 'Streams of living water shall flow out from within him.'
>
> "He was speaking of the Spirit which believers in him would receive later; for the Spirit had not yet been given, because Jesus had not yet been glorified."
>
> John: 7.37-39

Once more John makes the point that the glorification of Jesus (his death on the cross) is necessary before *the* Spirit can be released to the people. It is important for John, writing at least seventy years after Jesus' death on the cross, that Christians understand that the crucifixion was the necessary sacrifice without which God's will regarding the Spirit, and God's gift of faith, could never be realized. Only with Jesus' ultimate sacrifice could these be released. This is such an important part of John's theology these several generations after Jesus' death that, to get his point across, he has made it a part of a parable set back in Jesus' lifetime.

The above comment by Jesus led some of the people of Jerusalem to declare Jesus the expected prophet. Others insist he must be the long awaited Messiah. Because the Messiah was supposed to have been a descendant of David and from a family living in David's village of Bethlehem, this split the crowds. However, there was still so much support for Jesus that the police had left without attempting to arrest him.

Upon returning empty handed the police faced furious verbal chastisement by furious Pharisees who insisted the police had been misled.

> " Is there a single one of our rulers who has believed in him, or of the Pharisees? As for this rabble, which cares nothing for the Law, a curse is on them." Then one of their number, Nicodemus (the man who had once visited Jesus) intervened. "Does our law", he asked them, "permit us to pass judgment on a man unless we have first given him a hearing and learned the facts?" "Are you a Galilean too?" they retorted. "Study the Scriptures and you will find that prophets do not come from Galilee."
>
> John: 7.46-52

CHAPTER 24

THE UNAVOIDABLE CONFLICT

The opening of the eighth chapter of "The Gospel According To John" differs in various versions of the bible. The first eleven verses were obviously added later by other authors, but are accepted by many scholars as describing an event that might well have occurred. *The New Oxford Bible* includes these eleven verses in its opening of the chapter. *The New English Bible*, on the other hand, begins with verse number twelve, but includes the omitted verses as an addendum at the end of the gospel.

The verses in question relate the familiar story of Jesus defending a woman caught in adultery.

> Early in the morning he (Jesus) came again to the temple. All the people came to him and he sat down and began to teach them. The scribes and the Pharisees brought a woman who had been caught in adultery; and making her stand before all of them, they said to him, "Teacher, this woman was caught in the very act of adultery. Now in the law Moses commanded us to stone such women. Now what do you say?" They said this to test him, so that they might have some charge to bring against him. Jesus bent down and wrote with his finger on the ground.

> When they kept on questioning him, he straightened up
> and said to them "Let anyone among you who is without
> sin be first to throw a stone at her." And once again he
> bent down and wrote on the ground. When they heard
> it, they went away, one by one, beginning with the elders;
> and Jesus was left alone with the woman standing before
> him. Jesus straightened up and said to her, "Woman,
> where are they? Has no one condemned you?" She said,
> "No one, sir." And Jesus said, "Neither do I condemn
> you. Go your way and from now on do not sin again."
>
> John: 8.1-11

As the eighth chapter opens John has Jesus beginning to teach publicly, which from that point on makes serious confrontations with the political/religious authorities inevitable. It is this transition that presented later writers with an opportune spot for insertion of those first eleven verses. From this point on Jesus will be seen as being in direct conflict with the authorities on every important point that he makes in his teachings. We are seeing Jesus take his first deliberate step on the road to Calvary and the glorification John has described as the necessary culmination of Jesus' work.

Jesus' assertion that he is the "light of the world" is repeatedly challenged by Pharisees. When in response he says, "If you continue in my word, you are truly my disciples; and you will know the truth, and the truth will make you free," even some who had believed in him said: "We are descendants of Abraham and have never been slaves to anyone. What do you mean by saying, 'You will make us free'?"

> Jesus answered them, "Very truly, I tell you everyone
> who commits sin is a slave to sin. The slave does not
> have a permanent place in the household; the son has a
> place forever. So if the Son makes you free, you will be
> free indeed. I know that you are descendants of
> Abraham; yet you look for an opportunity to kill me,
> because you have no place in you for my word. I declare
> that I have been seen in my Father's presence; as for you,
> you should do what you have heard from the Father."

> They answered him, "Abraham is our father." Jesus said
> to them, "If you were Abraham's children, you would be
> doing what Abraham did, but now you are trying to kill
> me, a man who has told you the truth that I heard from
> God. This is not what Abraham did. You are indeed
> doing what your father does." They said to him, "We are
> not illegitimate children; we have one father, God
> himself." Jesus said to them, "If God were your Father,
> you would love me, for I come from God and now I am
> here. I did not come on my own, but he sent me.
>
> Why do you not understand what I say? It is because you
> can not accept my word. You are from your father the
> devil, and you choose to do your father's desires."
>
> John: 8.34-44

This is one more passage that can lead to confusion when read literally. Jesus says he is the son and that he is there on earth because God sent him. Yet this is the Jesus who John earlier introduced as the Logos incarnate. The Logos that existed "before the beginning", and at the beginning was with God.

When his listeners claimed to "have one father, God himself," Jesus tells them that the reason they cannot accept his word is that they are not children of God, but of the devil. A literal reader may accept this to mean the devil, an evil god, is actually their forefather. Keeping in mind what Jesus has meant by the term devil or Satan, leads figurative readers to a different conclusion. Jesus is saying that material desires for such things as wealth, position, power, and physical satisfaction make doubters find his words a threat to all they seek from life. They are "children" dependent upon those temptations and trespasses, which Jesus calls the devil, to give them a purpose in life.

These charges by Jesus led his opponents to condemn him as a Samaritan and as one possessed by a demon. For them, Jesus' miracles could only be the work of a demon. Jesus responded:

> "I do not have a demon; but I honor my Father, and you
> dishonor me. Yet I do not seek my own glory; there is
> one who seeks it and he is the judge. Very truly, I tell
> you whoever keeps my word will never see death." The

> Jews said to him, "Now we know that you have a
> demon. Abraham died, and so did the prophets; yet you
> say, Whoever keeps my word will never taste death. Are
> you greater than our father Abraham, who died? The
> prophets also died. Who do you claim to be?" Jesus
> answered, "If I glorify myself, my glory is nothing. It is
> my Father who glorifies me, he of whom you say, He is
> our God, though you do not know him. But I know
> him; if I would say I do not know him, I would be a liar
> like you. But I do know him and I keep his word. Your
> ancestor Abraham rejoiced that he would see my day; he
> saw it and was glad." Then the Jews said to him, "You
> are not yet fifty years old, and you have seen Abraham?"
> Jesus said to them, "Very truly, I tell you before Abraham
> was, I am." So they picked up stones to throw at him,
> but Jesus hid himself and went out of the temple.
>
> John: 8.49-59

With this passage confusion may continue to grow for the literal reader. Jesus now says he existed before Abraham, which would fit with his being the Logos. Yet he continues to proclaim himself inferior to God. Read figuratively, these confusing comments may be interpreted as merely a continuation of John's efforts to establish the divinity of Jesus the messenger. Whereas the writers of the three synoptic gospels moved quickly to bring Jesus' teachings to their readers, John has been placing greater emphasis on defining Jesus' role as God's messenger bringing light to the world.

John presents a firm belief that there is a mystical bond between the Christ and the Christians of faith, and that this bond or union is through the church which is Christ's church. This motivates John's entire gospel, as he makes clear near the conclusion of his gospel when as we noted earlier he writes:

> Now Jesus did many other signs in the presence of his
> disciples, which are not written in this book. But these
> are written so that you may come to believe that Jesus is
> the Messiah, the Son of God, and that through believing
> you may have life in his name."
>
> John: 20.30-31

In assuring people that there is a mystical bond between the Christ and Christians, but that this bond exists only through the church, John is not only stressing Jesus' role as the bringer of light. He is also telling his readers that the church must be supported as it is the means of connecting the individual with God.[133]

THE SHEPHERD AMID MORE SIGNS

Mark had collected oral traditions available by the time of Paul's death. Matthew and Luke later created stories of a virgin birth and expanded on the story of a physical resurrection of Jesus. In so doing, these two gospel writers created a Jesus arriving by miraculous birth and leaving after a miraculous resurrection. Arriving from where and going back to where? Matthew and Luke made it clear that the Jesus they depicted had come from God and returned to God, therefore was divine as was his message.

The birth and resurrection details of the gospels of Matthew and Luke were obviously additions of material not available to Jesus' mother, his brother James, Peter, Paul, all the other early founders of Christianity, and Mark who recorded what was being taught forty years after Jesus' death. The later additions of the birth and physical resurrection of Jesus first appear in the work of Matthew and Luke.

John, who does not follow the outline of the three synoptic gospels in developing his gospel, adds lengthy discourses by Jesus. If these additions are John's words, not those of Jesus, why then are they considered important? When keeping in mind the time when and the place where John's gospel was written, and most importantly the audience for whom it was written, the purpose for which John has his words and thoughts appear to be those of Jesus becomes clear to the figurative reader. John's gospel gives the reader a purpose for Jesus' appearance on earth. By the time John writes, Christian churches have been bringing the teachings of Jesus to their members for more than three generations. John does not repeat those teachings as recorded by

---

[133] This may well be a reason why church authorities included John, so different from the synoptic gospels, when drawing together the *New Testament*.

Mark, Matthew, and Luke. Instead he stresses the authority of Jesus as God's agent through still more signs, while expressing his (John's) theology through Jesus' words and actions.

Is John to be criticized for this portrayal of Jesus as the one expounding this theology? Not if one believes that John considers this to be an honest interpretation of Jesus' intent. At the same time, one must recognize that John's perspective of "Jesus' intent" cannot help but be influenced by Hellenistic thought, Gnosticism, and his own life experiences. This is one more part of the growth and development of man-made Christianity during the more than two centuries that passed between the crucifixion and the compiling of the *New Testament*.

The ninth chapter opens with another sign of Jesus' divinity, but then in the same opening passage it defines, in terms of John's theology, the purpose for Jesus' being.

As he went on his way Jesus saw a man blind from his birth. His disciples put the question, "Rabbi, who has sinned, this man, or his parents? Why was he born blind?" "It is not that this man or his parents sinned," Jesus answered; "he was born blind so God's power might be displayed in curing him. While daylight lasts we must carry on the work of him who sent me; night comes, when no one can work. While I am in the world I am the light of the world."

With these words he spat on the ground and made a paste with the spittle; he spread it on the man's eyes, and said to him, "Go and wash in the pool of Siloam (The name means 'sent'.) The man went away and washed, and when he returned he could see.

John: 9.1-7

Several points are made in this short passage. First, Jesus refutes the accepted belief that illnesses were God's means of punishing individuals. Blindness was not an act of punishment, but an opportunity for "God's power" to be displayed. Second, this becomes more than just another "sign" of Jesus' power when John has Jesus add that there was little time left to accomplish the task for which he was sent. "While I am in the world I am the light of the world".[134] Soon I will be gone. In the short span between now and my death, much is yet to be done.

Once more John highlights Jesus role as the light that has entered a dark world; a world in which people could not see their relationship to God. Without Jesus there is no light for them to find the path to salvation. As we noted earlier, for John salvation was the result of coming to know God's will; Jesus was the light that drove out that darkness that represented the lack of knowledge of God. Humans had to know themselves, to understand their true relationship with God. If they had this knowledge, and actually believed what had been revealed to them, they would make the right moral choices in their relationships with one another.[135]

John's theology, reflecting Hellenistic and Gnostic influences, is grounded on the belief that individuals must learn of their personal relationship to God; that a part of God is in each individual. Few people saw this relationship and the manner in which it would govern their behavior with regard to each other. They would not believe this just because John or any other human were to so preach. But, if their unawareness or even disbelief of this relationship were portrayed as a darkness throughout the world, only a light could make them aware of their relationship with God. Jesus, through his teachings, then becomes the light that makes it possible for people to see their relationship to God, and the way of life that God willed for them.

John's Jesus is the Logos incarnate. The Logos existed before the beginning. It was the purpose and plan for the world and life thereon. Therefore, Jesus was the light opening the eyes of those who were unaware that they had a purpose; showing them how to be a part in fulfilling God's purpose for their existence. This, people could accept when the light, a divine Jesus who as the Logos was the plan and purpose temporarily in human form, was the messenger.

A third point: Jesus sends the man to the pool of Siloam. To this man whose parents had been blind to the way of God, and who was himself blind, spiritual sight was given. He was healed by his faith in the word of Jesus and by baptism.[136]

---

[134] Other translations read "As long as I am in the world…"

[135] See pp. 6-7 of our earlier Chapter 22.

CHALLENGING THE SHEPHERD

The remainder of this chapter is devoted to the reaction of the Pharisees. They repeatedly challenge the man who had been blind, but now could see. They refuse to believe his story; repeatedly attempting to discredit it and him. When he continues to insist that he had been healed by Jesus they accuse him of being one of Jesus' disciples. If he had not been a sinner, they said, he would not be blind, and everyone knew God would not listen to sinners. When, despite this continuing harassment, the man still insisted he was telling the truth, his accusers expelled him from the synagogue.

Upon learning of the man's expulsion from the synagogue Jesus sought him out. A small crowd gathered round as Jesus spoke to him. Several Pharisees among the crowd were angered when they heard him say that he was the Son of Man. Addressing them Jesus said:

> "It is for judgment that I have come into the world – to give sight to the sightless and to make blind those who see." Some Pharisees in his company asked, "Do you mean that we are blind?" "If you were blind,' said Jesus, you would not be guilty, but because you say 'We see', your guilt remains."
>
> John: 9.39-41

This passage should be read carefully for John does not mean that judgment is the reason for Jesus coming into the world. Remember, he had earlier written: "God loved the world so much that he gave his only Son, that everyone who has faith in him may not die but have eternal life It was not to judge the world that God sent his Son into the world, but that through him the world might be saved," (John: 3.17.). *The New Oxford Bible* notes at this point: "Judgment was not the purpose, but the result of Jesus' coming. Belief opens the eyes

---

[136]   *The New English Bible* notes (fn. pg. 121 NT): spiritual sight as been conferred "through faith and baptism…..John wishes to associate Jesus and the pool, both sent by God; John sees baptismal symbolism in the incident."

of the spirit (*he who worshipped him*), unbelief blinds *the Pharisees*. Proud refusal to admit spiritual blindness demonstrates their *sin*."[137]

The New English Bible notes that the dialogue between Jesus and the man he had healed (verses 35-38) "is often viewed as reflecting the late first century baptismal interrogation of the neophyte."[138] We see here another example of how Christianity was growing as men added their thoughts to the gospels. This form of baptismal interrogation of neophytes would not come into being until decades after Paul and Barnabas had established the Gentile churches. But, to strengthen the theological point he is making John has considered it necessary to have it appear that Jesus first uttered these words sixty or more years earlier.

People throughout the Mediterranean world had for more than a thousand years referred to their gods and kings as shepherds of the people. It is therefore not surprising that, in this region where shepherding was one of the oldest tasks and where early Hebrew tribes had lived among various of those cultures, *Old Testament* prophets would also come to refer to God as the good shepherd.

John has built his tenth chapter around this familiar concept, and in this case Jesus is the good shepherd. The chapter opens with a parable.

> "Very truly, I tell you, anyone who does not enter the sheepfold by the gate but climbs in by another way is a thief and a bandit The one who enters by the gate is the shepherd of the sheep. The gatekeeper opens the gate for him, and the sheep hear his voice. He calls his own sheep by name and leads them out. When he has brought out all his own, he goes ahead of them, and the sheep follow him because they know his voice. They will not follow a stranger, but they will run from him because they do not now the voice of strangers." Jesus used this figure of speech (parable) with them, but they did not understand what he was saying to them.
>
> So again Jesus said to them, "Very truly, I tell you, I am the gate for the sheep. All who came before me are thieves and bandits, but the sheep did not listen to them. I am the gate. Whoever enters by me will be saved, and

---

[137]   Fn. p. 141 NT, *The New Oxford Bible*.
[138]   Fn. p. 122 NT, *The New English Bible*.

> will come in and go out and find pasture. The thief comes only to steal and kill and destroy. I came that they may have life, and have it abundantly.
>
> "I am the good shepherd. The good shepherd lays down his life for the sheep. The hired hand, who is not the shepherd and does not own the sheep sees the wolf coming and leaves the sheep and runs away – and the wolf snatches them and scatters them. The hired hand runs away because a hired hand does not care for the sheep. I am the good shepherd. I know my own and my own know me, just as the Father knows me and I know the Father. And I lay down my life for the sheep. I have other sheep that do not belong to this fold. I must bring them also, and they will listen to my voice. So there will be one flock, one shepherd. For this reason the Father loves me, because I lay down my life in order to take it up again. No one takes it from me, but I lay it down of my own accord. I have power to lay it down, and I have power to take it up again. I have received this command from my Father,"
>
> John: 10.1-18

When sheep were brought to corrals by more than one shepherd, a single gatekeeper could guard those flocks until the shepherds returned for their sheep. The gatekeeper, recognizing them, would let them enter the corral, where a shepherd's sheep would recognize his voice and come to him.

By saying Jesus' listeners did not understand this parable John has given a reason for adding the further parable in which Jesus is the gate.[139] All those who before the coming of Jesus had falsely claimed to be messiahs or bearers of the true word of God, were thieves who came to steal the sheep. But, Jesus says, I am the only gate through which you can enter into God's fold.[140]

---

[139] John believes this point is so important that he emphasizes it by repeating it in this second parable as if the listeners had not understood the first parable.
[140] *The New Oxford Bible* notes that as the good shepherd: "Christ provides (a) escape from the perils of sin, (b) freedom, and (c) spiritual sustenance (the bread, water, and light of life)." This note refers the reader to the promises of the parables in the preceding three chapters, fn. NT p. 142.

Among those to whom Jesus was speaking there were Pharisees and many faithful Jews familiar with Scriptural passages in which prophets spoke of God as the shepherd. Those prophets had promised that God would eventually come to lead his flock; and it is at this point that John is portraying Jesus as the good shepherd sent by God to fulfill this promise.

Readers should not forget that John is writing primarily for a Gentile audience, yet is referring to Jewish scriptures in a manner that will give authenticity to Jewish readers of his gospel. This point is demonstrated when he has Jesus saying he is the good shepherd who knows his own sheep as they know him, *but* that he also has other sheep (Gentiles) that he must bring into the fold.

John concludes this parable by once again having Jesus predict his own sacrificial death; the death John insists was necessary to save the world. "And I lay down my life for the sheep." When Jesus has brought the Gentiles into the fold, "there will be one flock and one shepherd. And, to achieve this task, for which Jesus says God has sent him, he will deliberately follow the path leading to his crucifixion.[141]

John concludes this chapter with Jesus being challenged at the celebration of Hanukkah by doubters who demanded that if he was the Messiah, he should say so quite plainly. Jesus responds by telling the non-believers that what he does is done in his Father's name and that those deeds are his credentials. Whether he is called Messiah or by some other title is not important. It is his works which are important for they reflect the purpose God has for mankind.

> "Because you are not sheep of my flock you do not
> believe…My own sheep listen to my voice; I know them
> and they follow me. I give them eternal life and they
> shall never perish; no one shall snatch them from my
> care. My Father who has given them to me is greater
> than all, and no one can snatch them out of the Father's
> care. My Father and I are one."
>
> John: 10.26-30

---

[141]   *The New English Bible* notes that Jesus' insistence that he is voluntarily laying down his life and has the right (power) to receive it back again reflects "a major motif that the anticipated crucifixion and vindication of Jesus are not imposed by human decision , but result from Jesus' *free* decision in obedience to the Father's will." Fn. NT p.123.

The unbelievers in the crowd picked up stones with which to stone Jesus for blasphemy. "You a mere man claim to be a god." To this John has Jesus pointing out that the Law as laid down in their Scriptures said that: "Those are called gods to whom the word of God was delivered – and the Scripture cannot be set aside."

This is an appropriate and strong ending of a chapter devoted to emphasizing the heart of John's theology, namely that Jesus acting for God is creating a bond between believers and himself. It again prepares John's audience to accept the point that after Jesus' death this union of Christians with God is through the church created to carry Jesus' message.

CHAPTER 25

DEEDS AND DISQUISITION

We have noted the major role parables played in the gospels of Mark, Matthew, and Luke. They served two purposes. They were used as illustrations of divine power in order to give credibility to the assertion that Jesus was the Son of God while at the same time serving as examples of the spiritually dead being reborn, of eyes and ears being opened to God's word, and of the healing of the spiritually crippled. In contrast John has until now avoided speaking of miracles, speaking instead of signs proving Jesus was the Logos incarnate. It is, therefore, a decided shift when he devotes his eleventh chapter to the raising of Lazarus, seen more as a miracle than a sign when read literally.

THE RAISING OF LAZARUS

John has Jesus arriving at the tomb four days after Lazarus died. According to Jewish belief the soul remained close to the body for three days before departing. By then corruption of the corpse would be apparent. This late arrival by Jesus assured his followers that Lazarus was indeed dead, and that his soul was no longer present. This, then, is not to be just another parable about the spiritually dead being born again.

When it was learned that Jesus was only about two miles from the home of Mary and Martha, the sisters of Lazarus, Martha set out to meet him.

> Martha said to Jesus, "If you had been here, sir, my
> brother would not have died. Even now I know
> whatever you ask of God, God will grant you." Jesus
> said, "Your brother will rise again." "I know that he will
> rise again," said Martha, "at the resurrection on the last
> day." Jesus said, "I am the resurrection and the life. If a
> man has faith in me, even though he die, he shall come to
> life; and no one who is alive and has faith shall ever die.
> Do you believe this?" "Lord, I do," she answered: "I
> now believe that you are the Messiah, the Son of God
> who has come into the world."
>
> John: 11.21-27

When Jesus, arriving at the tomb, had called for the stone to be rolled away Martha had protested, saying, "Already there is a stench." Jesus said, "Did I not tell you that if you have faith you will see the glory of God?" So they rolled away the stone

> Then Jesus looked upwards and said, "Father, I thank
> thee; thou hast heard me. I knew already that thou
> always hearest me, but I spoke for the sake of the people
> standing around, that they might believe that thou didst
> send me." Then he raised his voice in a great cry:
> "Lazarus, come forth." The dead man came out, his
> hands and feet swathed in linen bands, his face wrapped
> in cloth. Jesus said, "Loose him; let him go."
>
> John: 11.41-44

These passages may be read literally, the raising of Lazarus seen simply as one more miracle; but, when read figuratively they become a complicated message. The chapter began with Jesus receiving word that his friend Lazarus was ill. Jesus waited two days before taking action. It was then that he told his disciples he was going to go back to Judea, where Martha, Mary, and Lazarus lived; an announcement that was met with objections by his disciples who insisted that it was not safe for him to return to Judea where just recently men gathered to stone him to death.

When Jesus has told Martha that Lazarus will rise again she says: "I know he will rise again at the resurrection on the last day." But, when would the last day arrive? It had been promised by prophets and by false Messiahs for centuries, but there was still no sign that the last day was in any way approaching. Martha believed Lazarus would be raised on that last day, but would he lie dead for centuries before that occurred?

Readers should not forget that John's theology is grounded on the belief that individuals must learn of their personal relationship to God; that a part of God is in each individual. Previously in his ninth chapter John portrayed man's unawareness, or even disbelief, of this relationship as a darkness throughout the world in which only the Light could make them see their relationship with God. Jesus, through his teachings, becomes that light which makes it possible for people to see this relationship and the way of life that God willed for them.

Thus, John says, it is through Jesus that each individual is shown that she or he has a purpose, and that each has a part in fulfilling God's purpose for their existence. So it is through Jesus that individuals discover this relationship and attain salvation by living the life God has willed for them. It is through me that you are being saved, "I am the resurrection and the life."

Resurrection is not physical. Therefore the body may rest in the tomb, but the soul (spirit) is resurrected at the time of the death of the physical body. This is not unlike Paul's description of resurrection. In this parable Lazarus' physical rising from the dead becomes a means by which John is able to assure his readers that resurrection is through Jesus, i.e. through living the life Jesus says God has willed for each individual and in recognizing one's personal relationship with God.

Obviously, John could not know the exact words spoken almost seventy years earlier. So, why does he have Jesus saying that he knew God understood what he wanted without his having to pray aloud before Martha and her friends? It is for his readers that John has Jesus saying, "I spoke for the sake of the people standing around, that they might believe that thou didst send me." It is the readers of John's gospel who are the "people standing around" and who are being assured by him that Jesus had been sent by God.

John also uses the raising of Lazarus as the act that finally pushes the Pharisees and Sadducees to conclude there was only one way to deal with this threat to all they held as vital to their beliefs and way of life.

> Now many of the Jews who had come to visit Mary and had seen what Jesus did, put their faith in him. But some went off to the Pharisees and reported what Jesus had done.
>
> Thereupon the chief priests and the Pharisees convened a meeting of the Council. "What action are we taking?" they said. "This man is performing many signs. If we leave him alone like this the whole populace will believe in him. Then the Romans will come and sweep away out temple and our nation." But one of them, Caiaphas, who was High Priest that year said, "You know nothing whatever; you do not use your judgment; it is more to your interest that one man should die for the people, than that the whole nation should be destroyed." He did not say this of his own accord, but as the High Priest in office that year, he was prophesying that Jesus would die for the nation – would not die for the nation alone but to gather together the scattered children of God. So from that day on they plotted his death.
>
> John: 11.45-54

John has just said that the concerns of the Pharisees and Priests embraced far more than their personal positions. He has stressed their fear for the eventual survival of their religion and their nation, which would be a much stronger motive for extreme action. The three earlier gospels placed responsibility for Jesus' arrest, trial, and crucifixion on the high priests and other Sadducees, but John has made the Pharisees the major guilty party. We must remember that he is penning his gospel at a time of increasing concern over the role of Pharisees as Judaizers within Christian churches.

At this point, having described the role of the Pharisees, John says the Chief Priests and the Pharisees called for meeting of the Sanhedrin.[142] The High Priest who convened the meeting insisted that

---

[142]   Historians are divided as to the composition of the Council (Sanhedrin). Some describe it as a body of Sadducees, others say it was a body of Pharisees, and a third description has it a council of Pharisees and Sadducees. (continued)

Jesus must "die not for the nation alone but to gather together the scattered children of God." The scattered children, as contrasted to the chosen people, were the non-Jews of the world. This implies a belief among the Priests and Pharisees that eventually all Gentiles would be brought under Jewish religious law.

In the eyes of the High Priest, popular acceptance of Jesus' message was undermining the authority of their religion and its leaders, authority that was absolutely essential if the people of all nations were to be brought under the Law. If this happened Israel would fail in its role as God's servant by failing to bring all Gentiles into the fold. "So from that day on they plotted his death."

Large crowds had gathered outside the Temple and had filled the streets as Jesus rode into the city on the back of a colt. In John's version these throngs, having just learned of the raising of Lazarus, met him with palm fronds while shouting:

> "Hosanna! Blessings on him who comes in the name of the Lord! God bless the king of Israel! "
>
> John: 12.12-13

Observing this huge demonstration of faith in Jesus the Pharisees could only be strengthened in their conviction that Jesus was destroying their religion and that only by eliminating him could it be saved. They had already concluded that it was necessary to kill Lazarus as well "since it was on account of him that many of the Jews were deserting and believing in Jesus." (John: 12. 9-10)

> The Pharisees then said to one another, "You see, you can do nothing. Look, the world has gone after him."
>
> John: 12.19

John follows this decision by the Pharisees with a passage emphasizing once more his point that Jesus knew that he had to die if his message was to live.

Earlier gospels mention the membership as including scribes, elders and the chief priests. John speaks only of Pharisees and chief priests in this connection.

> Now among those who went up to worship at the festival
> were some Greeks. They came to Philip, who was from
> Bethsaida in Galilee, and said to him "Sir, we wish to see
> Jesus." Philip went and told Andrew; then Andrew and
> Philip went and told Jesus. Jesus answered them, "The
> hour has come for the Son of Man to be glorified. Very
> truly, I tell you, unless a grain of wheat falls into the earth
> and dies, it remains just a single grain, but if it dies it
> bears much fruit.
>
> John: 12.20-24

As we have earlier noted, unlike the authors of the three synoptic gospels John has not employed a biographical approach in describing the works of Jesus. As some biblical scholars have pointed out, the Jews of Palestine would have found it difficult to understand John's gospel. Greek influence as well as that of Gnostics is so evident throughout John that his theology would have been quite foreign to adherents of the theology of the Jews. And it was upon that Jewish theology that the three earlier gospels had based their chronicles of the "reforms" preached by Jesus. One should never lose sight of the fact that for John the Logos was the key to everything that existed.

> In the beginning was the Word (Logos), and the Word
> was with God. He was in the beginning with God. All
> things came into being through him, and without him not
> one thing came into being. What has come into being in
> him was life, and the life was the light of all people. The
> light shines in the darkness, and darkness did not
> overcome it.
>
> John: 1.1-5

This was the Logos Plato would have recognized and the Persians could have accepted. In John the Logos, by becoming flesh in the form of Jesus, replaces the Jewish role of Jesus as the Messiah found in the synoptic gospels. As the people on earth could not see the light, but lived in perpetual darkness, God had to send them light.

Sending this light, the Logos in human form, was a temporary measure only. Once the Logos had dispelled darkness, God would recall it.

In introducing his first chapter John referred to the Logos as "he" and "him"; yet elsewhere in his early chapters John makes it clear that he believed the Logos was the creative intelligence that brought all things into being; not a male in human form. These points may seem contradictory, but at this juncture John is speaking of the Logos as an intelligence not limited to a physical form.

Jesus continues:

> "Now my soul is troubled. And what should I say –
> Father, save me from this hour" No, it is for this reason
> that I have come to this hour. Father, glorify your
> name." Then a voice came from heaven, "I have
> glorified it, and I will glorify it again." The crowd
> standing there heard it and said that it was thunder.
> Others said, "An angel has spoken to him." Jesus
> answered, "This voice has come for your sake, not for
> mine. now is the judgment of this world; now the ruler
> of this world will be driven out. And I, when I am lifted
> up from earth, will draw all people to myself." He said
> this to indicate the kind of death he was to die. The
> crowd answered him, "We have heard from the law that
> the Messiah remains forever. How can you say that the
> Son of Man must be lifted up? Who is the Son of Man?"
> Jesus said to them, "The light is with you a little longer.
> Walk while you have the light, so that darkness may not
> overtake you. If you walk in the darkness, you do not
> know where you are going. When you have the light,
> believe in the light, so that you may become children of
> the light."
>
> John: 12.27-36

In his earlier passage John had stressed once more his point that the task for which Jesus (the Logos) had been sent among people could only be completed successfully through the crucifixion.

> "The hour has come for the Son of Man to be glorified.
> Very truly, I tell you, unless a grain of wheat falls into the
> earth and dies, it remains just a single grain, but if it dies

> it bears much fruit."
>
> John: 12.20-24

For John, Jesus as the Logos not only knew from the beginning that his time on earth in physical form would end with his execution; he did nothing to avoid it. He even threw challenges at the Pharisees that could only result in his eventual crucifixion. Without the world observing his death as a human martyr he knew his teachings could easily be forgotten in a few years. But, as the seed bears fruit only when it dies, John sees Jesus' death as determined by God before the Logos was ever sent in the form of Jesus to bring the light that would dispel the darkness in which all people lived. And the continued existence of light in the world depended on the crucifixion of Jesus.

In his concluding passage of the twelfth chapter John sums up the role Jesus sees for himself as the Logos incarnate.

> Then Jesus cried aloud: "Whoever believes in me believes not in me but in him who sent me. And whoever sees me sees him who sent me. I have come as the light into the world, so that every one who believes in me should not remain in darkness. I do not judge anyone who hears my words and does not keep them, for I came not to judge the world, but to save the world. The one who rejects me and does not receive my word has a judge; on the last day the word that I have spoken will serve as a judge, for I have not spoken on my own, but the Father who has sent me has himself given me a commandment about what to say and what to speak. And I know that his commandment is eternal life. What I speak, therefore, I speak just as the Father has told me."
>
> John: 12.44-50

* * * * * * * * * * * *

John opens his thirteenth chapter once more stating quite clearly his belief that Jesus knew he was about to give up his life to accomplish the purpose for which he had been sent to this world.

> Now before the festival of the Passover, Jesus knew that his hour had come to depart from this world and go to the father.
>
> John: 13.1

This frequent repetition of Jesus' awareness from the beginning that he was to be crucified and would return to God was not without purpose. John is making certain that his readers can not fail to see that the Logos that would return to God had to have been sent by God. Therefore, everything said and done by Jesus had a divine purpose. Thus John's insistence that Jesus was at all times keenly aware that his work would end on the cross complements and highlights John's main theme, that Jesus as the Logos in human form was being sent into this world for only as long as needed to establish the Light that would reveal God's purpose.

Having thus established Jesus as both the Logos and at this point the agent of God, John now has Jesus beginning to speak at length. The discourses that follow reveal what John sees as the real intent in all Jesus had said and done. By claiming they are Jesus' discourses John is using an approach acceptable to his Greek oriented audience, many of whom would reject the earlier gospels because of their more limited (parochial) Palestinian orientation and their heavy use of miracles as vehicles for Jesus' message. This is not unlike the earlier gospel writers creating the Sermon on the Mount (or the plain) to summarize in one easily understood unit all of what each considered to be Jesus' most important teachings. Authors of all four gospels were using whatever means, parables, symbols, or discourses that seemed to them most appropriate for getting across what they believed to be the real meaning of Jesus' life and message.

WITH THE END IN SIGHT

With his thirteenth chapter John begins what the *New English Bible* describes as Jesus' farewell discourses; the Last Supper being the setting for the first of these discourses. Jesus has risen from the table and, despite their protestations, has washed the feet of his disciples, after which he explains:

> "Do you know what I have done to you? You call me
> Teacher and Lord – and you are right, for that is who I
> am. So if I, your Lord and Teacher, have washed your
> feet, you also ought to wash one another's feet. For I
> have set you an example: you are to do as I have done to
> you. Very truly, I tell you servants are not greater than
> their master, nor are messengers greater than the one
> who sent them. If you know these things, you are
> blessed if you do them."
>
> John: 13.12-18

Just before washing the feet of his disciples, Jesus had given Judas a piece of bread dipped in wine. With this act John indicates that Jesus was aware that he was to be betrayed by Judas. Knowing that he had failed to convince Judas to abandon his intent to betray him, Jesus then tells him to leave, saying: "Do quickly what you are going to do." The other disciples were unaware of what this meant; thinking that as Judas was in charge of the common purse Jesus might be instructing Judas to purchase food for the coming festival. Jesus then tells them, "Now the Son of Man has been glorified." The betrayal has been set in motion. The cross is now inevitable.

When Jesus then tells his disciples he will be leaving them they naturally wish to accompany him. Where was Jesus going, they wanted to know, and why can they not accompany him. Jesus responds:

> "Where I am going, you cannot come. I give to you a
> new commandment, that you love one another. Just as I
> have loved you, you should love one another. By this
> everyone will know you that you are my disciples, if you
> have love for one another.
>
> John: 13.33-35

It is here that John includes Jesus' response to Peter's plea to accompany Jesus. "Will you lay down your life for me? Very truly, I tell you, before the cock crows, you will have denied me three times."

John's fourteenth chapter begins with a continuation of Jesus' remarks at the conclusion of the last supper. It is here that Jesus says he will be going to his father's house where he will prepare a place for the disciples. Immediately Thomas has a question and Jesus a response which John presents as a keystone in the foundation of the church.

> Thomas said to him, "Lord, we do not know where you are going. How can we know the way?" Jesus said to him, "*I am the way*, and I am the truth and I am life; no one comes to the Father except by me."
>
> John: 14.5-7

This was a period in which a myriad of religions and philosophies claimed to be the only way to approach or appeal to God. Recognizing this, John has made it clear that Jesus is the only conduit God has provided for humans to reach God; "No one comes to the Father except by me." Forget all others who may claim to represent God's will. Only by way of Jesus will you ever be able to approach God. The coming crucifixion and death of Jesus is the way Jesus will be returning to God who sent him, and by way of that crucifixion, Jesus is saying, I am opening the way for all who believe in me and what I have taught. John uses this statement to show the close relationship of Jesus to God that allows Jesus to speak for God.

John further emphasizes this relationship by having Philip say, "Lord show us the Father and we will be satisfied;" and by having Jesus respond:

> "Have I been all this time with you, Philip, and you still do not know me. Then how can you say, 'Show us the Father'? Do you not believe that I am in the Father and the Father in me? I am not myself the source of the words I speak to you; it is the Father who dwells in me doing his own work. Believe me when I say that I am in the Father and the Father in me; or else accept the evidence of the deeds themselves. In truth, in very truth I tell you, he who has faith in me will do what I am doing; and he will do greater things still because I am going to the Father. Indeed anything you ask in my name I will do, so that the Father may be glorified in the

> Son. If you ask any-thing in my name I will do it."
>
> John: 14.8-14

John is tightening the framework of the Christian church. He is saying by way of Jesus' discourse that there is only one way to approach and to have access to God. That way is, by implication, through the church created to carry Jesus' message through the ages. Readers of John, like the readers of Paul and the three earlier gospels, should step into the sandals of these men who devoted their lives to keeping Jesus' teachings alive through the perilous years of the early church.

The remainder of the fourteenth chapter and the fifteenth continue to show Jesus as the agent of God:

> "You heard me say to you, I am going away, and I am coming to you. If you loved me you would rejoice that I am going to the Father because the Father is greater than I."
>
> John: 14.28

John now shifts to a different illustration of the role of Jesus as God's agent. We have earlier noted John's deep concern over the activities of Pharisees who had become Judaizers within Christian churches. This should be kept in mind as one begins reading John's fifteenth chapter for though he is writing for a Hellenistic audience he now uses a symbolic reference to criticize Israel's failure as God's servant.

> I am the real vine, and my Father is the gardener. Every barren branch of mine he cuts away; and every fruiting branch he cleans, to make it more fruitful still. You have already been cleansed by the word that I spoke to you. Dwell in me as I in you. No branch can bear fruit by itself, but only if it remains united with the vine; no more can you bear fruit, unless you remain united with me.
>
> "I am the vine, and you are the branches. He who dwells in me as I dwell in him, bears much fruit; for apart from me you can do nothing. He who does not dwell in me is

398

> thrown away like a withered branch. The withered
> branches are heaped together, thrown on the fire, and
> burnt."
>
> John: 15.1-6

Pharisees and others familiar with the Scriptures could not miss the reference to Isaiah's, and other prophets', use of the vineyard as a symbol for Israel. As the people of Israel had been chosen to carry the word of God throughout the world but had failed to do so, Jesus is referring to himself as the true vine chosen to do what Israel had failed to do. Therefore, he is not denying the truth of the religion in which he had been brought up, but rather is saying I am doing what you as the chosen servants of God failed to do ("I am the real vine") bearing the message.

Repeated reference to Christians dwelling within Jesus and he in them describes a union which could only be realized through the church in which, through prayer and love for one another, Christians, through Jesus, also become bearers of fruit. John thus continues to offer reasons for the existence and the role of the Christian church, both as a rebuttal to Judaizers and other critics and as an invitation to non-Christians in the Hellenistic world. The remainder of the chapter is devoted to this same theme.

> "This is my commandment: love one another as I have
> loved you. There is no greater love than this, that a man
> should lay down his life for his friends. You are my
> friends, if you do what I command you. I call you
> servants no longer; a servant does not know what his
> master is about. I have called you friends , because I
> have disclosed to you everything I heard from my Father.
> You did not choose me, I chose you. I appointed you to
> go on and bear fruit, fruit that shall last; so that the
> Father may give you all that you ask in my name. This is
> my commandment to you: love one another."
>
> John: 15.11-17

Jesus warned that even as he has been hated so would his disciples be hated, and said this warning was to make them aware of the need to "guard against a breakdown" of their faith. Then, commenting in length about his leaving, he concluded by saying the hour of his leaving this world had come. Finally his disciples understood when he told them he came from the Father and was returning to the Father. They said:

> "Why, this is plain speaking; this is no figure of speech. We are certain now that you know everything, and do not need to be questioned; because of this we believe you have come from God"
>
> Jesus answered, "Do you now believe? Look, the hour is coming, has indeed already come, when you all are to be scattered, each to his home, leaving me alone. Yet I am not alone, because the Father is with me. I have told you all this so that in me you may find peace. In the world you will have trouble. But courage! The victory is mine; I have conquered the world."
>
> John: 16.30-33

* * * * * * * * * * * *

With the opening of his seventeenth chapter John goes back to his opening theme that Jesus is the Logos temporarily in human form. The chapter is in the form of a prayer, what the *New Oxford Bible* refers to as "Jesus' high priestly prayer."

> After Jesus had spoken these words, he looked up to the heaven and said, "Father, the hour has come; glorify your Son so that the Son may glorify you, since you have given him authority over all people, to give eternal life to all you have given him. And this is eternal life, that they may know you, the only true God, and Jesus Christ whom you have sent. I glorified you on earth by finishing the work that you gave me to do. So now, Father glorify me in your own presence with the glory that I had in your presence before the world existed."
>
> John: 17.1-5

In this brief passage John has summarized Jesus' role in this world and his relationship to God. But, once again in his attempt to present Jesus as the Logos (existing before the world existed) and as the Logos temporarily in human form, John can be confusing. If Jesus is the Logos that existed before all else, in other words was the creative intelligence that created the universe, what is its relationship to God? Readers may recall the first sentence of John's first chapter: "In the beginning was the Word, and the Word was with God, and the Word was God." Was the Logos with God, or was the Logos God? If the Word (Logos) is God, then Jesus as the Word in human form was God. Yet, Jesus speaks of God as the Father who sent him and who is now recalling him.

In presenting Jesus as existing as the Word before the " beginning", John is thus able to present Jesus as the Word incarnate in terms acceptable to philosophers of the Hellenistic world. As we have earlier noted, Greek philosophers had been discussing the role of the Logos for centuries before the arrival of Jesus. John then says the Word was with God. This places God at the beginning. From this point John adds, "and the Word was God. " Thus for his audience John is making God, as defined and worshipped by Christians, acceptable to much of the Hellenistic world.

Jesus' prayer continues through the rest of the seventeenth chapter. He asks for God's protection for the disciples after he has given up his worldly life and returned to the "Father", and for them to be successful in the mission he has assigned to them. This mission includes making the world understand that he is the "Son of God", to which he then adds:

> " But it is not for these alone that I pray, but for those also who through their words put their faith in me; may they all be one; as thou Father, art in me, and I in thee, so also they may be in us, that the world may believe that thou didst send me. The glory that thou gavest me I have given to them that they may be one, as we are one; I in them and thou in me, may they be perfectly one. Then the world will learn that thou didst send me, that thou didst love them as thou didst love me."
>
> John: 17.20-23

John concludes this prayer with an entreaty that Christians, that is the church universal, be successful. *The New Oxford Bible* notes that "Jesus' prayer for the church universal is that believers may be indwelt by the Father and the Son and express their unity in *love,* thus fulfilling its mission of leading the *world to believe.*" This is John's way of presenting the role of the church as it existed seventy years after Jesus' death, there having been no church until men had created it after Jesus 'death.

As we realize it was not possible for anyone to know seventy years later what Jesus may have said in his prayers, and knowing there was no church until after men like Paul and Barnabas had established it, it becomes necessary for readers to determine John's intent in these prayers. Mark, Matthew, and Luke created stories of miracles and other parables to bring what they considered the deeper meaning of Jesus' teachings to the people for whom they wrote. John in writing for his Hellenistic audience created these prayers as his means of bringing to his readers what he considered to be the intent of Jesus' message and the absolute necessity for a church created to perpetuate faith in Jesus and "the Father".

* * * * * * * * * * * *

With his eighteenth chapter John moves directly to the arrest and trial of Jesus. Jews did not have the authority to issue a death sentence; only Roman authorities could sentence a man to death. Jesus is, therefore, taken to Pilate. It is important to note that John said the priests and temple police who brought Jesus to Pilate did not enter Pilate's palace. As he explained, a Jew who entered the house of a Gentile would suffer ritual defilement which would bar them from the feast of Passover; therefore Pilate had to step out of his house to tell the high priests that:

> "I find no case against him. But you have a custom that I release someone for you at the Passover. Do you want me to release for you the King of the Jews?" They shouted in reply, 'Not this man, but Barabbas!' Now

402

Barabbas was a bandit.

John: 18.38-40

When Pilate's soldiers brought Jesus out wearing a purple robe and a crown of thorns, the chief priests and their temple police shouted, "Crucify him! Crucify him! (John: 19. 5-6) John has made it clear that this was no mob of Jewish citizens demanding Jesus' death, but only those priests and temple police who during the night had brought him to Pilate's house. They called for crucifixion, the Roman means of execution, whereas historically execution by Jews had been by stoning. This made the execution officially a Roman execution for which the priests could absolve themselves of blame once the huge crowds that had followed Jesus heard of the execution.

John once more turns to the scriptures, as had earlier gospel writers, to show that Jesus' execution was fulfilling those scriptures. Psalm 22 is a lament, a cry for help at a time of serious illness.

My God, my God, why have you forsaken me? Why are you so far from helping me, from words of my groaning?

...They stare and gloat over me; they divide my clothes among themselves, and for my clothing they cast lots.

Psalm 22: 1, 17-18

Readers should compare this with John's description:

When the soldiers had crucified Jesus, they took his clothes and divided them into four parts, one for each soldier. They also took his tunic; now the tunic was seamless, woven as one piece from the top. So they said to one another, "Let us not tear it, but cast lots for it to see who will get it." This was to fulfill what the scripture says, "They divided the clothes among themselves, and for my clothing they cast lots."

John: 19.23-24

John by means of this passage has implied that "Providence controlled even the soldier's behavior."[143] As did the other gospel writers John also adds:

> After this Jesus knew that all was finished, he said (in order to fulfill the scripture). "I am thirsty." A jar full of sour wine was standing there. So they put a sponge full of wine on a branch of hyssop and held it to his mouth. When Jesus had received the wine, he said, "It is finished," Then he bowed his head and gave up the spirit.
>
> John: 19.28-30

This passage also is added to show the reader that the manner of Jesus' death fulfilled the scriptures. Psalm 69, which begins with the words "Save me, O God," which is described both as a lament, probably written during the Babylonian exile, and as a prayer for deliverance from personal enemies, says in verse 21, "They gave me poison for food, and for my thirst they gave me vinegar to drink".[144]

John moves on to describe the resurrection of Jesus. In his version Mary Magdalene finding the tomb empty ran to inform the disciples. As Peter arrived he saw the linen wrappings lying there in such a manner as to indicate Jesus had somehow departed without having to have the wrappings unwound from his body. Here John must be read carefully. The tomb is empty which indicates a physical resurrection of Jesus. Over the years since Jesus had died rumors had spread that his body had been carried away by his disciples or by others. John adds that the wrappings had not been unwound. To carry away the body, but to leave the wrappings unwound was a physical impossibility. This emphasizes a miraculous physical resurrection; quite contrary to the spiritual resurrection preached by Paul and the early founders of the church.

Then John adds that the disciples returned to their homes. Mary, however remained and then saw two angels in the tomb. At that moment Jesus spoke to her, but she did not recognize him.

[143]   p. 155 NT fn. 24. *The New Oxford Bible"*.

[144]   Fn., p. 615, *The New English Bible*. Fn. p. 730 OT, *The New Oxford Bible*.

404

> Supposing him to be the gardener, she said to him, "Sir,
> if you have carried him away, tell me where you have laid
> him, and I will take him away." Jesus said to her,
> "Mary!" She tuned and said to him in Hebrew,
> "Rabbouni!" (which means Teacher). Jesus said to her,
> "Do not hold on to me, because I have not yet ascended
> to the Father. But go to my brothers and say to them. 'I
> am ascending to my Father, and to your Father, to my
> God and your God.'" Mary Magdalene went and
> announced to the disciples, "I have seen the Lord"; and
> she told them that he had said these things to her.
>
> John: 20.15-18

Mary Magdalene, of all persons, should have immediately recognized a physically resurrected Jesus. This leads John's readers to consider that he is saying this was not a physically resurrected Jesus, but rather a realization that faith in Jesus and his teachings would always be with her and the disciples.

Whereas John has up to this point been describing a physical resurrection, this further passage tends to imply a spiritual resurrection. "Do not hold on to me." Do not mourn me, the physical Jesus. Do not believe all is lost through my death. Do not believe all I have taught you died with my physical death. Instead, remember what I have taught; have faith in our Father, our God. If you have faith I will always be with you.

Earlier gospels had Jesus appearing before the disciples on the third day after his death. Read figuratively, this was the time when the disciples recalled his instructions about carrying the message and retaining faith in God through him. In spirit he would always be with them. His teachings would never die.

John differs in that he has Jesus appearing before the disciples later on the same day that they had found the tomb empty. As with Mary, Jesus was not immediately recognized by the disciples with whom he had been living and working daily for almost three years. Then the disciples rejoiced when they "saw" him.

> Jesus said to them again, "Peace be with you. As the
> Father has sent me, so I send you." When he had said
> this, he breathed on them and said to them, "Receive

> the Holy Spirit. If you forgive the sins of any, they are
> forgiven them; if you retain the sins of any, they are
> retained.
>
> John: 20. 21-23

This appearance by Jesus before his disciples may be read literally or figuratively. Remembering that people of that day spoke and wrote symbolically, a figurative reader may tie this passage in with a second appearance of Jesus which John uses to speak of the doubting Thomas who would not believe what he could not see. The message that one reading figuratively may find is in the words of Jesus as he says:

> "Put your finger here and see my hands. Teach out your
> hand and put it in my side. Do not doubt but believe."
> Thomas answered him, "My Lord and my God!" Jesus
> said to him, "Have you believed because you have seen
> me? Blessed are those who have not seen and yet come
> to believe."
>
> John: 20. 27-29

For one who reads figuratively this may provide a clarification of the earlier passage in which Jesus has "appeared" before the disciples. Jesus has just said, "Blessed are those who have not seen and yet come to believe." Is he referring to the other disciples whom he has sent on their mission as he had been sent by the Father? John has Jesus referring to his hands and his side. Yet this had been a Roman crucifixion. As noted earlier the purpose of crucifixion was slow strangulation from hanging by outstretched hands. Hands and feet nailed to a cross would completely defeat the purpose of the slow death of crucifixion called for by the priests and temple police. However, if John had not mentioned wounds there would have been no way to complete the parable contrasting a doubting Thomas with those who believed without seeing.

Reading figuratively, one notes John's oft repeated point that the crucifixion was absolutely necessary to preserve the message Jesus had brought from his Father, and that Jesus had always been aware of this necessity. Furthermore, John was well aware that his Hellenistic audience did not believe in physical resurrection. The emphasis placed on faith and belief in Jesus stands out as John completes this discussion of resurrection by having Jesus say, "Blessed are those who have not seen, and yet have come to believe." Thus the earlier appearance before the disciples as in earlier gospels may be seen as their realization that Jesus may have died, but that his teachings were still with them and the mission he had assigned them still lay before them. As they mourned they had come to realize this was not the end, but a new beginning. This, then, was truly a resurrection.

John concluded his gospel with these words:

> There were indeed many other signs that Jesus performed in the presence of his disciples, which are not recorded in this book. Those here written have been recorded in order that you may hold the faith that Jesus is the Christ, the Son of God, and that through this faith you may possess life by his name.
>
> John: 20. 30-31

With these last words John has made clear the purpose of his gospel. Clearly this was intended as the concluding statement of the gospel. Why then is there a twenty-first chapter? It is obviously written as an epilogue. A dictionary defines an epilogue as: "A short concluding section at the end of a literary work, often discussing the future of its characters." In view of John's concluding statement at the end of the previous chapter, what was the purpose of this epilogue?

THE EPILOGUE

There are biblical scholars who believe Chapter 21 was written well after John had completed his gospel which leads to the question of whether, as in the case of other gospels, this was a section added by other than the original author.

In the early years after Jesus' death the Apostles, following Jesus' last instructions, spread his message. In Jerusalem Jesus' brother James was in control of the "mother" church which operated more or less as a reformed branch of Judaism. Jesus had said he had come to reform and thereby strengthen the religion of his people. James had been assisted by Peter and others of that generation, and would not agree to the admission of Gentiles unless they submitted to Jewish religious law.

Paul's efforts to obtain the right to develop a church among Gentiles may have been complicated by some who hoped to establish a hereditary control of the "church." Yet even within the Gentile churches there rose contentious claims of authority over individual churches and regions in which the new religion was blossoming. As early as 48 to 58 AD Paul's letters were showing his concern, if not fear, over the results of struggles for leadership in churches he had established.

In the early years after Jesus' death the Apostles, being considered the personal messengers of Jesus, were looked upon as the ultimate authority in the growing church. But, with the death of the last Apostles who was to assume this authority? By then a hierarchy had already grown among the local and regional ministers. Paul had died in Rome in 67 AD. Peter had died three years earlier, also in Rome. With the death of the last of the Apostles competing factions and individuals vied to become the power that would wield authority over the already mushrooming hierarchy.

We earlier noted the efforts of Pharisees and other Jews within the church to bring it under the Law as a reform branch of Judaism. In cities, a senior presbyter often became the president or head of all the presbyters of that city. By the time Matthew and Luke wrote their gospels, leadership of the church, from the lowest levels to the highest, was in question, and a new figure of authority had risen; the bishop.

The church was consolidating its leadership in Rome where rival bishops were struggling for positions of authority. In Rome Peter, who had died several decades earlier, would become the symbol of that ultimate authority and would be known as the rock upon which the church would be based; ignoring the fact that it was Paul who wrested control of the religion from Peter and from the Jerusalem "church" that had limited Jesus' teachings to a reform role within synagogues under Jewish religious law.

Readers should not lose sight of these ongoing efforts to consolidate control of the church under bishops in Rome and their allies among other bishops. Jesus had died three generations before John wrote. Paul, Barnabas and others had created the Christian church among Gentiles. Peter and Paul had lived their last years in Rome which had become the organizing center of the new religion. As has been true of so many pioneering movements, organization had bred a bureaucracy, which leads to further questions about the epilogue to John's gospel.

Why the emphasis on Peter in the epilogue? Why this additional material about further appearances of Jesus before his disciples? How long after John had written the previous twenty chapters was this epilogue added? These questions call for the further question: what was the motive behind adding this twenty-first chapter?

Viewing that epilogue, not from a theological point of view, but from an historical, perspective, one can not ignore the political/religious environment in which it was written. It may have been written shortly after John had completed his twenty chapters. Or, it may have been added as late as when the *New Testament* was being compiled in Rome. Whether added shortly after the original ending of the gospel, or later, it does provide the basis for organizers in Rome. It gives them Peter, the rock.

> After breakfast Jesus said to Simon Peter, "Simon son of John, do you love me more than all else?" "Yes, Lord," he answered, "you know that I love you." "Then feed my lambs," he said. A second time he asked, "Simon son of John, do you love me?" "Yes, Lord, you know I love you." "Then tend my sheep." A third time he said, "Simon son of John, do you love me?" Peter was hurt that he asked him a third time, "Do you love me?" "Lord," he said, "you know everything: you know I love you." Jesus said, "Feed my sheep."
>
> John: 21.15-17

CHAPTER 26

THE ACTS AND EPISTLES

We have treated Paul's letters as a fifth gospel, which seemed appropriate for several reasons. Paul considered himself to be an apostle, and was so accepted by the growing church. Throughout his letters his developing theology is apparent, and his theological convictions became a major part of this new born religion. His letters were written before any of the other gospels. Mark, the first of the other gospel writers was recording not only material from Peter's sermons but also, having traveled with Paul and Barnabas, what was being taught in those early churches founded by Paul.

"The Acts of the Apostles", on the other hand, is a chronicle of the early development of the Christian church rather than an accounting of those works and teachings of Jesus upon which the church was founded. Nor is it a theological discourse as was John's gospel. In *Can Religion Survive Worship* we have urged readers to seek reasons for the gospel writers writing what they did within the political/religious climate of their times. We have further urged readers to seek the messages those writers were delivering within their parabolic approach. Important though they may be as part of the *New Testament*, lengthy discussion of "Acts" or of the epistles of later writers is a separate matter which would add little if anything to one's study of the gospels.

THE ACTS OF THE APOSTLES

Tradition has it that Luke was the author of Acts, and that he wrote it as a follow-up to "The Gospel According To Luke." The opening verses of Acts aim to make this quite clear.

> In the first book, Theophilus, I wrote about all that Jesus did and taught from the beginning until the day when he was taken up to heaven, after giving instructions through the Holy Spirit to the apostles whom he had chosen.
>
> Acts: 1.1-2

A reader need go no further than these introductory words of Acts before facing the first of the problems confronting him or her.

It is not possible to set an actual date for the writing of Acts. Until recently it was largely accepted that the "Gospel According To Luke" was written around 90 A.D. The date of the writing of Acts is considered by some biblical historians to be somewhere between 65 A.D. and 80 A.D.

Why is the date important? The content of Acts indicates lack of awareness of events occurring after 65 A.D. After chronicling Paul's years as a missionary and his house arrest in Rome, the author says nothing about Paul's death or the years immediately preceding his death. Paul arrived in Rome in 60 A.D. Acts concluding verse says:

> He lived there (Rome) two whole years at his own expense and welcomed all who came to him, proclaiming the kingdom of God and teaching about the Lord Jesus Christ with all boldness and without hindrance.
>
> Acts: 28.30

This means the chronicle of Acts ends with the year 62 A.D.; but Paul lived until 67 A.D. which could mean Acts was written as much as twenty-five or more years before the "Gospel According to Luke." In that case it would have predated Mark's gospel which could account for there being no mention of the gospels in what was intended to be a history of the early development of Christianity. That, in turn, implies that those opening verses of Acts which said this was Luke's second book were added later, sometime after the "Gospel According to Luke" had been written.

By 150 A.D. authorship of Acts was being attributed to Luke, a young physician who was supposed to have accompanied Paul during his travels in establishing Christianity among the Gentiles. This has been accepted throughout the centuries since then, but raises further questions. Why does the author of Acts say nothing of Paul's letters? Could he really have been close to Paul and still have had no knowledge of these important writings of Paul? Why does he not describe those years Paul spent in Arabia and Damascus before his arrival in Jerusalem? Why does the author of Acts, who was not present, give us such an elaborate dramatic description of Paul's conversion on the road to Damascus in contrast to what Paul describes as a quiet spiritual experience?

Such gaps and inaccuracies would indicate that the author of Acts relied on a variety of sources in his writing of Acts. For example, in his first fifteen chapters the author of Acts speaks as one who is reporting what he has heard from various sources. He refers to "they" and "them." Then in the eleventh verse of the sixteenth chapter he, for the first time, speaks of "we." Was this because the first time he was with Paul was when Paul was setting sail for Troas?[145]

Just how important are these inaccuracies and dubious descriptions? With all these inaccuracies and occasional dramatic exaggerations should one bother to read Acts?

Readers should continue to be aware of the writing style of authors when books of the bible were being written. Exaggerations were common in both the Old and the New Testaments, frequently being used to emphasize the credibility of a prophet, disciple, or apostle. This should not necessarily cast doubt on the value of the message the authors of most books of the bible were trying to bring to their readers. Authors would also describe events, such as the three times Paul's "miraculous" conversion was described in Acts, in as dramatic a way as possible in order to emphasize the importance of the event. This does not mean many of those events did not occur, though

---

[145] *Acts*, 16. 11. Was the author of Acts now quoting from a diary he had kept from that time on, or even from a diary made available to him?

in a less sensational manner; nor does it mean that most biblical "events" were only parabolic illustrations.

Why, with all these inaccuracies and doubtful descriptions should one bother to read Acts? Readers should be aware that this is chronicle written by someone who did not have first hand knowledge of most of the events about which he wrote, but relied on a variety of sources. At the same time the reader should appreciate that Acts does chronicle the early years of the growth of the young religion. As the *New Oxford Bible* notes: "Luke's purpose in writing was to awaken faith by showing the triumphant progress of the Good News and to defend Christians against the charge that they were destructive of Jewish institutions and a troublesome element in the empire."

The *New Oxford Bible* then notes that Luke's further purpose was to outline the role of the Holy Spirit in the creation and continuing growth of the Christian church. In doing this Luke provides a chronicle of the manner in which Christianity spread throughout certain "selected portions of the Mediterranean world. From every point of view, the New Testament would be infinitely poorer without the first book of church history."[146]

THE EPISTLES

The Epistles vary from apocalyptic writings to letters in which an author expands on his version of Christian theology. These writings give us insight into the development of early Christianity and the early church. Some are aimed at shoring up the faith of believers who appear to be close to abandoning their new religion. We must remember that in its early years this new religion was beset by rival religions and doubters of all kinds.

The epistles vary also in length from the half page second and third letters of John to the lengthy Letter to the Hebrews and the apocalyptic Revelations. These letters and epistles give the reader a view of how men were expanding both the theology of the young religion and the structure of the growing church. In this they are an important portrayal of how Christianity was being molded in those early years.

---

[146]   *The New Oxford Bible*, p,160 NT.

The first three gospels were "historical" and biographical accounts of Jesus and his teachings. John's gospel was a theological discourse presenting the nub of Jesus teachings to a Hellenistic audience. Paul's "gospel" countered deviations threatening the early development of Christianity among Gentiles. In this respect the five gospels (Paul, Mark, Matthew, Luke, and John) stand apart as the base upon which Christianity would grow. Important as they are for reasons just noted, the epistles do not alter that base. They may build upon it. They may affect the manner in which Christianity would develop, but they are not a part of the gospel base of the religion.

CHAPTER 27

CAN RELIGION SURVIVE WORSHIP

Like all religions, Christianity is man-made. It was James, one of Jesus' brothers, who along with Peter led an early reform sect within the religion of the Jews; a sect that included some of Jesus teachings and which is referred to as the first "Christian" church. They were particularly known for their insistence that all members of Paul's early churches be required to observe Jewish religious law. When Paul, Barnabas and others carried Jesus' teachings to the Gentiles and declared them free from that Law it was in a sense the first stage in the development of the new religion. No longer a sect of Judaism, it would then begin to grow as a new religion under the new name "Christian".

A MAN-MADE RELIGION

Paul's conversion occurred about eight years after the crucifixion. As we have noted, during his roughly four years in Arabia and Damascus, his two years with the Jerusalem "church", and throughout his years devoted to organizing Christian churches among the Gentiles his theology continued to develop. A little more than two years after Paul's death in Rome, almost forty years after the crucifixion, Mark gave the world its first gospel.

Jesus did not create a new religion; and at no time did he ever seek to create a new religion. He repeatedly insisted that he was trying to strengthen the religion in which he had been raised. Not until after his death would his teachings and various interpretations of the crucifixion become the base upon which others would build a religion to carry his message. Interpretations of those teachings not only varied among congregations spread over thousands of miles, but even among the writers of the gospels. It was not a religion to stand still in those formative years. It was home to a continually growing theology reflecting the growth of its missionaries; Paul being an excellent example of how rapidly that theology could develop in one short generation.

We must keep in mind that all theologies throughout the ages have reflected the political pressures of their times. As we earlier observed, churches being formed in Greece, Anatolia, and North Africa were influenced by other religions and philosophers; and conflicts within churches erupted over varying theological interpretations with increasing frequency. By the time Matthew and Luke penned their gospels, about sixty years after the death of Jesus, the addition of accounts such as those of a virgin birth and physical resurrection had been easily accepted into the growing collection of oral traditions.

The influence of the Stoics is found in Paul's theology, as is the influence of Gnosticism in the "Gospel According to John." Epistles continued to be written over the next two centuries; for example, the "Second Letter of Peter" was not written until around 150 A.D., some hundred and twenty years after the death of Jesus, and more than eighty years after the death of Paul. These later epistles reflected Christian theology as men had developed it by the time the authors of these epistles took up their pens.

Early leaders of this growing new religion did not agree on which gospels, letters, and epistles would become their "bible" until more than two and a half centuries after the death of Jesus; and not until Augustine (354-430) with his neo-Platonist philosophy did the western version of Christianity emerge. Thus, Christianity as practiced over the next eighteen hundred years would be based primarily on writings of men; writings from which, more than two hundred years after Jesus' death, other men would select a few which would be known as the *New Testament*.

We have little knowledge of what was included in the numerous "gospels" which those men decided not to include, or why that handful of men determined what should be the bible that is still the basis of Christianity almost eighteen hundred years later. Neither do we know why in the political/religious climate of the day those men in particular were chosen to determine what would become the *New Testament*.

We do know that there was conflict among the various bishops, congregations, and individuals seeking leadership positions in the multi-faceted "church". Rome, the capital of the Roman Empire, eventually became the center for disputes about how the new church should be organized and about which doctrines and theological interpretations would best guarantee central control of that religion. It was in this political/religious atmosphere that those early leaders determined what would be included in the *New Testament*.

We should not forget that during that first two hundred and fifty years of the growth of the Christian churches, while there was no *New Testament*, teachings were largely based on oral traditions. During those formative years when men were developing Christian theology and were determining what to teach there was no equivalent of the Christian Bible. It would be a few selections from these developing beliefs that would become the base upon which Christianity would grow.

As a religion that knew no national borders the growth of Christianity's theology in those young years of the church was extremely rapid; and would continue, though at a slower pace, through later centuries. Additions to Christian services such as the Apostles Creed (as revised by French monks more than six hundred years after the death of the apostles) would continue to the present century. Bishops, during the first centuries of Christianity, raised private armies, and when contradictory interpretations of "Christianity" grew heated some resorted to assassinations of their opponents.

It was not until three hundred years after Jesus' death on the cross that, under the Emperor Constantine, Christianity became a legal religion within the Roman Empire. Like Paul three hundred years earlier, Constantine recognized in Christianity the potential for unifying the ever quarreling and often warring ethnic and national groups within the Empire. But by then Christianity had itself become a theological battleground for church leaders differing over theological interpretations.

In 180 A.D., Irenaeus, bishop of Lyon, in his thesis *Adversus haereses*, refuted Gnosticism and its influences. From him came the theory of the necessity of salvation because, he insisted, the fall of Adam ended man's likeness to God. According to Irenaeus, Jesus had to be God in order to bring salvation to humans. The anti-Gnostic forces within the new church prevailed and Gnostic scriptures were destroyed. Only in the 1940's was a Gnostic library discovered in Egypt. This type of destruction of any scripture that might deviate from whatever was the prevailing belief at any one time accounts for the loss of many gospels and other writings, resulting in a selective preservation of writings by the time men were chosen to put the *New Testament* together.

About a century and a quarter later, Arian, a presbyter of the church in Alexandria and more a philosopher than a theologian, disputed Irenaeus' interpretation. He insisted that only God could be divine, having existed before the beginning and therefore was the creator of all else. Therefore, Jesus was "created" and could not be divine. Jesus would have a human body, but not a human soul. If Jesus had to grow and change from infancy to the time he began his teaching, he therefore had a beginning. Only God existed before the beginning. So, Jesus is "created"; only God existed before creation and was therefore "uncreated". To most church leaders this was one more heresy. To them Arian's interpretation made Jesus a demi-God, and such a theory would result in belief in more than one God (polytheism) rather than monotheism.

Under Constantine, leaders of the Arian movement were cast out of their churches; the resultant bitter intrigue leading to further divisions within the church. This is but one of hundreds of examples of the continuing struggle by opposing factions striving to mold Christianity into a form acceptable to them. By the fourth century a Roman (Western) tradition and an Eastern tradition were drifting apart. The Nicene Creed would be revised and revised until by the eleventh century it was adopted by the papacy. In their struggle to create a universal church, men were unwittingly sowing the seeds of its fragmentation.

By the sixteenth century Europe was stirring with unrest. Scientists were rejecting centuries old theories. Humanism was setting the stage for the Renaissance with its emphasis on individualism and freedom of thought. Restrictions of the Church increasingly chaffed as this revolt against medievalism grew. Men like the English theologian John Wycliffe and the Czech religious reformer Jan Hus had been outspoken in their criticism of abuses within the church.[147] It was

---

[147] Wycliffe (1330-1384) pressed hard for reform within the church, calling for an end to luxurious living and corruption among priests. Failing to obtain the

418

inevitable that this growing rebellion against the restrictions of the medieval centuries would eventually bring about the Reformation wherein new leaders like Martin Luther and John Calvin would move to the fore.[148]

It is important to note that these above examples of man-made changes in Christianity are but a very few of the many occurring before and during the Renaissance and continuing until the present. As the protestant churches evolved they in turn split over and over into denominations and sects within denominations and into factions within sects; these schisms being the result of men differing in their belief as to how Christianity should be practiced and how the Bible should be interpreted.

Few members of twenty-first century congregations have ever read the rules and regulations by which their particular denomination is governed. Yet it is these man-made rules that set each denomination apart from the others. Rules tell members what they must do and what they must not do, but do little to carry the message. The implication: "Obey the rules and you will be saved." Is there a hint of hypocrisy in this?

---

reforms he sought he took the matter to the British Parliament. Through his efforts the first English translation of the Bible was undertaken. He believed every man who could read should be able to refer to the Bible as the ultimate authority instead of the distrusted church authorities. Hus (John Huss, 1372-1415), learning of Wycliffe's efforts to reform the church from Czech students returning from Oxford, became the leader of the reformation movement, and the University of Prague its center. When promised safe-conduct by Emperor Sigismund, he came before the Council of Constance. There he refused to recant, and was burned at the stake, the Emperor having repudiated his promise of safe-conduct. Princes of the church then passed a resolution stating no promise of safe-conduct was binding when considered harmful to the church.

[148]   In churches organized by Paul early Christians sought to find God, to understand him, and to become a part of him. This required freeing oneself from all worldly desires that were obstacles to becoming one with God. Mysticism, as this type of religion came to be known, became a part of early Catholicism as preached by Augustine (354-430 AD). Mysticism continued its major role in Christianity until it gave way before the teachings of Thomas Aquinas (1224-1274 AD), who believed that blessedness was not achieved in this world, but rather in the world to come. His works reflected some Spanish-Arabic influence. By the 13th century, resistance to the growing use of materialistic rituals gave rise once again to mystics. Writings of the leading mystics of the 13th and 14th centuries were major influences in Luther's developing theology before and after his break with the Catholic church.

Amendments to those books of rules, whether referred to as church law, or orders, or by other titles, continue to be made even as this manuscript was being prepared. And it is such amending or refusal to amend that is continuing to split congregations. We might well ask: How many of those most vocal in their defense of those rules, or of those who insist upon a differing interpretation of the rules, think of those rules as reflecting "divine" authority rather than as continuing man-made rules? Whether a faction is defending or is calling for changes in these rules its members apparently fail to appreciate that they are members of a religion devoted to praising Jesus, and created in large part by Paul, both of whom called for freedom from the slavery of such man-made religious law.

SMOTHERING THE MESSAGE

If you are a Christian, what holy day or days do you next expect to observe? Will it be Ash Wednesday and Lent; or Maundy Thursday, celebrating Jesus' Last Supper with his disciples; or Good Friday, celebrating the day Jesus was crucified: or Easter, celebrating a physical resurrection of Jesus and a physical appearance before his disciples and friends; or the weeks of recognition of Jesus' ascension and the days which followed; or Christmas, celebrating a miraculous virgin birth? Each was created by men long after the death of Jesus; Christmas being an example of how many times one of these celebrations has been changed by men over the past twenty centuries since its first version was created in AD 336. For a clearer perspective of how holy days have become a part of modern Christian worship it may be helpful to review the variety of influences that have shaped just one of those holy days by tracing of the 2,000 year development of Christmas.

* * * * * * * * * * * *

The winter solstice brought fear into the life of primitive man. Days grew shorter; his sun was dying; but then with awe he saw days grow longer after December 21. By 2000 BC the Egyptians had ritualized this miraculous "rebirth" of the sun. Babylonians likewise celebrated this rebirth of the sun; a celebration which became known as Sacaea when later adopted by the Persians.

Greeks associated the god Cronus with this annual phenomenon. Later the merging of the Egyptian and Persian versions of the celebration of the sun's rebirth became the basis of the Roman holiday of Saturnalia (Saturn being in some ways the Roman counterpart of Cronus), which eventually grew to be a seven day celebration beginning on December 17. Like the Egyptians, Persians, and others the Romans decorated with greenery. Whereas the Egyptians used palm branches, evergreens, a symbol of survival, were used in all lands where they grew.

Saturnalia became the most joyous celebration of the year. Work was suspended. Slaves were allowed to act as free men for that week. Parties, games and feasts abounded. Evergreen trees, outdoors, not indoors, were decorated. Gifts were given. Candles were given and lit.

By 300 AD, men and women were abandoning mystery religions and emperor worship by the tens of thousands as they converted to Christianity. These early Christians, whose religion kept them from participating in the pagan celebration of Saturnalia, had by 336 AD established their own period of celebration and gift giving. December 25, the day after the end of the annual Saturnalia, was chosen as their holiday for gift exchange, decorations, and feasting. Coincidentally, December 25 was also the day that the Persian sun god Mithra's birthday was celebrated.

Eighteen years later (354) Pope Liberius declared that the festivities of December 25 should, for Christians, include a celebration of the Nativity – thus *Christmas* was born. This could not have happened at a time more likely to bring conflict between the church and the emperor. It was the time when the above noted Arian conflict was dividing Christians. The Council of Nicea had ended in 325. Twenty-five years later Constantius became emperor, and as an advocate of Arianism denounced both the decisions of the earlier Council of Nicea and the belief that Jesus was divine.

A year after he had declared that the celebration of the Nativity should be added to the December 25th celebration, Pope Liberius was exiled by the emperor, until he later gave in and signed a condemnation of the decisions of the Council of Nicea. The inclusion of the celebration of the Nativity in the December 25 celebration was banned by the emperor.

Christmas was celebrated during the Middle Ages (476-1453) as Christianity spread throughout Europe. The tribes of Scandinavia and

Germany had long celebrated the annual return of the sun, which fitted well with their conversion to Christianity. (Evergreens, their symbol of survival, were most appropriate while celebrating the rebirth of the sun and the birth of Jesus.) When adopting Christianity they also brought other such customs as burning the Yule log amid raucous celebrations.

By the last centuries of the Middle Ages Christmas had become a bawdy celebration little resembling a celebration of the Nativity. Protesters of corruption within the church and of the excesses of priests increased in numbers as did their demands for reforms. As part of their reformation attempts to return to what they believed practices were in the early days of Christianity, Protestants abolished Christmas as an immoral celebration. In England by the 17th century there were an increasing number of reformers who were not satisfied that the Church of England had sufficiently removed traces of popery from its establishment. The most effective of these groups seeking further purification of the church became known as Puritans; among whose demands was the banning of Christmas which had once more become a rowdy and bawdy festival.

Parliament, under great pressure to cleanse the Church and its priests of their remaining excesses, eventually took up arms. The resulting civil war between the royal army and the armies of the Parliament, and the execution of Charles I, brought about Puritan control of the government under Oliver Cromwell. Pre-civil war Puritans had demanded a presbyterian form of government, but with Cromwell's death in 1658   conservative elements among the Puritans supported restoration of the monarchy and an episcopal polity.

It was during the height of their influence that the Puritans succeeded in having Puritan colonies established in the New World. In these American colonies, under strict religious control, Christmas was banned as an immoral celebration. Later settlements were divided on this policy. Dutch settlers and their churches banned Christmas whereas Catholic settlements and those dominated by the Church of England celebrated the holiday.

It would be in the early 1800s that Christmas would begin to be celebrated in New York once more as a gift giving celebration and a time of joy. Five years after the end of the American Civil War, Congress and President Grant would pass and sign legislation making Christmas a legal holiday.

Even in the twenty-first century Christmas crèches demonstrate confusion in the acceptance of the gospel stories. Matthew says Mary and Joseph lived in a house in Bethlehem where Jesus was born and to which the wise men came bearing gifts. Luke says Joseph and Mary lived in Nazareth and traveled to Bethlehem for a census registration (which actually took place when Jesus was 12 or 13 years old).[149] Upon arriving in Bethlehem there being no place for them in the inn, Jesus was born in the manger where shepherds would find him. Most crèches include a manger, but also include both Matthews's wise men, and Luke's shepherds. The point to be noted here is that every effort is being made to celebrate a virgin birth, but even in the twenty-first century not one word of the message of the teacher is celebrated. Yet most Christians are completely unaware of the many interpretations and celebrations of Christmas created by men over the almost 2000 years leading up to the current celebrations.

* * * * * * * * * * * *

From this tracing of the development of one holy day we might well ask: To how many Christians will it occur that all the above noted Christian holy days were created by men to celebrate some phase of the life of the teacher, but that not one of these "holy" times is devoted to his teachings? Have fears of the gospel writers been realized? (John: 4. 48-49: "Will none of you ever believe without seeing signs and portents?")

New generations of Christians may well wonder whether worship of the teacher is all there is to Christianity. Does it require nothing of its believers other than ritualizing that worship? Do the vast majority of Christians believe the purpose of their religion is to do no more than provide an opportunity to praise a miracle performing teacher, while giving little, if any, attention to what he taught? Do they see religion as no more than an attempt to achieve salvation through worship of a messenger; a messenger whose message they may consider beautiful but too idealistic for the practical world? True, some prayers of praise are addressed directly to the "Father" who "sent the messenger." But even they are usually offered in the manner of medieval subjects humbly and worshipfully petitioning their king.

---

[149]   Depending on the month Jesus was born. According to Luke the shepherds were in the fields with their sheep. That would mean late spring or summer as sheep grazed during that period but were kept in pens where they could be fed during the colder months.

Churches post signs listing the hour of their "Worship Service"; always the emphasis on worship. How many worshippers reduce the "creative intelligence" to the mere image of a man? "Reduce" is the proper term for conceiving such a limited image of the creative intelligence they worship. Is not the creative intelligence worshippers call God being demeaned by attributing to their God the weakness of a human-like ego requiring constant adulation? Worship reduces that which is worshipped to the level of the worshipper. The worshipper assumes that what would please him would also please the one being worshiped. Worshippers, not only Christians, reduce their God to the point where he fills the role of an oriental potentate before whom they bow and sing praises.

Christians in the "developed" Western world who attend church services might well consider the content of those services. Note the hymns, the choral offerings, the readings of psalms, the prayers of the pastor and the congregation; prayers all too often being mini-sermons. Add to these the further rituals of praise, and time taken for collection of offerings and announcements of church activities. All but a relatively few minutes of that brief weekly service are devoted to praising the one they call the messenger or to making requests of God through prayer in the name of the messenger.

Among clergy who attempt to apply the teachings of the *New Testament* to current affairs there are unfortunately those who succumb to the temptation to select and interpret passages that will support what the pastor sincerely believes is the correct political, economic, or other social position his congregation should support.

In beautiful stained glass windows of churches, basilicas, and cathedrals we see a virgin Mary holding an infant Jesus, or a Jesus bathed in rays from above, or a similar scene drawn from one of the various versions of Jesus' life. Some sanctuaries are home to beautiful statues of Mary and Jesus with candles and incense offered in worship of God or Jesus. The messenger dominates. *But where is his message?*

How many congregations sit through this weekly ritual for the comfort and the feeling of security it gives them? Prayers for forgiveness may leave them refreshed for the coming week. But, where is the message? What are they going forth to do? How close to the teachings of the teacher will they live that next week? Without the message, the teacher's life and his sacrifice on the cross are robbed of their meaning. He is praised for dying on the cross, but not for the message he held to so firmly that he knew it would lead to his crucifixion; the crucifixion John insisted that Jesus realized was necessary to keep the message alive.

In all of this we find what is now and will in the next several decades become a major source of further schisms among the congregations of the Christian churches. Not only will it result in congregations being split, but will increase the numbers departing from the ranks of Christianity.

It is the smothering effect of worship on the message of the teacher.

CAN RELIGION POSSIBLY SURVIVE WORSHIP ?

The more highly developed a nation becomes, the less chance there is for religions within that nation to survive worship. In the United States, for example, so much has happened just in the lifetime of the oldest members of Christian congregations. As those older members stepped into the twenty-first century they could look back to a childhood and youth when the airplane and the radio were in their infancy, and the automobile had only begun to be built with self-starters instead of hand cranks. In their lifetime they saw the first home radios, the first commercial aircraft, the Great Depression, rural electrification, the Second World War, the building of a massive highway infrastructure over which hundreds of thousands of huge semi-trailers rolled each day, the first television, the first man on the moon, anti-biotics, streets lined with skyscrapers, nuclear energy, great discoveries by archaeologists, the discovery of plastics, the first computers, and crews of men and women looking down at our globe from their space stations.

Add to these all those new labor saving household appliances and materials (e.g. automatic washing machines and dryers, dishwashers, permanent press garments, disposable diapers), and all the super store offerings of clothing and processed foods provided previously through labor intensive tasks in the home; all of which have freed tens of millions of women for productive careers outside the home and time for much needed creativity that would enhance society.

All these and so many other changes are taken for granted by the youngest generation to have entered the twenty-first century. Throughout the centuries past each new generation has stood on the shoulders of the previous generation. And those have been shoulders of generations justly proud of having met and conquered so many challenges in their lifetimes. But, it is all too common for previous generations to fear and even resent the new ideas, the political and economic changes, and the general way of life of the next generation, even when those changes are possible only because they are built on the firm foundation of that older generation's shoulders.

Burnings of witches and heretics, and prerogatives of the seventeenth century nobility were not only discarded, but were condemned by generations born in the eighteenth century. Ways of life considered proper in the eighteenth century were cast aside in the nineteenth century, during which accepted practices of the previous five thousand years, such as slavery, were declared immoral. Racial and gender discrimination of previous millennia were attacked and greatly reduced by younger generations of the twentieth century. So, why should it be expected that the young generations of the twenty-first century will be the first to fail to develop new ideas and beliefs as a result of their increased knowledge?

But, what of religion? Will it play an important role as they travel their road into the future, or will it fall by that roadside?

Grandparents of that oldest generation of Christians entering the twenty-first century, even those grandparents born in cities of the rapidly developing Western world, lived their childhoods in agriculturally dominated cultures. In America the great majority of those grandparents, whether they attended rural one or two room schoolhouses or city schools, did not continue their education to the point of completing high school. Most did not even complete the elementary grades. Even fewer in Europe received that much education.

The youth who entered the twenty-first century are not only completing their high school education, but millions will be attending the several thousand colleges and universities in the United States. Throughout most of the developed world this is a growing pattern. These young people are observing space exploration throughout our solar system. A heaven depicted as a physical home in the skies above the earth is no longer believable for their generation.

They are studying molecular biology, geology, geophysics, newly researched ancient history, archaeology, anthropology, nuclear engineering, and fields available only to a tiny minority of their grandparent's generation. An explosion of technology in the western world hurled the generations of the twentieth century from the horse and buggy of 1900 into the space age of 2000. Another, even greater explosion; an explosion of knowledge is sweeping the youth of the Western world forward in the twenty-first century.

As young people entering the twenty-first century grow to adulthood amid this knowledge explosion they can not help but be disillusioned -- *if* -- they are given no other reason for being Christians than to worship Jesus. As they learn that supposed virgin births were common among gods, religious leaders, emperors, pharaohs, and heroes two thousand years ago, how can they be expected to accept as literal truth the story of Jesus being born of a virgin? Will they be faced with an older generation's insistence that Christianity must be based on the belief that its messenger was born of a virgin? Is that all that Christmas will celebrate, when it could be celebrating the birth of the beliefs the messenger brought?

When these new generations realize that even as Paul and his fellow missionaries were founding Christianity they were insisting that resurrection was spiritual, not physical, will these new generations still be expected to accept as literal truth the parables of Matthew and Luke in their descriptions of a physically resurrected Jesus walking amid his disciples and friends?

With their knowledge of modern biology and medicine, can they be expected to believe diseases were caused by demons hiding within the bodies of their victims? With their knowledge of the physical and natural sciences, how can they be expected to accept literal beliefs in miracles, especially as all other religions during Jesus' lifetime attributed similar miracles to the ones they worshipped? Will the insistence of their elders that they accept such parables as literal truth deny them the message wrapped in those parables?

Yet, all those things that new generations will be unable to accept or believe have for two thousand years been the basis for worship of the Christ of Christianity. Those are the beliefs and practices that are the basis of the religion they find their parents' churches still practicing. As long as churches remain places of worship rather than sanctuaries in which new generations can gather to learn the meaning of the Kingdom of God and to find faith in the way of life taught by Jesus, main-line churches can expect to see such erosion of their membership that most may well cease to exist within the first half of the twenty-first century.

In reviewing the crisis facing Christianity and Christian churches in the developed world we have noted the role of various clergy and clerical patterns for sermons. But, what of the many clergy whose sermons are aimed at shining light on the teachings of Jesus so that each individual in his or her congregation can use his or her own judgment as to how life should be lived? They are devoting their efforts to keeping those teachings alive.

Unfortunately their credibility and the credibility of their efforts are increasingly doubted by the newer generations. All too often a well developed fifteen or twenty minute sermon is surrounded by much longer rituals of worship that are no longer acceptable to younger generations. The message is smothered and lost. Individuals who no longer find the literal belief in a virgin birth, physical resurrection, the Logos incarnated, and numerous other miracles to be credible are supposed to sit through the worship of those very things, and then are expected to accept the credibility of the minister or priest. The best of messages by the best of ministers can be smothered by the cloud of doubt and disbelief created by the rituals and myths of worship which surround them.

Insistence that the gospels be accepted literally as an accurate history and biography, and that the miracles attributed therein to the messenger require that he be worshipped, is creating a generation of atheists. We of the twenty-first century with the literal mindedness of the scientific age fail to step into those sandals of the people who populated the Middle East two thousand years ago. When we do try to empathize with them we still carry the baggage of the literal-minded with us into an age in which people were symbolic-minded. For several millennia the stories around campfires and the legends about various heroes and gods and what we would refer to as history were woven around symbols. They were not intended to be taken as literal fact. For the people of those ages symbols carried more meaning, were more expressive of what they believed, than any literal (factual) account.

It was around 400 A.D. that Augustine declared that if a passage in the bible contradicted what was accepted as proven scientific fact, then that passage should be seen as a symbolic illustration or as a parable. It was not until the 1600s when the so called scientific revolution was sweeping Europe that Christians began to insist that like scientific fact the bible should be seen as a saga of facts. During the three hundred years that followed churches promulgated the belief that all within the bible was to be accepted literally. This was to assure it of the same acceptance as proven scientific fact.

A twenty-first century literal reading of the gospels closes the eyes and ears of the reader to what the authors of the gospels were saying. In our age of scientific rationalism, insistence on a literal reading of the gospels will continue to swell the ranks of atheists. Our younger generations deserve a better legacy.

THE FORK IN THE ROAD

The choice facing the older generation of church leaders is whether their churches will continue to be temples built for adoration of the messenger or whether they will become houses for teaching his message. It is not the intent of *Can Religion Survive Worship* to criticize those who have received comfort from services devoted to worship. Acceptance of the gospels as a literal history containing an accurate biography of Jesus has carried Christianity this far since the scientific revolution. It has kept alive faith in the messenger and the Father. But now Christians are approaching the fork in the road.

Within main-line protestant churches any move toward a more figurative approach to the Bible will be viewed by many older members as betrayal of their faith. If they are unable to stem even a slight shift toward a more figurative interpretation of the Gospels, many will move to evangelical churches preaching the authority of the Gospels as read literally, or may be drawn by charismatic preachers to the growing number of Pentecostal churches

At the same time resistance by those insisting upon the authority of the Gospels as read literally can only turn away younger generations. The evangelicals and Pentecostals will take one fork in the road; the remaining churches taking the other fork. However, all too many of the church leaders and elders who remain in those shrinking main line churches will try to hold to a minimum the shift from a literal to a figurative search for the message. If they succeed they may well be found traveling their fork of the road with younger passengers increasingly dropping by the wayside. In 2010 news media reported research by the Pew Foundation had found: "Young Americans are dropping out at an alarming rate of five to six times the historic rate; thirty to forty percent having no religions today as contrasted to five to ten percent a generation earlier." Eventually, with the passing of the older generations, and the alienation of the younger generations, there may be no more passengers.[150]

Even as those main line protestant churches that fail to meet the challenging changes of the twenty-first century fade away, the evangelicals will temporarily grow in numbers. Likewise, Roman Catholic churches that seek to restore the hierarchy of faith that existed in earlier centuries may lose many of their younger members in developed countries, but may nonetheless not suffer an immediate decline in overall membership.[151]

In the United States, for example, the twenty-first century opened with a new awareness of the impact of recent and continuing waves of immigrants from developing countries. The vast majority of these new arrivals are either evangelicals or Roman Catholics. As their children complete years of higher education in their new homeland and begin their working careers they, like other younger generation Americans (who are all descendents of earlier generations of immigrants), will begin to question acceptance of the Gospels as literal history and as a literal biography.

MEETING THE CHALLENGE

Even as congregations continue to shrink in main-line churches throughout the developed states of the world, the great majority of their remaining members refuse to heed or accept this as a valid warning that their churches are not likely to survive beyond the next twenty-five to fifty years. However, leaders of those same main-line denominations recognized the writing on the wall well before the turn of the century.

---

[150] Recent surveys indicate a relatively rapid rise of atheism in the United States, led by the increase of atheism among young people. As of 2007, approximately one of every five young people was a declared atheist, about 30% more than the number of adults who have adopted atheism. Adopted is the appropriate term as atheism has been labeled the world's fourth largest "religion", (*The Economist*. Nov. 30, 2007, Special Report: Religion).

[151] A Pew research project found that one-third of American Roman Catholics who were born in the United States had left the church before the middle of the first decade of the 21st century. However, in the United States, by 2008, Latin American immigrants had replaced this loss to a point that accounted for roughly one-half of the Catholic membership below the age of forty.

Within seminaries preparing clergy, and at the upper levels of denominational administrations, staffs have been scrambling in an increasingly urgent search for panaceas.

For centuries, with the exception of Episcopalian and some Lutheran clergy, most protestant clergy never donned a robe. Their sanctuaries were relatively subdued, with the exception of stained glass windows. During the last quarter of the twentieth century, as many of those same churches sought ways to attract new members and to stem their steady decline in membership, services became more elaborate. Clergy adopted robes. Candelabra were introduced into the sanctuaries where none had been before. Rituals were added to open the services. Church décor grew more elaborate. Some observers commented that in their efforts to preserve their religion, churches were resorting to ceremonies not too different from those of the middle-ages, services which aimed to hold people in reverent, even fearsome, awe of God.

Some main-line congregations have added to their services what they consider to be ecumenical outreach. Their clergy often select from a variety of colorful robes, stoles, and crucifixes for different occasions. Psalms are sung by a cantor. Multiple candles are lit on the dais during the opening of the service, and during prayers of the pastor. High held banners lead choirs as they parade through the aisles to open the service. Not one, but several, mini-sermons guised as prayers offer praise in the form of confessions and requests for help in being subservient and more conscious of the power they are praising.

Services in some large churches have become spectaculars, leaving the impression that their leaders believe the more elaborate the pageantry, the more likely they will be able to stem the loss of members. Every moment is squeezed for the last drop of worship. *But, where is the message?* Are awe and meditation compatible? If not, are the material displays of worship self-defeating? Are they distractions from the message of the teacher?

Ministers of main-line churches who use scripture to support their ideas of what is politically or socially correct may believe they are using the teachings of the gospels to guide their congregations along the "right path." But, the same scriptural passages are used by pastors on the right and the left of the political spectrum as bases for sermons aimed at leading their congregations to support what the pastor sincerely believes is socially, politically, economically or religiously the Christian thing to do. Yet the minister's knowledge of such fields is all too often restricted to the same twenty minute newscasts as are the members of his congregation. The interpretation of that input cannot help but be filtered through the unconscious biases of the pastor concerned. Wearing clerical garb does not shield clergy from contracting many of the same secular biases held by the laity. Unfortunately, all too often prayers label as wrong those whose opinions differ by calling on God to forgive them.

Where is the attempt to present the message to the people in such a manner that *they may then use their individual judgment in finding the way to live according to those teachings*? Do our current practices represent a drifting back to the pre-reformation era when the church, rather than the faith of individuals, was considered the source of salvation? If so, does this account for the growing use of pageantry in services? Are we once more faced with the conflict Jesus and later Paul found between faith and the "Law"? Do the "Laws" of today, namely denominational rules and regulations and the resultant limiting of Christianity for millions of individuals to a Sunday ritual, reflect that same conflict? Do most Christian churches lack confidence in the ability of their members to live their lives according to the teachings of the gospels unless told by clergy what they must do? Is that why so little time is given to the actual message?

Meanwhile, huge arenas are being filled with congregations hanging on every word of evangelical and Pentecostal ministers. Roman Catholic churches are being urged to return to Latin in their service. Though few would admit it, there is an air of desperation among main-line protestant and Roman Catholic leaders in Europe and the United States. The first decade of the twenty-first century had witnessed the closing and consolidation of churches at a record rate as their congregations dwindle.

Churches with a fundamentalist interpretation of Christianity also face a limited future. Immigration and the shift of older members of main-line churches to churches offering a more literal interpretation of the Bible also have their limits. It may well be only another generation or two before even the evangelical churches, for reasons noted above, will begin to feel the pressures being felt by main-line churches during the first decades of the twenty-first century.[152] Christian churches in Africa and Latin America will face these same

---

[152] As *Can Religion Survive Worship* was being completed even the evangelical churches in the American southern states were reporting a heavy loss of younger members.

challenges when their countries reach the stage of development the Western developed nations reached as they entered the twenty-first century.

As churches seek a way to staunch the hemorrhaging of their membership they need to look not to the past, but to the future, which means to the generations who will be making religious choices that will determine the course of their lives and the future of the entire world.

Carrying the teachings of Jesus into the future without the rituals of worship and the literal acceptance of the myths and legends springing from parables is a challenge. If turning houses of worship into houses for the teaching of Jesus' message is too great a challenge to be met by churches, what vehicle can replace the rituals of worship to carry into the future the teachings of the one they have worshiped? If Christians cannot meet this challenge, they will be responsible for the failure of their religion to survive.

Worship has existed largely because it has promised to carry rewards such as a good life and salvation. Otherwise, why worship? Worship in that sense becomes selfish, reward seeking. Can Christians ever become so unselfish that they can forego what they conceive of as the rewards of worship, and instead see Christianity as living according to the teachings of Jesus as reported in the gospels and the letters of Paul? And this can not be done without seeking the deeper messages within the parables.

If rituals, processes, and procedures are put aside and the message becomes the way of life of people, what is to become of churches and clergy that have existed primarily to preside over those rituals, processes, and procedures? What will be the vehicle carrying the message?

Where do Christians go from here?

This is the challenge.

It is time to look for the answer.

Made in the USA
Charleston, SC
27 June 2012